International Political Economy Series

Series Editor: Timothy M. Shaw, Visiting Professor, University of Massachusetts Boston, USA, and Emeritus Professor, University of London, UK

Manuela Nilsson and Jan Gustafsson (*editors*)
LATIN AMERICAN RESPONSES TO GLOBALIZATION IN THE 21st CENTURY

Leo Panitch and Martijn Konings (*editors*)
AMERICAN EMPIRE AND THE POLITICAL ECONOMY OF GLOBAL FINANCE

Eul-Soo Pan
THE INTERNATIONAL POLITICAL ECONOMY OF TRANSFORMATION IN
ARGENTINA, BRAZIL, AND CHILE SINCE 1960

Julia Sagebien and Nicole Marie Lindsay (*editors*)
GOVERNANCE ECOSYSTEMS
CSR in the Latin American Mining Sector

Henry Veltmeyer, James Petras and Steve Vieux
NEOLIBERALISM AND CLASS CONFLICT IN LATIN AMERICA
A Comparative Perspective on the Political Economy of Structural Adjustment

Henry Veltmeyer, James Petras
THE DYNAMICS OF SOCIAL CHANGE IN LATIN AMERICA

International Political Economy Series
Series Standing Order ISBN 978–0–333–71708–0 hardcover
Series Standing Order ISBN 978–0–333–71110–1 paperback
(*outside North America only*)

You can receive future titles in this series as they are published by placing a standing order. Please contact your bookseller or, in case of difficulty, write to us at the address below with your name and address, the title of the series and one of the ISBNs quoted above.

Customer Services Department, Macmillan Distribution Ltd, Houndmills, Basingstoke, Hampshire RG21 6XS, England

The Future of Entrepreneurship in Latin America

Edited by

Esteban R. Brenes
INCAE Business School, Costa Rica

and

Jerry Haar
Florida International University, USA

First published 2012 by
PALGRAVE MACMILLAN

Palgrave Macmillan in the UK is an imprint of Macmillan Publishers Limited,
registered in England, company number 785998, of Houndmills, Basingstoke,
Hampshire RG21 6XS.

Palgrave Macmillan in the US is a division of St Martin's Press LLC,
175 Fifth Avenue, New York, NY 10010.

Palgrave Macmillan is the global academic imprint of the above companies
and has companies and representatives throughout the world.

Palgrave® and Macmillan® are registered trademarks in the United States,
the United Kingdom, Europe and other countries.

ISBN 978–0–230–27918–6

This book is printed on paper suitable for recycling and made from fully
managed and sustained forest sources. Logging, pulping and manufacturing
processes are expected to conform to the environmental regulations of the
country of origin.

A catalogue record for this book is available from the British Library.

Library of Congress Cataloging-in-Publication Data
The future of entrepreneurship in Latin America / edited by Esteban R.
Brenes, Jerry Haar.
    pages cm. — (International political economy series)
Includes bibliographical references and index.
ISBN 978–0–230–27918–6
1. Entrepreneurship—Latin America. 2. Latin America—Economic conditions—
1982– I. Brenes, Esteban R., editor of compilation. II. Haar, Jerry, 1947– editor
of compilation.
HB615.F8785 2012
338'.04098—dc23   2012009557

Printed and bound in Great Britain by
CPI Antony Rowe, Chippenham and Eastbourne

Contents

List of Figures

List of Tables

Foreword

The perennial question every entrepreneur asks himself or herself is: "How can I not only survive in the marketplace but thrive, even under adverse business conditions?" For entrepreneurs in Latin America and the Caribbean, the challenges are exceptionally daunting, given the plethora of volatile political and economic forces and factors – not just in their own region but elsewhere in the world, as well. My own experience as a successful entrepreneur in the Latin American region has led me to conclude that *knowledge* – informal as well as formal, technological as well as tacit – is the most important tool entrepreneurs can employ to succeed in business.

Economic reforms in 1990s Latin America embraced the contemporary trend of dynamic interdependency sweeping the world, with the United States and Great Britain in the vanguard. Countries could no longer maintain vertical integration within borders, protected by high tariffs. As trade barriers rapidly came down, local businesses faced global competitors overnight. The shift was a dramatic one, and entrepreneurs changed gear into "survival mode." While many small and medium-sized businesses went under, many others successfully adapted, reformulating business plans, management, and operations. Large firms, as well, were not immune from this brave new world of market competition. A great many instituted sweeping changes in their firms' strategies, structures, and operations. As a result, they not only survived but thrived – ironically providing lessons for firms in industrialized nations as these enterprises continue to grapple with the impact of a lingering recession.

In tandem with the economic reforms and liberalization measures in Latin America, multinational companies from North America, Europe, and Asia accelerated their use of breakthrough technologies in manufacturing processes, production, and operations. Moreover, they increasingly deployed these technologies to the Latin American region – now more competitive than in the past. The subsequent transfer of technology, through purchase, licensing, or joint venture collaboration, gave rise to a new crop of indigenous global competitors from the region known as *multilatinas*, including Cemex, Embraer, and Concha y Toro.

The region's industrial titans are household names, yet there is little acknowledgement of how they interact side by side with a myriad of small firms and the thousands of microenterprises that form a large part of the informal economy. True, there is a huge gap in the resources the latter can access; but it is the smaller firms that are overcoming this challenge and, in turn, are contributing to a positive outlook for the Americas.

Vision and leadership on the part of business and government – working together – hold the necessary tools for change as Latin America catches up with the housing, communications, infrastructure, education, social, and health care needs of the population. Together, they have managed to teach important lessons in areas deemed exclusive to developed economies such as pension funds and enterprise privatization.

I have had the good fortune to participate as an entrepreneur in several subregions of Latin America. These included pioneering enterprises in automotive production in Mexico; launching the start-up of a publishing house, which introduced a voucherless payment system for catalogue sales and the first edition of *Entrepreneur Magazine* in Spanish, when the term was little understood worldwide; and participating in the turnaround of Chile's LAN Airlines, now a case study for the world's airline industry.

Recently I have ventured into one of the most exciting new technology businesses in the region – mobile financial services. This new service promises not only greater economic independence for the general population, but empowerment of the local entrepreneur and, overall, holds an unimaginable source of economic growth and wealth for our countries.

These past experiences lead me to believe that the editors Brenes and Haar have produced an invaluable publication, both timely and relevant, as Latin America is on the verge of developing a truly middle-class society, with entrepreneurs playing an increasingly important role in the region's growth and development. The reader, whether academic, practitioner, or policymaker, will gain a greater, more intimate understanding of the complex structure and workings of entrepreneurship and its future in the Latin America. I am extremely proud of the work of the Eugenio Pino and Family Global Entrepreneurship Center in the College of Business Administration at Florida International University. From their renowned, annual Americas Venture Capital Conference to workshops and mentoring services to start-ups, established entrepreneurial enterprises, and family businesses, these activities and their research endeavors, such as *The Future of Entrepreneurship in Latin America,* serve as invaluable contributions to the discussion, understanding, nurturing, and promotion of entrepreneurship in the Americas.

Boris Hirmas Said
Chairman, Tres Mares

Preface

Esteban R. Brenes and Jerry Haar

What do these citizens of the Western Hemisphere have in common?

- R. Marcelo Claure – Bolivian native who is the founder, chairman, president, and CEO of Brightstar Corp., a multibillion-dollar leader in value-added distribution and supply chain service and solutions in the wireless industry.
- Roberto Silva – resident of Rio's Rocinha *favela* where he owns and operates an upholstery shop.
- Steve Aronson – US-born ex-coffee broker, living in Costa Rica where he founded Grupo Britt in 1985 and turned it into a social and environmentally conscious leader in gourmet coffee with Britt-branded products distributed in four countries and over 80 Britt stores in eight countries.
- German Efromovich – a Brazilian entrepreneur born to a family of Polish Jews in Bolivia, raised in Africa, Chile, and in São Paulo, Brazil; he held many odd jobs, including selling encyclopedias before consolidating a multibillion-dollar oil and aviation empire.
- Maria Elena Ibáñez – Colombian-born, Miami-based businesswoman who founded and sold a series of technology companies and currently distributes her own brand of Hispanic food products.
- Maria Gomez – owner operator of a bakery in Petare, one of Caracas's poorest neighborhoods.
- Carlos Argüello – Guatemalan developer of cutting-edge digital media whose Studio C credits include *Armageddon, The Chronicles of Narnia,* and other Hollywood productions.

They are all *entrepreneurs* – creative individuals who develop, launch, maintain, and expand a venture or enterprise. They are, as Howard Stevenson of Harvard Business School asserts, highly dedicated and relentless in their pursuit of opportunity without regard to the resources currently under their control.

The unstoppable, expanding force of globalization has created boundless opportunities and enormous challenges for rich and poor nations, companies large and small, in all sectors, and in all lines of business pursuit the world over. Entrepreneurship is almost always associated with individuals such as the late Steve Jobs, Richard Branson, Ricardo Salinas, Stan Shih, and Ratan Tata. However, sectors (information technology), industries (biotechnology, digital media), regions (Silicon Valley, Canada's Waterloo region, South Korea's Daedeok Techno Valley), and entire nations (Taiwan, Israel, Singapore) also shape, and are shaped by, the force of entrepreneurship. While no government can mandate the creation of entrepreneurs, government does play a role of incalculable importance in forming an environment that facilitates or impedes entrepreneurship.

The most widely recognized survey of entrepreneurship at the national level, the Global Entrepreneurship Monitor (GEM), acknowledges that, depending upon economic circumstances, there will be opportunity entrepreneurs and necessity entrepreneurs, the latter a characteristic of deteriorating economies such as Venezuela, Cuba, Ghana, and Uganda.

For emerging market entrepreneurs, in particular, the business environment impacted by governmental policies and actions is felt acutely. The latter include (*see* Haar and Price 2009, de Soto 2000, Fukuyama 2011):[1]

- Fiscal and monetary policies
- Tax and regulatory regimes
- Education and workforce quality
- Labor laws
- Credit access
- Infrastructure and logistics
- Technology and innovation
- Legal systems
- Public safety

While much has been written – and continues to be – on economic development in emerging markets and less so on entrepreneurship in emerging markets, precious little has addressed entrepreneurship in Latin America. Therefore, we decided to fill the void with this volume. As professors, researchers, and consultants with extensive experience in the private and public sectors (Esteban R. Brenes formerly served as Minister of Science and Technology and Minister of Agriculture in Costa Rica), both of us have maintained a lifelong commitment to business and economic development in Latin America and unswerving faith in the entrepreneur as the personification of grassroots capitalism.

The book is organized as follows. The first chapter presents and examines the emergence of today's entrepreneurial world. This includes forces and factors, the economic milieu; globalization and social and political factors; challenges and threats to entrepreneurship; and the case of entrepreneurship in Latin America. The remainder of the book comprises case studies of entrepreneurship in eight key countries: Argentina, Brazil, Chile, Colombia, Costa Rica, Mexico, Peru, and Venezuela. Although Costa Rica is not one of the "big emerging markets" in Latin America, we chose to include that nation since it stands out as a beacon of technology entrepreneurship catalyzed by Intel's decision to invest in Costa Rica in 1996, choosing the tiny country to locate originally US$300 million semiconductor assembly and test plants, investing many more millions in the following years.

We would like to thank our contributors who dedicated countless hours in researching and writing original contributions to entrepreneurship in specific Latin American countries. Esteban R. Brenes is grateful for the support of INCAE Business School and to entrepreneur Steve Aronson in whose name he holds a chair in strategy and agribusiness; to his wife, Laura, and sons, Esteban and David, for their support and patience during the long months of work on the volume; and to colleagues Alvaro Ramos Chaves, Daniel Montoya, Méduar Cerda Duarte, and José Miguel Paez Lucero. Jerry Haar thanks the College of Business Administration and the Programme for Technology and Management for Development at the University of Oxford and its director Dr Xiaolan Fu that hosted him as a visiting fellow in the summer of 2011. He also thanks his wife, Barbara, and son Eric for their love and steadfast support through yet another (fifteenth) book. We both thank Boris Hirmas Said, Chairman of Tres Mares, SA, for his generous support in aiding the publication of the volume; Faquiry Díaz Cala; Professor Timothy Shaw, editor of the International Political Economy Series of Palgrave Macmillan; Alexandra Webster and Christina Brian for their editorial guidance; Philip Tye for his copyediting; and Chris Cecot for indexing. Their responsiveness and guidance through the process of manuscript submission and acceptance were invaluable.

Note

1. *See* Jerry Haar and John Price, eds., *Can Latin America Compete?* (New York and Basingstoke: Palgrave Macmillan, 2009); Hernando de Soto, *The Mystery of Capital* (New York: Basic Books, 2000); and Francis Fukuyama, *Falling Behind: Explaining the Development Gap Between Latin America and the United States* (New York: Oxford University Press, 2011).

References

De Soto, Hernando. 2000. *The Mystery of Capital*. New York: Basic Books.
Fukuyama, Francis. 2011. *Falling Behind: Explaining the Development Gap between Latin America and the United States*. New York: Oxford University Press.
Haar, Jerry and John Price (Eds). 2009. *Can Latin America Compete?* New York and Basingstoke: Palgrave Macmillan.

Notes on Contributors

Esteban R. Brenes is currently the Steve Aronson Full Professor of Strategy and Agribusiness and Chairman of the Strategy Department at INCAE Business School. Previously, he was Dean of INCAE Business School from 2002 to 2007 and also served as a visiting professor at the Ross School of Business at the University of Michigan. Dr Brenes has authored over 50 case studies, academic papers, and journal articles in the fields of strategic management, international business, and family business. In addition to his academic work, he is the President of BAC y Asociados a consulting firm in corporate strategy, mergers and acquisitions and family business management. Between May 1998 and June 2000 he served as Minister of Science and Technology and Minister of Agriculture for the Government of Costa Rica. He received his doctoral degree in agricultural economics, international trade and marketing from the University of Florida.

Jorge Carneiro is Assistant Professor of Strategy and International Management at the Pontifical Catholic University of Rio de Janeiro, Brazil. He obtained his PhD in Business Administration from the Federal University of Rio de Janeiro. He is the Editor-in-Chief of the *Brazilian Administration Review* and a member of the Scientific Committee of the Strategy Division of ANPAD, the Brazilian Academy of Management. His PhD thesis received the Best PhD dissertation in Business Administration Award 2008 from the Brazilian Ministry of Education. His research interests include strategic management, international business, and organizational performance measurement.

Angela da Rocha is Associate Professor of Marketing and International Business at the Pontifical Catholic University of Rio de Janeiro (PUC-Rio) and Director of NUPIN, the Center for International Business Research. Before joining PUC-Rio, she has been a faculty member at the Federal University of Rio de Janeiro for 30 years before she retired, where she was for two terms the dean of the Coppead Graduate School of Business. She obtained her PhD from IESE Business School, Spain. She has nine books published in Brazil and numerous articles in international and Brazilian journals including *Entrepreneurship and Regional Development, Entrepreneurship Theory and Practice, Journal of International Entrepreneurship, Journal of International Business Studies* and *International Marketing Review*.

Jorge Ferreira da Silva is Associate Professor of Strategy and Quantitative Methods at the PUC-Rio and Vice-Dean of Graduate Programs at IAG Business

School. He is the President of ANPAD, the Brazilian Academy of Management, and is one of the top researchers ranked by the National Council for Scientific and Technological Development (CNPq). Dr Da Silva has published in national and international journals, such as the *Journal of Business Research, Journal of International Entrepreneurship, Latin American Business Review*, and *Brazilian Administration Review*. Prior to his academic career, Dr Da Silva was a vice-president of several leading Brazilian firms in the information technology area. He holds a PhD in industrial engineering from PUC-Rio.

Ana Cristina Gonzalez is Assistant Professor at Universidad de los Andes School of Management in Bogotá, Colombia. She holds a BSc in industrial engineering, a Master's in economics from Universidad de los Andes and a Master's in Management from Tulane University. She is a PhD candidate in management at Tulane University. Her research interests include entrepreneurship and corporate governance in family businesses. She coordinates the Universidad de los Andes STEP Project, an international research network led by Babson College that explores the entrepreneurial process of family businesses that create value across generations.

Jerry Haar is Associate Dean, Director of the Pino Entrepreneurship Center, and Professor at the College of Business Administration in Florida International University. He is also a non-resident research fellow at the Vale Columbia Center on International Sustainable Development at Columbia University. Formerly associated with the North-South Center, University of Miami, he has held visiting appointments at Wharton, Harvard, Oxford, Stanford, and the American Enterprise Institute. He was also a research associate at Columbia University and a Fulbright Scholar at the Fundação Getúlio Vargas in Brazil. A former Director of Washington Programs for the Council of the Americas, Dr Haar has written or co-written 14 books, including *Can Latin America Compete?* and *Winning Strategies for the New Latin Markets* and has consulted for both small companies and multinational firms. He holds a PhD from Columbia University.

Gonzalo Jiménez is Director of the Family Business Center at the Universidad Adolfo Ibáñez in Santiago, Chile, where he holds the Albert von Appen Chair in Family Business. A professor of strategy in the graduate program, he is an entrepreneur and founder and chairman of Proteus, a management consulting firm with large corporate clients throughout South America. He holds an economics degree and a master's in finance from Universidad de Chile, and an MBA from Ponts et Chaussées – one of France's leading *grandes ecoles*. The first Chilean Luksic-Rockefeller Visiting Scholar at Harvard University, Gonzalo Jiménez is completing his doctorate degree at the University of Liverpool.

Victoria Jones is Associate Provost for Global Engagement at Seattle University. She was Associate Dean for International Relations in Brazil at the Escola de Administração de Empresas de São Paulo da Fundação Getulio Vargas and at the business school of the University of Texas at San Antonio. She holds a PhD from Cornell University, an MA from the University of Pennsylvania Annenberg School, and a BA from the University of Southern California. She teaches and researches in the areas of international marketing and international management.

Oswaldo Morales-Tristán is an assistant professor of Management in the Graduate School of Business at ESAN University, Lima, Peru. He holds a PhD in International Studies from the Graduate School of Asia Pacific Studies, Waseda University, Japan, an MBA from ESAN University, a Master in Corporate Law from the University of Lima, and a Licentiate in Law from the University of Lima. His research interests include organizational culture, strategic management, and entrepreneurship. He is currently working on cultural change processes and their impact on long-term business performance.

Keiko M. Nakamatsu is a research associate in the Center for Entrepreneurship at ESAN University. She holds an MBA from ESAN University and an MD from the National University of San Marcos. Her research interest focuses on entrepreneurship. She is the coauthor of the GEM reports in Peru.

Roman E. Porras is the former coordinator of the Entrepreneurship Center at INCAE Business School (where he graduated from the MBA program). He is also member of Nicaragua's entrepreneurial network, and a collaborator at the Secretary of Science and Technology from Panama (SENACYT). Porras was awarded the first prize in the 2004 technological innovation contest from Council of Science and Technology from Nicaragua (CONICYT). He was also awarded the second prize for a business plan contest organized by the Presidency of Nicaragua in 2006. He is now a corporate credit risk analyst in the Nicaraguan banking industry.

Maria Pradilla is assistant director of international programs in the College of Business Administration at Florida International University and a Juris Doctor candidate in the University's College of Law. She holds a bachelor degree in economics and international business from Loyola University in New Orleans and a master's in international business from Florida International University. Her applied research interests cover competitiveness, entrepreneurship, innovation, international commercial law particularly in the areas of litigation, arbitration, and mergers and acquisitions. An entrepreneur, she is the founder and president of a successful ballroom and Latin dance studio in Alexandria, Virginia.

Aramis Rodriguez is a researcher and professor at IESA Entrepreneurship Center. A PhD candidate in entrepreneurship sciences at Nebrija Universidad, Spain, he is also a marketing specialist. Aramis is part of the team that coordinates the GEM in Venezuela, and the Global STEP Project for family business. His current research is mainly focused on corporate entrepreneurship, small medium enterprises, and entrepreneurial orientation of family business.

Luis J. Sanz is a finance and entrepreneurship professor and associate dean at INCAE Business School, one of the leading business schools in Latin America, and Director of INCAE's Entrepreneurship Center. A consultant in finance, corporate governance, and family business, Luis Sanz is widely published in books and academic journals and has been quoted in the *Wall Street Journal* and other business media. He was a member of the Investment Committee of Agora Partnerships, a social capital venture fund in Nicaragua. He also served as an external director of CAMM Brokers in Costa Rica. He holds a PhD in economics from the University of Pennsylvania.

Jaime Serida-Nishimura is a professor of Information Systems and Management in the Graduate School of Business at ESAN University, Lima, Peru. He holds a PhD in Business Administration from the University of Minnesota, an MBA from ESAN University, and a BSc in Industrial Engineering from the National University of Engineering. His research interests include entrepreneurship, innovation management, and IT strategy. He leads the GEM research project in Peru. He is currently Dean of the Graduate School of Business and the General Director of the Center for Entrepreneurship at ESAN University.

Roberto Vainrub is Managing Director of Financial Partners Capital Management, a corporation principally engaged in providing financial advice. He formerly served as Vice President of IESA business school in Caracas, Venezuela, and is the founder of its Center for Entrepreneurship. In addition to an extensive management career in the financial services industry and service on corporate boards, Dr Vainrub has three decades' experience in academics – teaching in executive education programs and authoring several books and a number of articles in publications such as *Harvard Business Review*. He holds an MS from Stanford University and a PhD in industrial engineering from Universidad Católica Andrés Bello in Caracas.

Rafael Vesga is Assistant Professor at Universidad de los Andes School of Management in Bogota, Colombia. He holds a bachelor degree in economics from Universidad de los Andes, a Master of Science in Public Policy and Management from the H. John Heinz III School of Public Policy and Management at Carnegie Mellon University and a Master in Management from Tulane University. He is a PhD candidate in management at Tulane University. His research interests are entrepreneurship, innovation, and strategy. He coordinates the entrepreneurship group in charge of research, service, and teaching efforts, including the GEM initiative.

1
Introduction: The Emergence of an Entrepreneurial World

Jerry Haar
Florida International University

Esteban R. Brenes
INCAE Business School

Entrepreneurship and the multitude and variety of entrepreneurs who are shaping the post-industrial global economy have become mainstream. The quest for new products and new processes ranges from microlending arrangements by organizations such as Acción and the Kenyan Women's Finance Trust, to "cloud computing," which is making a significant impact, in particular, on the health-care industry. These also include new firms known as "born global" enterprises whose first markets are not their home country, but the world (e.g. Skype), and large multinational stalwarts such as Walmart, Cemex, Volkswagen, and Telefónica whose entrepreneurial approach to sourcing, supply chain management, and logistics has become the industry standard.

Forces and factors shaping an entrepreneurial world

Increasing competition from globalization, the rise of Asia, the proliferation of and broader access to technology and communications, expanded access to credit, and a growing consumer class empowered to decide what they buy, when, how, and at what price, have combined to create a new business environment where the playing field for trade, commerce, and investment is dynamic and challenging.

Just what are the key forces and factors that are shaping this new entrepreneurial world? How do they interact? What are the implications for producers and consumers?

The macroeconomic milieu

The global financial crisis, which began in the late fall of 2008, continued through much of 2010 in the industrialized nations before an incremental recovery began to take shape. The post-financial crisis economic environment is one characterized by a multispeed recovery, with emerging economies intact, for the most part, and industrialized nations recuperating minimally or even losing ground, as witnessed by the PIIGS group of nations (Portugal, Ireland, Italy, Greece, and Spain). This disparity is even occurring within regions. To illustrate, in Asia, Japan's growth rate averages 2 percent compared to nearly 6.5 percent for Vietnam. In Europe, the comparison is 1.7 percent for Germany versus 4.5 percent for the Slovak Republic.[1]

One collateral impact of the financial crisis is that financial conditions today are more difficult than before the crisis. Bank capital remains a constraint on growth, affecting consumers and smaller firms in particular. Combined with increases in sovereign risk premiums and rising public deficits and debt in industrialized nations, it will be quite some time before robust economic growth resumes worldwide. Falling revenues, the continuing recession in the housing market, fiscal crises at the state and municipal levels of government, and unfunded liabilities of social security, pensions, and health pose grave threats not just to the United States but to other economies as well. Although industrialized nations are suffering this malaise, emerging economies are not free of severe challenges, including asset bubbles in housing, a surge in corporate and consumer debt, overheated economies with their inflationary impacts, and the prospect of imposing higher interest rates to prevent a financial meltdown.

Alarming though this scenario may appear, there are many bright spots – enduring ones – in the economic environment, which give cause for optimism among entrepreneurs. These include access to capital (albeit more restrictive since the global financial crisis), a generally low inflationary environment worldwide, an increase in consumer spending among all economic classes, and a greater openness and integration in global commerce.

Globalization in all its ramifications

Globalization is raising the competitive stakes for everyone, particularly in the rich world, and it is being driven by developing economies. Developing countries are becoming hotbeds for business innovation with innovations such as US$3000 cars, US$300 computers, and US$30 mobile phones that provide nationwide unlimited service for just 2 cents per minute; all of which are changing the traditional view that innovation happens in the developed world and is then transferred to the developing world.[2] Further, it is not only innovation of products, but also innovation of systems of production and distribution, supply-chain management, recruiting, and retention; essentially every business process and model is being reinvented.

The most important factors in the globalization of entrepreneurs are technology and the falling costs of communications.[3] The success of entrepreneurship is driven by technological changes such as the personal computer, the mobile phone, and the Internet. These changes have democratized entrepreneurship.[4] Entrepreneurs can come from anywhere in the world and can reach customers anywhere from the day they open their doors. Thanks to the Internet, entrepreneurs can cheaply and quickly start a company and reach millions of potential customers from anywhere in the world. Similarly, mobile phones have revolutionized communications and business, particularly in developing countries where the infrastructure for landlines is poor or nonexistent. In Bangladesh, Grameen Bank provides microfinancing for Bangladeshi women, called phone ladies, who carry mobile phones with long-lasting batteries and sell time on their phones to local villagers. There are over 270,000 of these phone ladies in Bangladesh.[5]

Another factor that has traditionally transformed and shaped internationalization is foreign direct investments (FDI), which is now flowing to China in a disproportionate amount. For entrepreneurs, the "China price" presents tough competition, and as a result only the most competitive and efficient entrepreneurs survive. India, on the other hand, has led the internationalization of information technology.[6]

An obvious consequence of globalization is that local companies, able to quickly and cheaply experience what is happening around the globe, are dreaming big dreams, driven by a mixture of ambition to expand worldwide and fear that cheaper competitors will penetrate the market. The number of companies from BRIC countries (Brazil, Russia, India, and China) on the *Financial Times 500* more than quadrupled between 2006 and 2008, from 15 to 62.[7] But this change is not just supply driven; customers in developing countries are also getting richer faster than their developed country counterparts, and as a result are demanding more products and services. However, consumers in emerging markets are hard to reach, tend to be more varied and volatile than those in mature markets, and do not yet have strong brand loyalty. Companies in these markets have an advantage over their Western counterparts and are able to connect with potential customers through strategies such as product demonstrations in department stores.

Some notable examples of successful entrepreneurial companies from emerging markets that have become multinationals are Lenovo and South African Breweries. Lenovo did not exist in 1990, yet five years ago it bought IBM's personal computer business and is now the fourth-largest PC maker. Similarly, South African Breweries was a local brewer in 1990 and today is one of the top three largest beer companies in the world.

Another major change brought about by globalization is the rise of "born global" firms. Many entrepreneurs start global, rather than starting local and expanding globally. "Born global" firms not only find opportunities for their products or services globally, but they also search for materials, talent, and factors of production globally. For example, EyeView is a company that uses "rich media" (a combination of video and audio) to teach customers how to use websites. Most of EyeView's customers are international, the company is now headquartered in Tel Aviv, and its founders are originally from Boston, Sydney, and Tel Aviv.[8]

Trade and investment integration

Globalization has also had an impact on trade and investment worldwide. Countries' economies are more interdependent than ever before. Another factor shaping the entrepreneurial world is the explosion of global trade. During the period 1995–2007, worldwide merchandise exports have grown from US$5.2 billion to US$13.9 billion, while trade in services has grown from US$1.2 billion to US$3.36 billion.[9] In 2009, China became the leading exporter of merchandise in the world, overtaking Germany; while the US remained the world's leading importer.[10] Of particular note is the trade growth from and among developing nations, which in 1995 represented only 18 percent of total exports, while in 2007 it grew to 29 percent.[11] Fueling this trade has been the growth of trade agreements – whether free trade agreements such as the US–Singapore FTA or the Trans-Pacific Strategic Economic Partnership – customs unions such as Mercosur, bilateral investment treaties (trade-related), or other accords aimed at reducing tariff and non-tariff barriers. Since 2001 the number of free trade agreements alone has grown from 95 to 188.[12]

As a result, changes in one economy can have severe repercussions in the economies of its neighbors, as well as more distant countries. For example, high government deficit and debt levels in several high-income countries create volatility in international financial and commodity markets. The main impact for developing countries is a generalized decline in stock market valuations and an increase in global currency volatility. Similarly, when the euro depreciates in relation to the US dollar, it benefits exporters in countries tied to the euro while hurting those tied to the dollar.

On the investment side, the financial crisis in Europe and the post-recession lending environment in the US have not had a major effect on developing nations' access to capital. While these countries' sovereign interest rate premiums have widened, they are still lower than their October 2008 peak. It is true that bank lending to emerging economies remains depressed, as high-income banks continue to recapitalize and strengthen their balance sheets; however, capital markets have exhibited resilience and both portfolio and foreign direct investment are on the upswing.

Expansion of credit worldwide

The global financial crisis, which began in the fall of 2008, destroyed US$50 trillion in wealth, the equivalent of one year of world Gross Domestic Product (GDP).[13] While bank credit contracted in nearly all countries in at least one of the eight months after the crisis hit; subsequent performance in the expansion of bank credit has been as markedly uneven – in fact polarized – as the overall recovery itself. Certain nations such as Germany, India, Thailand, Peru, and Poland have witnessed a credit expansion, while others – particularly France, Greece, Mexico, Turkey, and Venezuela – have experienced a significant contraction.

The extensive liquidity expansion that fueled the credit boom of the first half of the decade, and contributed to the bubble and bust in financial markets, is history now. Interbank lending rates have returned to normal levels, and emerging market sovereign interest rate premiums have declined. However, credit will be more scarce and expensive in years to come. Presently, though, global liquidity has been expanding modestly and lending to natural-resource-rich countries is likely to remain robust, while developing countries in particular are likely to rely more on domestic financial intermediation.[14]

Social development changes

Proliferation of both middle class and bottom of the pyramid sectors

Emerging markets are characterized by population size and growth. Today there are far more middle-class consumers in the world's emerging market nations than in the West and their combined purchasing power, sophistication, and confidence are growing by leaps and bounds. While many of the advanced economies are seeing a slow recovery due to large debt, emerging economies are expanding rapidly and are becoming more important in the worldwide recovery. According to the US Department of Commerce, emerging market economies will represent more than 75 percent of expected growth in world trade in the next two decades.[15]

Emerging markets in Asia are less vulnerable to market fluctuations because they tend to be cash rich, and therefore less reliant on debt. In these countries, the potential for middle-class growth is tremendous and, it is expected that as early as the next decade, it could quadruple. Goldman Sachs has estimated that the emerging markets' middle class will be 800 million by 2013, which will mean that the BRIC countries will have a total middle class larger than the population of western Europe, USA, and Japan combined.[16]

In China, it is estimated that 70 million consumers have the same buying power as the average American household, and this number is expected to quadruple in the next 25 years. If that projection holds true, in 25 years China's middle class will be as large as the total US population is today. Similarly, in India there is a middle-class market segment of about 180 million people, which is nearly equal to that of the United States. Further, it is projected that India will add between 75 million and 150 million new middle-class consumers within the next 25 years, bringing the total middle-class population in India to between 240 and 320 million people.[17]

These new middle-class consumers have an appetite for Western goods and are open to global trade. Consequently, there is a growing demand for Western-style goods and services such as high-technology products and automobiles. The growing middle class is going to be the major consumer of new cars and it is estimated that by 2020 China could be buying more cars than the United States, and that Brazil and India could be buying more cars than any of the G7 countries. US multinationals like General Electric, Procter & Gamble, DuPont, and General Motors expect more than half of their future growth to come from emerging markets.[18]

Corresponding to the rise in personal consumption, the governments of emerging markets continue to spend billions of dollars on infrastructure projects and improvements. The World Bank estimates that more than US$2 trillion will continue to be spent on infrastructure in emerging markets over the next ten years. Thus, emerging markets not only have an increasing per capita income, a large consumer market, and a growing middle class with a high purchasing power; but also firms and government have important needs, such as raw materials and machine tools, to develop industrial and agricultural potential.

As a result of the growing middle class, the traditional pyramid population model found in a less developed country, where the very large base represents the majority of the population with a low per capita income and the narrow apex depicts the limited number of rich people, is changing in the emerging economies. In these economies, the population is better represented by a diamond shape where the middle class represents the wider middle area of the diamond because the size of the middle class exceeds in number that of the other socio-economic clusters. These countries will, therefore, mature into newly industrialized economies – an intermediate step towards becoming developed countries.

In the next decade there could be a major shift in emerging markets, whereby at least five emerging economic powers could take their place among the world's top ten largest economies. These economies will pose tremendous opportunities in fast-moving consumer and services markets because they have a huge population.

Occupational emancipation of women

Another important shift occurring in the world's population today is that women are becoming more independent and are creating and running businesses across a wide range of countries and under varying circumstances. Female entrepreneurship is an increasingly salient part of the economic makeup of many countries and is a key contributor to economic growth in low/middle-income countries, particularly in Latin America and the Caribbean. Interestingly enough, the gender difference is more pronounced in high-income countries but persists throughout all regions, with European and Asian low/middle-income countries showing a greater gap than the Latin American and Caribbean low/middle-income countries.[19]

Although GDP is important, there are other important factors in entrepreneurial activity such as regional and cultural differences. Also, having a social network that includes other entrepreneurs as well as perceptual factors such as optimism, self-confidence, and reduced fear of failure are factors that contribute to the rise of women entrepreneurs. Conversely, many of the obstacles that women entrepreneurs encounter are the lack of collateral, their domestic responsibilities, limits on their mobility, and limited access to finance. For these reasons, women tend to be concentrated in small and medium-sized businesses, their business contacts are mainly sourced through personal connections, and their businesses are often in the service industries; this further hinders their ability to obtain financing, because these types of businesses are harder to evaluate.

In South Africa, for example, women entrepreneurs faced major barriers accessing finance as they made up only 5 percent of clients in the Black Economic Empowerment Equity Fund. However, some initiatives have been taken to increase the access of women entrepreneurs to financial instruments, including regular banking, debt financing, and equity financing. For example, Standard Chartered, an international bank, has introduced women-focused marketing in its regular banking services particularly in countries where women have had a lower rate of formal engagement with banks. Similarly, Sero Lease and Finance Ltd, a women's leasing and finance company in the United Republic of Tanzania, offers women borrowers, even those without credit history and collateral, access to the use of capital equipment and other equipment or products needed for their businesses. At a regional level, the European Network to Promote Women's Entrepreneurship aims to raise the visibility of existing women entrepreneurs and to create a favorable climate to increase the number of women entrepreneurs and the size of existing women-led businesses.

All these organizations have had a positive impact for women entrepreneurs. International Labor Organization (ILO) data suggests a very gradual reduction in the gender segmentation of labor markets since the 1980s. In 2000, there were far fewer occupations in which over 80 percent of the workforce was either female or male. Overall, women are increasingly found in the services sector, which in 2008 accounted for 46.3 percent of all women's employment, compared to 41.2 percent of men's employment.

Immigration

Immigrants are key to promoting entrepreneurial activity because they not only bring with them their economic output such as creating innovation, start-ups, and new jobs; but also, and perhaps more importantly, they bring their thirst to improve their lives and achieve something better. But not all immigrants are alike. According to Basch and Blanc-Szanton, some immigrants can create a transnational culture, which is defined as the "processes by which immigrants build social fields that link together their country of origin and their country of settlement."[20] Transnational entrepreneurs represent a large proportion, often the majority, of self-employed people in immigrant communities. This cultural theory suggests that ethnic and immigrant groups are equipped with culturally determined features such as dedication to hard work, membership of a strong ethnic community, economical living, acceptance of risk, compliance with social value patterns, solidarity and loyalty, and orientation towards self-employment. These features provide an ethnic resource that can facilitate and encourage entrepreneurial behavior and support ethnic self-employment.

Contemporary transmigrants are similar to middleman minorities in that they have native speaker fluency in two languages, which distinguishes them from immigrants, who lose their foreign language fluency within three generations. Further, transmigrants form diasporas, just as middleman minorities do. However, because of transnationalism, it is argued, ethnic groups that were never middleman minorities can now make up diasporas as well; and these diasporas are easier to maintain because of globalization. For example, Brazilians or Filipinos have access to diasporas such as were previously available only to middleman minorities like the Jews, Armenians, or Chinese.

Further, contemporary transmigrants also have international social capital that provides access to enforceable trust, which in turn hugely simplifies international trade. For example, enjoying international social capital, a Haitian transnational residing in New York City can much more easily buy and sell goods from a co-ethnic in Port-au-Prince, confident that invoices will be paid or, if unpaid, can be informally collected without recourse to the law. In New York, a number of Haitian entrepreneurs have established family-run restaurants, record shops, groceries, laundromats, dry cleaners, garages, and travel and real estate agencies. Additionally, many Haitian factory workers participate in Sann, a rotating credit association that serves as an informal savings and loan agency for illegal immigrants; and those with legal status also use it as a quick source of capital for investment purposes.

Political shifts

Governments ranging from socialist to free market are realizing that entrepreneurship is crucial to their global economic survival and are actively supporting and promoting entrepreneurial activity. Denmark, although a socialist government, is actively open to entrepreneurship. The government is trying to embrace capitalist globalization, while maintaining its traditionally generous welfare state. The government has created a network of growth houses – ready-made offices that provide start-ups with consulting advice, legal services, conference rooms, and other advantages that large companies enjoy. Additionally, the government has created Vaekstfonden, a public venture capital fund that promotes education for entrepreneurship. As a result, Denmark is now ranked fifth for ease of doing business by the World Bank and is home to 20 percent of Europe's biotechnology companies, as well as many thriving clean-energy technology, fashion, and design industries; as a proportion of GDP, Danish companies attract more venture capital than companies in any other European country.[21]

On the other side of the spectrum is Singapore with its free-market government. The government has done everything in its power to assist entrepreneurs and, as a result, Singapore ranks no.1 in the world for ease of doing business according to the World Bank's league table. Singapore's government has invested heavily in digital media, bioengineering, clean technology, and water purification. It has also created a public venture capital fund that has resulted in more than 5 percent of Singapore-based companies receiving funding from venture capital.[22] In addition, schools teach the virtues of entrepreneurialism from an early age.

For countries such as Israel, entrepreneurship is a matter of survival. Israel is home to 4000 high-tech companies, more than 100 venture capital funds, and a growing health-care industry, and it has the world's highest ratio of PhDs per capita – mostly engineers and scientists.[23] In Israel, it is common for young Israeli professionals to start a business with friends they met in the army, where they were trained in teamwork and improvisation, and also became more risk-tolerant – traits that make them ideal for entrepreneurial endeavors.

These countries set an example and help spread the entrepreneurship seed to neighboring countries, for example Arab countries copying Israel's model and other European countries following in Denmark's footsteps. However, it is not only developed countries that are leading the way in entrepreneurship; emerging economies such as India and China are becoming hotbeds of innovation.

India is a great example of an emerging country that is putting its resources into supporting entrepreneurship. India not only thrives in technology with companies like Infosys, but its other industries are also doing very well. For example, Bollywood produces 1000 films per year that are watched by 3.6 billion people (compare to Hollywood: 700 films and 2.6 billion viewers).[24] Another example is the Narayana Hrudayalaya hospital in Bangalore, which is turning heart surgery into a "Wal-Mart like" business. India's strategy is to reverse its brain drain. India has drawn heavily on its expatriate population living in the US (about 1 million) to kick-start its entrepreneurial economy. In 2003–5, some 5000 tech-savvy Indians with over five years of experience in the US returned to India. Further, India's higher education is so competitive that only 1 in 75 applicants is accepted. Therefore, the focus has turned towards producing entrepreneurs rather than technicians.

China's transformation from communism to entrepreneurialism is even more amazing. In 2006, when the Vice-Premier visited the US, she took over 200 entrepreneurs with her. The Central Party School offers special courses for entrepreneurs. China is similar to India in that many Chinese live in the US, particularly Silicon Valley, and the Chinese government is doing everything possible to lure them back to China – such as upgrading universities, setting up science parks, working with foreign institutions, and welcoming foreign companies. So many Chinese expatriates have indeed returned that in Silicon Valley this phenomenon is called "B2C" (back to China). In general, most Chinese entrepreneurs have focused on "knock offs," or successful replications of Western companies or products, and marketing them in China. For example, Baidu is similar to Google, Dangdang to Amazon, and Taobao to Ebay. But although these companies replicate the Western counterpart's business concept, the management methods are innovative. There are also product innovators such as Alibaba, which sells Chinese goods from all areas in China to other businesses.

In both China and India, government still gets in the way through bureaucracy and corruption; however, these countries continue to push the envelope, and competition is so fierce within their own borders that businesses must innovate in order to survive. Like Asia, Latin America is a region with high potential for entrepreneurial activity. However, in Latin America a clear demarcation exists between those governments that are "business friendly," such as Colombia and Brazil, and those that are hostile towards business, such as Venezuela and Ecuador.

In Venezuela, President Hugo Chavez's twenty-first-century socialism hinders entrepreneurial activity, because the state forces entrepreneurs to depend on state or bank financing for their formation, and on state or public company contracts for their survival. Further, the government has an inherent dislike of business people, particularly those who exhibit capitalist attributes such as initiative, risk-taking capacity, and the ability to coordinate the factors of production and promote business success in the market in order to make a profit. Venezuela's twenty-first-century socialist policies also affect entrepreneurship in other ways; for example, the use of oil revenue for the primary accumulation of a modern capitalist system means that entrepreneurs in the oil revenue system already have their earnings assured because of protection, contracts, incentives, overpricing, preferential dollars, and non-reimbursed loans.[25] As a result, these "entrepreneurs" do not have the need, desire, or know-how to compete in uncertain markets. In the long run, these socialist policies will lead to an erosion of entrepreneurial activity in Venezuela.

Another regime that may be construed as "anti-market" or at least not very hospitable to private enterprise is Ecuador. Government policies stifle businesses to such an extent that Ecuador ranks 99th out of 132 countries in terms of the obstacles to business presented by government administrative requirements, such as permits, regulations, and reporting. Further, the INSEAD Global Innovation Index ranked Ecuador 122nd out of 132 countries in innovation input and 128th in innovation potential.

On the other hand, Colombia's policies have become more pro-market, and as a result entrepreneurial activity is growing. Colombia's government is making huge investments in infrastructure and it has entered into free trade agreements (FTAs) with Canada, Chile, and Andean and Central American countries. While the FTA with the US is waiting for approval from Congress, Colombia has a commercial agreement that allows tax rebates on goods exported from Colombia to the US. Further, Colombia has made reforms to its tax regime and other areas of doing business, including being the first country in Latin America to have laws relating to investor protection. Another aspect of Colombia's environment that presented problems for entrepreneurial activity and overall investment was security. However, after 2002 the Colombian government put security at the top of the agenda, and kidnappings and murders reduced drastically.

The most pro-market country in Latin America is Brazil. It has an annual budget of US$20 billion to support innovation through various instruments and institutions, and it is developing projects that range from submarines to aircraft, as well as space research. Brazil possesses a satellite launching center and was the only country in the southern hemisphere to form part of the team responsible for the construction of the International Space Station. The country's principal innovative strengths, however, lie in deep-sea oil exploration, tropical agriculture, and regional aircraft manufacturing, in which world-class technologies have been developed. Further, Brazil has the most entrepreneurial population in the world, as measured by the percentage of the population who create enterprises, where one adult in eight starts their own business. On the domestic front, the Brazilian government appears to be making great efforts to encourage innovation through rigorous IP protection and an integrated network of institutions, laws, and norms. However, Brazil still has a long way to go. Despite recent improvements, education and infrastructure still lag behind those of China or South Korea, government coordination of innovation policies often lacks coherence, and institutions tasked with managing innovation processes, such as the Intellectual Property Agency (INPI), still tend to be bureaucratic and inefficient.

Forces and factors that threaten and challenge entrepreneurship

Entrepreneurship is crucial for the development of emerging economies because entrepreneurs are engines of investment, employment, and innovation. Therefore, it is important to determine what factors encourage the appearance of entrepreneurs. For example, a well-developed financial sector, strong contract enforcement, and investor protection will be positive factors at the social level. At the individual level, factors such as individual attitudes to risk and personal exposure to an entrepreneurial culture become more important.

Entrepreneurship is not created spontaneously. The proper environment for entrepreneurs requires well-functioning methods that nourish profitable entrepreneurial projects but avoid subsidizing unprofitable ones. The factors that threaten and challenge entrepreneurs can be classified into two categories according to their source:

- *Government and political challenges*: Local in nature, these have to do with enduring structural and institutional problems, public safety, and political leadership.
- *Globalized challenges*: These threats are not country-specific but are the result of global behavior. These include anti-market backlash, wealth gaps (inequality), underdevelopment of financial markets, and risk aversion.

Government and political challenges

Competitive small and medium enterprises (SMEs) in the formal sector generate substantial economic growth and job creation in developing countries. However, in some countries, up to 80 percent of economic activity is in the informal sector. This is a concern because informal sector firms do not pay taxes or social services for workers. This is often due to excessive bureaucracy and regulation. In addition, the recent global financial crisis made access to credit more difficult, lowered demand, slowed international trade, and lowered employment levels. This encourages the move of many formal entrepreneurs into the shadows of the informal sector.[26]

Enduring structural and institutional problems

During 2009, in reaction to the crisis, some governments (China, the Republic of Korea, Malaysia, and the Russian Federation) addressed the threat of informality and encouraged economic recovery through regulatory reforms aimed at making it easier to start and operate a business. Those reforms included strengthening property rights and improving the efficiency of commercial dispute resolution and bankruptcy procedures. This underscores the need to overcome enduring structural and institutional problems to achieve higher levels of economic development through entrepreneurship. Seven of these potential problem areas, discussed below, are particularly notable.

Government bureaucracy, corruption, and support to entrepreneurship

The Global Competitiveness Report[27] defines competitiveness as the set of institutions, policies, and factors that determine the level of productivity of a country. These elements also determine whether entrepreneurship will arise.

Bureaucracy plays a major role. However, Brazilian entrepreneurs seem to have a much lower appetite for risk. This is because, in Brazil, starting a business takes 152 days and 18 different procedures. Therefore, Brazilian entrepreneurs show an unsurprising willingness to bend the law. "Good entrepreneurship in Brazil is the ability to navigate around the bureaucracy,"[28] suggests Simeon Djankov. Eduardo Giannetti da Fonseca, an economist, concurs: "If Bill Gates had started Microsoft in a garage in Brazil, it would still be in the garage." The behavior of Brazil's entrepreneurs is not hard to explain. What is hard to explain is their existence.

Eastern Europe and Russia lag behind other emerging regions in entrepreneurship. This delayed development is partially explained by institutional deficiencies such as poorly enforced property rights, high taxation, and burdensome regulation. All these deficiencies are a legacy of the Soviet state sector. These states often interfere in an arbitrary manner in private sector firms and industries, to the detriment of new private ventures.[29] Another issue that reflects these shortcomings is the high level of corruption in these countries. Corruption is consistent with low scores on entrepreneurship. The level of corruption can be treated as a proxy for overall institutional quality and explains further the lag in entrepreneurship.

Infrastructure

It is tempting to think of infrastructure only in its physical aspects, such as roads and ports. Indeed, the World Bank emphasizes this aspect in its *Doing Business Report 2010* with indicators such as access to electricity. But entrepreneurs also need non-physical infrastructure such as training and government support for new businesses.

In physical infrastructure, the most marked contrast today is between India and China. Both are fast-growing countries and have seen enormous improvements in the lives of millions of middle-class Indians and Chinese. However, while investors are enthusiastic about China's investments in infrastructure (e.g. the fast train from Beijing to Shanghai, or the third terminal at Shanghai Pudong airport), millions of Indians are not benefiting from the boom because of the lack of physical infrastructure, especially in rural areas. To reduce the gap, the Indian government must increase investment in rural roads, logistics, cold storage chains, and electricity.

Beyond physical infrastructure, there are at least five additional dimensions of infrastructure that support entrepreneurship: government support, business support services, family–business harmony, physical facilities, financial support, and information services.[30] Hence, cookie-cutter infrastructure strategies to promote entrepreneurship are not feasible. For example, physical facilities help the most with market expansion, but resource aggregation and technological improvement are mostly determined by the quality of information services.

In a similar vein, high-tech entrepreneurial development, like nanotechnology and clean-energy technology, requires laboratory space and expensive scientific equipment. Ideally, this space should be available through collaborations between universities and off-campus incubators or accelerators. But the need for these sorts of relationships is still larger than the supply.

For any country to be in the forefront of the technology revolution – to be the leading producer, not just the leading consumer – it must have the facilities in place to develop ideas into ready-to-market products. Once a new idea or solution to a problem is recognized, the invention's viability must be researched and protected either with patents or secrecy. That protection enables a new or existing company to spend a significant amount of time developing the invention into an innovation – that is, a new, commercialized product. Scientific innovations, especially in very sophisticated technological fields, have several barriers within the commercialization cycle. Infrastructure is perhaps the greatest hurdle to commercializing high-tech inventions.

High-tech infrastructure such as incubators or accelerators is now available in developing countries like China, India, Brazil, and Chile that invest in this kind of infrastructure. Chile has Innova-CORFO, a government initiative which is financed from mining taxes.[31] CORFO helps high-tech projects with seed capital and technical support (e.g. it brings in experts from abroad). It not only supports individual innovation projects, but also business incubators and technological consortia.

Another example is Costa Rica's promotion of franchises. The government is interested in franchises as a type of formal SME (small and medium-size enterprise) that strongly generates employment.[32] Mexico experimented earlier with this same model as a way to quickly expand businesses, but it was not until 2007 that real financial support was provided with Mexico's National Franchise Program. Today Mexico is ranked seventh worldwide in franchises.

Workforce

Modern economies have shifted away from traditional low-skilled manufacturing towards a knowledge-based economy that relies heavily on human capital. Most entrepreneurs are finding it difficult to get enough skilled workers, especially in developing countries. A classic example is

India, where low-productivity agriculture still employs around 60 percent of Indian workers but contributes less than 20 percent of GDP. Ideally, this workforce should be transferred to the fast-growing services and manufacturing sectors,[33] but Indian entrepreneurs cannot find the required skills in this labor pool. The Indian government must increase its investment in education and skills formation.

Dynamic modern economies also require flexibility to hire and dismiss workers. Rigid regulations protect some jobs but discourage entrepreneurs from hiring. In Latin America, making regulations more flexible would lead to an average net increase of 2.1 percent of total employment[34] because increased dismissals would be more than compensated by increased hires (possibly by entrepreneurs). Furthermore, there should be an increase in productivity as workers are reallocated to where they are most productive. Unemployment insurance, which is designed to protect workers who lose jobs rather than protect the jobs themselves, may be more effective than rigid labor laws both in protecting workers and creating jobs. For example, Table 1.1 shows how much additional labor could be employed if the rigidity of labor laws in some countries of Latin America were decreased.

Table 1.1 Job rotation statistics

	Net Percentage change in employment if labor regulations more flexible	Additional hires as percentage of employment if labor regulations more flexible	Additional dismissals as percentage of employment if labor regulations more flexible
Argentina	2.8	5.1	2.3
Bolivia	3.3	7.2	3.9
Chile	0.8	1.7	0.9
Colombia	5.3	6.7	1.4
Ecuador	1.9	3.4	1.5
El Salvador	0.7	1.6	0.9
Guatemala	1.5	2.5	1.0
Honduras	0.3	1.1	0.8
Mexico	1.0	1.4	0.3
Nicaragua	0.0	0.4	0.4
Panama	0.4	1.7	1.3
Paraguay	4.0	8.8	4.8
Peru	3.1	3.8	0.7
Uruguay	3.9	5.4	1.6
Averages	2.1	3.6	1.6

Source: Enterprise Surveys. Calculations based on data from Enterprise Surveys. Weights are used in the calculation of country-level statistics to approximate the values that would be obtained by using a census of firms. The net percentage may not equal the hiring percentage minus the dismissal percentage due to rounding error.

Credit

It is said that good projects will find the money for their development. In reality, competition for resources with other potential businesses is fierce. Entrepreneurs have a hard time accessing formal credit since they often lack a credit history. Even if the entrepreneur has access to formal credit, this is usually more expensive in developing countries than in developed ones. The alternatives to credit are business angels, venture funds, and/or developed capital markets. Again, those options are available mostly in developed economies. In developing countries the main funding sources are personal funds and/or the funds of family members of the entrepreneur.

Nevertheless, there are exceptions. In Chile, CORFO provides direct financial support focusing on two main areas – research and business development. In Costa Rica, two state-owned banks, Banco Nacional and Banco Popular, have been funding SMEs successfully for ten years. They have become experts in serving these types of enterprises, and loans to that sector have been growing very fast. A similar role has been played by private banks in many developing nations.

In southwestern Nigeria, cooperative thrift and credit societies have evolved over time to provide credit and develop the entrepreneurial ability of owners of microenterprises. There is evidence that entrepreneurial ability and business success improve significantly in members of the cooperatives.[35]

Taxation

Taxation policies and payment systems affect new businesses in two different ways: complexity of the tax system and the impact of taxes. Brazil is the poster child of complexity. It takes 2600 hours for a medium-size business to keep up with its taxes each year and the same hypothetical business would pay 69 percent of its second-year profits in tax, if it played by the rules and did not receive special tax breaks.[36] Eastern and Central Europe discourage entrepreneurial activity both because of high taxation and state expenditure that absorb economic resources, which then become more expensive and difficult to access by the private sector.

It is traditionally said that redistributive taxation is bad for growth, because it reduces the incentive to engage in physical capital accumulation (i.e. why work hard if the extra money is going to be taxed?). More recent work challenges this story.[37] Consider a world where all economic growth comes from entrepreneurs' effort (which is higher than that of employees because moral hazard disappears). There are three types of jobs and two types of people. All unskilled people become low-skill employees. Skilled people can become entrepreneurs or high-skill employees.

As in the traditional story, taxes are potentially discouraging for successful entrepreneurs. But at the same time, redistribution creates a social insurance net that makes skilled people less afraid of becoming entrepreneurs. If this second effect is strong enough, then redistributive taxes stimulate entrepreneurship and growth. If the stimulus to growth is large enough, the negative income effect of taxes is cancelled out by the much higher overall income that skilled people will receive (either as entrepreneurs or skilled workers). Note that unskilled workers are always better off with redistributive taxes.

The social insurance effect of redistributive taxes is stronger in the presence of imperfect credit markets. This suggests that developing countries would be good candidates to use redistributive taxes to encourage entrepreneurship. In developed countries, the reduction in returns to entrepreneurs through higher taxes dominates the social insurance effect because workers already have good social insurance through other mechanisms.

Costa Rica used a tax system to promote diversification of its economy during the 1980s and 1990s. Taxes for investment in nontraditional businesses were reduced. New investments could be deducted, with some restrictions, from the income tax for a number of years. This kind of strategy can be used for short periods of time.

Cultural issues

The decision to become an entrepreneur is affected by values, beliefs, and social institutions.[38] Some societies consider entrepreneurs undesirable and people are discouraged from following this path. In former Soviet countries, schools and universities trained people to become bureaucrats so that even today, it is hard for young people to become entrepreneurs. In other countries, business people are not respected because they have shown improper behavior in that society in the past. Countries with a clear view of the importance of entrepreneurship for growth and success should work at changing the attitude of their population, and encourage them to accept entrepreneurs, and even consider them as heroes.

Coverage for natural disasters

In countries with a high risk of natural disasters, such as hurricanes, earthquakes, and floods, the availability and reasonable cost of insurance for these events are essential for new enterprises. The government response to disaster is also crucial. In Peru, there is collective insurance that is paid based on weather conditions: less or more rain than expected, ocean water temperature deviating from normal ranges, among other things. Chile began reforms aimed at eliminating barriers to the creation of SMEs, providing tax incentives (exemptions, reducing taxes), making available new credits for SMEs, and reducing bureaucratic costs in the life cycle of a company, among others.

Public safety

Developing countries frequently have a weak state unable to provide security. Guatemala's efforts to combat civilian insecurity in 2005 cost approximately US$2.4 billion, equivalent to 7.3 percent of its GDP.[39] When a country is so unsafe, entrepreneurs face additional costs to operate in comparison with other parts of the world. Those costs are either possible direct losses to firms due to violence, or expenditure in security and insurance to prevent such losses.

In Latin America one-third of the companies studied suffer from one or more incidents of crime annually. The comparable figure for Eastern Europe and Central Asia (ECA) is one-fifth. Relatively well-off large firms are more likely to be victims of crime than small firms, but losses due to crime as a percentage of annual sales are bigger for small firms. Figure 1.1 shows significant differences in the cost of security and crime across countries. In Honduras, expenses and losses as a result of violence exceed 4 percent of annual sales, four times the figure for Chile.

Corruption often takes center stage in African discussions. Even Barack Obama – who has relatives in Kenya – said "My cousin in Kenya can't find a job without paying a bribe."[40] But the data in Figure 1.2 suggests that the average cost of crime and security in Africa (2.7 percent of sales) should be as much a cause for concern as corruption (3.1 percent),[41] with some variation across countries.

Political leadership

Certain countries have regimes hostile to private enterprise. Entrepreneurs fear arbitrary actions and laws that affect the normal operations of enterprises.

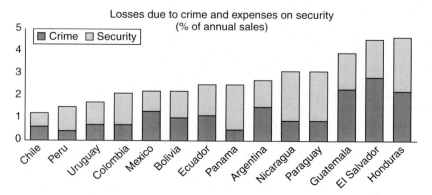

Figure 1.1 Firms in Honduras spend or lose four times as much as firms in Chile
Source: Enterprise Surveys.

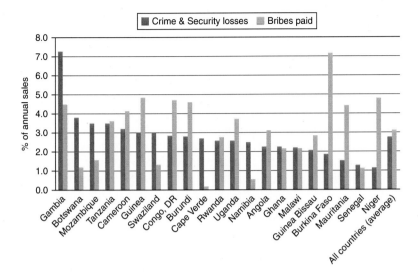

Figure 1.2 Crime, security, and corruption in Africa
Source: Enterprise Surveys. Crime and security losses above include losses to firms due to crime and their expenses on security (averaged over all firms surveyed). Surveys for the various countries were conducted at different points of time between 2005 and 2007.

Such actions can be as drastic as nationalization of entire industries, as in Venezuela, which had a free business environment for decades. At the beginning, the Venezuelan government wanted to exercise control over natural resources and other strategic industries. Later it wanted to ensure food security and distribution. Today it is about controlling public communications. Because of these risks, any new businesses developed in countries like Venezuela are less willing to commit large amounts of resources. This implies less employment and economic development.

Globalized challenges

Entrepreneurs all over the world are affected by market failure and other elements, which are specific to where an entrepreneur comes from and that may put him at a disadvantage versus other entrepreneurs that come from better environments.

Anti-market backlash emanating from the global recession

Over the last 20 years, the world economy has opened up more than at any other time in history. With the recent economic crisis the idea of protectionism has come back. The old protectionist arguments focused on the need to preserve jobs, nascent industry protection, or food security. The new protectionist arguments are about weakened domestic industries that survived the crisis and now demand government protection from what they call "foreign devils."

Protectionism due to the crisis is not reserved to emerging economies. Even the USA, long the pillar of free trade and globalization, has engaged in it, particularly in agriculture. Large American firms are outsourcing services in countries like India or China. In the context of the crisis and job losses, this outsourcing is generating an anti-India, anti-China and, in general, an anti-emerging economies backlash.[42] Governments might be compelled to establish restrictions and create legal difficulties for companies that outsource, and also create new import requirements to protect the industrial sector from foreign competitors. For example, the USA put taxes on Chinese products, specifically Chinese tires and steel pipes. This kind of strategy can lead to a form of deglobalization. For example, Latin America has not been hit so hard by the recession, but its openness to business has deteriorated significantly.

Especially worrisome is the fact that the recent financial crisis will create a market backlash supported by the creation of a "state capitalism": the US government is no longer "pushing" the market but is instead "driving" the market. For example, investment banks that were supposed to go broke were saved, even though there was not really any money available to save them. Therefore, when the economy begins to rise again, it will be with "government-picked" instead of "market-picked" industries.

These anti-market movements are more likely in developed economies; but even India, which benefits from outsourcing, could face an internal backlash. Political parties could exploit rural misery to build their own power bases, straying from sound economic policies towards populism. Governments may shy away from necessary but unpopular reforms. This could lead to a back-door return to the days of socialist policies and excessive controls on industry.

The wealth gap

Economic inequality is not good for entrepreneurship. Getting well-qualified workers becomes more difficult; government bureaucracy and corruption tend to increase; and innovation possibilities and financing opportunities become scarcer. Equality in an economy that is performing well is optimal for entrepreneurs, given that more people will have access to education, enough resources to spend, and are willing to take more entrepreneurial risks. Equality in itself is not necessarily a good result. For example in 2010, Venezuela was the most successful Latin American country in reducing the wealth gap, but achieved this by using policies that made everybody poorer than the previous year.

Income inequality can be measured by the Gini coefficient both at country and at world level. This coefficient compares the real distribution of income with the distribution in a hypothetical perfect society. As shown in Figure 1.3, it is based on the Lorenz curve, which plots the cumulative income held by the bottom *x* percent of the population.[43] When the whole world is considered, by the end of 2008 (before the financial crisis) the richest 10 percent of adults in the world were in possession of 85 percent of global household wealth. Of course, they were in the wealthiest and most developed economies: half of them lived in Japan or the USA.[44] After the economic crisis of 2008–9, the wealth gap within countries might have increased because low-income people were hit the hardest. But the crisis also hit developed countries especially hard, so worldwide inequality between countries may also have been reduced (see Figure 1.4).

Although inequality is not good for entrepreneurship, many entrepreneurial activities directed towards the bottom of the pyramid meet with great success. Inclusive growth presents opportunities not just for good politics but also for good business. Finding profitable solutions to problems can bring new avenues of growth for many industries such as health care, education, infrastructure, and agriculture. A good example is ITC, a diversified

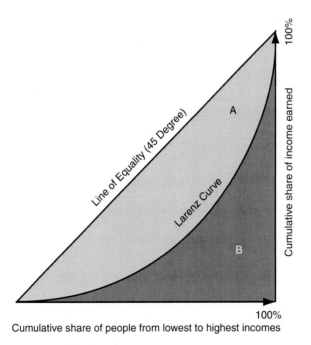

Figure 1.3   Gini index construction
Source: www.udel.edu/johnmack/frec834/development.html. The Gini index is equal to the area marked A divided by the sum of the areas marked A and B.

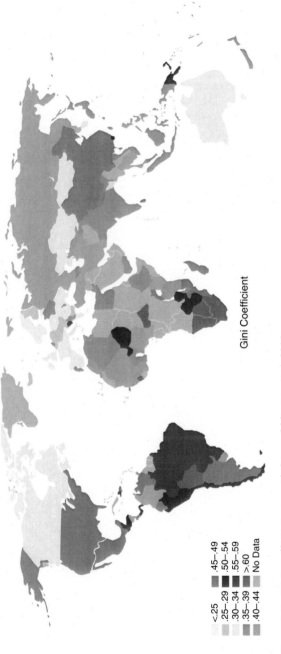

Gini Coefficient

<.25 .45–.49
.25–.29 .50–.54
.30–.34 .55–.59
.35–.39 >60
.40–.44 No Data

Figure 1.4 Gini coefficients around the world by country, 2009
Source: CIA – *The World Factbook* 2009.

Indian company that also sells packaged foods. Its "e-Choupal" project (Choupal meaning "meeting place" in Hindi) now provides the world's largest rural digital network, with 6400 centers covering 4 million farmers in 40,000 villages. It provides farmers with information on prices and best practice, helps them to procure quality inputs, and buys their produce directly. Without intermediate buyers, farmers earn more and procurement costs for the company are lower. Therefore, countries should pursue equality to improve entrepreneurship, but savvy businessmen can find opportunities in unequal environments.

Essentially, entrepreneurship is the key to break the vicious cycle of low growth and high inequality. More than half of the richest 1 percent of US households are those of entrepreneurs. Similar proportions are found for the whole world.[45] Entrepreneurship and wealthy entrepreneurs are essential for economic growth; if the right incentives are applied they can become a motor for innovation by increasing labor force productivity, creating job opportunities, and accessing financial services that could further develop sleepy financial markets. The awakening of financial markets would then increase opportunities for less wealthy entrepreneurs.

The absence of a financing culture

Access to economic resources is fundamental for any business plan during all its stages. Without access to loans, companies cannot grow. Growth would depend only on their capacity to generate excess cash. Loan availability for entrepreneurs depends on cultural factors and on society's savings in financial institutions.

Developing economies often have a culture that refuses to finance entrepreneurs. This could be related to risk aversion, or rooted in regional values that prevent people from making sacrifices for just "a possibility" of a successful new business. Furthermore, financial institutions might be mistrusted. This lack of trust translates into fewer savings available for financial institutions to loan to entrepreneurs. Domestic financial markets then remain underdeveloped, which is yet another threat (see Figure 1.5).

Mistrust is not only a problem for financial institutions. If disposable income is very low, people tend to consume most of their income and there will be few savings. The problem tends to intensify in poorer countries, sometimes even leading to negative saving rates as in Middle East and North African countries.[46]

One of the reasons is that there is greater volatility in the growth of consumption than in the growth of the economy, and that the volatility is higher in developing economies (see Figure 1.6 and Table 1.2). Given the higher level of consumption the saving rates are very low. Financial institutions are affected by this volatility, which keeps them underdeveloped; this

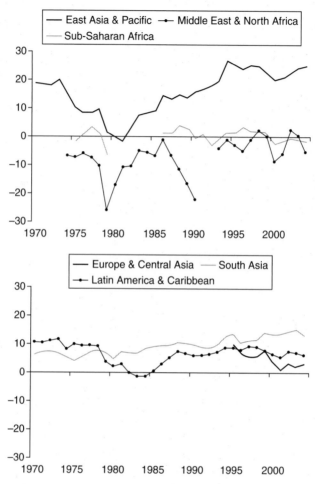

Figure 1.5   Adjusted net saving rates by region (% of GNI), 1970–2004
Source: World Bank Statistical database. data.worldbank.org.

then affects the economy, and a cycle is formed. Business angels, venture funds, and developed capital markets are crucial in order to break this cycle and remove credit restrictions for entrepreneurs, in particular for emerging economies.

Key players in the entrepreneurial environment

The environment in which entrepreneurs create, develop, operate, manage (and sell or close) their enterprises is a complex and dynamic one; outside

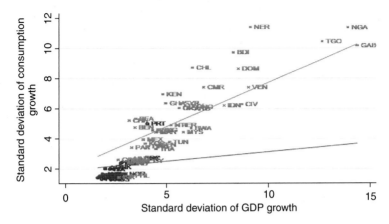

Figure 1.6 WDI data, 1960–2007. Regression lines of standard deviation of consumption growth on standard deviation of GDP growth of developed (dark line) and developing (brighter line) countries respectively. Developed countries cluster around the lower left corner which means that both consumption and GDP growth volatility are low. Developing countries spread out towards the upper right, which means that both volatilities are higher

Source: Chen H. 2009. Underdevelopment of Financial Markets and Excess Consumption Volatility in Developing Countries, University of Zurich, February 10.

Table 1.2 Standard deviation for consumption growth and output growth and their ratio for WDI data (1960–2007). All numbers are percentages. σ_c and σ_y are standard deviation for consumption growth and output growth, respectively. σ_c/σ_y is their ratio. Standard errors are in parentheses

	σ_c	σ_y	σ_c/σ_y
Developed countries	2.155	2.403	0.896
	(0.46)	(0.31)	(0.07)
Developing countries	5.385	4.503	1.197
	(0.34)	(0.19)	(0.05)
Defference	3.23	2.101	0.302
	(0.57)	(0.36)	(0.08)

Source: Chen H. 2009. Underdevelopment of Financial Markets and Excess Consumption Volatility in Developing Countries, University of Zurich, February 10.

institutions and groups participate, facilitate, and shape this environment and impact how, when, and why creative small business people succeed (or fail). The players in this milieu include various types of entrepreneurs, governmental agencies, financial institutions, universities and research laboratories, multinational enterprises, and non-governmental organizations (NGOs).

Entrepreneurs of all stripes

Formal vs. informal

The key player in the entrepreneurial environment is the *entrepreneur* himself. The first method of categorizing the entrepreneur's firm is to identify whether it is formal or informal. The former comprises officially registered, established businesses that pay taxes, comply with regulations, and adhere to other governmental requirements. The vast majority of entrepreneurial firms in industrialized nations fall into this category. On the other hand, informal businesses are those that are not taxed or monitored by governmental authorities (federal, state, or local) and are not included in a nation's gross national product. In all developing nations, small businesses – in essence, self-employment – comprise a larger share of informal employment than wage employment. Regionally, informal employment exceeds 80 percent in sub-Saharan Africa (excluding South Africa; 70 percent if that nation is included) and over 60 percent in North Africa, Latin America, and Asia.[47]

Be that as it may, governments are working diligently to create an easier, more efficient, more equitable, and more transparent environment to enable informal businesses to become formal. Guatemala, Jordan, and Sri Lanka witnessed an increase of more than 20 percent in the number of new business registrations, after the introduction of a modernized system enabling businesses to register online. Many of these businesses already existed in the informal economy, but moved to the formal one once it became easier to register. In some countries it takes about three months to register a new company in the traditional manner, versus ten minutes if it is done online. These processes also help to differentiate legitimate enterprises from shadowy ones, in addition to helping governments collect taxes.[48]

Opportunity vs. necessity

Another classification of entrepreneurs is "opportunity" versus "necessity." The GEM[49] asserts that entrepreneurs can either be "pushed" or "pulled" into entrepreneurship. Those "pulled" are opportunity entrepreneurs, while those "pushed" are necessity entrepreneurs.[50] Two major drivers of opportunity entrepreneurs are the quest for independence, and the desire to increase their income as compared to that of an employee. Necessity entrepreneurs do not have a choice because they may not have any other way to earn a living.

In the GEM studies, all high-income countries are ranked highly on opportunity-driven entrepreneurship. The most important factor in terms of motivation to find opportunities is the desire to be independent. Other factors include differential taxation of employers versus employees, and attitudes toward individual wealth creation and accumulation. In emerging markets, Chile and Uruguay are the only two examples of low- or middle-income countries with high opportunity-driven entrepreneurship. In Latin America, entrepreneurs seek increased income, rather than independence. The situation varies, with some countries showing a priority for income as the high motivator and others manifesting independence as the main driver.

GEM's 2009 report, surveying 54 countries, found that the global economic downturn that began at the end of 2008 reduced the number of people who thought there were good opportunities to start a business in many parts of the world. This increased the proportion of necessity-driven entrepreneurs – people starting businesses because they felt they had no other choice.

Social entrepreneurs

Social entrepreneurship is no longer a niche within the business world. The idea of using business to create social and environmental value alongside profits has reached nearly every sector of the economy. The uniqueness of social entrepreneurs is their dedication to blurring the distinction between making money and offering charity.[51] Some use the profits from their main business to cross-subsidize their charitable work. For example, India's Aravind Eye Care System performs 250,000 eye operations a year, and 60 percent of their work is performed for free. Others build their companies with the express intention to target a social issue. For example, entrepreneur Vinod Kapur in India developed the Kuroiler, a multicolored chicken resistant to disease, capable of surviving on scraps, fighting off predators, and producing twice as much meat as a regular chicken. He has built an entire supply chain around this chicken, including breeding specialists and vendors who sell them across rural India. Another example is Shane Immelman of South Africa who built a company by trying to bring the benefits of education to poor schoolchildren in that country. He invented the lapdesk, a desk which sits on the child's lap and is covered with advertisements. He distributes these for free to the schoolchildren in his home country, and is now also getting orders from other countries.

Intrapreneurship

Traditionally entrepreneurs were identified with independent individuals who have the drive and desire to be their "own boss." However, many entrepreneurs reside within large firms. Some of these firms recognize the value of these latent entrepreneurs and promote their entrepreneurial spirit within their organization. Thus, intrapreneurship, or corporate entrepreneurship, is the practice of a corporate management style that integrates risk-taking and innovation approaches, as well as the reward and motivational techniques that are more traditionally thought of as being the province of entrepreneurship.

One of the first examples of intrapreneurship was the PR1ME Leasing Division created by Howard E. Haller and Paul Renne. PR1ME Leasing Division enabled PR1ME Computers to more easily finance its sales by increasing the sales volume and profit margin on super minicomputer sales, as well as shortening the sales cycle. Further, in various cases, intrapreneurs also have a profound impact on society. For example, in the 1980s 3M funded the project that became perhaps the most widely used intrapreneur-developed product today: 3M's Post-it Notes(TM).[52] Intrapreneurship, however, is not exclusive to companies in developed countries, but can be found in companies around the globe. For example, the Indian division of Cadbury's, the chocolate giant, altered its formula so that its Indian chocolate would have a higher melting point than chocolate sold in Europe; which is particularly important in a nation where refrigeration is not always available.[53] Another such example is Vodafone Group plc, a telecommunications multinational corporation (MNC) based in the UK, which provides services in over 30 countries. Within its network, Vodafone created a mobile payment method for Kenyan and Afghan customers known as the M-PESA. This program allows customers to make remote transactions from one mobile phone to another, without having a bank account. As a testimony to creativity, some intrapreneurs have even identified consumer needs outside our planet. This is the case of Arla Foods, a Danish MNC, which partnered with NASA to develop dairy products that were taken into space for astronauts' consumption in 2005.

Robert C. Wolcott and Michael J. Lippitz have developed four models of corporate entrepreneurship, focusing on the idea that there is no one single approach to intrapreneurship. The first is the Enabler model, where the company provides funding, as well as senior executive attention to prospective projects. Next is the Producer, where the group with a mandate for intrapreneurship is established and fully supported by the company. The Advocate model is when the company promotes corporate entrepreneurship, while intentionally providing modest budgets and assigning organizational ownership for the creation of new businesses. Last but not least, is the Opportunist, when the company has no definite approach to intrapreneurship, relying on both internal and external forces for the allocation of resources and concept selection.[54]

Family firms

Family firms are characterized by the concentration of ownership, control, and often key management positions among family members, even after the retirement of the firm's founders. These types of firms are generally found in countries with weak legal structures where trust between family members may function as a substitute for lackluster corporate governance and contractual enforcement.

Examples of successful family firms can be found in Latin America with big family consortiums such as Grupo Votorantim in Brazil, Grupo Carso and Inbursa in Mexico, Grupo Luksic in Chile, Brescia in Peru, and Tenaris Siderca. The stability and resilience of these family firms have been put to the test when, contrary to what American scholars predicted would happen, these firms were successful even after reaching Wall Street. Their success was mainly a result of their flexibility and ability to adapt, as well as the fact that they have had to overcome many restrictions and counterproductive policies in the economies from which they emerged. For example, in many of these countries access to credit is difficult; thus, credit between related firms continues to be one of the main ways to access capital.

The main problem that family firms face is the potential inability to professionalize the management function, which could be problematic when it comes to finding a successor. However, most successful family firms have found ways to address this problem. For example, the Brazilian Grupo Odebrecht maintains a continuous search for management talent, and one of management's main goals is to train an effective successor.[55] In general, the most successful firms in Latin America are family conglomerates, a trend that seems likely to persist in years to come.

Financial institutions

Corporate venturing

The private equity and venture capital financial model was initially developed in the US and, thus, designed for the US institutional environment. However, other countries have begun to imitate it in response to the needs of local entrepreneurs. One such example is Brazil. The Brazilian venture capital model shares many similarities with the US one, such as an industry composed mostly of independent organizations, where capital management comes mostly from institutional investors, capital is heavily concentrated regionally and in a few organizations, investments are made within a close geographical distance, and software and IT are preferred sectors. The main differences between the two models are that in Brazil, investments are concentrated in more advanced stages of corporate development because credit is scarce; thus, few leverage buyouts (LBOs) take place. Also, there is a low level of sector specialization; there is a demand for commercial partners and strategic buyers for portfolio companies because of the concentration of firms in Sao Paulo's financial district; and arbitration is generally preferred because of the inefficiency of the legal system.[56]

Brazil, however, is not the only example of a developing private equity and venture capital model in the region. In a new study by the Latin American Venture Capital Association (LAVCA) and the Wharton School, over 100 private equity and venture capital firms reported making 184 investments in Latin America in 2008, totaling over US$4.4 billion. Five countries (Brazil, Mexico, Colombia, Peru, and Chile), all of which have achieved or neared investment grade status in recent years, dominated the regional private equity landscape by being home to almost 80 percent of the companies that received private equity investments in 2008. According to this study, the majority of capital raised for Latin America went to regional funds (21 percent) and to fund managers based in the two largest markets: Brazil, which captured 48 percent of funds raised, and Mexico, with 15 percent. Peru and Colombia were also represented, with three new funds raised in each of those two markets and several managers aiming to close on commitments in the first half of 2008.

Further, according to the Emerging Markets Private Equity Association, fundraising for private equity funds focusing on the developing world stands at US$35.3 billion through the first half of 2008; this represents a 68 percent increase over the same period last year and is on course to break last year's year-end record of US$59 billion. The funds that have seen the greatest increase are those focusing on Asia and Africa, while those focusing on Eastern Europe, the Middle East, as well as Latin America have respectively declined.

Venture capitalists

In general, venture capitalists are decreasing their overall investing dollars, focusing on their best companies and increasing their allocation to later-stage investments, which allows late-stage companies to shorten their venture capital gestation period by exiting sooner. Overall, the total volume of venture capital investment in the world was estimated at 0.2 percent of GDP in 2001. As the process of globalization continues, venture capitalists are adapting their strategies accordingly. The main focus for venture capitalists is China – so much so that in their minds "there is China, and then there is the rest of the world."[57]

Further, the focus of venture capitalists has begun to shift in recent years, and they now exhibit tremendous investment interest in clean technology and life sciences to the point where two thirds of venture capitalists from the Americas (excluding the US) plan to increase their clean technology investments. This shift in focus seems to be caused by an increase in local government interest in clean technology, which provides further incentives to venture capitalists.

Angel investors

For entrepreneurs in developing countries, angel investors are critical to achieving success. Angel investors provide "[in]formal venture capital-equity investments and non-collateral forms of lending made by private individuals… using their own money, directly in unquoted companies in which they have no family connection."[58] These investors are crucial in bridging the gap between a start-up and the kind of growing company that a venture capitalist would consider, because angel investors are generally less risk-averse than formal venture capitalists. Angel financing fills the gap between informal cash infusions from the 3Fs: friends, fools, and family, and later financing from venture capital firms, which, because of their high transaction costs, do not engage in small investments. Further, because business angels usually have entrepreneurial backgrounds, they are known to be hands-on investors, contributing their skills, expertise, knowledge, and contacts in a variety of informal and formal roles.

In 2010, at the World Business Angels Association conference it was announced that the new Asociación Latinoamericana de Redes de Inversionistas Ángeles (Latin American Association of Angel Investors) was created to encourage angel investor involvement in Latin America. The founding members come from nine different Latin American countries: Argentina, Brazil, Chile, Colombia, Costa Rica, Mexico, Panama, Peru, and the Dominican Republic. The organization, which is supported by the Inter-American Development Bank, has as its mission the promotion of investments and networks that contribute to the strengthening of a culture of entrepreneurship, in order to support economic development, job creation, and wealth creation in the Americas.

Investment banks

The main business of investment banks is to intermediate between issuers and investors through the functions of mergers and acquisitions (M&A) advisory services and underwriting of securities issues. They also provide trading and investing in securities and asset management. Yet, the investment banks' core function lies in the "origination" of large and complex financial instruments that expose them to market risks and imply that their business relies predominantly on the short term. The source of revenue for investment banking is shifting as a result of globalization. In 2009, the US accounted for 46 percent of total investment banking revenue, down from 56 percent a decade earlier. Europe accounted for nearly a third of the total, a proportion which has remained relatively stable during this period. Asian countries, however, have increased their share from 14 to 21 percent in the last decade.[59] This trend will most likely continue, as investment conditions in developing Asian countries continue to improve. Further, as market conditions improve, investment banks will not be able to rely to the same extent on fees generated by financial restructuring. Rather, commodities trading in emerging markets and continuing industrialization of China and other Asian countries as well as funds from the Middle East are likely to become a more important source of investment banks' business in the coming years. On the other hand, a low-interest-rate environment, along with an increase in corporate confidence and less volatile markets, should help to facilitate a pickup in M&A activity.

In terms of efficiency of investment banking around the world, very little information is available. The Swiss bank UBS is considered one of the leading investment banks in the developing nations. For example, in China, UBS spent US$210 million for a 20 percent stake in Beijing Securities as of 2007. The transaction is one of only two agreements between a foreign investment bank and a domestic securities firm that the Chinese government has approved. Similarly, in Asia, UBS was involved in the US$11.1 billion acquisition of Hutchison Essar by Vodafone, which was the biggest ever takeover involving an Indian company. Further, UBS was involved in the biggest M&A transaction in Korea; the Shinhan/LG Card deal. In Russia, UBS's presence has strengthened as a result of a joint venture with local player Brunswick Securities in 1997, which it later bought in 2004. UBS has also had a presence in the Middle East for 40 years; in 2007 it received a license to set up a branch in the Dubai International Financial Center. In Latin America, UBS was an adviser and financial provider to Brazilian iron ore producer CVRD in its hostile takeover of Canada's Inco, which at US$19.3 billion is the largest cross-border M&A transaction involving a Latin American company. In Central and Eastern Europe, UBS's standout transactions include the first RMBS (residential mortgage-backed securities) in Ukraine for Privatbank and the first ECP (Euro commercial paper) in Kazakhstan for Kazkommertsbank. However, as strong as UBS is in the world, according to World's Best Investment Banks 2010, the best investment bank in Latin America is Citi, while its equivalents are Morgan Stanley in Asia, Bank of America Merrill Lynch in Central and Eastern Europe, and Standard Bank in Africa.[60]

Universities and research labs

Strong educational systems are crucial in the development of a successful entrepreneurial environment as they provide training for potential entrepreneurs and foster research that can lead to commercial breakthroughs. Through proper funding and adequate administration of research labs and activities, universities provide a rich environment for entrepreneurs to succeed. Entrepreneurial countries such as the US have strong and vibrant education systems, particularly in higher education. Conversely, those countries where higher education and research are lacking generally exhibit low levels of entrepreneurial activity. For example, as a region, Latin America fares poorly, with an R&D to GDP ratio of 0.5 percent, which is a fifth of South Korea's, one-third of China's, and half that of India. Brazil, Mexico, and Argentina produce fewer patents in a year than Johns Hopkins, Columbia, and Harvard universities do combined. Despite this gloomy assessment, to stimulate R&D, multinational firms have become more active in the region. Microsoft, IBM, Kodak, Telefónica, and Hewlett-Packard are among those companies partnering with the region's universities. Another encouraging sign is the dramatic improvement of private universities, particularly Church-related ones in the region, which have been upgrading their faculties, revamping curricula, and investing more resources in infrastructure and operations. Higher education institutions are also partnering more with US, Canadian, and European universities.

Nevertheless, some public universities and research institutes in the region stand out. For example, in Brazil, where technological research is still carried out mainly by public universities and research institutes, the most prominent are the Oswaldo Cruz Institute, Butantan Institute, Aerospace Technical Center, the Brazilian Agricultural Research Corporation, and the INPE. The most fruitful and innovative research is being carried on in the biosciences, including biotech, at institutes like the University of São Paulo.

Another way in which universities further cultivate the students' entrepreneurial skills is through university- and corporate-sponsored competitions. The Premio Jóvenes Emprendedores competition sponsored by Uruguay's Santander Universidades seeks to monetarily reward those students with the most viable, well-organized new business plan. Similarly, in Central Europe, the Hungarian Central European University (CEU) Labor Project was the local organizer of the CAED 2008 International Conference on Comparative Analysis of Enterprise Data.

University students are also encouraged to become responsible business leaders. Students In Free Enterprise (SIFE) is a non-profit organization that maintains an international network of students, academics, and business leaders available to partner universities. This network is meant to mobilize university students to make a difference in their communities, while becoming entrepreneurs. Through annual competitions, participating students apply business concepts to developing outreach projects that improve the standard of living for people in need, while being evaluated by business leaders who serve as judges.

In Asia, some of the leading business schools such as the James Cook University and the Management Development Institute of Singapore offer BA degrees in business management and entrepreneurship, as well as BSc degrees in entrepreneurship and management. The SIM University offers an executive master's in technology entrepreneurship.

The African higher education system relies heavily on public funding. A lack of state funding and subsidies has already shown detrimental consequences. Nevertheless, some of the technologically leading universities in Africa are University Cape Town, Stellenbosch University, and University of Pretoria.

Multinational firms

Some MNCs, with a much larger monetary sum in profits than the GDP of certain countries in which they operate, can influence business environments in a myriad of ways. A few MNCs, such as the US food chain McDonald's, provide entrepreneurial opportunities around the world through their franchise system, as is the case in Latin America and the Caribbean where the chain sold 1500 restaurants for US$700 million to licensee and businessman Woods Staton. Similarly, Sony's recent investments in Paraguay, Guatemala, and El Salvador enable business ventures that also include entrepreneurship opportunities.

Another effect of MNCs is a result of the individual needs of certain subsidiary CEOs as they struggle to survive and face termination and relocation to the low-cost Eastern bloc and Asia. Through interviews conducted with the CEOs of different subsidiaries, four reinforcing strategies are seen as trends commonly used to enhance their position, as well as to foster a climate for entrepreneurship. These include taking risks, being proactive, being innovative, and halting the penalization of failure. These four trends shape entrepreneurs in the making, while they are still under the MNCs' support and have access to their resources. Employees must then be proactive, acting on, rather than reacting to, their environments. Innovators are always admired as they seek new perspectives on old problems.

Partnerships of MNCs with governments and NGOs have also been profitable ventures. This is the case of Cisco and Accenture, as they both joined the Egyptian Education Initiative (EEI), a partnership between the Egyptian government and the World Economic Forum, aiming to maximize the potential for collaborative public–private partnerships to achieve educational goals. Cisco was in charge of developing a program to teach small- and mid-size business owners to use different advanced technologies, in order to promote their business strategies of becoming more competitive and innovative. However, the new *Business Essentials Course* needed to be translated into Arabic (from the original English version), as well as modified to fit the needs of the local population. Therefore, they sought another partnership with Accenture Development Partnerships, a non-profit organization within Accenture (a global management consulting, technology services, and outsourcing company), that provides high-quality consulting services to donors, non-governmental organizations and other non-profit entities working in developing countries.

The knowledge of MNC employees is also praised, with many of them assisting at entrepreneurial competitions held at universities in order to maximize the success rate of the entrepreneurs with whom they work. Fidelity Asia Ventures (FAV), the Asian venture capital arm of Fidelity International

Ltd, is a key sponsor of the annual China Business Plan Competition, held by the Smith School's Dingman Center for Entrepreneurship. Since its inception in 2005, it has attracted more than 600 entries and awarded more than US$195,000 in cash and prizes, making it one of the largest and most influential entrepreneurship competitions in China.[61]

Governments

Governments play a crucial role in promoting the entrepreneurial environment. For example, by implementing policies to achieve aims like transparency, convenience, and rule of law (similar to those laid out by the World Bank in its *Doing Business* reports, governments can emulate at least two qualities of some of the world's most successful entrepreneurial clusters: a vibrant higher education system, and an environment open to outsiders. In the US, for example, approximately 85 percent of all high-growth business created in the past 20 years was launched by college graduates.[62] Further, the three most entrepreneurial spaces have been those inhabited by the Jewish, Chinese, and Indian diasporas.[63] This shows that educated émigrés are at the cutting edge of innovation; thus, openness to outsiders is crucial in developing a successful entrepreneurial environment.

Most governments, however, make the same basic mistake when attempting to promote entrepreneurship: assuming that there is only one successful model of an entrepreneurial cluster. It is important to realize that it would be impossible to recreate Silicon Valley without its two world class universities (Berkeley and Stanford) and a big financial center (San Francisco). Instead, each area should concentrate on its own particular strengths. *The Economist* identifies three successful entrepreneurial ecologies. These are the "anchor-firm," "driven by crisis," and "local-hero." In the anchor-firm model, one big player provides experience to employees who then decide to go it alone and nurture dozens of suppliers. For example, Hindustan Unilever is a food and personal care giant that employs 45,000 women across India to market its goods to 150 million consumers in rural areas. These saleswomen not only earn income, but they also learn about products, prices, and marketing, sending a ripple of entrepreneurship throughout rural India. Secondly, in the driven-by-crisis model people become entrepreneurs when the economy stops supplying jobs, as it did in San Diego during the 1990s and local start-ups like Qualcomm were founded. Finally, the local-hero model occurs when a local entrepreneur sees an opportunity, starts a business, and turns it into a giant. Earl Bakken, who founded Medtronic in Minneapolis in 1949, is an example of the local-hero model. In addition, there are three other major components to a successful entrepreneurial model. These are the role of chance, the importance of culture, and the impact of economic policies.

NGOs

Non-governmental organizations apply the philosophy of "don't give a fish, but teach how to catch the fish" when assisting new entrepreneurs to become successful. Several UN agencies such as the World Bank, the IMF, the UNDP, as well as regional development banks, Oxfam and Doctors without Borders from USAID, provide resources, technical assistance, financing, and managerial education. In addition, some of these NGOs also transfer or loan funds from wealthier countries to poorer countries, mainly for large public works and infrastructure projects; these contribute to capacity-building in developing countries. Within the regional development banks we find the Inter-American Development Bank, which is the primary development financing source for Latin America and the Caribbean.

Some of this assistance is focused on the young, as is the case of ACODEP (Asociación de Consultores para el Desarrollo de la Pequeña) in Nicaragua, which has designed a program to teach entrepreneurial skills to recent college graduates. Others see poor entrepreneurs as their priority, such as CREDIT (Cambodia Rural Economic Development Initiatives for Transformation), which provides sustainable financial services to 48,035 families, with loans outstanding of US$29.61 million. Furthermore, some NGOs such as MFI (Microcredit Foundation of India) focus on women. MFI promotes sustainable economic prosperity particularly among women. By establishing Madura in 2006 as a private, for-profit enterprise that worked for socioeconomic change, the new face of the MFI was able to lower operational costs, while leasing out loans at one of the lowest interest rates, between 18 and 21 percent on diminishing balances, compared to market rates of 25–40 percent. In fact, Madura topped the Forbes list for being the world's most cost-effective microfinance organization in the world in 2007.[64]

As with the MFI, other NGOs are becoming entrepreneurs in their own right to curtail the limitations presented by donor funding. In newly independent states, NGOs are generating resources through self-financing enterprises. Some examples are Ekocenter, a coordinating body for environmental NGOs in the Balkans that is using a publishing and an organic wine project to generate income; and the Organização de Ajuda Fraterna, a center for street children in Brazil that covers all of its annual expenses from the sale of furniture and hospital equipment, while simultaneously providing job training and income for its constituents.[65]

Like these, there are a myriad of NGOs all over the world helping small entrepreneurs, who because of their size are politically disadvantaged, to start their own businesses and learn the necessary skills to be successful. Further, NGOs act as a "lobbying" agent for small entrepreneurs to reduce subsidies and national regulations that discriminate against imports and, by implication, entrepreneurial activity. Access to foreign markets, trade agreements, and rules provide incentives for entrepreneurs to take advantage of opportunities for innovation and new market development on a global scale.

The case of Latin America

Entrepreneurship in the context of neo-liberal reform is vividly illustrated in the case of Latin America within the context of the "Washington Consensus." The Washington Consensus was established during the last part of the 1980s. The idea behind it was to orient policymakers in the developing world, and particularly to help weak Latin American economies recover from the debt crisis. The consensus focuses on macroeconomic issues such as finance and trade, by improving banking systems, and keeping interest and exchange rates reasonable. It also suggested that investment in infrastructure and basic education would increase through privatization and deregulation.

The Washington Consensus boosted entrepreneurship through measures that improved the economic environment. For example, fiscal discipline contributes to macroeconomic stability, and investment in human and physical capital empowers potential entrepreneurs. However, the Consensus failed to reproduce a vital element of the US economy: "support for entrepreneurship." Schramm proposes a four-sector model[66] in this regard, consisting of:

(a) *High-impact entrepreneurs*: people who start businesses need not be scientists or inventors of new products themselves.
(b) *Large mature firms*: new companies require money, skilled people, and other resources. US entrepreneurs often obtain these things from mature firms, and US corporations have learned to use new companies as reliable sources of innovation.
(c) *The government*: it uses some of its tax revenues to foster new businesses.
(d) *Universities*: they generate a constant flow of ideas for new businesses.

Governments, especially those in developing countries, are less efficient compared to the market in allocating resources. Entrepreneurs acting through markets and supported by market-friendly institutions are usually the best agents to achieve economic growth and development. For example, import substitution and export promotion policies had an impact on development, but supporting entrepreneurship and its aggressive resource allocation and mobilization would have generated a more tech- and innovation-based economic growth.[67] Additionally, entrepreneurs fill in

Table 1.3   Economic Liberty Index

11	Chile	49	Costa Rica	99	Honduras
33	Uruguay	59	Panama	113	Brazil
39	El Salvador	77	Paraguay	138	Argentina
41	Peru	79	Guatemala	147	Bolivia
45	Colombia	90	Dominican Republic	175	Venezuela
48	Mexico	98	Nicaragua		

Sources: *The Wall Street Journal* and the Heritage Foundation, January 2011.

the gaps left by incomplete and underdeveloped markets through positive externalities such as demonstration effects, knowledge dissemination, and network externalities.

An entrepreneurship-based development strategy that creates the institutions and incentives for productive, innovative entrepreneurship can positively impact growth and development in developing countries by: (1) removing many of the distortions currently present in their markets, (2) encouraging human capital development, (3) better allocating scarce resources through market processes and, (4) providing employment alternatives to the public sector.

There have been important improvements in Latin America over the last decade in all areas of interest of the Washington Consensus, especially Brazil in basic education (even if it remains below the OECD average). Exceptions such as Venezuela, Paraguay, Nicaragua, Bolivia, and Ecuador still need institutional development, clear regulation for certain industries, infrastructure, and basic education. See Table 1.3, where the economic liberty index includes measures for economic openness, regulatory efficiency, the rule of law, and competitiveness.

The Washington Consensus approach to development – which stresses privatization of state-owned companies and the freeing up of local business environments to help existing firms – has already had a positive impact on large firms. But more needs to be done to induce a real symbiosis between established firms and universities with entrepreneurs. Latin American countries must establish conditions that allow entrepreneurship to flourish: favorable business policies and regulations and access to investment and human capital.

Macroeconomic stability as the anchor of entrepreneurship

Macroeconomic stability, understood as openness of finance and trade, good banking systems, reasonable interest and exchange rates, and stable tax structures, is important for new firms. Expectations and perception have much to do with the choice of becoming an entrepreneur. Entrepreneurs expect to succeed despite the statistical odds against it. Furthermore, their perception of all other opportunities must be such that those other opportunities are less desirable than attempting to create a business on their own.

External macro factors determine the likelihood of success between the entrepreneur's two choices: entrepreneurship or traditional employment. For example GDP growth, which is an indicator of the economy's health, is correlated with the level of entrepreneurship. Another is unemployment: during periods of relatively high unemployment, individuals fear suffering extended periods of unemployment or underemployment (a position that does not maximize a person's potential productivity). These individuals may find entrepreneurship more attractive.

Tables 1.4 and 1.5 show total GDP and GDP per capita of several Latin American nations. Fortunately, inflation is now far more controlled in this group of countries, decreasing from an average of 48 percent per year in the 1980s to only 11.1 percent in 2008 and 7.6 percent in 2009.

Latin America has exhibited high growth potential as well as high sensitivity to increases in aggregate demand, but its economies have been prevented from realizing their full potential by the generalized adoption of contradictory macroeconomic policies, even within the Washington Consensus. However, there has been a recent shift in countries like Chile, Colombia, Brazil, Mexico, Uruguay, Peru, Costa Rica, and Panama that are now making great progress in realizing their full potential.

Idle resources such as unemployment and underutilization of invested capital are two very important measures for potential growth. As we can see in Table 1.6, it is a fact that labor unemployment is widespread in the

Table 1.4   GDP annual rates of growth (%)

Year	Argentina	Brazil	Chile	Colombia	Mexico	Uruguay	Venezuela
1997	8.1	3.3	6.6	3.4	6.8	5	6.4
1998	3.9	0.1	3.2	0.6	5	4.5	0.3
1999	−3.4	0.8	−0.8	−4.2	3.8	−2.8	−6
2000	−0.8	4.4	4.5	2.9	6.6	−1.4	3.7
2001	−4.4	1.3	3.4	1.5	0	−3.4	3.4
2002	−10.9	1.9	2.2	1.9	0.8	−11	−8.9
2003	8.8	0.5	3.9	3.9	1.4	2.2	−7.7
2004	9	4.9	6.2	4.8	4.2	11.8	17.9
2005	9.2	2.3	6.3	5.1	3	6.6	9.3
2006	8.5	4	4.6	6.7	4.9	4.3	9.9
2007	8.7	6.1	4.6	6.9	3.3	7.5	8.2
2008	6.8	5.1	3.7	2.7	1.5	8.5	4.8
2009	0.9	−0.2	−1.5	0.8	−6.5	2.9	−3.3

Sources: World Bank, World Development Indicators. http://www.worldbank.org/ (2006–9) and www.eclac.org (1997–2005).

Table 1.5 Per capita GDP annual rates of growth (%)

Year	Argentina	Brazil	Chile	Colombia	Mexico	Uruguay	Venezuela
1997	6.9	1.7	5.1	1.5	5	4.3	4.2
1998	2.7	−1.4	1.9	−1.3	3.3	3.8	−1.6
1999	−4.4	−0.7	−2	−6	2.1	3.6	−7.8
2000	−1.8	2.9	3.2	1.1	5	−2.2	1.8
2001	−5.4	−0.2	2.2	−0.3	−1.5	−4.1	1.5
2002	−11.7	0.4	1	0.2	−0.7	−11.7	−10.5
2003	7.8	−0.9	2.8	2.1	0	1.5	−9.3
2004	8	3.4	5	3.1	2.7	11	15.8
2005	8.2	0.9	5.2	3.4	1.6	5.8	7.5
2006	7.4	2.8	3.5	5.1	3.8	4.1	8
2007	7.6	5	3.5	5.3	2.3	7.2	6.4
2008	5.7	4.1	2.6	1.2	0.5	8.2	3.1
2009	−0.1	−1.1	−2.5	−0.6	−7.5	2.5	−4.8

Sources: World Bank, World Development Indicators. http://www.worldbank.org/ (2006–9) and www.eclac.org (1997–2005).

Table 1.6 Unemployment rates (%)

Year	Argentina	Brazil	Chile	Colombia	Mexico	Uruguay	Venezuela
1997	14.9	5.7	6.1	12.4	5.4	11.5	11.4
1998	12.9	7.6	6.4	15.3	4.7	10.1	11.3
1999	14.3	7.6	9.8	19.4	3.7	11.3	15
2000	15.1	7.1	9.2	17.2	3.4	13.6	13.9
2001	17.4	6.2	9.1	18.2	3.6	15.3	13.3
2002	19.7	11.7	9	17.6	3.9	17	15.8
2003	17.3	12.3	8.5	16.7	4.6	16.9	18
2004	13.6	11.5	8.8	15.4	5.3	13.1	15.3
2005	11.6	9.8	8	14	4.7	12.2	12.4
2006	9.5	8.4	6.0	12.7	3.2	10.6	9.3
2007	9.2	9.3	7.2	10.9	3.4	9.2	7.5
2008	7.3	7.9	7.8	11.7	4.0	7.6	7.4
2009*	8.7	8.1	9.6	12.0	5.5	7.6	7.9

Sources: World Bank, World Development Indicators. http://www.worldbank.org/ (2006–8) and www.eclac.org (1997–2005), *https://www.cia.gov/library/publications/the-world-factbook/index.html.

region. Even worse, open unemployment figures do not tell the whole story, because precarious or informal employment is very common. The estimated figures of informal employment as a percentage of the labor force for selected countries were as follows at the beginning of the past decade: Argentina, 42.5 in 2002; Brazil, 46.2 in 2001; Mexico, 47.2 in 2002; Uruguay, 45.7 in 2002; Venezuela, 56.5 in 2002. The figure was high even in Chile

(32.5, in 2000), where the rate of growth has been well above the regional average for about more than two decades.

The existence of unused resources, which would suggest substantial growth potential, is also shown in capacity utilization data. According to Banco de Mexico's surveys, in 2003 firms used only about 72 percent of their capacity, and that rate never exceeded 75 percent in the 1996–2003 period. In Brazil, even in 2004, when their highest rate of GDP growth in first part of the decade was recorded, capacity utilization reached only 82.7 percent. In Argentina, the degree of utilization of capacity in the manufacturing industry has remained below 72 percent between 2004 and 2006 in spite of fast economic growth.[68]

To overcome stagnation and employ these idle resources it will be necessary to reconstruct the state's capacity to implement pro-growth policies. Short-term macroeconomic policies to reduce unemployment and to increase the degree of capacity utilization should be used to promote the generation of profits for firms and to awaken entrepreneurs' "animal spirits." Short-term expansionary policies should be coupled with measures to improve competitiveness and avoid balance-of-payments problems. Some of this actually occurred during the 2009 crisis. Alternatives to the liberal program (Washington Consensus) will fail unless a pro-growth strategy, which includes both short- and long-term policies such as sustained increases in effective demand and prioritized investments in strategic sectors and branches of the economy, is adopted.

Additionally, there are some elements that must be carefully monitored: continued capital influx to the region makes local currencies more expensive, which in turns affects the export competitiveness and local prices. The dependence on remittances and tourism in Mexico, Central America, and the Caribbean made them especially vulnerable to the economic performance of the USA. To make matters worse, European deleveraging could diminish FDI, especially from Spain and Portugal. With its recent macroeconomic stability, known idle resources, and recent forecasted growth for the next few years, Latin America is a promising ground for new businesses and the growth of entrepreneurial activities.

Asymmetrical impacts of reform and the resulting backlash in Andean countries: Venezuela, Ecuador, Bolivia

Most countries in Latin America followed macro policies oriented towards improving stability and healthy growth. These policies also strengthened democracy, which impacted how countries managed the 2009 crisis: "we find strong evidence that positive perceptions of government economic performance and of the national economy are a major determinant of support for democracy and the political system."[69] However, there have been backlashes in Venezuela, Bolivia, and Ecuador, which introduced certain reforms towards what some call the new twenty-first-century socialism. How does socialism encourage or discourage entrepreneurship in Latin America?

Venezuela's President Hugo Chávez was re-elected in December 2006 with over 60 percent of the vote. During the campaign and ever since, he has insisted that voting for him amounts to supporting twenty-first-century socialism, although he never offers a very precise definition of it. The core of his campaign consisted of more public spending, not unlike the first term of his arch-rival Carlos Andrés Pérez.

Despite experiences around the world with state inefficiency, the centerpiece of the new socialism is the renationalization of the backbone of the economy: communications, energy, mines, and hydrocarbons, and perhaps later also food, tourism, banking, and education, declaring them to be "strategic," critical to "national security," among other arguments. Nationalized industries cannot have entrepreneurial activity.

During the 1980s the Sandinista government of Nicaragua engaged in nationalization of industries. One of the main problems they faced afterwards was lack of management capacity. Under the new socialism all these big state-owned companies will act very differently in the markets compared with a privately owned firm, because of political interference.

Privately owned firms exist under these regimes, such as new non-state or only partially state economic units that may possibly produce directly for the market. Even then, it will be a domestic market that is well protected by the government. In addition, the most extreme countries are already talking about increasing the say of the government in companies' decision processes. For example, the government may appoint directors to the board.

Under political uncertainty and without incentives to create their own company, potential entrepreneurs will seek to reduce their risk, look for a job with a non-state or state-owned local company or if they can, leave the country. The entrepreneurial spirit is difficult to kill in short periods of time, but the longer these regimes persist, the harder it will be to see entrepreneurial activities in those countries.

There have been some recent turning points, such as Bolivia's infamous increase of fuel prices. Evo Morales argues that they have to use international prices to stop illegal imports. This is a powerful argument since for the first time in his government they recognize they are not alone; there is a real-world economy. It is also an important message for the new socialism community.

Entrepreneurship and FDI across nations in Latin America

Companies from Latin America have sharply increased their outward foreign direct investment (OFDI) since 2003, as we can see in Figure 1.7.

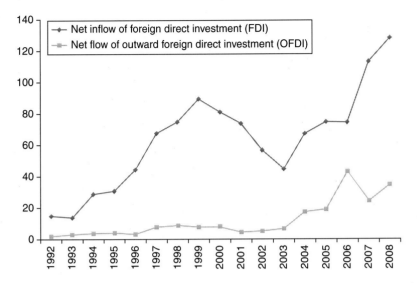

Figure 1.7 Latin America and the Caribbean: inward foreign direct investment and outward foreign direct investment, 1993–2007 (billions of dollars)
Source: Economic Commission for Latin America and the Caribbean (ECLAC), estimates on the basis of official figures as of May 15, 2009.

This investment has gone to other Latin American countries as well as overseas.

During the last decade, Latin American firms have become more international. Many now operate in many different countries. As we can see in Figure 1.8, within-region FDI has increased rapidly from the period 1999–2003 to the period 2004–8. The most active countries in this new way of doing business are Mexico, Brazil, and Chile. This intraregional FDI partially fell in 2009 due to the crisis. However, it will recover and continue growing during the next decade.[70]

This intraregional cross-country entrepreneurship is relatively new and its growth benefits from a new business regionalization mentality, which comes from better understanding of other countries, improved transportation options, and more political and macroeconomic stability. Liberalization policies and FTAs from around the region had an important effect on this process. In addition to the general improvement in business conditions, some countries are actively encouraging FDI for entrepreneurs with interesting ideas. For example, Chile has a program in which it offers up to US$40,000 for the development of an idea and a visa (open to all nationalities) for one year, renewable automatically, for entrepreneurs who come to live and develop their businesses in Chile.[71]

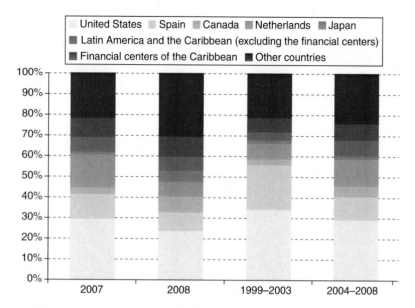

Figure 1.8   Latin America and the Caribbean: origins of foreign direct investment, 1999–2008 (billions of dollars)
Source: Economic Commission for Latin America and the Caribbean (ECLAC), estimates on the basis of official figures as of May 15, 2009.

The emerging middle class

The middle class, another socio-economic segment that is a driving force, is growing all over the world, from 430 million people in 2000 to 1.2 billion by 2030. China and India will contribute two-thirds of that growth. In Latin America, Brazil, and Mexico are the countries that will contribute the most to the rise of the emerging middle class. While GDP growth has been only moderate in Mexico, poverty has fallen from 37 to 14 percent over the last ten years. A growing middle class reflects better levels of education and therefore more productivity in the labor force.

Large reductions of poverty levels accelerate the growth of a mass consumer market. The increase in purchasing power and improved living conditions not only make established markets grow. They also generate new business opportunities for entrepreneurs. Moreover, a solid middle class means that politicians will be held accountable for maintaining and expanding progress rather than catering to elites and ignoring the plight of the poor striving for their own middle-class lifestyle. In that vein, Figure 1.9 portrays the annual disposable income – current and projected – for six major emerging markets.

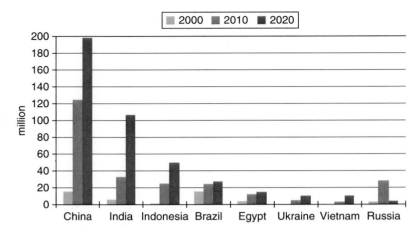

Figure 1.9 Households with annual disposable income of US$5000–15,000 in selected economies, 2000–20
Source: Euromonitor International from national statistics. Data for 2010 and 2020 are forecasts.

The emerging middle class will eventually become interested in other issues that in the long run will contribute to stability and sustainability of the countries with positive consequences for entrepreneurship. Middle-class members are more concerned than members of the base of the pyramid about democracy, religion, the environment, and general life satisfaction.[72] Entrepreneurs can profit from addressing those concerns.

Multiple market segments

The Latin American market is composed of more than 35 countries populated with over 560 million consumers, many of them with similar characteristics, origins, and shared language (Spanish and Portuguese). It is a market that is rich in natural resources and also hungry for technology and creative ideas, products, and services. This creates an extraordinary opportunity for entrepreneurs around the region. In the 1960s and 1970s when markets were totally closed, the opportunities for entrepreneurs were limited to their home countries. During that time, large and very profitable companies diversified into different businesses, leaving little space and opportunities for new entrepreneurs.

Today's openness and integration of Latin American markets allow companies to identify market segments that are similar in several countries, and with minor adjustments they can approach those groups. Companies can grow and gain economies of scale that are important for their competitiveness. These multinational companies from the region are called "multilatinas".[73] This is not to say that integration is complete. Marketers launching regional campaigns based solely on research in their own country may fail disastrously. Local cultural nuances still hold significant value. Most companies are taking those differences into consideration to reach their niches. The opportunities to expand regionally are growing as new trade agreements among countries come into effect. The most exciting process today is the potential integration of the capital markets of Chile, Peru, and Colombia. This implies that integration in Latin America may be going beyond trade issues.

The spirit of enterprise: opportunity and necessity entrepreneurs in the new millennium

There must be a sense of spirit involved when deciding to become an entrepreneur, a spirit that forces somebody to be really passionate about what he does, and also very ambitious, innovative, and with high levels of perseverance. Culture influences both economic development and the spirit of entrepreneurship. Latin America's religious history is one which manifests a preference for the poor over the rich, making the rich feel like sinners, as opposed to other religions that actually prefer the rich and successful and where being rich is a blessing. In the latter case, both the rich and the poor have a strong incentive to improve their condition, thus promoting an entrepreneurial society. In the former case, if rich people are sinners, this inverts the value of work, as in Latin America, where entrepreneurs are suspect while manual laborers are not since they must work to survive.

Spanish and British colonies distributed uninhabited land differently. In the former, all land was claimed by the Crown. In the latter, it was available to those who would work it. An exception to the Spanish rule was Costa Rica, where land was distributed by the government in the colonial period to produce coffee. This historical accident may partially explain the broader middle class in Costa Rica.

Low levels of entrepreneurship in Latin America are often blamed on, and viewed as part of, the Iberian Peninsula heritage[74] – a past-obsessed heritage that sees no use for thriftiness, perceives competition as aggression, lacks trust in fellow citizens, and encourages low compliance with laws, norms, and authority. Another factor is the pervasiveness of socialism from the late 1950s until now. It was at its strongest in Cuba then, and is in Venezuela today, but in many other countries socialism has strongholds in government employees, unions, or public universities and occasionally has reached power in governments.

Those influences affect the way the population has regarded entrepreneurs and business people. Instead of looking at them as a source of employment and development, they are seen as something negative for society. High inequality and exclusion play important roles in that attitude. During the "fat cow" years of the 1960s and 1970s, many Latin American entrepreneurs prospered and grew with government support and protection from imports, at a high cost for society, and did not do anything in compensation.

The spirit of entrepreneurship has been growing all over Latin America as it has opened up and market economies have shown some benefits. Attitudes change as countries prosper and their populations enjoy better education, health services, and living conditions. Of course, the change is strong in Chile and Mexico but not in Cuba, Venezuela, Bolivia, and Ecuador. Governments now help emerging businesses; universities collaborate more with the business community; and people work harder as they recognize that their prosperity is based on their individual effort and no longer expect that prosperity just from government.

Nevertheless, entrepreneurial spirit is not enough to become an entrepreneur. As Herrera and Brown observe: "When somebody is trying to swim: you may have a great desire to swim in the sea but if you don't know how to swim and you just throw yourself in the water, two things can happen: Either you move forward with great difficulty, guided by your instincts, or you simply drown."[75] So the entrepreneur should keep in mind the importance of knowledge and learning as well as the right economic and political environment.

The (de)evolving family firm

In Latin America, entrepreneurs often come from families active in business. This is partly because these families have substantial resources, networks, and capabilities to develop new businesses, either within the family firm or as spin-offs. Hence, family businesses represent over 90 percent of the firms in Latin America.

The STEP Project[76] has found, by looking at the history of Latin American family firms, that the generations after the business founders remain highly entrepreneurial. However, there are ways to contribute to those entrepreneurial processes within the family and the family firm. Among these are being an exemplary entrepreneur for younger generations, motivating and incentivizing entrepreneurship, and transmitting entrepreneurial values over generations. Successful families use entrepreneurial action as a strategy for growth. They also encourage innovation within the firm as an extension of the family values that inspire entrepreneurship. Less successful firms have leader-centered cultures and lack world-class corporate governance, two flaws that limit entrepreneurship.

The complex array of forces and factors that shape entrepreneurship is one that permeates the environment of all countries. This is especially true of Latin America's big emerging markets and Central America's most stable and democratic nation, Costa Rica. Each is addressed in this volume by experts who are intimately familiar with the entrepreneurial milieu of these countries.

Argentina

Maria Pradilla's chapter on Argentina presents an overview of entrepreneurship in that country, including its historical roots and trajectory. First, the chapter presents the entrepreneurial environment in that nation with a focus on the main macroeconomic variables that affect the growth and development of small business enterprises. This is followed by a section that hones in on the challenges and opportunities for entrepreneurs in Argentina. That is followed by two case studies of successful Argentine entrepreneurs who founded "born global" businesses – enterprises for whom external markets are their main or even exclusive focus of commercial activity. Pradilla also addresses the often neglected but critically important role that entrepreneurship education plays in preparing a workforce that can harness and manifest the skills that education in entrepreneurship can provide. The development of small business incubators and business plan competitions are encouraging signs that the outlook for entrepreneurship in Argentina is brighter than a decade ago.

Brazil

Da Rocha, Ferreira de Silva, and Carneiro focus on the analysis of both institutional facilitators and obstacles to the growth of new ventures in Brazil, using case studies of two successful companies in distinct sectors of the economy – a software developer, and a manufacturer and retailer. While these were successful cases, the writers illustrate how two distinctive strategies enabled these firms to triumph in difficult economic times. The institutional facilitators they mention are the availability of financial and human capital and an adequate regulatory framework. Conversely, there are factors that impede entrepreneurial activity, such as high levels of corruption. The writers argue that the existence of government policies and institutions that favor the development of an environment supportive of entrepreneurship is of critical importance, in fact a prerequisite to new venture formation and survival.

Chile

Chile is indisputably perceived as the top performer in the Latin American region with respect to macroeconomic environment, political risk, and clear and transparent access to information, which gives confidence to invest and provides a healthy environment for entrepreneurs. The nation unilaterally embarked upon neo-liberal economic reform nearly a decade before other countries in Latin America and the Caribbean. Not surprisingly, Chile possesses a host of positive characteristics that make it the most recommendable place in the region to start and run a business.

Nevertheless, the country confronts many challenges that need to be addressed for it to become a truly entrepreneurially oriented country.

Jiménez and Usach address this issue, including the contradictions of a society that does not encourage risk-taking and has little tolerance of failure, yet overwhelmingly respects and admires business success among entrepreneurs.

Colombia

This chapter indicates that there is a high prevalence of both necessity and opportunity entrepreneurship in Colombia. However, there are few results yet in terms of the presence of high-potential entrepreneurial ventures, of the kind that could lead the country into a new stage of economic development. It also presents an interesting discussion about unique government and institutional policies especially established to promote entrepreneurship, which have had very good results so far. The case of CB Group, a cosmetics company, is presented to illustrate some of the strong and weak points of what is called the Colombian entrepreneurial ecosystem. At the end, the chapter offers recommendations for strengthening the entrepreneurial ecosystem and the development of Colombia as an entrepreneurial economy.

Costa Rica

This chapter's focus is on how Costa Rica is transforming a knowledge society into a knowledge-based economy. Entrepreneurial activities are growing, especially in the IT sector. This is happening even as constraints exist, starting from a lack of financing with not many options for angels or venture capital, a thin stock market, and not enough products from the banking system to support start-ups. Additionally, even though human resources are well trained there seems to be a lack of entrepreneurial drive and a large number of bureaucratic inefficiencies. The chapter presents how the IT industry has been growing during the last decade, from a few firms to 290, with industry reported sales of over US$200 million. Two very interesting cases are presented: Mora and Beck, which discusses the process of angel financing, and Fair Play Labs, who ended up producing games for Nintendo among others. The chapter finishes by discussing the challenges for entrepreneurship in a transition economy.

Mexico

This chapter describes the reasons why Mexico has become an interesting environment for entrepreneurship. It argues that opportunities for employment might not be a good option given the low salary levels and the lack of real employment benefits. Therefore, many consider self-employment or being an *empresario* as a better opportunity, which in addition, is actually seen as a good activity by society. Business informality is common and in most cases those businesses are usually more profitable than formal companies, as a result of government bureaucracy and environmental complexity. Staying small, informal, and working together with the family networks is a strategy that leads to just enough success for many Mexican entrepreneurs. The chapter presents many mini cases of several entrepreneurial ventures from around the country; among others, the southern Zapatistas' business network, the history of Grupo Liverpool and how Grupo Azteca and its CEO Ricardo Salinas created an entrepreneurial culture.

Peru

In the case of Peru, Nakamatsu, Morales, and Serida provide a comprehensive assessment of the socio-economic and political environment for entrepreneurship in that country. Peru was able to weather the storm of the global financial crisis of 2008–10 and adopted an economic stimulus plan that preserved job creation and public investment. At the same time, the government took measures to improve the regulatory and investment environment for both multinational firms and small- and medium-sized enterprises alike. The writers point out that the level of necessity entrepreneurs has declined precipitously, since the economy has been improving steadily over the last decade, and the number of opportunity entrepreneurs is growing at twice the rate of the former. They delve deeply into microfinance as a stimulus of entrepreneurship and highlight Peru's gastronomic boom with a case study of Roky's Chicken and Grill.

Venezuela

Roberto Vainrub and Aramis Rodriguez's chapter on Venezuela presents and analyzes the historical and cultural factors that have manifested an impact on entrepreneurial activity in Venezuela, followed by a review of the economic and political developments that shape the country's business environment. Measures of entrepreneurship during periods of economic, financial, and regulatory volatility are examined. It is revealed that year after year, Venezuela has ranked among the world's top countries in terms of early entrepreneurial activity as measured by the GEM. Annually, as many as 3 million people, approximately 22.8 percent of Venezuelan adults, start a new business or run a recent start-up. The writers then describe the best practices of key players who grew their business under turbulent conditions. Among the cases they highlight are Casa Hellmund, Grupo Sambil, Chocolates El Rey, and the Cisneros Organization. The chapter concludes by presenting a number of challenges currently faced by investors in Venezuela, together with the opportunities within reach of entrepreneurs with vision, determination, commitment, and endurance.

Notes

1. World Bank, *Global Economic Prospects: Fiscal Headwinds and Recovery*. Washington, DC: World Bank Group, Summer 2010.
2. A. Wooldridge, "The World Turned Upside Down," *The Economist*, April 15, 2010: 2.
3. A. Wooldridge, "Global Heroes," *The Economist*, March 14, 2009, http://www. economist.com/node/13216025?story_id=13216025.
4. A. Wooldridge, "An Idea Whose Time has Come," *The Economist*, March 14, 2009, http://www.economist.com/node/13216025.
5. Ibid.
6. J. Haar and J. Meyer-Stamer, *Small Firms, Global Markets: Competitive Challenges in the New Economy*. New York: Palgrave Macmillan, 2008: 11.
7. A. Wooldridge, "The World Turned Upside Down," *The Economist*, April 15, 2010: 1.
8. "Magic Formula," *The Economist*, March 12, 2009, http:// www.economist.com/ node/13216077.
9. World Bank, *World Development Indicators 2009*. Washington, DC: World Bank, 2009.
10. World Trade Organization, *International Trade Statistics 2010*. Geneva: World Trade Organization, 2010.
11. Ibid.
12. World Trade Organization, "Some Figures on Regional Trade Agreements Notified to the GATT/WTO and in Force," http//rtais.wto.org/UI/publicsummarytable.aspx.
13. C. Loser, "Global Financial Turmoil and Emerging Market Economies: Major Contagion and a Shocking Loss of Wealth?," Centennial Group, Asian Development Bank, 2009: 7.
14. World Bank, *Global Economic Report 2010*. Washington, DC: World Bank Group, 2010: 76.
15. S. Singh, *Handbook of Business Practices and Growth in Emerging Market*. Hackensack, NJ: World Scientific Publishing, 2010: 257.
16. S. Pelle, *Understanding Emerging Markets: Building Business BRIC by Brick*. New Delhi: Tejeshwar Singh, 2007: 35–36.
17. J. A. Caslione and A. R. Thomas, *Growing your Business in Emerging Markets: Promise and Perils*. Westport: Quorum Books, 2000: 31.
18. Antoine W. van Agtmael, *The Emerging Market: How a New Breed of World-Class Companies is Overtaking the World*. New York: Free Press, 2007: 20.
19. United Nations, *2009 World Survey on the Role of Women in Development*. New York: United Nations, 2009.
20. Leo-Paul Dana, *Handbook of Research on Ethnic Minority Entrepreneurship*. Cheltenham, UK: Edward Elgar, 2007: 5.
21. "Lands of Opportunity," *The Economist*, May 12, 2009.
22. Ibid.
23. Ibid.
24. "The More the Merrier," *The Economist*, May 12, 2009.
25. Raúl González Fabre, "Five Little Problems with Venezuela's Brand of 21st Century Socialism," *Envio*, March 2007, http://www.envio.org.ni/articulo/3673.
26. World Bank, *Doing Business 2010*. Washington, DC: World Bank Group, 2010.
27. World Economic Forum, *Global Competitiveness Report for 2010–2011*. Geneva: World Economic Forum, 2010.
28. S. Djankov, "Betting the Fazenda, a Different Kind of Risk-Taking," *The Economist*, March 6, 2008.

29. Global Entrepreneurship Monitor (GEM), *2010 Global Report*. Wellesley, MA: Babson College, 2010.
30. J. Liao, H. Welsch, and D. Pistrui, "Entrepreneurial Expansion Plans: an Empirical Investigation of Infrastructure Predictors," *New England Journal of Entrepreneurship*, Spring 2009: 19–33, http://proquest.umi.com.ezproxy.fiu.edu/pqdweb?did=1703 453311&sid=29&Fmt=3&clientId=20175&RQT=309&VName=PQD.
31. CORFO, *2010 Annual Report*. Santiago: Corporación del Fomento de la Producción, 2010.
32. L.D. Quirós, "Costa Rica promueve las franquicias como política pública para el desarrollo," *Revista Summa*, October 26, 2010.
33. "Policy: Still Poor, Mostly," *Business Asia*, November 3, 2008.
34. World Bank, *The Effects of Rigid Labor Regulations in Latin America*. Washington, DC: World Bank Group, 2009.
35. B. Adekunle, *The Impact of Cooperative Thrift and Credit Societies on Entrepreneurship and Microenterprise Performance*. University of Guelph, 2007.
36. World Bank, *Doing Business 2010*. Washington, DC: World Bank Group, 2010.
37. C. García-Peñalosa and J. Wen, "Redistribution and Entrepreneurship with Schumpeterian Growth," *Journal of Economic Growth*, 13, 1, 2008: 57.
38. L. Harrison and S. Huntington, Eds. *Culture Matters: How Values Shape Human Progress*. New York: Basic Books, 2000.
39. C. Munaiz and A. Mendoza, *The High Price of Violence*. Rome: Inter Press Service, 2007.
40. J. Tapper and S. Miller, "Political Punch. 'My Cousin In Kenya Can't Get a Job Without Paying a Bribe': Obama Tells African Leaders to Get Their Houses in Order," *ABC News*, July 10, 2009. http://blogs.abcnews.com/politicalpunch/2009/07/my-cousin-in-kenya-cant-get-a-job-without-paying-a-bribe-obama-tells-african-leaders-to-get-their-ho.html.
41. World Bank, *Enterprise Surveys*. Washington, DC: World Bank Group, 2010.
42. D. Karl, "America's New Anti-India Backlash," *Bloomberg BusinessWeek*, May 13, 2010. http://www.businessweek.com/globalbiz/content/may2010/gb20100513_405539.htm.
43. More equal distributions yield Gini coefficients closer to 0, more unequal distributions of income yield values closer to 1. Within countries Gini coefficients vary from 0.23 (Sweden) to 0.70 (Namibia).
44. W. Naudé and J.C. MacGee, "Wealth Distribution, the Financial Crisis and Entrepreneurism," *WIDER Angle Newsletter*, March, 2009. http://www.wider.unu.edu/publications/newsletter/articles/en_GB/10-03-2008-feature-article/.
45. Ibid.
46. World Bank Statistical Database.
47. Kristina Flodman Becker, *The Informal Economy*. Stockholm: Swedish International Development Agency, 2004, 5.
48. Leora Klapper, Raphael Amit, Mauro F. Guillén, and Juan Manuel Quesada, "International Differences in Entrepreneurship," in *Entrepreneurship and Firm Formation across Countries*, Ed. Josh Lerner and Antoinette Schoar, Chicago and London: The University of Chicago Press, 2010, 129.
49. Global Entrepreneurship Monitor, *2007 Executive Report*, January 18, 2008, http://www.gemconsortium.org/download/1293546602093/GEM_2007_Executive_Report.pdf.
50. Global Entrepreneurship Monitor, *2009 Global Report*, April 14, 2010, http://www.gemconsortium.org/download/1293549742796/GEM%202009%20Global%20Report%20Rev%20140410.pdf.

51. Nick Dewar, "Saving the World," *The Economist*, March 12, 2009.
52. John S. DeMott and Rosemary Byrne, "Here Come the Intrapreneurs," *Time*, February 4, 1985.
53. Alonso Martinez and Ronald Haddock, "The Flatbread Factor," *Strategy + Business*, Spring 2007.
54. Robert C. Wolcott and Michael J. Lippitz, "The Four Models of Corporate Entrepreneurship," *MIT Sloan, Management Review*, 49, 1, October, 2007.
55. Eduardo Thomsom, "Cuestión de Família," *America Economía*, August 2008.
56. Leonardo de Lima Ribeiro, Antonio Gledson de Carvalho, "Private equity and venture capital in an emerging economy: evidence from Brazil," *Venture Capital*, 10, 2, 2008: 111–126.
57. Deloitte, *Global Trends in Venture Capital – 2010 Global Report*. New York: Deloitte, 2010.
58. Global Entrepreneurship Monitor, *2009 Global Report*, April 14, 2010.
59. *Banking 2010*, International Financial Services London (February 2010), http://www.ifsl.org.uk/media/2372/IFSL_Banking_2010.pdf, 8.
60. "World's Best Investment Banks 2010," *Global Finance*, April 19, 2010.
61. "Chinese Entrepreneurs Win More than $50,000 in Cash and Prizes in International Business Plan Competition," University of Maryland, Robert H. Smith School of Business (October 29, 2008), http://www.rhsmith.umd.edu/news/releases/2008/102908.aspx.
62. "Magic Formula," *The Economist*, March 12, 2009.
63. Ibid.
64. Sumaiya Khan, "The Accidental Entrepreneur," *India Today,* April 7, 2010.
65. Lee Davis, "The NGO Entrepreneur: Nonprofit in Purpose, For-Profit in Approach," ISAR Resources for Environmental Activists, December 9, 2010.
66. C. Schramm. "Building Entrepreneurial Economies," *Foreign Affairs*, 83, 4, 2004.
67. Z. Acs and N. Virgill, "Entrepreneurship in Developing Countries," *The Jena Economic Papers*, 2009.
68. All the estimates come from ECLAC and *Revista de Economía Poíítica* 28, 3, 2008.
69. Mitchell Seligson and Amy Erica Smith, Eds. *Political Culture of Democracy*. Nashville: Vanderbilt University, 2010.
70. United Nations Economic Commission on Latin America and the Caribbean, *Foreign Direct Investment in Latin America and the Caribbean*. Santiago: ECLAC, 2008.
71. Area Development Online, "Start-Up Chile Seeks Innovative Entrepreneurs," July 28, 2010.
72. Pew Global Attitude Project, 2009. *The Globe's Emerging Middle Classes: Views on Democracy, Religion, Values and Life Satisfaction in Emerging Nations*. February 12, 2009. http://pewresearch.org/pubs/1119/global-middle-class.
73. For an in-depth analysis of *multilatinas* see: Alfonso Fleury and Maria Tereza Fleury, *Brazilian Multinationals*. New York: Cambridge University Press, 2011; Alvaro Cuervo-Cazurra, "The multinationalization of developing country MNEs: The case of multilatinasm," *Journal of International Management*, 14, 2, 2008: 138–154; Robert E. Grosse and Luiz F. Mesquita, eds., *Can Latin American Firms Compete?* New York: Oxford University Press, 2007; and Fernando Robles, Françoise Simon, and Jerry Haar, *Winning Strategies for the New Latin Markets*. Englewood Cliffs, New Jersey and London: Prentice-Hall and Financial Times, 2003.
74. H. Herrera and D. Brown, "Entrepreneurial Spirit in Latin America," *Universia-Knowledge@Wharton*, interview, March 19, 2008.
75. Ibid.

76. STEP Project: Several business schools from the region are coordinating, with Babson College, in a study to improve understanding of transgenerational entrepreneurship.

References

Acs, Z. and N. Virgill. 2009. *Entrepreneurship in Developing Countries*. The Jena Economic Papers, Jena, Germany. http://www.wiwi.unijena.de/Papers/jerp2009/wp_209_023.pdf.

Adekunle, B. 2007. *The Impact of Cooperative Thrift and Credit Societies on Entrepreneurship and Microenterprise Performance*. Guelph: University of Guelph.

Area Development Online. 2010. "Start-Up Chile Seeks Innovative Entrepreneurs." July 28.

Business Asia. 2008. "Policy: Still Poor, Mostly." November 3.

Caslione, J.A. and A.R. Thomas. 2000. *Growing your Business in Emerging Markets: Promise and Perils*. Westport: Quorum Books.

CORFO. 2010. *2010 Annual Report*. Santiago: Corporación del Fomento de la Producción.

Dana, L. 2007. *Handbook of Research on Ethnic Minority Entrepreneurship*. Cheltenham, UK: Edward Elgar.

Davis, L. 2010. "The NGO Entrepreneur: Nonprofit in Purpose, For-Profit in Approach." ISAR Resources for Environmental Activists, December 9.

De Lima Ribeiro, L. and A.G. De Carvalho. 2008. "Private Equity and Venture Capital in an Emerging Economy: Evidence from Brazil." *Venture Capital*, 10, no. 2.

Deloitte. 2010. *Global Trends in Venture Capital – 2010 Global Report*. New York: Deloitte.

DeMott, J.S. and R. Byrne. 1985. "Here Come the Intrapreneurs." *Time*, February 4.

Dewar, N. 2009. "Saving the World." *The Economist*, March 12.

Djankov, S. 2008. "Betting the Fazenda, a Different Kind of Risk-Taking." *The Economist*, March 6.

The Economist. 2009a. *Globalization Stalled: How the Global Economic Upheaval Will Hit the Business Environment*. The Economist Intelligence Unit, May.

The Economist. 2009b. "Lands of Opportunity." May 12.

The Economist. 2009c. "Magic Formula." March 12.

The Economist. 2009d. "The More the Merrier." May 12.

Flodman Becker, K. 2004. *The Informal Economy*. Stockholm: Swedish International Development Agency.

Global Entrepreneurship Monitor (GEM). 2008. *2007 Executive Report*. January 18.

Global Entrepreneurship Monitor (GEM). 2010. *2009 Global Report*. April 14.

Global Finance. 2010. "World's Best Investment Banks." April 9.

González Fabre, R. 2007. "Five Little Problems with Venezuela's Brand of 21st Century Socialism." *Revista Envío*. Universidad Centroamericana. March.

Haar, J. and J. Meyer-Stamer. 2008. *Small Firms, Global Markets: Competitive Challenges in the New Economy*. New York: Palgrave Macmillan.

Harrison, L. and S. Huntington, Eds. 2000 *Culture Matters: How Values Shape Human Progress*. New York: Basic Books.

Herrera, H. and D. Brown. 2008. *The Spirit of Entrepreneurship in Latin America*. Universia-Knowledge@Wharton, interview, March 19.

Interbank, Annual Reports, 2009.

International Financial Services London. 2010. *Banking 2010*. February.

Karl, D. 2010. "America's New Anti-India Backlash." *Bloomberg Business Week,* May 13.

Khan, S. 2010. "The Accidental Entrepreneur." *India Today,* April 7.

Lemer, J. and A. Schoar. 2010. *Entrepreneurship and Firm Formation across Countries.* Chicago and London: The University of Chicago Press.

Liao, J., H. Welsch, and D. Pistrui. 2009. "Entrepreneurial Expansion Plans: an Empirical Investigation of Infrastructure Predictors." *New England Journal of Entrepreneurship*, Fairfield, 12, no. 1, Spring: 19–33.

Loser, C. 2009. "Global Financial Turmoil and Emerging Market Economies: Major Contagion and a Shocking Loss of Wealth?" Centennial Group, Asian Development Bank.

Martinez, A. and R. Haddock. 2007. "The Flatbread Factor." *Strategy + Business,* Spring.

Moore, V. 2009. "Nano Entrepreneurship." *Mechanical Engineering,* New York, 131, no. 4.

Munaiz, C. and A. Mendoza. 2007. *The High Price of Violence.* Rome: Inter Press Service.

Naudé, W. and J.C. MacGee. 2009. *Wealth Distribution, the Financial Crisis and Entrepreneurism.* WIDER Angle newsletter, March.

Pelle, S. 2007. *Understanding Emerging Markets: Building Business BRIC by* Brick. New Delhi: Tejeshwar Singh.

Pew Global Attitude Project. 2009. *The Globe's Emerging Middle Classes: Views on Democracy, Religion, Values and Life Satisfaction in Emerging Nations.* February 12.

Quirós, L.D. 2010. "Costa Rica promueve las franquicias como política pública para el desarrollo." *Revista Summa,* October 26.

Schramm, C. 2004. "Building Entrepreneurial Economies." *Foreign Affairs,* New York, 83, no. 4, Jul/Aug: 104.

Seligson, M. and A.E. Smith, Eds. 2010. *Political Culture of Democracy.* Nashville: Vanderbilt University.

Tapper, J. 2009. "Political Punch. 'My Cousin in Kenya Can't Get a Job without Paying a Bribe': Obama Tells African Leaders to Get Their Houses in Order." ABC News, July 10.

United Nations. 2009. *2009 World Survey on the Role of Women in Development.* New York: United Nations.

United Nations Economic Commission on Latin America and the Caribbean. 2008 *Foreign Direct Investment in Latin America and the Caribbean.* Santiago: ECLAC.

University of Maryland. 2008. "Chinese Entrepreneurs Win More than $50,000 in Cash and Prizes in International Business Plan Competition." October 29.

Van Agtmael, A.W. 2007. *The Emerging Market: How a Breed of World-Class Companies is Overtaking the World.* New York: Free Press.

Wolcott, R.C. and M.J. Lippitz. 2007. "The Four Models of Corporate Entrepreneurship." *MIT Sloan Management Review,* 49, no. 1, October.

Wooldridge, Adrian. 2009a. "An Idea Whose Time has Come." *The Economist,* March 14.

Wooldridge, Adrian. 2009b. "Global Heroes." *The Economist,* March 14.

Wooldridge, Adrian. 2010. "The World Turned Upside Down." *The Economist,* April 15.

World Bank. 2010a. *Doing Business 2010: Reforming through Difficult Times.* Washington, DC: World Bank.

World Bank. 2010b. *Global Economic Prospects: Fiscal Headwinds and Recovery.* Washington, DC: World Bank Group.

World Bank Statistical Database.

World Bank. 2009. *World Development Indicators 2009*. Washington, DC: World Bank Group.

World Bank. 2010a. *Global Economic Report 2010*. Washington, DC: World Bank Group.

World Bank. Summer 2010b. *Global Economic Prospects: Fiscal Headwinds and Recovery*. Washington, DC: World Bank Group.

World Bank. 2011. *Global Economic Prospects: Navigation Strong Currents*. Washington, DC: World Bank Group, January 12.

World Bank Group. 2009. *The Effects of Rigid Labor Regulations in Latin America*. Washington, DC: World Bank.

World Bank Group. 2010. *Enterprise Surveys*. Washington, DC: World Bank.

World Economic Forum. 2010. *Global Competitiveness Report for 2010–2011*. Geneva, Switzerland.

World Trade Organization. 2010. *International Trade Statistics 2010*. Geneva: World Trade Organization.

2
Entrepreneurship in Argentina

Maria Pradilla
Florida International University

The objective of this chapter is to present an overview of the entrepreneurial environment in Argentina. First, this chapter examines the overall macroeconomic and entrepreneurial environment in Argentina and analyzes how changing conditions have affected entrepreneurial activity. Then, the chapter focuses on the challenges and opportunities that entrepreneurs face in Argentina and evaluates how a successful entrepreneurial company overcame these challenges and took advantage of the opportunities. Finally, the chapter presents the outlook for entrepreneurship in Argentina and posits a series of recommendations for improving the entrepreneurial environment.

Argentina's macroeconomic and entrepreneurial environment

This section will discuss the broad macroeconomic environment in Argentina as well as the more specific regulatory and cultural conditions that affect entrepreneurial activity. To illustrate the effects of these different forces on the entrepreneurial environment in Argentina, the results from the 2009 GEM report on Argentina's entrepreneurship will be used.

Over the past two decades, Argentina's economy has undergone severe challenges. In the early 1990s, after a period of stagflation, the government pegged the peso to the US dollar; limited the growth in the money supply; and began a process of trade liberalization, deregulation, and privatization. Although during those years inflation dropped and GDP grew, the economy began to crumble in 1995, and by 2001 Argentina's economy collapsed. In 2002, Argentina defaulted on its debt, GDP shrunk even further, unemployment reached 25 percent and the peso depreciated 70 percent after being devalued and floated. These changes in macroeconomic conditions affected firm creation and closure as illustrated by Figure 2.1. In 1996, there were 377,000 firms in Argentina, but as a result of the crisis, firm creation

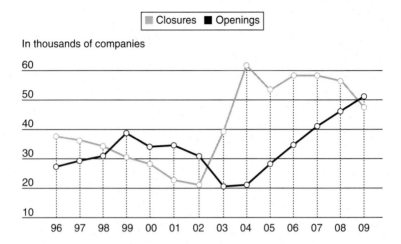

Figure 2.1 Companies in Argentina
Source: Clarin.com from OEDE-MTEYSS.

declined from close to 40,000 in 1996 to approximately 20,000 in 2002, bringing the total number of firms to 356,000 (Kantor 2011).

The economy began to rebound in 2003, growing at around 9 percent annually between 2003 and 2007, and 7 percent in 2008. However, Argentina was not immune to the global recession and, in 2009, economic growth slowed to 0.8 percent. High economic growth resumed in 2010, and GDP expanded by 9.2 percent. Accordingly, firm creation was at its highest in 2003 but began a downward trend up to 2009. Between 2009 and 2010, 49,000 new firms were created but 53,000 firms closed, bringing the total number of firms to 487,600 (Figure 2.1). The Economist Intelligence Unit predicts that over the next five years, Argentina's economic growth will slow from an estimated 6.7 percent GDP growth in 2011 to only 3.5 percent in 2015, which is likely to also decrease firm creation and increase firm closures (EIU 2011).

Inflation, unemployment, and overall economic uecertainty and fear are also factors that contribute to economic instability, which stifles entrepreneurial activity. Although inflation has decreased since 2004 (Figure 2.2), making it more attractive for entrepreneurs to begin new ventures, Argentines are still reluctant to start new firms because there is an overall distrust about whether the economy will continue to improve and stabilize. On the other hand, unemployment in Argentina has decreased below 8 percent and, according to the Economist Intelligence Unit, will continue to decrease over the next three years.

Overall, the year 2010 ended with good results in terms of growth, public finance, and to a lesser extent inflation, providing a strong impetus to

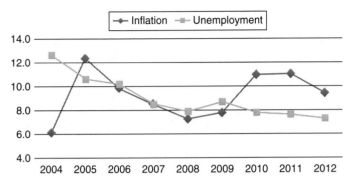

Figure 2.2 Argentina's inflation and unemployment rate
Source: EIU (2011).

continue that trend in 2011 and contributing to the launch of new ventures. However, the economic environment is still unstable, and entrepreneurs as well as investors may still be reluctant to "dive in" and start or support new ventures. A longer period of growth and stability is necessary to build trust in the minds of investors and entrepreneurs, and to be able to determine whether the positive trend will continue because, even though the current results confirm the positive macroeconomic trends of the past couple of years, promoting entrepreneurial activity requires ample periods of stability in order for potential entrepreneurs to gain the necessary confidence and to decide to take advantage of the available opportunities.

Findings from the 2009 GEM Report

According to the GEM, the overall rate of early stage entrepreneurial activity in 2009 was 14.68 percent compared with 16.5 percent in 2008, a return to 2007 levels when it was 14.4 percent (GEM 2009). However, Argentina's Total Entrepreneurial Activity (TEA) is above the overall average of GEM countries which is 11.8 percent, but below the Latin American average of 17.62 percent (GEM 2009). Nevertheless, Argentina's TEA decline to 2007 levels shows that entrepreneurs are still wary of launching new businesses.

Paradoxically, the entrepreneurial culture in Argentina is growing and has become a part of the overall makeup of Argentina's society, as illustrated by the GEM report. The results of the GEM estimated that approximately 1 out of 7 Argentines between 18 and 64 years of age are involved in some type of entrepreneurial activity and 7 out of 10 Argentines believe that being an entrepreneur is a desirable career choice (GEM 2009). However, in 2009, public perception regarding the opportunities to develop new businesses declined and showed that only 40 percent of Argentines thought that there are good opportunities to start a business within the next six months. In general, the young and more educated Argentines are slightly more optimistic than other groups (GEM 2009).

A troublesome finding presented by the GEM report is that necessity entrepreneurs have increased in proportion to opportunity entrepreneurs. This finding is consistent with the inference that economic conditions must improve and stabilize more to solidify a sense of confidence and trust by potential entrepreneurs. Further, research shows that opportunity entrepreneurship adds more to a country's economic environment than necessity entrepreneurship because the former is more closely related with innovation in favorable economic conditions. In Argentina, the proportion of the entrepreneurial activity motivated by necessity was 47 percent of the total TEA in 2009, compared to 38.4 percent in 2008, 32.2 percent in 2007, and 26 percent in 2006. The 2009 rate is close to the 2002 rate, when the index was 50 percent. Conversely, opportunity entrepreneurs still represent over 50 percent of all entrepreneurs (GEM, 2009). The 2009 necessity index was high compared, for example, with the 23 percent measured in the US, or when compared to other Latin American countries such as Peru (28 percent), Colombia (34 percent), and Uruguay (22 percent) (GEM 2009).

Further, a factor that may benefit the opportunities for entrepreneurial activity is new technology use. In terms of new technology use, Argentina is in the top five Latin American countries along with Chile, Uruguay, and Colombia. In 2009, 29.3 percent of entrepreneurs in Argentina used new technologies. Technology is one of Argentina's competitive advantages, as demonstrated by its high proportion of the usage of new technology as compared to countries with much higher TEA such as Brazil, which has a much lower technology application at only 18 percent (GEM 2009).

Additional factors that affect the entrepreneurial environment are government policy, financial markets, liberalization of markets, social norms, cultural factors, and education. Government policy and financial markets are the weakest of these factors in Argentina, while the rest are considered the greatest strengths. As with most economies, the most critical factor for entrepreneurs is access to capital. In Argentina, 32 percent of all GEM's respondents estimated they would need between US$3000 and US$10,000 to start their venture and 48 percent responded that they would provide the necessary capital to start their venture (GEM 2009). Similar to previous years, major investments in the early stages are carried out by the three Fs: friends, family, and fools.

The GEM findings show that a trend in the entrepreneurial environment in Argentina is not yet clearly defined, and therefore the results appear paradoxical. For example, although unemployment is decreasing, the percentage of necessity entrepreneurs is increasing. One of the reasons is that the economic environment in Argentina is still unstable and entrepreneurs are not yet ready to trust the seemingly improving trend, but rather they seem cautiously optimistic about the future.

Challenges and opportunities for entrepreneurs in Argentina

Argentina is one of the Latin American countries that enjoys great natural resources, an educated population, and an innovative and entrepreneurial culture. Over the years, the government has begun to realize the importance of entrepreneurial activity in the overall economic growth of the country, and has begun to implement policies that foster entrepreneurial activity. Nevertheless, Argentina ranks 115 out of 183 countries in ease of doing business as reported by the World Bank, behind Mexico (35) and Peru (36), but ahead of Brazil (127) (World Bank 2011). However, unlike Brazil, where indicators show that doing business has become easier since 2006, in Argentina the report shows that, in some areas, doing business has become more difficult. Figure 2.3 shows Argentina's position in *Doing Business 2011* relative to other economies in the world and Latin America.

One of the main challenges facing Argentina's entrepreneurs is the overall regulatory environment, including procedures to start a business, paying taxes, and overall corruption in the country's institutions. Argentina's entrepreneurs face additional challenges in protection by the rule of law and in securing capital. In Argentina, however, entrepreneurs can take advantage of a series of opportunities related to the population's high-risk tolerance and entrepreneurial culture, the availability of an educated workforce, its institutions of higher education and business incubators, and the double-digit growth of certain sectors such as technology and tourism.

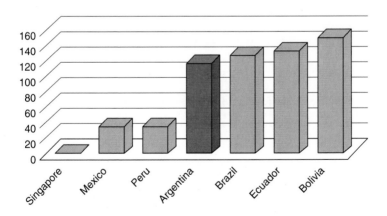

Figure 2.3   Ease of doing business – global rank
Source: World bank – Doing Business Report 2011.

Challenges

1. Regulatory environment

One of the main challenges in Argentina is its cumbersome regulatory environment. Starting a business requires over a dozen different procedures and may take months to complete. These numbers present a difficult challenge for entrepreneurs starting a new business. Argentina's ranking in "Starting a Business" is 142 out of 183 countries, falling behind other Latin American countries such as Peru (54), Mexico (67), and Brazil (128). This result is mainly due to the number of procedures it takes to start a business. In Argentina, it takes 14 procedures to start a new business, while it takes only 6 in both Peru and Mexico. Table 2.1 shows the cost, amount of time, and number of procedures necessary to launch a new business.

In relation to the Latin American and Caribbean region, where on average it takes less than 10 procedures to start a new business, Argentina falls behind with 14 procedures. However, in terms of the number of days required to start a new business, Argentina fares much better than the average in Latin America, taking only 26 days versus close to 60 days in other countries.

The tax burden and its multiplicity of procedures prove frustrating and costly for those who start a new enterprise. According to the *Doing Business* Report, Argentina ranks 143 out of 183 countries in paying taxes, behind Ecuador (81), Peru (86), and Mexico (107). Argentinian companies must pay a myriad of taxes such as value added tax at 21 percent, subway tax at 10 percent, corporate income tax at 35 percent, and social security contributions at 23 percent among others. As a result, Argentina has one of the highest tax rates in Latin America, as illustrated in Figure 2.4.

Corruption has been an endemic problem in many Latin American countries, and Argentina has not been immune to it. Argentina ranks 105 out of 178 countries in the 2010 Transparency International Corruption Perception

Table 2.1   Starting a business in Argentina

Starting a Business	Doing Business 2008	Doing Business 2009	Doing Business 2010	Doing Business 2011
Rank	N/A	N/A	137	142
Procedures (number)	13	14	14	14
Time (days)	30	31	26	26
Cost (% of income per capita)	9.7	9	11	14.2

Source: World Bank – Doing Business 2011.

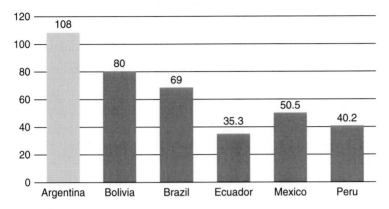

Figure 2.4 Total tax rate (% of profit)
Source: World Bank – Doing Business Report 2011.

Index, with a score of 2.9 out of a possible 10 (10 highly clean, 0 highly corrupt) (Transparency International 2010). In relation to its Latin American counterparts, Argentina ranks behind Chile (21), Uruguay (24), and Brazil (69) among others. Even though Argentina has strong anti-corruption regulation, it is offset by uneven enforcement and a weak judiciary. In 2009, Santoro cited statistics from Argentina's Center for the Investigation and Prevention of Economic Crime disclosing that in the last 25 years, out of the 750 corruption cases tried, it has taken an average of 14 years to reach resolution (Santoro 2009).

Argentina's high level of corruption and cumbersome regulatory environment are stifling forces in the development of its entrepreneurial environment. Argentina's Transparency International ranking for the previous three years indicates that there no measures have been taken to bring Argentina out of its high level of corruption. Corruption control, therefore, is one of the main challenges facing Argentina that must be addressed in order to improve the entrepreneurial environment and promote new firm creation.

Rule of law

Rule of law indicates economic agents' confidence level and their commitment to society's laws and rules, and in particular the quality of contract enforcement, property rights protection, the police, and the courts. The rule of law is important for entrepreneurship in two ways. First, it is connected with availability of financing because investors require some assurance that their money will be used and repaid as agreed. Thus, corporate financing may critically be affected by the type of legal rules and their enforcement

(La Porta et al. 1996). Second, the rule of law is associated with economic growth and entrepreneurship through the provision of security of person, security of property and enforcement of contracts, checks on government, and checks on corruption (Haggard and Tiede 2011).

The Worldwide Governance Indicators (WGI) report projects aggregate and individual governance indicators (including rule of law) for 213 economies over the period 1996–2009 (Kaufmann et al. 2010). The results of the assessment of rule of law carried out by the WGI for Argentina in the last five years show a decrease in the final score, which indicates a decline in Argentina's position in the world. Argentina's level of corruption has increased and its position has declined from 135th in 2005 to 150th in 2009.

A possible reason for this decline can be the origin of Argentina's legal code. Legal rules change in different countries based on how they were formed. Commercial laws have developed as a result of two broad traditions: common and civil law. Common law countries, like the United States and the United Kingdom, developed from judges making decisions on how to solve specific issues, and thus are based on precedent and not codes. Conversely, civil law comes from rules developed by legal scholars and derives from French, German, or Scandinavian traditions (La Porta et al. 1996). In general, common law provides the strongest protection for investors, while civil law, particularly that derived from French law, provides the least protection. As a result, common law countries have developed stronger and more sophisticated financial markets that enhance the economy's ability to bear risk by spreading that risk over a large number of investors. This is critical for promoting entrepreneurship and economic growth (Federal Reserve Bank of St. Louis 2004). Argentina's civil code derives from French law, and as such investor protection is low and the country has not developed sophisticated capital markets. Rather, financing has remained concentrated mainly in a few banks.

Nevertheless, Argentina ranks better than most Latin American countries in enforcing contracts. The World Bank ranks Argentina 45 out of 183 economies in enforcing contracts, ahead of Peru (110), Brazil (98), and Mexico (81) among others (World Bank 2011). The presence of efficient contract-enforcing rules is important in improving the rule of law because it provides a sense of stability and increases investor confidence, thereby counteracting, at least to some extent, the negative effects of the high level of government corruption and the lack of well-developed capital markets.

Securing capital

Access to capital, both to start and to grow a business, is one of the biggest challenges facing entrepreneurs. In developing countries such as Argentina where financial markets are not well developed, securing capital is a much harder task. Generally, entrepreneurs fund their start-ups with their own capital or capital raised through the 3Fs: friends, family, and fools. Banks are the next biggest source of financing. Finally, venture capitalists and angel investors are also sources of capital, particularly for ventures in the technology and energy sectors.

In Argentina, sources of nonbank finance in Argentina are limited. After the government nationalized the country's 14-year-old private pension fund system (worth US$29 billion) in November 2008, investor confidence was badly shaken by a perceived deterioration of regulatory stability and contractual security. The private pension funds were the largest institutional investors in the country and the nationalization negatively impacted on an important supply of investment in local capital markets (EIU 2010).

Access to credit (banks). Over the years, Argentina's financial system has shrunk from 205 banks in 1994 to only 85 in 2007. Most of these banks are located in Buenos Aires, and the largest 10 hold 70 percent of the assets, 74 percent of the deposits, and 67 percent of total loans (Ascua 2008). Although lending to the private sector has increased since 2004, credit outstanding as a percentage of GDP is still approximately 15 percent, which is quite low by international standards. Further, even the prime rate, which hit 67 percent in 2002, has been declining and is still hovering around 17–20 percent (17 percent in the first half of 2010) (Banco Central 2010). The high cost of money, coupled with a tight credit situation, negatively affects entrepreneurs who are ready to start their business but cannot secure funding for their projects. Therefore, it is not surprising that in Argentina many companies are not able to get off the ground, and even if they do, they are not able to survive because of the inadequacy of the financial system.

Venture capital. As is the case in most Latin American and other developing countries, the climate for private-equity and venture-capital investments in Argentina is weak. But Argentina falls behind even in comparison with other Latin American countries. For example, in terms of the overall environment for venture capital and private equity investments, Argentina tied for tenth place among 12 Latin American countries in the 2010 Scorecard prepared by the Economist Intelligence Unit on behalf of the Latin American Venture Capital Association (LAVCA) (EIU 2010).

One of the main reasons why Argentina lags behind is its increasingly complex and high-tax environment, which stifles venture capital and private equity activity. In 2009, the city of Buenos Aires passed a higher capital-gains tax and an extended stamp tax. Additionally, as mentioned earlier, the nationalization of the private pension funds in 2008 removed a large and important source of funding from venture capital and private equity activity. Other obstacles and deterrents to attracting start-up and buy-out investments are the perception of corruption in politics (EIU 2010).

Some sectors, however, remain attractive to private investors in spite of the obstacles presented above. The most attractive sectors for investors in Argentina are information technology, as well as life sciences and entertainment. In information technology, most investments are targeted at software development, outsourcing, video games, and social media (EIU 2010). Silicon Valley investors, such as Riverwood Capital, have become interested in Argentina's new information technology ventures. Francisco Alvarez Demalde, founding partner at Riverwood, says that "within Latin America, we regard Argentina as a very attractive country for off-shore IT services" (LAVCA 2010).

Angel investors.   The availability of angel investors in Argentina is also limited and has not kept up with the increasing number of start-ups. Nevertheless, 2011 is poised to be the most active year in Argentina regarding angel investments since the stock market crash in 2008 (Ergo 2011). One reason is that, as has occurred in the US and Europe, groups that promote investment by angels have begun to spring up in Argentina. The objective of these groups is to create a framework of trust in which investors feel more secure, because credibility in financial matters is one of the major pitfalls that Argentina must overcome to achieve a real growth of angel investments (Ergo 2011).

Among the groups that promote angel investment in Argentina are the Business Angels' Club and the Entrepreneurs' Club of Emprear. The Business Angels' Club was created by IAE alumni and its goal is to promote the emergence of new entrepreneurs and to increase investment awareness in those who have the capital to invest. Similarly, the Entrepreneurs' Club also promotes new entrepreneurs and investments. It also holds regular meetings where projects are presented and organizes training programs for investors and entrepreneurs (Ergo 2011).

Additionally, international angel investors have noticed the growth in Argentina's information technology sector and have begun to invest in new and young ventures. Angel Gambino, an angel investor and serial entrepreneur, has invested in Latin America's online social network Sonico. Sonico's operation is based in Argentina even though the bulk of its customers are in Brazil because of the lower costs of operating in Argentina.

Access to capital for Argentine entrepreneurs is still a challenge, and personal networks and banks are still the primary source of financing. However, in certain sectors, such as information technology, Argentina's entrepreneurs are beginning to attract international venture capital and angel investors.

Opportunities

Despite the existing challenges entrepreneurial activity in Argentina has begun to thrive, in part as a result of an entrepreneurial culture, a large and educated workforce as well as an increasing trend in entrepreneurial education, and the double-digit growth of certain sectors of the economy such as technology and tourism. Therefore, Argentina is placed 16th out of the 20 most entrepreneurial countries in 2009 and third in the Mercosur region (GEM 2009).

Culture

Historically, entrepreneurial opportunities in Argentina were only available to those fortunate to have benefitted either from a family inheritance or connections with the authorities (Ortmans 2010). As early as in the 1990s, scholars reported that Argentina did not have any policies to support or subsidize entrepreneurial activity, and that risk analysts did not know how to evaluate a new business, particularly in the technology field or any other new industry (Kantis et al. 2000). Entrepreneurship was not regarded by the masses as a viable career option, and thus was not a part of the country's makeup. This viewpoint on entrepreneurship began to change in the 1990s, and today Argentina's entrepreneurial culture is on an upswing.

Argentina's angels are contributing to the entrepreneurial culture by providing expertise along with funds. Beyond that, Argentina has developed a highly visible and important entrepreneurship culture focused on innovation and change (Ortmans 2010). As discussed previously, one out of seven Argentines are involved in some type of entrepreneurial activity and seven out of ten believe that being an entrepreneur is a desirable career choice.

Some of the most important factors that make Argentina an ideal place for entrepreneurial ventures are its highly educated population, the vast availability and variety of natural resources, the outstanding scientific-technological endeavors, the manifold untapped production niches, and a regional market (Mercosur) with growing integration (Economy and Business 2008). The availability of a highly educated population is reflected in the country's positioning as an important global player in IT-related industries, with the presence of companies such as Globant, which will be discussed later in the chapter. Argentina's creative workforce and businesses have also attracted international companies to invest in the country. For example, Google cited Argentina's emerging entrepreneurial spirit as a main factor in its decision in 2007 to base its Latin American operations in Buenos Aires (Ortmans 2010).

Entrepreneurship and education

Education is important both to form an entrepreneurial culture and foster entrepreneurial activity, as well as to provide an educated and highly skilled labor force from which entrepreneurs draw talent. The latter is one of Argentina's competitive advantages as its labor force is highly educated. On the other hand, entrepreneurial education in Argentina, like in most Latin American countries, still lags behind that of developed countries such as the United States. Higher education in Argentina mainly focuses on training students for a professional career as employees and not towards fostering creativity and encouraging entrepreneurship (Postigo and Tamborini 2002).

The concept of education includes social capital, the development of networks between entrepreneurs and institutions, availability of institutional support such as incubators to assist entrepreneurs, and the characteristics of the educational system (for example, entrepreneurship in educational programs, action-oriented learning, and attitude to risk). In particular, networks play a key role in the entrepreneurial process, from identifying the business opportunity to mobilizing resources for starting a business (Shapero 1984, Johanisson 1988). Education for entrepreneurship at universities is extremely important because the critical age for incubating and creating a new venture is between 25 and 35 (Postigo and Tamborini 2002).

In Argentina there are 47 public and 46 private universities dispersed around the country, offering undergraduate and graduate degrees. Although education for entrepreneurship did not start until the 1990s, approximately 33 percent of the public institutions and 20 percent of the private ones are engaged in some activity related to entrepreneurship (Postigo and Tamborini 2002). Interestingly, as Postigo notes, universities in Argentina have focused their programs on education "for" entrepreneurship, rather than "about" entrepreneurship, by providing courses, seminars, research programs, and incubators that target potential entrepreneurs and students who already have a venture idea. This trend may be a result of the high unemployment rate and Argentina's stagnant economy over the past 20 years.

Further, most private institutions have business plan contests and the public ones have incubators. For example, the entrepreneurship center at the Universidad Argentina de la Empresa (UADE) witnessed the participation of 147 business plans in the university's annual Business Plan Contest in 2011 (UADE 2011). This contest began ten years ago and is one of the most important in Argentina.

Another leader in entrepreneurship education is IAE, a leading business school with a long-standing presence in research, teaching (undergraduate and graduate), service, and networking with entrepreneurs, angel investors, and venture capitalists. Clubs, business contests, and mentoring programs are also well-integrated into the school's entrepreneurship center. However, it is important to stress that few institutions of higher education have research programs or allocate resources to training their staff on entrepreneurship-related topics.

Additionally, business incubators also play an important role in the development of new businesses because they are designed to reduce start-up costs and train entrepreneurs in business practices. At the same time, business incubators connect entrepreneurs to markets and generally assist them in finding financing opportunities for the new ventures (Robinson 2008). This combination enables entrepreneurs to pursue their business interests, and therefore greatly influences the volume and quality of opportunities to start new businesses. Argentina has incubation activity, but it is not nationally coordinated and is scattered among different cities and universities.

According to Robinson (2008), there are an estimated 10–15 business incubators in Argentina, while there are over 299 in Brazil. In Buenos Aires, the city government sponsors only two incubators, a general incubator focusing on most types of businesses and a design incubator. As a result of a lack of national support, Argentina has developed an unofficial entrepreneurship and business incubation organization in Buenos Aires, which is comprised of universities, government officials, business managers, and other entrepreneurs (Robinson 2008).

Argentina, particularly Buenos Aires, has made tremendous strides in the last two decades in launching entrepreneurship centers, hosting business plan competitions, and encouraging business incubators. Nevertheless, availability of entrepreneurship education still remains scarce and must continue to improve in order to truly foster the growth of entrepreneurial activity. There are still a limited number of institutions, mainly in Buenos Aires, that offer education either "for" or "about" entrepreneurship.

1. Growth by sectors

Information technology. The Argentine Information technology (IT) market is the second largest in Latin America. Despite the current economic crisis, the total value of spending on IT products and services was over US$3.8 billion in 2010 and will approach US$6.2 billion by 2014. Per capita IT expenditures are expected to rise from US$94 in 2010 to US$147 in 2014 as the market approaches pre-2001 crisis levels. Argentina's IT spending will grow by 13 percent annually over 2010–14 (PR-Inside.com 2010).

Similarly, technology is the sector with the highest number of young entrepreneurs in Argentina, specifically in areas related to the Internet, video games, mobile phone applications, and social networks. For example, the average age of an entrepreneur in the video game sector is 27 (Kozak 2011).

In technology, particularly the Internet, Argentina's entrepreneurs have excelled. By early 2000, Argentina was at the forefront of Latin America's Internet bubble with high-profile IPOs and Argentinean entrepreneurs and start-ups breaking into the international arena (LAVCA 2010). A decade later, Argentina has been able to expand into many IT-related industries, and is now positioned as a global player in the industry in areas such as software development, business process outsourcing, Internet business, video games, and online social gaming (LAVCA 2010). As a result, a number of Silicon Valley investors have begun to invest in Argentina's new companies, such as the case of Argentina's technology leader, Globant (described later in the chapter).

Further, angel investors are taking notice of Argentina's entrepreneurial activity in the IT sector and have begun to invest. For example, Angel Gambino – angel investor and serial entrepreneur – has invested in Sonico, a social network company with over 48 million subscribers (LAVCA 2010). A developing niche within Argentina's IT industry is social gaming, which has spurred a frenzy of interest from international investors. This in turn has created a push for Argentinean entrepreneurs to continue to innovate and remain at the cutting edge of this Internet technology with companies such as MetroGames, Popego, and Socialmetrix (LAVCA 2010).

Tourism. Another industry that is growing rapidly, and thereby presenting opportunities for entrepreneurs, is tourism. "We are working in tourism, one the best sectors to develop a new business. This is a sector that grows more than 10 percent per year. There is clearly a lot of opportunity in tourism-related business," said Damián Habib, partner of IGGY (Habib 2010). This 10 percent growth projection is expected to continue until 2020 and is well above the average world growth projection of 4.1 percent per year (*Leisure & Travel Week* 2010). INDEC recorded 2.3 million foreign tourist arrivals in 2007, a 12 percent increase from the previous year. Traditionally, Argentines have long been active travelers within their own country, and account for over 80 percent of tourism. However, international tourism has also seen healthy growth, almost doubling since 2001. Foreign tourists come from all over the world, but mainly from Brazil, Uruguay, Chile, US, and Spain. In 2010, the 103,993 tourists from Brazil represented a 385 percent growth compared to the same period a year earlier. Similarly, there were 94.8 percent more tourists from Uruguay in July 2010, 73.2 percent more from Chile, and 14.8 percent more from Spain, than in July 2009 (Antonelli 2010).

The World Economic Forum estimated that, in 2008, tourism generated around US$25 billion in economic turnover, and employed 1.8 million people. Further, around 4.6 million foreign visitors arrived in 2007, yielding a positive balance vis-à-vis the number of Argentines traveling abroad. This rapid growth, and positive trend, has opened up new opportunities for Argentine entrepreneurs in all areas related to tourism and hospitality.

Successful entrepreneurs: the case of Globant

Some of Argentina's entrepreneurs have been able not only to take advantage of existing opportunities, but also to bypass the existing challenges and rise to become global leaders in their industry. This is the case of Globant, where its founders began with a successful entrepreneurial idea and have been able to take advantage of the social capital, human capital, and technology available to break down the obstacles in getting access to finance and bypassing bureaucratic barriers.

Globant is a software development and IT outsourcing company based in Buenos Aires and founded in 2003 by four Argentinean entrepreneurs: Martín Migoya, Martín Umarán, Guibert Englebienne, and Néstor Nocetti (Globant 2011). These entrepreneurs launched the company with a US$1000 investment, and after only seven years have grown the company to become one of the top 10 software companies in the world with revenues in excess of US$60 million and over 2000 employees.

Globant's founders, all engineers with prior work experience in a variety of multinational companies, came together in 2003 and took advantage of their personal and professional network of contacts to start the company. (*See* Appendix 2.1 for founders' biographies.) After seeing the growth in India's outsourcing market, Globant's founders decided to replicate it. During the first year, Globant posted revenues of US$3 million and hired over 70 employees (Mukami et al. 2006). The year 2005 was key for Globant when it was selected as Endeavor Entrepreneur and was recognized as the Best Services Exporter by Export. Additionally, in the same year, the Sloan School of Management of the MIT wrote a case about Globant. Among Globant's customers are Google, Coca-Cola, Disney, LinkedIn, and Nike. Globant anticipates that for 2011 it will earn between US$80 and US$90 million in sales and will have over 3000 employees (Endeavor.org 2011).

These events propelled the company forward and placed it in the sights of two US-based venture capital firms: Riverwood Capital and FTVentures. In 2008, Globant received US$13 million in joint investment from these firms, and in 2011 it received an additional US$15 million (Endeavor.org 2011). The key to having been able to secure financing from these companies is a result of Globant's rapid and successful growth and the exposure generated by its Endeavor connection.

Globant's growth has been impressive; it has achieved revenue growth of over 884 percent since 2004 (Endeavor.org 2011). By 2007, the company had reached revenues of US$22 million and by 2010 the company's revenues were estimated at US$60 million (Endeavor.org 2011). To achieve its dramatic growth, Globant has actively engaged in an aggressive acquisition strategy, with a clear goal of being listed on the Nasdaq Exchange. For example, in 2008, Globant purchased Accendra, an Argentinean software developer, for US$2 million and Openware, a former Argentinean competitor in the IT services and security, for US$1.5 million in cash and stock (*La Nación* 2008).

An aspect that sets Globant apart from its competitors is its innovative human resources policies, which are tailored to meet the needs and expectations of its employees. For example, similarly to what successful giant Google does, Globant's offices offer gym, yoga, and massage sessions, a climbing wall, a ping-pong table, a soundproof music room and a wide choice of leisure areas and equipment that makes the place comfortable, relaxed, and fun (Weigert 2007). As a result of these policies, Globant is able to attract the most talented individuals in Argentina and has a low rate of employee fluctuation, a common phenomenon in most companies involved in the technology industry (Ergo 2011).

Globant's founders have been able to take advantage of their experience and network, as well as the country's availability of a highly educated labor force and a depreciated local currency. Additionally, Globant's founders bypassed many of the country's bureaucratic issues by focusing on an industry based in a "virtual world" and were able to capitalize on the cultural proximity between Argentina and the "West," an aspect of doing business with which Indian companies struggle.

Outlook and conclusion

Argentina's positive macroeconomic results in the past couple of years present a positive environment for entrepreneurial activity. Argentina's per capita GDP of US$15,871 (purchasing power parity) is one of the highest in the region, even after the effects of the 2002 recession and peso devaluation. However, this number is still only 33 percent to that of the US, showing the clear room for growth and potential for Argentina to "catch up" with developed countries.

The time is ripe for Argentina and its entrepreneurs to take advantage of Latin America's resilience in weathering the 2008 world economic crisis, the increase in overall FDI investment, and the increase in exports. More specifically, Argentine entrepreneurs seem to have higher aspirations and confidence in their ability to build sustainable and innovative companies. For example, Oscar Alvarado, CEO of El Tejar, focuses on building a company that concentrates on people, the community, and longevity, rather than merely short-term profitability. In turn, this Argentinian company continues to grow, generating over 44 percent internal rate of return (Ernst & Young 2010).

Further, Argentina's large internal market and highly skilled labor force are additional positive factors affecting entrepreneurial activity in the future. Argentina, with its 41 million people, is economically about the size of Washington, DC, with its 5.3 million people. The potential opportunity for growth is almost unfathomable.

However, it does not matter how much creativity, brilliance, drive, commitment, and resources an entrepreneur may possess; external factors – mainly government policy – will contribute in large part to the success or failure of entrepreneurial ventures. Some of the policies needed to further foster entrepreneurial activity in Argentina are:

- reducing the amount of time and complexity of procedures to start a business,
- improving access to capital and the terms and conditions for borrowing and attracting investment,
- simplifying taxation and labor policies,
- improving the quality of the operation of the judicial system and implementing policies to combat corruption,
- continuing to implement policies that improve macroeconomic variables such as GDP growth and inflation, and
- reducing the size and scope of the informal economy.

The outlook for Argentina's entrepreneurs is bright. However, the degree of success hinges on whether the government continues to implement policies to address both the macroeconomic issues as well as the internal regulatory framework.

Appendix 2.1   Biographies of Globant's founders

Martín Migoya, CEO

Martin has extensive experience in business management, sales, and marketing. As Globant's CEO, his focus is to drive revenue, objectives, and profitability. He oversees the company's long-term objectives, planning, and analysis. Prior to co-founding Globant, Martin was Director of Business Development and Latin America's Regional Business Manager at a large consulting and technology services company, developing the IT and ERP markets in Brazil and Argentina. He was instrumental in managing and developing high-technology businesses related to SAP and the Internet, with customers like Procter & Gamble, Renault, and Roemmers Laboratories. Previously, Martín worked as Project Manager for REPSOL-YPF, Argentina's largest oil and gas company. Martin has lived and worked in Argentina, Brazil, Mexico, and the UK. He holds a degree in electronic engineering from La Plata University and a master's degree in business administration from CEMA University.

Guibert Englebeienne, CTO

Guibert has extensive experience in the information technology and communication industries. As Globant's CTO, Guibert is in charge of the software production process, and the creation and management of strategic company technology partnerships. Prior to co-founding Globant, Guibert was a scientific researcher at IBM and later the CTO for CallNow.com Inc., a telecommunications company based in New York providing international callback services through the Internet. He also conceived and developed a US-patented technology powering a service named 2Speak, to use the Internet to anonymously connect two parties through phone lines. Guibert was responsible for the phone-chat implementation in Chinadotcom Co., owner of the biggest Asian Internet portals. He has also worked as an IT development manager outlining and developing software for tax collection through Internet governmental portals. Guibert has lived and worked in Argentina, the US, Venezuela, and the UK. He holds a degree in computer science and software engineering from UNICEN University.

Martin Umaran, COO

Martin has extensive experience in executive and business management for technology industries. As Globant's COO, Martin is responsible for the delivery of products and professional services, and is actively involved in capacity growth and process initiatives. Prior to co-founding Globant, Martin was CEO for Neuwagen, a company focused on selling cars to the customers of Caja de Ahorro y Seguro (Argentina's largest insurance company). He also worked at several technology companies as senior business manager. At Santander Bank, he was responsible for their CRM implementation initiative. He also negotiated, implemented, and operated a state-of-the-art tax collection system in several Venezuelan cities. At YPF Ecuador, Martin worked as a manager of facilities automation and maintenance. He also worked at Roman Logistics, where he managed several projects for the Argentinean offices of Ford, GM, and Unilever. Martin has lived and worked in Argentina, Ecuador, Venezuela, and the UK. He holds a degree in mechanical engineering from La Plata University and a master's in business administration from IDEA University.

Nestor Nocetti, VP of Innovation Labs

Nestor has a considerable amount of experience in the information technology industry, both in operational and advisory roles. As Globant's VP of Corporate Services, Nestor is in charge of determining the structure for business consolidation and expansion, aligned with the corporate objectives and vision. Prior to co-founding Globant, Nestor worked as Internet manager in an Argentinean information technology company, where he specialized in Internet marketing and web portal localization with customers like EMC, a world leader in information storage, and Techint, an engineering and procurement services provider. He also worked on several projects related to geographic information systems for Light Rio de Janeiro, electricity providers in Brazil, and UTE, and a public electricity provider in Uruguay. He worked as a consultant on issues related to IT development, strategy, and operations in the oil and gas market, for ENAP Chile, and YPF Argentina. Nestor has lived and worked in Argentina, Chile, and Brazil. He holds a degree in electronic engineering from La Plata University and a degree in business direction from IAE University.

Source: Mukami et al. (2006).

Note

The author wishes to thank Marcelo Barrios of UADE Business School for his invaluable contribution to this chapter.

References

Antonelli, N. 2010. "Argentina's Tourism Industry Booming." *Infosurhoy*. September 14. http://www.infosurhoy.com/cocoon/saii/xhtml/en_GB/features/saii/features/main/2010/09/14/feature-02.

Ascua, R. 2008. "Evaluation of Risk Factors in the Financing to New Companies in the Vision of Argentine Entrepreneurs." In *2008 International Council for Small Business World Conference*, http://www.smu.ca/events/icsb/proceedings/chalg6f.html.

Banco Central de la República Argentina. 2010. *Programa Monetario 2011*. http://www.bcra.gov.ar/pdfs/polmon/Programa%20monetario%202011.pdf.

Economist Intelligence Unit (EIU). 2010. "Country Finance Argentina 2010." London, October 2010.

Economist Intelligence Unit (EIU). 2011. *Country Report – Argentina*. London, May.

Economy and Business. 2008. "Argentina, a Country of Entrepreneurs." May 2008. http://www.en.argentina.ar/_en/economy-and-business/C603-argentina-a-country-of-entrepreneurs.php.

Endeavor.org. 2011. http://www.endeavor.org. Accessed on May 20, 2011.

Ergo, L. 2011. "Angel Investment Outlook in Argentina: 2011." Altmarino blog. January 26. http://www.altamirano.org/startups-2/the-angel-investments-outlook-in-argentina/.

Ernst & Young. 2010. *Entrepreneurship and Innovation: the Path to Growth in Latin America*. Boston, Mass: Ernst & Young Global Limited, UK.

Federal Reserve Bank of St. Louis. 2004. *Rule of Law and Economic Growth*. International Economic Trends. August. http://www.research.stlouisfed.org/publications/iet/20040801/cover.pdf.

Global Entrepreneurship Monitor (GEM). 2009. *Global Entrepreneurship Monitor 2009*. Argentina Report. Buenos Aires.

Globant. 2011. retrieved January 28. http://www.globant.com.

Habib, D. 2010. Partner at IGGY interviewed in Buenos Aires. December.

Haggard, S. and L. Tiede. 2011. "The Rule of Law and Economic Growth: Where are We?" *World Development* 39, no. 5: 673–85.

Johanisson, B. 1988. "Designing Supportive Contexts for Emerging Enterprises." Växjö University.

Kantis, H, P. Angelelli, and F. Gatto. 2000. "Nuevos emprendimientos y emprendedores en Argentina: de que depende su creación y supervivencia?" Interamerican Development Bank and Instituto de Industria from the Universidad Nacional de General Sarmiento, August.

Kantor, D. 2011. "Secuela de la crisis: se redujo la cantidad de empresas en el país." Clarin.com. May 15. http://www.ieco.clarin.com/economia/Secuela-crisis-redujo-cantidad-empresas_0_481152125.html.

Kaufmann, D., A. Kraay and M. Mastruzzi. 2010. *World Governance Indicator (WGI)*. The World Bank Group. http://info.worldbank.org/governance/wgi/index.asp.

Kozak, D. 2011. "Emprender es un Viaje de Ida." *El Guardian*. May 19.

La Nación. 2008. "Dos Empresas de Software se unen para Entrar en el Nasdaq." June 20. http://www.lanacion.com.ar/nota.asp?nota_id=1023009.

La Porta, R., F. Lopez-de-Silanes, A. Shleifer, and R. Vishny. 1996. "Law and Finance." National Bureau of Economic Research. Cambridge, Mass. July.

Latin American Venture Capital Association LAVCA. 2010. "Executive Briefing: Argentina Builds Momentum as a Global IT Hub." July 14. http://lavca.org.

Leisure & Travel Week. 2010. "Business News; Argentina Tourism Booming, to Grow by 10% Annually Until 2020." NewsRx. Atlanta, Ga. October 9.

Mukami, S., R. Premo, Roger, I. Trantcheva, and E. Yeager. 2006. "Globant: Leading the IT Sourcing Revolution in Latin America." http://www.slideshare.net/enendeavor/globant.

Ortmans, J. 2010. "Start-ups Continue to 'Bloom' in Argentina." *Entrepreneurship.* September 13. http://www.entrepreneurship.org/en/Blogs/Policy-Forum-Blog/2010/September/Start-Ups-Continue-to-Bloom-in-Argentina.aspx.

Pr-inside.com. 2010. "Argentina Information Technology Report Q3 2010." July 26. http://www.pr-inside.com/argentina-information-technology-report-r2024129.htm.

Robinson, D. 2008. "The Development and Diffusion of Business Incubation Capabilities in Five Emerging Markets in South America." Networks Financial Institute at Indiana University, Working Paper. July. http://www.networksfinancialinstitute.org/Lists/Publication%20Library/Attachments/118/2008-WP-08_Robinson.pdf.

Postigo, S. and M. Tamborini. 2002. "Entrepreneurship Education in Argentina: the Case of San Andrés University." Paper presented at Internationalizing Entrepreneurship Education and Training Conference, Malaysia, July 8–10. http://www.udesa.edu.ar/files/img/Administracion/DTN27.PDF.

Santoro, D. 2009. "Corrupción: Argentina Sacó Otra Mala Nota en el Ranking Global." Clarin.com. November 17, 2009. http://www.ieco.clarin.com/economia/Argentina-ranking-global-mala-saco_0_154784530.html.

Shapero, Albert. 1984. "The Entrepreneurial Event." In C. A. Kent (Ed.), *The Environment for Entrepreneurship*, pp. 21–40, Lexington, Mass.: Lexington Press.

Transparency International. 2010. *Corruption Perception Index Report 2010.* http://www.transparency.org/policy_research/surveys_indices/cpi/2010/results.

Universidad Argentina de la Empresa (UADE). 2011. www.uade.edu.ar.

Weigert, W. 2007. "Globant Opens a New Development Center in La Plata." Press release. http://www.globant.com/Content/Media_Room/Press_Releases/display.html?articleFile=/news/press_releases/La_Plata.html&urlBack=/Content/Media_Room/Press_Releases/&year=2007.

World Bank. 2011. *Doing Business in Argentina. Making a Difference for Entrepreneurs.* Washington, DC: World Bank.

3
Entrepreneurship in Brazil: The Role of Strategy and the Institutional Environment

Angela da Rocha, Jorge Ferreira da Silva, and Jorge Carneiro*
Pontifical Catholic University of Rio de Janeiro

The impact of the institutional environment on entrepreneurship is still not fully understood, particularly in reference to developing countries. In these countries changes can occur in a rapid and unpredictable manner, creating periods of high turbulence, which can negatively impact the creation and development of new ventures (Ahlstrom and Bruton 2010). It is believed, therefore, that economic stability is an important factor in stimulating entrepreneurial activity, while at the same time turbulence tends to discourage it (Haddad 2008).

Furthermore, the literature indicates that certain elements of the institutional environment can act as facilitators, such as the availability of financial and human capital and of an adequate regulatory framework. Other factors, such as high levels of corruption, can have a deleterious effect on entrepreneurial activity (Bowen and De Clercq 2008). Therefore, the existence of government policies and institutions that favor the development of an environment supportive of entrepreneurship is considered a critical prerequisite (Audretsch 2007, Spencer et al. 2005).

Even so, it is possible for entrepreneurs still to succeed when confronted with institutional environments that are both turbulent and detrimental to new ventures. Moreover, different strategies can lead to better results in terms of growth and profitability, also depending upon company resources (Zou et al. 2010).

This chapter seeks to analyze both the institutional facilitators and obstacles to the growth of new ventures in Brazil, using longitudinal case studies of two successful companies in distinct sectors of the economy: Totvs, a software developer, and O Boticário, a manufacturer and retailer of perfume and cosmetics. Both are successful, but each employed different strategies that have enabled their growth in a turbulent environment.

Comparing Brazil to other countries

Entrepreneurship can be significantly different among various countries as a result of historical, cultural, and societal characteristics. The GEM conducts an annual study of 18 to 64-year-old residents of multiple countries. This study presents the possibility of comparing some behavioral aspects of Brazilian entrepreneurs with those in other countries, such as Latin American (LA) and the BRIC countries (Bosma and Levie 2010). The countries selected for this particular comparison have a similar development level according to the GEM criteria.

Attitudes and perceptions of entrepreneurial behavior

Attitudes and perceptions towards entrepreneurial activities can play an important role in promoting or discouraging entrepreneurial behavior. A comparison across countries, which can provide enlightening insights, appears in Table 3.1.

Latin American countries score higher than other emerging countries in entrepreneurial attitudes and perceptions, as measured by the GEM study (Bosma and Levie 2010). Among these countries, Chile, Colombia, and Peru show higher levels of entrepreneurial orientation, as indicated by higher percentages of people both perceiving opportunities to start a new business

Table 3.1   Attitudes and perceptions of entrepreneurial behavior in selected LA and BRIC countries, 2009

Country	Perception of business opportunities (%)	Perception of having the capabilities to start a business* (%)	Afraid to fail (%)	Intend to start a new business[†] (next 3 years) (%)	Perception of high social status of entrepreneurs (%)
Brazil	47	53	31	21	80
Other LA countries					
Argentina	44	65	37	14	76
Chile	52	66	23	35	70
Colombia	50	64	29	57	74
Peru	61	74	32	32	75
Uruguay	46	68	29	21	72
Other BRIC countries[‡]					
China	25	35	32	23	77
Russia	17	24	52	2	63

*Among those perceiving good opportunities to start a business.
[†]Among those not yet involved with entrepreneurial activities.
[‡]India is not included in the GEM study.
Source: Bosma and Levie (2010).

and having the intention of founding a business in the next three years. As to the self-perception of having the required capabilities to run a business, Brazil scores lower than other LA countries in the study, but higher than China and Russia. In general, except for Russia, levels of perceived social status of entrepreneurs are quite similar, with Brazil ranking first.

Entrepreneurial activities

Brazil tends to be well placed in most studies on entrepreneurial activity. Compared to the other countries examined in Table 3.2, Brazil has the fourth-largest percentage of both new and established businesses. Nevertheless, when considering opportunity as the source of entrepreneurial drive, Brazil surpasses all the countries studied, with the exception of Uruguay.

Discontinuation rates of entrepreneurial businesses are lower in Brazil than in every other country examined, except for Russia. The GEM 2009 study (Bosma and Levie 2010) also collected data on reasons for discontinuation, as perceived by business owners. Between 2007 and 2009, 32 percent of the discontinuation of Brazilian businesses was caused by an inability to generate enough profits, and 23 percent by a lack of access to financial resources. Less than 2 percent of Brazilian entrepreneurs left their businesses because of retirement or opportunity to sell the business (which are among the most common reasons in developed countries).

Two additional results of the study are indicative, however, of lack of competitiveness of these ventures. First, Brazil shows the lowest percentage of innovation content of new businesses among all the countries monitored by GEM. This is explained in part by the lack of an R&D tradition in the country

Table 3.2 Entrepreneurial activity in selected LA and BRIC countries, 2009

Country	Early-stage entrepreneurial activity (%)	Established business ownership rate (%)	% of necessity-driven entrepreneurship	% of opportunity-driven entrepreneurship	Discontinuation of business (previous 12 months) (%)
Brazil	15.3	11.8	39	48	4.0
Other LA countries					
Argentina	14.7	13.5	47	37	6.2
Chile	14.9	6.7	25	42	6.4
Colombia	22.4	12.6	34	45	7.1
Peru	20.9	7.5	28	42	7.1
Uruguay	12.2	5.9	22	57	4.9
Other BRIC countries					
China	18.8	17.2	48	29	6.6
Russia	3.9	2.3	29	37	2.2

Source: Bosma and Levie (2010).

and a shortage of qualified labor. Second, Brazil also shows one of the lowest percentages of customers from international markets served by new ventures. This last finding could be explained by the fact that Brazilian firms face more obstacles when internationalizing: (i) Brazil is a continental-sized country insulated within its borders by formidable geographic obstacles, which fosters a domestic mentality (as opposed to a global mind-set) and increases the cost of transportation; (ii) the country is a traditional exporter of commodities and has little tradition in exporting high-tech products, which are the typical exports of an international new venture (Dib et al. 2010); (iii) the lack of innovation reduces the ability of new ventures to go international; (iv) government policies historically have dampened export efforts of Brazilian firms (Iglesias and Motta Veiga 2002, 2005, Da Rocha and Da Silva 2009).

Furthermore, the attractiveness of a large and expanding domestic market, increasingly demanding new products and services, as well as the appreciation of the Brazilian currency (the real) during the last five years, are additional impediments to internationalization. Even so, there have been recent changes in these dynamics. Of the total number of mergers and acquisitions in foreign markets conducted by Brazilian businesses during the first semester of 2010, 75 percent were undertaken by small and medium-sized businesses (Aguilar 2010).

External facilitators and obstacles to entrepreneurship in Brazil

Environmental conditions can foster or hinder entrepreneurship in a country. The GEM 2009 study provides an overview of the most important facilitators and obstacles to entrepreneurship in selected LA countries, according to an evaluation by national specialists (Table 3.3).

Major obstacles to the development of entrepreneurial firms in Brazil were indicated by specialists to be inadequate national policies and regulation, as well as deficiencies in primary and secondary education. This latter aspect is also a shortcoming for all other selected LA countries, and impacts the quality of their labor force. According to the research, the most important facilitators of entrepreneurship in Brazil are a dynamic domestic market; the existence of, and access to, adequate physical infrastructure; and social and cultural norms favoring entrepreneurship. In fact, with the exception of Uruguay and Argentina, a favorable social and cultural environment is shared with other LA countries.

Brazilian entrepreneurs have their own view of the obstacles faced in creating and developing their businesses. For example, Sebrae (the Brazilian organization for the development of micro and small firms) commissioned a study by Vox Populi (2007), a public opinion research institute, which

Table 3.3 Obstacles to and facilitators of entrepreneurship in selected LA countries, 2009

Countries	1	2a	2b	3	4a	4b	5	6	7a	7b	8	9
Brazil		–	–	–					+		+	+
Argentina		–	–	–	+		+		+			
Chile		+		–		–				–	+	+
Colombia	–			–	+	–					+	+
Peru		–		–	+	–					+	+
Uruguay				+	–			+		–	+	–

Notes: 1 = financial support; 2a = national policies; 2b = regulation; 3 = government programs; 4a = education (primary and secondary school level); 4b = education (post-school); 5 = R&D transfer; 6 = commercial infrastructure; 7a = dynamic domestic market; 7b = domestic market openness; 8 = access to the physical infrastructure; 9 = cultural and social norms. Obstacles are indicated by a minus (–) sign and facilitators are represented by a plus (+) sign.
Source: Bosma and Levie (2010).

showed that Brazilian entrepreneurs representing both surviving and closed small businesses considered the following five obstacles as the most important faced by their firms: excessive taxes, lack of qualified labor, lack of operating income, lack of demand, and fierce competition. Although apparently conflicting, specialists and business owners are in fact agreeing from different perspectives: government policies and regulation should aim at reducing taxes and provide access to loans at lower interest rates, while the lack of qualified labor results from the educational deficit in Brazil. As for lack of demand and aggressive competition, these obstacles conflict to some extent with the specialists' view of a dynamic domestic market (an aggregated view), suggesting that certain market segments where entrepreneurial firms compete are stagnant (a firm's perspective).

The institutional environment for entrepreneurship in Brazil

Even though entrepreneurial activity in Brazil has traditionally been supported by cultural and social norms, the institutional environment has not been as favorable to the establishment and growth of entrepreneurial ventures in recent decades. On the contrary, were it not for the individual aspirations of entrepreneurs and their determination, it is quite possible that the country would not have had, in the early years of the twenty-first century, successful large companies that are still guided by their founders.

Possibly the greatest proof of the competence and persistence of Brazilian entrepreneurs, who founded their companies in the last three decades, was their survival of the challenges presented by the turbulent environment of the 1980s and the early 1990s. This turbulence was not only represented by consecutive economic crises, but above all else by abrupt variations in macroeconomic performance. For example, during this period GDP growth rates changed from around –4 percent in 1981 to +8 percent in the mid-1980s, falling back to –4 percent in 1990 and growing to +4 percent in the mid-1990s. Inflation rates varied enormously, from 65 percent in 1986 to an astronomical 1800 percent in 1989 before falling to around 10 percent during the late 1990s. Furthermore, during the 1980s (referred to as the "lost decade" in Latin America), in Brazil, there were 4 different currencies, 7 monetary stabilization plans, 53 changes in price control rules, 17 changes in exchange rules, 13 wage policies, 20 plans for dealing with the external debt problem, and 18 projects to cut federal expenses (Serra 1990). In addition, the opening of the Brazilian market to foreign products challenged the ability of domestic firms to adapt to a new and globalized environment. The average tariff was reduced from 57.5 percent in 1987 to 30.5 percent in 1990, and to 11.2 percent in 1994 (Bonelli and Pinheiro 2008).

Starting in 1994, a new economic stabilization plan, known as the "Real Plan," was successful in reducing inflation to acceptable levels. This plan laid the foundations on which the country could achieve greater development in the first decade of the twenty-first century. The turbulent environment of the previous decades was replaced by one more favorable and supportive of entrepreneurship.

The entrepreneurs who survived this test were thus able to take advantage of the opportunities that came from changes in the institutional environment, achieving high growth rates for their companies. Among the macro changes that stand out were increased economic stability and a reduction in government interference. Some other changes to the institutional environment were especially auspicious for entrepreneurship.

Foremost among them was the growing availability of capital for nascent businesses. The increase in seed funds and venture capital, even though in a relatively limited scope, also stimulated entrepreneurial activities. Private equity funds have invested a total of 36 billion dollars between 2001 and 2010 in Brazil, and this amount continues to increase. Government funds were also available, such as the "Programa Inovar" (Program for Innovation), a seed fund managed by FINEP, the primary agency financing innovation in Brazil. This program provided for up to 70 percent of financial needs, requiring private investors to supply the other 30 percent (Lethbridge and Fogaça 2010). In addition, Brazil has been attracting the attention of international private equity funds interested in investing in Brazilian companies with entrepreneurial characteristics. Finally, during more advanced stages of corporate development, an initial public offering (IPO) is a viable alternative that can allow medium-sized Brazilian companies the opportunity to have access to financial resources to stimulate growth.

Another relevant change occurred in regulation, with the approval of various legal instruments intended to support small businesses. In 1996, federal tax filing for smaller companies was simplified under the "Lei do Simples" (Simple Law). For its part, the Federal Statute of Micro and Small-sized Enterprises of 1999 brought in a series of benefits in the administrative, social pension, credit, and labor areas. The General Law of Micro and Small Companies of 2006 amplified some of these benefits, particularly in terms of lowering administrative bureaucracy and exemption of fees. This law also assisted smaller companies to make successful bids for public contracts. Finally, in 2007, several federal, state, and city taxes that were applied to smaller businesses were unified and reduced.

Institutional support for innovation has also shown progress. The Law of Innovation of 2004 permitted companies to access grants and subsidized-interest loans from the Fundo Nacional de Desenvolvimento Científico e Tecnológico (National Fund for Scientific and Technological Development). Prior to this, such access was limited to universities and research institutes. FINEP developed specific programs to meet the need to fund innovation in small and medium-sized private companies. Substantial resources were also allocated to the development of business incubators and technology parks. In 2009 there were around 400 business incubators in Brazil, as compared to 1000 in the USA and 500 in China. Brazil ranked fourth in the world in the number of incubators, behind only the US, Germany, and China (Chandra and Fealey 2009). In addition, around 60 technology parks were established in the country by 2007 (Anprotec 2008).

Even though these changes have increased competitiveness and facilitated the creation and development of new ventures, the quality of the institutional environment still makes entrepreneurial activities difficult. This is particularly true regarding the high cost of credit, high tax levels, rampant corruption, and excessive bureaucracy. The problems in accessing credit are less today than in the past, but the economic policies adopted by Brazil to correct structural distortions in public expenditure and control inflation made it necessary to keep interest rates high. This directly impacts small and medium-sized companies, who have greater difficulty in gaining access to subsidized-interest loans from BNDES, the National Bank for Economic and Social Development.

The tax burden in Brazil is high, especially when compared to other countries. In 2006 for example, the tax burden in Brazil was 35.2 percent of GDP, as compared to 34.6 percent in Germany, 25.4 percent in the US, 24.6 percent in South Korea, and 18.5 percent in Mexico. More so, the tax burden has shown a historical tendency to grow, increasing almost 60 percent in the last two decades. In response to this situation, many companies resort to tax evasion; it is estimated that 65 percent of small-sized, 49 percent of medium-sized, and 27 percent of large-sized companies evade taxes in some manner. Furthermore, undeclared revenues are believed to represent 25 percent of all income in Brazilian companies (Amaral et al. 2009). This situation creates opportunities for corruption, and also reduces companies' ability to use these funds for further investment.[1]

Corruption, for its part, has an indirect impact on business growth because it results in a lower quality and quantity of public goods, such as transportation infrastructure, which increases logistics costs. It also affects economic efficiency by allowing private economic agents to distort legitimate and healthy competition among firms (Gonçalves 2008).

Finally, a complex and redundant bureaucracy not only means high administrative costs for businesses, but also reduces competitiveness due to the lengthy time necessary to open and close businesses, and makes it difficult to conduct certain business operations, such as foreign trade. As a consequence, the World Bank ranks Brazil 127th out of 183 countries in terms of difficulty in establishing a business (World Bank 2010).

Leadership and strategy: cases of successful Brazilian companies

Despite all of the issues facing entrepreneurial firms in a still adverse institutional environment, there are numerous examples of Brazilian companies managed by their founders that have achieved prominence from both a national and international perspective. Two such successful cases are included in this chapter as illustrative examples.

Case 1 – Totvs: building the largest Latin American software firm

Totvs is the largest Brazilian and Latin American software applications firm and the seventh-largest world developer of integrated management systems. It is also one of the 50 most internationalized Brazilian companies and among the top 1000 companies in the world in R&D investment. In 2009, the company was operating in 23 countries, with a gross revenue of US$630 million and around 9000 employees.[2]

How did a Brazilian company in the software industry become capable of competing on a par with multinational industry leaders, such as Oracle and SAP? The growth trajectory of Totvs is an example of an entrepreneurial leader's vision and a well-conceived strategy, which avoided head-on competition with multinational corporations.

A short history

Totvs's[3] origins date back to the early 1970s, to the foundation of Siga by entrepreneur Ernesto Haberkorn. At the time, Siga was a São Paulo-based company offering data processing services. In 1978 an engineering student, Laércio Cosentino, started working at the company as a trainee. Just four years later, at only 22 years old, Cosentino was promoted to general manager, with the mission of conducting a company reorganization (Cosentino et al. 2001).

In 1983, in order to cater to the new market of personal computers, Cosentino, in partnership with his boss, founded a new company, Microsiga, which later became Totvs. The new venture was initially dedicated to developing software for microcomputers, under the controversial Information Technology (IT) Law of 1984,[4] which guaranteed Brazilian companies a protected market for their products, shielding the infant industry from international competition. Despite government protection, Microsiga remained small and inconsequential in the sector until the beginning of the 1990s.

With the end of the market reserve for IT products in 1992, a new strategy was designed by corporate management with the intent of achieving leadership in its industry segment. Accordingly, during the 1990s, the company implemented several actions that enabled it to expand its geographic scope and accelerate growth. Some of the actions included opening franchises both in Brazil and abroad, creating foreign subsidiaries, obtaining international certifications, and investing in R&D. During the first decade of the twenty-first century, besides intensifying its previous actions, Totvs began a series of acquisitions that gave it the desired leadership position in the Brazilian market. The most important events in Totvs's development are presented in Table 3.4.

The company consistently achieved outstanding results. According to its website, "since inception, Totvs has been recording net income and positive cash generation despite the adverse economic scenarios in Brazil's recent past." Figure 3.1 presents the evolution of Totvs's gross revenue. Even though there was significant growth starting at the end of the 1990s, the last five years' revenues show strong acceleration, a result of the aggressive acquisitions policy adopted since 2005.

In fact, Totvs experienced uninterrupted two-digit growth rates from 2005 to 2010, coming through the global economic crisis of 2008–9 with high performance levels. Such results came from expanding the client base (both organically and through acquisitions), increasing the average revenue gained per client, and boosting product sales (Dezem 2010). The market value of the company surpassed US$500 million at the time it joined Bovespa, the São Paulo Stock Exchange, in 2006 and reached around US$2.7 billion in 2010. Attracted by its success, several American technology capital funds have invested in the company, controlling around 10 percent of its capital by 2010 (Valenti 2010).

Corporate governance practices at Totvs are considered highly advanced, especially in comparison with other Brazilian firms. Even before it

Table 3.4   Totvs's timeline

Year	Events
1983	Foundation of Microsiga Software
1990	Opening of the first franchise in Brazil
1996	Certified ISO 9001
1997	Opening of the first foreign subsidiary, Microsiga Argentina
1998	Entrance of Advent International Corporation as a business partner (25% stake in Microsiga)
2003	Acquisition of Sipros (Mexico) and the opening of Microsiga Mexico
2005	Acquisition of Logocenter
	Recapture of Advent's stock
	Entrance of Bndespar as a partner (16.7% stake in Totvs)
	International certification
	Creation of Totvs-BMI, a consulting firm
2006	Name of parent company changed from Microsiga Software SA to Totvs SA
	Incorporation of Logocenter
	Public offering of Totvs stock on the Bolsa de Valores de São Paulo (BOVESPA)
	Acquisition of RM Sistemas, with a business unit in Portugal
2007	Acquisition of all Totvs-BMI capital, along with a name change to Totvs Consulting
	Acquisition of Midbyte (software for the retail sector) and BCS (software for the legal sector)
	Joint venture (called TQTVD) with the company Quality for middleware production for digital TV
	Creation of the subsidiary EuroTotvs, based in Portugal
2008	Creation of the Totvs franchise system
	Acquisition of Datasul
2010	Acquisition of the remaining 45% of the stock in TQTVD joint venture
	Acquisition of SRC, owner of software development franchises linked to Datasul

Source: Compiled by the authors.

joined Bovespa, which only occurred in 2006, the company was awarded the Corporate Governance Award 2005 from the Instituto Brasileiro de Governança Corporativa (IBGC, or in English, the Brazilian Corporate Governance Institute), for unlisted companies. In 2009, it obtained first place in IR Global Rankings, being nominated for the Best Corporate Governance in Technology.[5]

The leader behind the strategy

Controversial chief executive and co-founder of Totvs, Laércio Cosentino, has been described as a tough-minded executive: demanding, arrogant, intransigent, and obsessed with efficiency. A brilliant strategist, he is also an

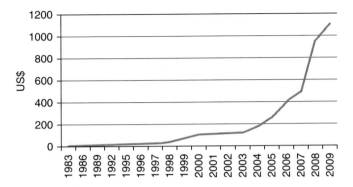

Figure 3.1 Totvs's gross revenue
Source: Company website.

implacable negotiator: "good luck to anyone who crosses his path" (Fusco 2008). Cosentino has been said to be personally involved in every major negotiation undertaken by Totvs, in particular, acquisitions. It was almost inevitable that top executives from acquired companies left soon after coming on board at Totvs, possibly because their management styles diverged.

Cosentino's leadership had a strong positive impact on investors' perceptions, as measured by the company's continued increase in market value. According to the leading business magazine *Exame*, he is "the most important name in the country's technology industry" (Fusco 2008). He was also nominated as the "businessman of the decade," "the most prominent businessman in the Americas" in 2008, and as the "most prominent businessman of the information technology and services segment" in 2007 by three other business publications.[6]

A winning strategy

Totvs's extraordinary growth was the result of a deliberate strategy, very well conceived, with perfect timing and a deep understanding of competitors' behavior. The strategy rested upon three pillars: segmentation, innovation and internationalization.

Segmentation: focus on small and medium-sized companies. The strategy adopted by Totvs in the Brazilian market was deliberately centered on conquering small and medium-sized companies as clients, a market segment left largely unexploited by foreign multinationals operating in Brazil. According to a survey conducted by Fundação Getúlio Vargas, Totvs served 38 percent of the companies operating in Brazil that used enterprise resource planning (ERP) systems, versus 25 percent for SAP and 17 percent for Oracle, its primary foreign competitors (Bouças 2010). According to the company website, it had a 65 percent share in the Brazilian small and medium-sized enterprise segment and 31 percent for the Latin American market, making it the second largest supplier of ERP in Latin America.

Serving the small and medium-sized enterprise segment was considered a competitive advantage by Totvs management, because the segment provided high growth potential due to a low degree of penetration by competitors; regular entry of new companies, many of which experienced rapid growth themselves; low insolvency levels (after the first four years of a company's life); and a growing need for new software products. In addition, by choosing to participate in this segment, Totvs avoided direct competition with industry giants. This strategy allowed Totvs's fast growth without confronting the multinationals, whose interest in the segment only became manifest after Totvs had already consolidated its leadership.

In order to conquer this segment, Totvs developed highly flexible products that could be adapted to the specific needs of clients. The company also offered a larger product portfolio than its competitors, which led a top manager from a global competitor to comment: "Totvs has a long list of coinciding, superimposed products" (Dezem 2010). In addition, Totvs adopted flexible payment options, considered more suitable for the segment's characteristics.

Totvs's revenues originated from a large number of individual clients; in October 2010, its 100 largest clients were responsible for only 18 percent of its revenue. The other 26,000 clients contributed the remaining 82 percent. Moreover, its clients were found across many sectors of the economy, a diversification which helped absorb potential impacts from problems affecting specific industries. Even though its focus remained oriented to the small and medium-sized enterprise segment, in 2009 it began to conquer significantly more large-sized clients, who spontaneously sought out Totvs. In October 2010, large clients represented 15 percent of the company's annual net revenue, as compared to only 5 percent three years before (Valenti 2010).

Innovation: among the world leaders. Totvs declares itself to be "the only company in Latin America to develop and own its proprietary technological platform for software, which gives it a high level of flexibility, interface (with different software, networks, databases and others) and freedom in the choice of platform, topology, connection and database."[7]

Investment in R&D at Totvs reached US$60 million in 2009, almost twice as much as invested in the year before (US$35 million). In 2010, Totvs became one of the select group of the top 1000 companies in the world that invest most in R&D. The importance of this position is even greater considering the relatively small number of Brazilian companies also ranked, such as Petrobras, Vale, and Embraer (Valor Econômico 2010).

Internationalization: focus on Latin America. The company's internationalization started in 1997, with the opening of its first foreign subsidiary, Microsiga Argentina. However, it was only in 2003 with the acquisition of Sipros from Mexico and the founding of Microsiga Mexico that the company had foreign operations beyond commercial activities. The choice of the LA market was because of the perceived similarities between these countries and Brazil in the software applications segment for small and medium-sized firms: a large number of small competing software companies, each one having low levels of market penetration. In this manner, without directly confronting the multinationals, there were attractive market opportunities for a company that wished to pursue aggressive growth in the segment.

In 2006, the acquisition of RM Sistemas gave Totvs a business unit in Portugal, which would be the embryo for EuroTotvs, founded in 2007 and headquartered in Portugal. From this base, the company began to enter the European market; it also controlled a franchise operation in Angola (Brunhara 2009).

The internationalization process continued in 2010 with the formation of a multinational management team. The first foreign top manager was the Argentinean Carlos Maiztegui, who had sold his software company, Meya, to Datasul, which was later acquired by Totvs. In 2010, he was responsible for the expansion of Totvs franchises in South America. Even though Totvs already had partnerships in Bolivia, Chile, Uruguay, and Paraguay, initial contacts were made in Peru and Ecuador to establish new partnerships (Brigatto 2010).

Relationships with other companies: acquisitions, franchising, and strategic alliances. Totvs had an aggressive policy of acquiring competitors, combined with a well-structured franchise system of local software companies, and the development of strategic alliances with global leaders.

Totvs's acquisition policy was carried out based on three criteria. First of all, companies that were candidates for acquisition should offer a broad client base that could be integrated into Totvs's own client base, allowing broader market share. Secondly, these companies should be developers of ERP or vertical software modules, maintaining a consistency in Totvs's product portfolio and keeping the focus on the business segments in which the company competed. Finally, it should be possible to encompass them in the Totvs business model (called the Expanded Business Model), which included consulting and outsourcing. Between 2005 and 2010, Totvs acquired several companies that met such criteria, with the most important acquisition being that of its main Brazilian competitor, Datasul, in 2008 (Fusco 2008).

The use of franchising was combined with Totvs's own distribution channels, resulting in a hybrid system. The franchises permitted partnering with local entrepreneurs, who had better knowledge of local markets than Totvs, and also required less investment. These were mainly used in markets with lower concentration of clients and that were more difficult to control, such as medium-sized cities in Brazil and other LA countries. Wholly owned operations, in contrast, were located for the most part in urban areas, with high concentration of clients, which demanded greater attention from the company.

Strategic alliances were made with global leaders, such as Dell, Microsoft, IBM, Intel, Oracle, and Novell, through commercial- and technological-based agreements. Such alliances allowed Totvs to interact with the most advanced R&D centers in the world, in addition to their benefits for corporate partners. As an example of the success of these alliances, Totvs was chosen as IBM's Best Partner in the Americas at the IBM Excellence Awards in 2007; in 2008 Totvs was awarded the "Best Partner – Innovation That Matters" award of IBM, for the development of the software Totvs Notes Integration, which permits users to access Totvs's ERP directly from Lotus Notes 8.1.[8]

Overcoming obstacles and capitalizing on facilitators.   The way in which Totvs was capable of overcoming restrictions imposed by the institutional environment in Brazil, at the same time benefitting from the facilitators offered, can be considered exemplary. Totvs was favored by government support of the IT industry in Brazil, but also had to confront the difficulty in accessing financial resources to support its growth, the scarcity of qualified labor in the country, and the competition from large MNCs.

Totvs benefitted from government policies and programs aimed at the IT sector, seen as a priority by various administrations. The company was founded during a period of strong protection of the domestic IT industry, coinciding with the beginning of the market reserve for IT products developed in Brazil. From the perspective of Totvs's management, the impact of the market reserve was positive, because it allowed domestic companies to develop in a market that up until then had been dominated by multinationals. Nevertheless, this protection did not lead to Totvs's expansion. Quite the contrary, it was only with the end of market protection that the company defined an aggressive growth strategy to conquer the Brazilian market, taking advantage of the inertia of other firms in the industry to move forward as the market reserve ended.

Starting in 1993, the National Software Export Program, Softex, created auspicious conditions for the development of software companies. One of the characteristics of this program, coordinated by CNPq, was the availability of a special line of credit for software companies, managed by FINEP and supplied by BNDES.

Insufficient access to resources to finance growth has been, without a doubt, one of the primary obstacles faced by entrepreneurial firms in Brazil. In the first years of Totvs's existence, access to banks was difficult, given that the company's products were intangible and it did not have property to offer as collateral, as noted by the company's Vice President of Finance: "The bankers could not see a factory, or products leaving the production line" (Adachi and Tavaglini 2010).

In 1998, the international private equity fund Advent acquired 25 percent of Microsiga (Cosentino et al. 2001); these resources were used to finance organic growth. By the time it left the company in 2005, Advent had received an adequate 100 percent return on its investment. That same year, Bndespar, a holding company associated with BNDES, injected funds in the company, which permitted Microsiga to start acquiring local competitors. The following year, with the expansion of the Brazilian capital market, the company, newly renamed Totvs, issued an IPO and was listed on Bovespa, the São Paulo Stock Exchange. These resources allowed the acquisition of RM, the third largest developer of management software in Latin America (Adachi and Tavaglini 2010). In 2007, two further acquisitions were undertaken: Midbyte (serving the retailing sector) and BCS (focused on the legal business segment). Later came the acquisition of Datasul, financed by an issuing of bonds and by BNDES funds. In recent years, Totvs has gained easy access to financial resources, due to its size and availability of collateral, in addition to being able to access capital markets both in Brazil and abroad.

Another limitation faced by entrepreneurial firms in Brazil has been the lack of qualified labor. In the case of Totvs, this limitation was less severe, due in good part to using university-level professionals, while Brazil's greatest deficit has been in well-trained low to medium-level employees. In spite of this, corporate management was aware of the importance of human capital in achieving market leadership, and invested in training, both from a technical and a managerial point of view. For example, each year since 2005, around 500 employees have received subsidies for graduate fees of 50–100 percent of the total cost (Saraiva 2010). Its concern for human resource management enabled Totvs to receive various recognitions, among which are: The 100 Best HR Suppliers of 2010, from *Gestão & RH* magazine, and 2007 Best Company to Work For in IT & Telecom, from the Great Place to Work Institute. Between 1998 and 2005, Totvs was chosen seven times by the business magazine *Exame* as one of the best Brazilian companies to work for.[9] Due in part to these recognitions, the company has been able to attract more talent than its domestic competitors.

Summarizing, Totvs's strategy permitted it to be successful despite the challenges stemming from the institutional environment; at the same time the company knew how to take advantage of the opportunities presented by this same environment. Such a strategy made it one of the most success-ful Brazilian companies in the 2000s. It stands out as an example of how an entrepreneurial firm can deal with an adverse environment, and use the obstacles to its advantage.

Case 2 – O Boticário: building the largest cosmetics franchise chain in the world

O Boticário[10] is one of the leading Brazilian companies in the perfume and cosmetics sector. Founded in 1977, at the height of the "Brazilian economic miracle," the company navigated the turbulence of the 1980s and first half of the 1990s to become the largest franchise system of perfume and cosmetics in the world.

Surfing the turbulence of the Brazilian economy

O Boticário was founded in 1977 by Miguel Krigsner, with the goal of estab-lishing a pharmacy in the city of Curitiba, the capital of the southern Brazilian state of Paraná. The initial investment was only 3000 dollars, borrowed from relatives. Perceiving an opportunity in the market for products with natural ingredients, Krigsner decided to offer small quantities of cosmetic products produced in the pharmacy with this positioning, targeting the middle to upper-middle segment of the market (Freire and Da Rocha 2002).

During that time, strong import restrictions favored the development of a domestic industry. The luxury segment, at the beginning of the 1980s, represented roughly 20 percent of the Brazilian market and was controlled by international brands: Helena Rubinstein, Max Factor, and Revlon. Another segment dominated by multinationals was door-to-door sales, which represented another 20 percent, with Avon having an estimated 75 percent market share. Finally, there was the popular cosmetics segment, in which both domestic and multinational brands competed. Multinational companies had production facilities in Brazil in response to import restric-tions and high tariffs (Schmidt and De Mello 1983).

During the 1970s, a new strategic group appeared within the perfume and cosmetics industry. It was formed by Brazilian manufacturers who used natural ingredients, such as Natura (founded in 1969) and O Boticário. Both firms targeted the upper-middle segments of the market. Natural cosmet-ics were perceived as "softer, less aggressive, with fragrances inspired by the countryside, and rustic but tasteful packaging, which sought to stand apart from the 'industrialized' concept and seek inspiration from nature" (Freire and Da Rocha 2002: 112). This positioning strategy differed from that adopted by multinational companies in the Brazilian market, whose prod-ucts were perceived as being more "industrialized." The natural cosmetics companies grew rapidly during the 1980s, helped by import barriers. As two large multinationals – Revlon and Yardley – exited the Brazilian cosmetics market, there were more opportunities for the domestically owned companies to increase their market share.

Steady growth of consumer demand led O Boticário to expand. In 1982, Krigsner established an industrial plant in order to manufacture products on a larger scale than had been possible with the pharmacies. Additionally, to achieve national coverage he developed an exclusive distribution system based upon franchising, starting in 1980.

The opening of the Brazilian market to imported products, at the beginning of the 1990s, had a severe impact on the industry. The average tariff on imported perfume and cosmetic products dropped from 85 percent in 1991 to 18 percent in 1995. The market was flooded with an "avalanche of imported products" (Abihpec 2010: 18). Domestic companies were forced to become more competitive, by focusing primarily on restructuring and cost reductions.

Top management at O Boticário had already anticipated market liberalization, and had overseen a reorganization and professionalization of the franchise system between 1987 and 1992. Even so, other actions were necessary to reduce costs, such as the adoption of a new cost control system and renegotiations with suppliers. Another important step was a revision of the market positioning of existing lines to achieve a better match between company offerings and consumer desires (Mano 2003).

The advent of the Real Plan in 1994 changed the dynamics of the industry, extremely sensitive to fluctuations in consumers' discretionary income. In addition, stabilization of the economy stimulated investment and firms' growth. Up until this point in time, company management was typical of a family-run business characterized by a bloated management structure and limited monitoring of performance. A sharp downturn in profitability alerted corporate management of the need to restructure the company. A re-engineering program was conducted in 1998, leading to a much leaner structure. The firm became more professional and results-oriented, without losing its customer focus. Logistics were also revised in order to reduce costs. As a result, the company increased its revenues by 50 percent and was back to profitability (Mano 2003).

After 2000, O Boticário showed continuous growth, and experimented with other distribution channels. In 2002 it started selling over the Internet; in 2007 it test-marketed telephone sales in northeast Brazil; and in 2009 a division was created to initiate direct consumer sales using a door-to-door system. This last move aimed at reaching lower-middle-class consumers, who had been largely ignored by the company until then. This segment was becoming the largest and most dynamic of the Brazilian economy.

Table 3.5 presents the company's timeline, highlighting important developments during its existence.

Table 3.5   O Boticário's timeline

Year	Events
1977	Founding of a pharmacy under the name O Boticário
1980	Opening of the first franchised storefront
1982	Inauguration of the first manufacturing plant
1984	Implementation of a national marketing program
1986	First store abroad located in Portugal
1987	The company's stores reach 1000
1987–92	Restructuring and professionalization of the franchise system
1990	Creation of the O Boticário Foundation for the Protection of Nature
1998	Reengineering program. Changes in the distribution system, eliminating distributors
2001	The company's stores reach 2000
2002	Adoption of new methods for controlling franchises Initiation of Internet-based sales
2007	Telephone-based sales in northeast Brazilian states
2009	Beginning of direct, door-to-door sales
2010	The company's stores reach 3000

Source: Compiled by the authors.

In 2008 O Boticário sales were US$450 million and the franchise chain revenues were US$1.2 billion. Only one year later, in 2009, company sales were estimated to have reached US$860 million and the franchise network sales were over US$2 billion.[11] By 2010, the company directly employed 1700 people and had 915 franchisees, with more than 3000 stores (O Boticário 2010).

Wisdom and prudence in leadership

Krigsner was born in Bolivia to immigrant Jews fleeing from Nazi Germany. He graduated as a pharmacist, which gave him the knowledge necessary to open, at the age of 27, his first pharmacy. After 30 years as CEO, in 2008 Krigsner became Chairman of the Board; he owned 80 percent of O Boticário's stock. His brother-in-law, Artur Grynbaum, was nominated CEO of the firm; he held the remaining 20 percent of company stock (Fusco 2010).

One of Krigsner's characteristics was his permanent concern with human relations. He stated in an interview (Exame 2007):

The most important thing within a company and in corporate life are the human relations that you build. You must build relationships based on trust (...) It is necessary, in my opinion, that people who work for you see the company as a way to fulfill their personal dreams, and not just the dream of owner. This philosophy ... is the basis of O Boticário's success.

His growth philosophy was based on the belief that "the best growth is that which is slow, balanced and harmonic." In his judgment, at several times O Boticário grew too fast, making it necessary to take corrective steps. Even so, he believed that businessmen should take risks, "according to the magnitude and speed that the firm can handle" (Exame 2007).

Krigsner stands out among Brazilian businessmen for his sense of social responsibility and ethics in business. In 2002, when he was nominated Entrepreneur of the Year by Ernst and Young, he stated:

> O Boticário offers a standard of corporate citizenship. My dream was not to build a cosmetics company, but a Brazilian institution. (...) From the moment that a domestic firm achieves this size, it has to accept other types of responsibilities. (...) Businessmen, not only the government should help to improve the social conditions in the country.[12]

He was one of the founders of the Institute for Retail Development, a non-profit organization created in 2004 by businessmen to fight retail-store tax evasion. He also established the O Boticário Foundation, dedicated to environmental causes. Krigsner was nominated International Retailer of the Year by the National Retail Federation of the United States in 2006, for his leadership, creativity, and innovation in the retail sector. In 2007 he was honored in the Hall of Fame of Atualidade Cosmética, the most important cosmetics industry recognition in Brazil (O Boticário 2010).

A strategy aimed at conquering the Brazilian market

O Boticário was created to serve the large Brazilian perfume and cosmetics market that grew at rates between 15 and 20 percent throughout the 1970s (Schmidt and De Mello 1983). In 1996, the Brazilian market was estimated at US\$4.7 billion, reaching US\$8 billion by 2006, and almost US\$13 billion by 2009. It is the third largest cosmetics consumer market in the world, with 8.1 percent of global consumption, following the United States and Japan, and surpassing China (Abihpec 2010).The size and dynamics of the Brazilian market made it the target of O Boticário, notwithstanding small incursions into international markets. Its growth strategy has been oriented around creating a network of exclusive franchised stores, developing a strong brand name, and pursuing innovation, with strong emphasis on corporate social responsibility.

Gaining access to the Brazilian market. The most crucial element for O Boticário's growth was the adoption of a selective distribution strategy based upon franchising. Such a strategy allowed O Boticário, in its first years, to avoid the obstacles to accessing traditional distribution channels for perfume and cosmetics: on one side, department stores dominated by international brands, and, on the other, supermarkets and drugstores saturated with established brands targeting the mass market. Moreover, the franchise network generated brand awareness and consolidated the brand's positioning by means of an exclusive and differentiated distribution channel. It was also a way to grow more rapidly by using third-party resources.

O Boticário's model was rapidly copied by other domestic companies that competed in the natural cosmetics segment. An exception was O Boticário's main rival, Natura, which from 1974 adopted the door-to-door sales model (Freire and Da Rocha 2002).

The franchise expansion was so successful that by 1987 the company had around 1100 franchised stores throughout Brazil. However, in the next two years the company reorganized its franchise system, reducing the number of stores from 1100 in 1987 to 800 in 1989. Even so, in 1992 it surpassed the previous high when it reached 1200 franchises.[13] Growth in the retail network, virtually all franchise-based,[14] continued steadily after the year 2000 (Figure 3.2).

Almost until the end of the 1990s the company used a national distribution system consisting of 21 distributors. This system initially proved efficient, but it also distanced the company from its retail operations. Therefore, as management became aware that this practice generated a lack of control over franchisees and a detachment from end customers, it was decided to distribute directly to the franchised stores. This change allowed the company to be closer to the market, reducing inventory levels, and

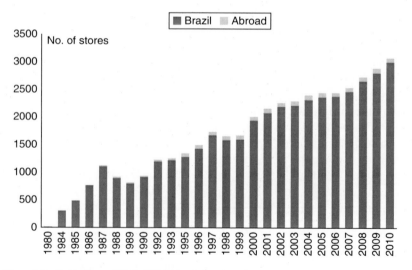

Figure 3.2   Evolution of O Boticário's retail network
Sources: Before 2000, compiled from several newspaper and business magazines; after 2000, company website.

improving communication with franchisees. In 2002, the company adopted a new method to control franchise performance. In parallel, it created a team of consultants to help franchise owners (Mano 2003).

By 2005, O Boticário had 45 percent of all cosmetics and perfume franchised stores in Brazil (Ribeiro and Melo 2006). In 2010, the company had almost 3000 stores, mostly franchised. The company was recognized as the best franchise chain in Brazil in 2008; it had also been chosen as the best in the perfume and cosmetics category for four consecutive years by the business magazine *Pequenas Empresas, Grandes Negócios*. Also in 2008, the design of its stores was recognized by the International Council of Shopping Centers as the best in Latin America. In 2009 and 2010, it received the Seal of Excellence in Franchising from the Brazilian Franchising Association (O Boticário 2010).

Developing brand image. The second pillar of O Boticário's strategy was the development of a strong brand image. At its beginning, the company relied primarily on word of mouth to bring new customers into the small pharmacy. In 1979 it opened a store in Curitiba's airport, which played an important role in building brand awareness among those who traveled into and out of the city. As the company developed its network of exclusive retail stores, the brand name became well-known.

Since 1984 O Boticário had invested in national advertising in Brazilian women's magazines, and later in television commercials. In the 2000s, the company started to use the Internet, especially social media, such as Orkut and Facebook. In 2009, marketing expenditure reached approximately 10 percent of its revenues.[15]

Creating innovative, high-quality products. The company has developed and launched several innovative products. It was the first in the world to produce a fragrance with wine alcohol in 2004. In 2006, it was the first Brazilian company to use nanotechnology in the development of anti-aging cosmetics. In 2008 the company inaugurated an advanced Molecular Biology Laboratory, with research facilities dedicated to the study of the skin's aging process (O Boticário 2010).

O Boticário's innovativeness was recognized with several awards. In 2005 the company conquered all perfume categories at the Atualidade Cosmética Awards, considered the most important of the industry in Brazil. In 2010 it was recognized as the fifth most innovative company in the country by the business magazine *Época Negócios*, being lauded for its pioneering application of nanotechnology in cosmetics and for instilling a culture of innovation (O Boticário 2010).

Investing in corporate social responsibility. O Boticário's image is strongly associated with corporate social responsibility. The company gives 1 percent of its net revenue to the O Boticário Foundation for the Protection of Nature, founded in 1990. Social actions are developed in local communities where the company operates, or on a regional or national scale. The company conducts several environmental education programs in partnership with schools, universities, NGOs, and government. It also patronizes the maintenance of the Botanical Gardens in its home city of Curitiba and owns natural reserves in Brazil, dedicated to protecting the natural flora and fauna of local ecosystems. The Foundation participates in the Climate Observatory, a Brazilian network of NGOs and social movements, and it is also a founding member of the Curitiba Forum on Climate Change (O Boticário 2010).

Up until 2008, the O Boticário Foundation had supported 1170 environmental conservation projects undertaken by 350 organizations throughout Brazil, with investments exceeding US$8 million. In recognition of its efforts in supporting the environment, the Foundation has received 47 awards (O Boticário 2010).

Going abroad: not yet a priority

The strong presence of O Boticário in the Brazilian market contrasts with a minor international presence. In 2009, only 2.5 percent of its stores were located abroad.[16]

The company's internationalization process began in 1986 with the opening of its first store in Portugal. This was followed by entering several markets, including some with high cultural distance such as Saudi Arabia, Australia, and South Africa, diffusing management attention and company resources. The initial management expectation was that after a few years the company would become a large Brazilian multinational. This, however, has not happened. The only market in which the company succeeded in establishing a network of retail stores was Portugal, a country with low cultural distance to Brazil. Even there, a series of errors forced management to rethink the entire operation (Naiditch 2007, Freire and Da Rocha 2002).

The main reason for failure in the firm's internationalization process was the lack of adequate managerial and financial resources, which had been fully engaged in the domestic market, allocated to international operations. Nevertheless, international expansion will soon become mandatory if O Boticario's growth is to continue, as expansion in the domestic market reaches saturation. Internationalization, up to now seen as a secondary issue, will then become one of management's primary concerns.

An independent and cautious trajectory

Summing up, O Boticário grew under the protection of high tariff barriers that impeded the entry of imported products, but permitted inward foreign direct investment. Therefore, domestic firms still had to compete with foreign multinationals, thus forcing O Boticário to adopt differentiation strategies and invest in alternative marketing channels, a strategy that was soon copied by local competitors. To protect its competitive advantage, O Boticário invested in the development of brand image. The use of franchised stores not only allowed the firm to expand rapidly with third-party capital, minimized risks, and guaranteed market access, but also made it possible to overcome limitations of the institutional environment in terms of well-trained managers; franchise owners tend to be more entrepreneurial, innovative, and market-oriented than a typical store manager would be if hired by the company.

O Boticário's growth, except for market protection in the first decade of its existence, did not benefit from government policies and programs. Its strategy was always cautious, never moving faster than its strengths allowed, and taking a step back when necessary, in order to protect the company from the oscillations and challenges of the institutional environment.

Lessons from history

What can be learned from the cases of Totvs and O Boticário? The two companies grew and survived in a turbulent environment, but they were to some extent shielded from foreign competition by government policies that protected infant industries. Both firms were forced to adapt to the abrupt changes in the Brazilian economy that came about during the first part of the 1990s, and became sizable companies in their respective industries. However, even though they faced the same macroeconomic conditions, an analysis of the two trajectories reveals almost opposite strategies with distinct timing. Such differences cannot be explained simply by entrepreneurial decisions, but also by diverse industry environments.

The environment of the perfume and cosmetics industry was characterized by government policies hostile to foreign products. Such policies made domestic companies equal with the multinationals operating in Brazil in terms of their cost factors (although the large MNCs had access to financial and human resources that were not available to small, local companies). In fact, before market liberalization Brazilian subsidiaries of foreign multinationals had also become inefficient as compared to their counterparts in more competitive markets. Thus there was space for the development of domestic firms that were nevertheless exposed to competitive pressure from the multinationals established in the country.

O Boticário knew how to adroitly exploit market opportunities, developing a brand with a touch of sophistication and offering quality products aimed at the middle to upper-middle classes. The opening of the Brazilian market did not impact O Boticário, but mostly the outlets serving the high-end segment, which was originally the domain of duty-free stores. The challenge faced by O Boticário in the post-liberalization period was essentially how to increase its competitiveness and transform itself into a more efficient company by adopting new management techniques.

Increased efficiency is an expected outcome of market liberalization. In the Brazilian case, however, a study showed that the impact among sectors varied greatly. Specifically in the pharmaceutical, hygiene, and cleaning products industry, in which O Boticário competed, the increase in productivity was lower than the patterns observed in other industries (an annual average of 1.7 percent between 1990 and 2000, versus 4.8 percent for chemical products and 7.1 percent for rubber products) (Bonelli and Pinheiro 2008).

In the context of its industry, O Boticário's performance is therefore even more striking. Its growth, when measured by the increase in the number of franchises, shows a smooth progression, with small but steady steps throughout its existence. (The only exception was a short period in the middle of the 1980s when there was a consolidation of the franchise system.) Its growth rate did not seem to be affected by the opening of the market, but the profit margin did suffer somewhat, forcing a reorganization and the adoption of new management methods.

Totvs experienced a different situation. Up to the beginning of the 1990s, the IT industry was protected by a government policy reserving the market for domestic firms. This made it practically impossible to import hardware but left room for the development of software applications, because the basic software was proprietary and exclusive of the closed architecture of hardware that had been authorized for the country. In fact, the software applications market ended up being reserved as well, due to the fact that the software had to be developed to adhere to the platforms (both hardware and basic software) that were available in Brazil.

The IT market reserve also had a distinct impact on small entrepreneurial companies because it eliminated direct competition with multinationals. This stimulated inefficiency and complacency and, in some cases, encouraged unethical and corrupt behavior. But the market reserve did create a labor market with qualified professionals, providing incentives for the training of technicians, researchers, and academicians, often in leading research centers abroad. It was within this context that Totvs matured. However, during the entire time the market was closed it remained a small company indistinguishable from any other.

The end of the market reserve caught most companies by surprise. There is evidence that many businessmen in the IT industry believed it would never happen, even though all of the political and economic indicators pointed in this direction (Fonseca et al. 2010). Totvs management, however, was prepared to respond quickly to the change.

Totvs based its strategies on two critical environmental factors: first, the end of the market reserve, in which the large, incumbent firms within the local software applications industry were strongly dependent on Brazilian hardware manufacturers (closed architecture and basic proprietary software); second, the growing tendency worldwide for hardware as a "commodity," having in common a basic software platform (for example, IBM-PC with DOS/Windows, client/servers with Unix). Totvs targeted its new offering at the universal platforms, which were not dependent on specific hardware, and was assisted by the inertia of incumbent firms, which had developed path-dependent behavior encouraged by market protection. With market liberalization, Totvs was able to become one of the industry leaders, and with proper financial leverage (initially provided by an international private equity fund and Bndespar, later by an IPO), was able to extend into new segments via the acquisition of competitors. Totvs then had an accelerated growth trajectory, particularly after the year 2000.

These considerations show how the strategies adopted were influenced by the specificities of each industry and how government protection in each industry produced distinct results. Regarding the Brazilian institutional environment, the two cases provide evidence that the entrepreneurs knew how to take advantage of opportunities to overcome existing obstacles with well-designed strategic actions.

Finally, it should be noted that there were striking differences in leadership style between the entrepreneurs that led the two companies: Cosentino, bold and inflexible; and Krigsner, cautious and oriented to human relations and social responsibility. Their strategies and philosophy were radically opposed: rapid growth through acquisitions on one side, slow and organic growth on the other. These strategic choices had a strong impact on their companies' growth trajectories, even while influenced by the institutional environments of the country and of their respective industries.

The future of entrepreneurship in Brazil

This study, though restricted to the cases and industries analyzed, allows some insights into the future of entrepreneurship in Brazil. The starting point for evaluating the potential for entrepreneurial activity in Brazil is its conformity to social and cultural norms. The high social status of entrepreneurs makes this career attractive to young people, just like the two entrepreneurs described in this study. This is a powerful force behind any government policy or program aimed at fostering entrepreneurship in Brazil.

The partial removal of barriers to entrepreneurial activities occurred relatively recently in Brazil, mostly with the opening of the market during the first half of the 1990s. However, there is evidence that the potential for transformation based upon these changes has already diminished, and further changes are necessary to enable a new cycle of growth and increased productivity. Even though it has consistently been suggested that Brazil is still a country relatively closed to international trade (Haddad 2008), additional reduction in tariff barriers seems less urgent than the development of policies to strengthen and improve the conditions for doing business in Brazil, which has the advantage of generating less resistance from interest groups than further market liberalization.

Among these policies it is important to highlight investment in education and training, investment in innovation, tax reductions, simplification of bureaucracy, credit at low interest rates, and a reduction in the requirements for collateral. All of these are obstacles to the growth of small entrepreneurial ventures today. Such changes are urgent and are perceived by entrepreneurs as the most important barriers to the growth and survival of their businesses. Other actions that are just as relevant, but the impact of which is less visible, include improvement of logistical infrastructure, security, legal procedures, and public services, which have been referred to as "Cost Brazil," severely undermining the competitiveness of Brazilian firms.

Notes

* The authors acknowledge the support of Pronex/Faperj/CNPq in this research.
  1. The funds would show up on the books as expenditure or investment, when they were never listed as income.
  2. Company site (http://www.totvs.com).
  3. From the Latin, meaning "everything"; it is pronounced "totus."
  4. It is worth noting that Law 7232 of October 1984, known as the Information Technology Law, was not the first mechanism for protecting the IT market in Brazil. Various other resolutions and government regulations had limited the freedom of foreign capital in this sector since 1976 (Erber 1983, 1986).
  5. Company site.
  6. *Consumidor Moderno, America Economia* and *Valor Econômico*, respectively (company site).
  7. Company site.
  8. Company site.
  9. Company site.
  10. The name "O Boticário" means "The Apothecary" in English, which refers to the old profession of natural pharmacists, prior to the advent of modern pharmacology.
  11. Sales data were compiled from several articles in newspapers and business magazines.
  12. Interview with Miguel Krigsner, September 2, 1992 (company document).
  13. Compiled from several sources.
  14. The company does not reveal the breakdown of company-owned and franchised stores. The last available data indicated that the company directly owned 58 stores in 2009.
  15. Company site (http://internet.boticario.com.br/portal/site/internetbr/).
  16. Seventy-three stores out of a total of 2883.

References

Abihpec. 2010. *"Panorama do Setor 2010,"* http://www.abihpec.org.br/conteudo/ Panorama_do_setor_20092010_Portugues_12_04_10.pdf, date accessed October 25, 2010.

Adachi, V., and F. Tavaglini. 2010. "Bolsa Aciona a Transformação Mais Radical," http://www.valoronline.com.br/impresso/116772/, date accessed November 7, 2010.

Aguilar, A. 2010. "Cenário é Favorável para Transações no Brasil e no Exterior," *Valor Econômico* December 12: F6.

Ahlstrom, D., and G.D. Bruton. 2010. "Rapid Institutional Shifts and the Co-evolution of Entrepreneurial Firms in Transition Economies." *Entrepreneurship Theory and Practice* 34, no. 30: 531–54.

Amaral, G.L., J.E. Olenike, L.M.F. Amaral, and F. Steinbruch. 2009. *"Estudo sobre Sonegação Fiscal das Empresas Brasileiras,"* http://www.ibpt.com.br/img/_ publicacao/13649/175.pdf, date accessed October 15, 2010.

Anprotec. 2008. *Parques Tecnológicos no Brasil: Estudo, Análise e Proposições*. Brasília: Abdi; Anprotec.

Audretsch, D. 2007. *The Entrepreneurial Society*. Oxford: Oxford University Press.

Bonelli, R., and A.C. Pinheiro. 2008. "Abertura e Crescimento Econômico no Brasil." In O. De Barros and F. Giambiagi (Eds.), *Brasil Globalizado*. Rio de Janeiro: Elsevier.

Bosma, N., and J. Levie. 2010. *"2009 Global Report"*, http://www.gemconsortium.org, date accessed September 5, 2010.

Bouças, C. 2010. "Parceira Brasileira da Microsoft Busca Expansão no Exterior," http://www.valoronline.com.br/impresso/idc/2409/304909/, date accessed November 5, 2010.

Bowen, H.P., and D. De Clercq. 2008. "Institutional Context and the Allocation of Entrepreneurial Effort." *Journal of International Business Studies* 39: 747–67.

Brigatto, G. 2010. "Companhias Nacionais Avançam no Exterior," http://www. valoronline.com.br/impresso/tecnologia-telecomunicacoes/103/120603/, date accessed November 5, 2010.

Brunhara, A.J. 2009. "Processo de Internacionalização da Totvs: um Estudo de Caso da Aquisição da Mexicana Sipros." Unpublished MBA dissertation, Pontifícia Universidade Católica do Paraná, Curitiba.

Chandra, A., and T. Fealey. 2009. "Business Incubation in the United States, China and Brazil: a Comparison of Role of Government, Incubator Funding and Financial Services." *International Journal of Entrepreneurship* 13 (Special Issue): 67–86.

Cosentino, L., E. Haberkorn, and F. Cícero. 2001. *Genoma Empresarial*. São Paulo: Editora Gente.

Da Rocha, A., and J.F. Da Silva. 2009. "The Internationalization of Brazilian Firms: an Introduction to the Special Issue." *Latin American Business Review* 10: 61–71.

Dezem, V. 2010. "SAP Planeja Expandir Serviços no Brasil e Exportar Inovação," http://www.valoronline.com.br/impresso/oracle/2267/31473/, date accessed October 7, 2010.

Dib, L.A., A. Da Rocha, and J.F. Da Silva. 2010. "The Internationalization Process of Brazilian Software Firms and the Born Global Phenomenon: Examining Firm, Network, and Entrepreneur Variables." *Journal of International Entrepreneurship* 8: 233–53.

Erber, F.S. 1983. *O Complexo Eletrônico: Estrutura, Evolução Histórica e Padrão de Competição*. Texto para discussão. Rio de Janeiro: IEI/UFRJ.

Erber, F.S. 1986. *Padrões de Desenvolvimento e Difusão de Tecnologias*. Texto para discussão. Rio de Janeiro: IEI/UFRJ.

Exame. 2007. "As Fórmulas do Boticário," http://exame.abril.com.br/revista-exame-pme/noticias/as-formulas-do-boticario-m0137534, date accessed October 15, 2010.

Fonseca, C.E.C., F.S Meirelles, and E.H. Diniz. 2010. *Tecnologia Bancária no Brasil: Uma História de Conquistas, uma Visão de Futuro.* Rio de Janeiro: FGV.

Freire, C., and A. Da Rocha. 2002. "Paradoxo da Distância Cultural: O Boticário em Portugal." In A. Da Rocha (Ed.), *As Novas Fronteiras: a Multinacionalização das Empresas Brasileiras.* Rio de Janeiro: Mauad.

Fusco, C. 2008. "Ele é Duro na Queda," http://portalexame.abril.com.br/revista/exame/edicoes/0933/tecnologia/ele-duro-queda-408279.html, date accessed October 7, 2010.

Fusco, C. 2010. "Ele vai bater à sua Porta," http://exame.abril.com.br/revista-exame/edicoes/0968/negocios/noticias/ele-vai-bater-sua-porta-58119?page=1&slug_name=ele-vai-bater-sua-porta-558119, date accessed October 7, 2010.

Gonçalves, C.E.S. 2008. "Produtividade e instituições no Brasil e no mundo: ensinamentos teóricos e empíricos." In O. De Barros and F. Giambiagi (Eds.), *Brasil Globalizado.* Rio de Janeiro: Elsevier.

Haddad, C.L.S. 2008. "Em Favor de uma Maior Abertura." In O. De Barros and F. Giambiagi (Eds.), *Brasil Globalizado.* Rio de Janeiro: Elsevier.

Iglesias, R. M., and P. Motta Veiga. 2002. "Promoção de Exportações via internacionalização das Firmas de Capital Brasileiro." In A. C. Pinheiro, R. Markwald, and L. V. Pereira (Eds.), *O Desafio das Exportações.* Rio de Janeiro: Banco Nacional do Desenvolvimento Econômico e Social.

Iglesias, R. M., and P. Motta Veiga. 2005. "Investimento das Firmas Brasileiras no Exterior: Algumas Hipóteses e Resultados de uma Pesquisa entre Exportadores." In C.A. Hemais (Ed.), *O Desafio dos Mercados Externos: Teoria e Prática na Internacionalização da Firma,* vol. 2. Rio de Janeiro: Mauad.

Lethbridge, T., and G. Fogaça. 2010. "É Capitalismo em Estado Puro." *Veja* 44, no. 23: 21–30.

Mano, C. 2003. "Crescimento Sustentável," http://exame.abril.com.br/revista-exame/edicoes/0789/empresas/noticias/crescimento-sustentavel-m0044558, date accessed October 25, 2010.

Naiditch, S. 2007. "Vinte e Um Anos de Erros," http://exame.abril.com.br/revista-exame/edicoes/0903/negocios/noticias/vinte-e-um-anos-de-erros-m0139963, date accessed October 25, 2010.

O Boticário. 2010. "Perfil Empresarial," http://internet.boticario.com.br/portal/site/institucional, date accessed October 25, 2010.

Ribeiro, F.C.R., and P.L.R. Melo. 2006. "O Processo de Internacionalização da Rede de Franquias O Boticário no Mercado Norte-Americano." *Anais do Workshop sobre Internacionalização de Empresas.* São Paulo: FEA/USP.

Saraiva, J. 2010. "Por MBA, Funcionário Assume Compromisso de Não Deixar a Empresa," http://www.valoronline.com.br/impresso/carreira/120/121972/, date accessed October 5, 2010.

Schmidt, A.M.R., and R.C. De Mello. 1983. *Nota sobre a Indústria Brasileira de Cosméticos,* Caso nº 15A183534. Rio de Janeiro: Central Brasileira de Casos.

Serra, J. 1990. "Existe uma Saída." *Veja* 23 (August): 62–63.

Spencer, J., T.P. Murtha, and S.A. Lenway. 2005. "How Governments Matter to New Industry Creation." *The Academy of Management Review* 30, no. 2: 321–27.

Valenti, G. 2010. "Grandes Empresas Compram Mais da Totvs e Puxam Receita," http://www.valoronline.com.br/impresso/investimentos/119/328655/, date accessed November 5, 2010.

Valor Econômico. 2010. "Cresce Participação do Brasil," http://www.valoronline.com. br/impresso/empresas/102/331173/, date accessed November 11, 2010.

Vox Populi. 2007. *"Fatores Condicionantes e Taxa de Mortalidade das MPEs,"* www. sebrae.com.br, date accessed September 5, 2010.

World Bank. 2010. *"Doing Business 2010: Reforming through Difficult Times,"* www. doingbusiness.org, date accessed October 21, 2010.

Zou, H.Z., X. Chen, and P. Ghauri. 2010. "Antecedents and Consequences of New Venture Growth Strategy: an Empirical Study in China." *Asia Pacific Journal of Management* 27, no. 3: 393–422.

4
Entrepreneurship in Chile

Gonzalo Jiménez
Escuela de Negocios, Universidad Adolfo Ibañez

Chile is arguably the best performer in the LA region in terms of a stable macroeconomic environment, lack of political risk and clear and transparent access to information, which gives the confidence to invest and provides a healthy environment for entrepreneurs (*see* Figure 4.1). The country has a set of positive characteristics that makes it the most recommended place in the region to start and run a business (*see* Table 4.1). Nevertheless, there are many factors that need improvement before we can consider Chile a truly entrepreneurship-oriented country.

Based on the World Bank's 2009 rankings, we can say that Chile is the most business-friendly country in LA. Chile is currently positioned as a leader economy among the other LA countries, due to its stable and sustainable growth. The country is well known for having an open market system, with numerous FTAs, and also a transparent government and efficient regulations. All of these characteristics have been critical to entrepreneurs, providing an adequate environment to start a business.

Chile has the highest GDP among all the other LA countries (4.4 percent annual growth) and Santiago was ranked the second-best city in LA in which to do business, only scoring slightly lower than São Paulo and beating Miami according to the 2009 *América Economía* business magazine ranking.

Geoff Lewis (2007) wrote an article for *Fortune Small Business* magazine proposing a list of countries ranging from the most to the least friendly to small business entrepreneurship, giving equal weighting to the World Bank data and the GEM, an annual study produced by Babson College and the London Business School. Chile is ranked as No.16, and the next-ranked LA countries are Jamaica at No. 21; Peru at No. 26; and Colombia at No. 29; as shown in Table 4.2.

Chile has a heterogeneous micro and small business sector, which is superior to the LA average, with 38 percent of total national employment (almost 2.3 million people). Small businesses typically enter industries that

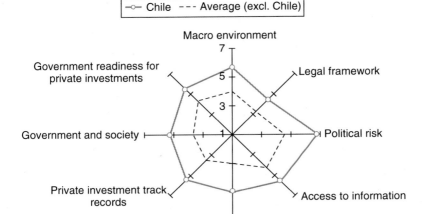

Figure 4.1 Investment attractiveness, Chile vs. Latin America
Source: Mia et al. (2007: 22).

Table 4.1 Investment Attractiveness Index by Pillars, of Chile and other countries

Infrastructure Private Investment Attractiveness Index			Subindex I: General investment environmental factors			Subindex II: Infrastructure investment specific factors		
Rank	Country	Score	Rank	Country	Score	Rank	Country	Score
1	Chile	5.46	1	Chile	5.60	1	Chile	5.25
2	Brazil	4.40	2	Mexico	4.57	2	Brazil	4.35
3	Colombia	4.33	3	Brazil	4.45	3	Peru	4.28
4	Peru	4.23	4	Columbia	4.42	4	Columbia	4.23
5	Mexico	4.04	5	El Salvador	4.34	5	Uruguay	3.73
6	Uruguay	4.02	6	Uruguay	4.31	6	Venezuela	3.64
7	El Salvador	3.97	7	Peru	4.18	7	El Salvador	3.60
8	Guatemala	3.64	8	Dominican Republic	3.98	8	Mexico	3.51
9	Argentina	3.41	9	Guatemala	3.82	9	Guatemala	3.45
10	Venezuela	3.37	10	Argentina	3.81	10	Bolivia	3.31
11	Bolivia	3.34	11	Bolivia	3.37	11	Argentina	3.01
12	Dominican Republic	3.33	12	Venezuela	3.11	12	Dominican Republic	2.69

Source: Mia et al. (2007: 22).

present fewer obstacles and have less diversification, compared to large businesses.

With a pro-business government, entrepreneurship has definitely acquired a more important role, becoming a more relevant topic on the government

Table 4.2   Most and least friendly countries to small business

Rank	Country	FSB score
1	New Zealand	2.03
2	United States	2.01
3	Canada	1.99
4	Australia	1.93
5	Singapore	1.88
6	Hong Kong, China	1.86
7	United Kingdom	1.85
8	Ireland	1.85
9	Denmark	1.75
10	Iceland	1.75
11	Norway	1.70
12	Sweden	1.64
13	Japan	1.64
14	Finland	1.60
15	Thailand	1.60
16	Chile	1.59

Source: *Money CNN* magazine, June 2007.

agenda. Even though Chile is a business-friendly country, there is still a lot of room for improvement on policies and institutions that regulate and protect businesses, especially small ones. The entrepreneurship environment still faces many difficulties and lacks some basic protection and incentives to flourish.

According to the Inter-American Development Bank (Agosin and Ortega 2009), there are some important factors that have been identified to explain this distinctive environment favorable to entrepreneurship:

Trade liberalization and strong exchange rate depreciation following the military coup of 1974; subsidies to specific sectors (especially forestry); the entrepreneurial activity of the state through a semi-public venture-capital-cum-research and development (R&D) undertaking, Fundación Chile; state-sponsored accumulation of production factors indispensable for the development of specific sectors (agricultural and forestry sciences); and the encouragement of foreign direct investment (FDI) in specific sectors where the country had undeveloped potential and has a comparative advantage, carried out through debt-equity swaps in the mid to late 1980s, which favored investment in pulp and paper sectors.

An additional and interesting aspect that makes Chile an attractive place to do business is all the export opportunities that have arisen during the past few years, especially in the mining, food, and forestry sectors. Only after the opening up of the economy in the late 1970s – with falling tariffs that made producers look at export markets, and the availability of foreign exchange to import capital equipment suitable for export production – did large volumes of exports become feasible. As shown in Figure 4.2, in Chile more than 40 percent of the established entrepreneurial efforts have clients abroad.

An example of successful exports is the Chilean wine industry, reaching more than 100 countries. Wine, a product that began to be exported in significant volumes in the mid-1980s, is now a major industry with exports close to US$1 billion, going all the way from bulk, commodity wine to product differentiation, now well known as a "good value for money product" and aiming to position some brands in the premium wines segment, where monopolistic competition is fierce and product quality and brand image are essential for success (Agosin and Ortega 2009). The evolution of wine exports is shown in Figure 4.3.

Chile has some advantages to produce and export wine, such as excellent geographical conditions, with a perfect climate of hot days and cold nights for flavorful vines for many wine varieties – such as Chardonnay,

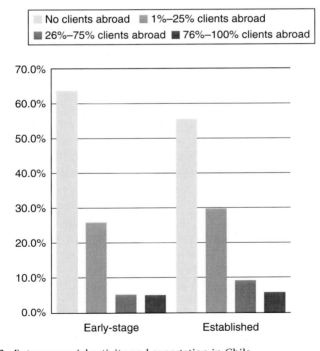

Figure 4.2 Entrepreneurial activity and exportation in Chile
Source: GEM (2009: 60 (Chile)).

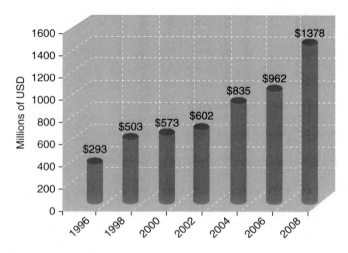

Figure 4.3   Evolution of Chilean wine exports
Source: InvestChile, Corfo, 2007.

Carmenere, Cabernet Sauvignon, Sauvignon Blanc, Merlot, Syrah – highly skilled professionals, good infrastructure, and sanitary conditions. "There are approximately 350 vineyards in Chile, exports are about 69 percent of wine production to more than 130 countries" (Agosin and Ortega 2009).

Economics

The Chilean economy was not as badly affected by the 2008 financial crisis as other countries were, a result of the stringent rules and precautions taken by the Central Bank, which was well prepared when the crisis hit the economy. The Central Bank of Chile was prudent enough to build up reserves in a period in which the exchange rate was below fundamentals and global financial markets were under extreme stress. This helped to minimize the effect of the crisis in the country. In spite of that, financial markets were altered, reducing access to funding and impacting on the national currency. According to the GEM (*see* Figure 4.4) people found it more difficult to start and develop their businesses and acknowledged there were fewer economic opportunities.

During the past decade, the Ministry of Economics has been promoting entrepreneurship and innovation nationwide. At the time of writing, the current Minister of Economics, Juan Andrés Fontaine, is visiting California with a group of young featured entrepreneurs in order to establish promising relationships between entrepreneurs, authorities, universities, investors, research and development institutions and so on. Efforts are being made to encourage

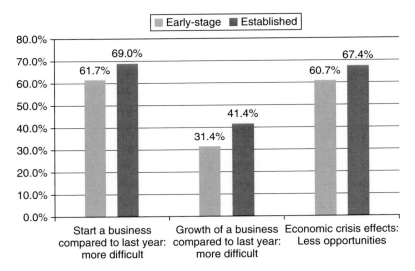

Figure 4.4 Effects of the economic crisis in Chile
Source: GEM (2009: 65 (Chile)).

Chileans to take risks and innovate through their businesses, and situations like the recent successful rescue operation of 33 miners have opened other countries' eyes to the valuable human and technical potential of Chile.

Political framework

"In Chile, a new business is able to begin operations within a shorter period of time, with less paperwork, and having to spend less money than in any other Latin American country" (World Bank 2009). Taking ideas from the design stage on the drawing board to an operating company is simpler and more cost-effective in Chile than anywhere else in the region.

As reported by the Governance Indicators Database (DataGov), Chile is superior to the rest of the countries in the LA countries, leading the ranking in most measured variables. Chile scores 1.24 in government effectiveness, compared to the region's 0.01 average. It also scores 61.7 in budget transparency compared to the regional 48.1. As for progress of the country, Chile scores 65 compared to 35.78, and has a 5.66 in the Public Institutions index compared to 4.16 for Latin America.

Low corruption and high transparency levels make Chile a good example of fair regulations as reported by the World Economic Forum's Global Competitiveness Index shown in Table 4.3, which is a measure of the institutions, policies, and factors that determine the level of productivity of a country.

Table 4.3   Regulatory efficiency in Latin America

Regulatory Efficiency		
Rank	Country	Score (Out of 7)
1	**Chile**	**5.0**
2	El Salvador	4.0
3	Mexico	4.0
4	Colombia	4.0
5	Uruguay	4.0
6	Dominica Rep.	3.7
7	Guatemala	3.7
8	Brazil	3.6
9	Peru	3.6
10	Argentina	3.3
11	Bolivia	3.0
12	Venezuela	2.0

Source: Mia et al. (2007: 17).

The Chilean political framework positively influences entrepreneurship through a set of supportive and restrictive microeconomic policies that encourage the development of the country. GEM measures for government policies and programs were created with the aim of improving entrepreneurship. The worst evaluated factor is the question about how easy it is to comply with all the paperwork required to start and run a new business, with 94 percent of the individuals answering negatively. This is followed by 82 percent of the people who consider it very difficult to meet all the norms, authorizations, and regulations needed for start-ups. Another item poorly evaluated is that the government apparently does not offer advantages to small businesses competing against large companies (GEM 2009).

On the other hand, an advantage of the political system is that the different regulations and taxes are predictable and stable, providing a basis for people to operate. Even though Chile has been improving every year, the worst-ranked factors are the more important ones in terms of entrepreneurship (difficulty in starting a business, getting the paperwork done, funding, and so on). The main challenge for the government is to encourage business activity by improving conditions for entrepreneurs.

As regards government programs, they have experienced a dramatic improvement in the last few years. Factors like the number of programs aimed at promoting entrepreneurship and the resources available for them have made the process more effective. Both business incubators and science and technology parks appear to have had a positive impact on the environment. These relatively new business services help emerging businesses to maximize their success by providing advice, resources, networking, and

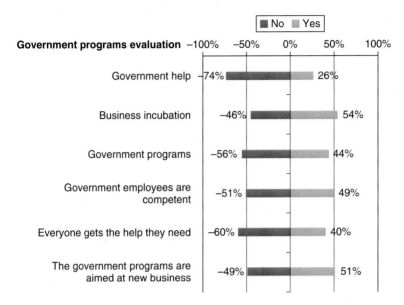

Figure 4.5 Evaluation of government programs
Source: GEM (2009: 77 (Chile)).

so on, assisting them to set up a satisfactory business model. Incubators develop their business model by focusing on variables that have been found critical for success in the experience of other countries and of local entrepreneurs. Incubators are committed to maximize start-up wealth creation and community impact. Networking is crucial in this phase in order to provide technical and market knowledge, and incubators are skilled at linking new start-ups with the wider business community.

As shown in Figure 4.5, entrepreneurs do not consider that government support for new and growing businesses can be easily obtained, especially through state agencies. They also believe that few receive support when creating a new business. These negative factors are somehow moderated by the general belief that state agencies discriminate by focusing on the potential of the business project, prioritizing innovative ones with high potential. The reason for this criterion is that innovative businesses act as role models for other businesses, encouraging them to innovate as well, and generating a competitive dynamism. Simultaneously, they have a higher potential to grow rapidly and contribute to the economy by generating new and higher-quality employment.

As Figure 4.5 shows, the main concern is the level of aid, estimated to be insufficient, but the broad quality evaluation is quite neutral.

Social environment

The social perception of entrepreneurship in Chile has historically never been positive, but this vision has become more neutral over the years. GEM studies demonstrate that the society does not encourage entrepreneurs to take risks, and there exists very little and often no tolerance of failure. It is judged in a negative light when an entrepreneur does not succeed in a project. In developed countries, there is the opposite perception, as entrepreneurs who have tried to start many businesses without success are considered more experienced, knowledgeable, and prepared to accept difficulties.

People also believe that the national culture does not foster innovation and creativity, but it has been becoming more important since the government created the Innovation Council specifically to promote innovative entrepreneurship. Another measure to help improve this situation is InnovaChile, an organization belonging to Corporación de Fomento a la Producción (CORFO), which executes policies that promote innovative entrepreneurship.

On the other hand, the society has a positive appreciation of entrepreneurship in some other aspects. Businesses successes are well respected, admired and have prestige, with 87 percent approval; and entrepreneurs are seen as very capable and competent people. Being an entrepreneur is considered to be a desirable career by 70 percent of people (GEM 2009).

Characteristics of entrepreneurs

In Chile, "14.9 percent of the adult population between 18 and 64 years old ... consider themselves an entrepreneur in early stages, while 6.7 percent define themselves as an established entrepreneur" (GEM 2009). Several characteristics can be observed in the typical Chilean entrepreneur according to GEM:

- **Motivation:**
  There are two main motivations why people decide to start a business. The first is the opportunity to increase their income, to achieve personal accomplishment by doing new things and gain greater independence. On the other hand, entrepreneurship is also embarked on when people need to earn enough money to live on and maintain their income.

  During the last year, entrepreneurships developing as opportunities went from 6.23 to 7.06 percent; and those caused by necessity increased from 1.86 to 2.4 percent (GEM 2009). Overall, the majority of Chilean entrepreneurs decide to start a business motivated more by opportunities rather than by necessity; this is encouraging but still requires a good entrepreneurial environment in order to be effective.

- **Age:**
  The Chilean economy is based on efficiency, focused on allocating resources where they will be maximized. In this type of economy, the majority of entrepreneurs start their businesses when they are 25–34 years old, followed by the 35–44 age group. Specifically, in Chile entrepreneurs in the early stages are mostly 25–34 and 35–44 years old, while the number of established entrepreneurs increases with age, the largest group being that aged 55–64 years, followed by the 45–54 age group. This behavior is in accordance with the life cycle and the working experience a person gains with age (GEM 2009).

  In Chile, "the average age to start a business is 37.5 years, and 47.6 years to be an established entrepreneur" (GEM 2009). As shown in Figure 4.6, the average ages in Chile are slightly higher than the average observed by GEM analysis, being 36.4 years in the early stages and 39.1 years in the settled ones.

- **Gender:**
  The relationship between gender and entrepreneurship is linked to the culture and people's habits. There is usually a small gap between men and women in developed countries, while in some countries it is not usual for women to work or develop their own projects.

  In Chile, there has always been more entrepreneurship among men than among women, the latter starting at later ages. Comparing gender

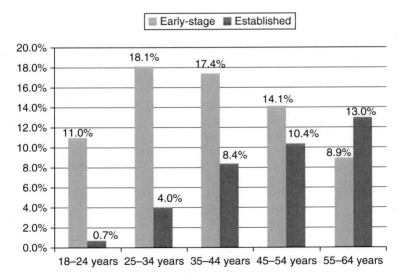

Figure 4.6 Entrepreneurial age brackets in Chile
Source: GEM (2009: 44 (Chile)).

activity for entrepreneurship in the early stages, we find 17 percent of men and 12.6 percent of women starting businesses. Now, when comparing settled businesses the gap is even wider, with 9 percent of men and 4.6 percent of women as entrepreneurs.

Studies show that there is no noticeable bias regarding education and work participation between men and women in Chile. This is promising for entrepreneurship gender equity (GEM 2009).

- **Education level:**
People who become entrepreneurs by necessity usually have lower education levels than people who look for opportunities to start businesses. Almost half of Chilean entrepreneurs have achieved not only the mandatory education level but also some years of different higher education levels: 5 percent of entrepreneurs in the early stages have a graduate school degree, 16 percent have completed a university degree and 9 percent have an incomplete university education; 14 percent of entrepreneurs in this stage have a technical degree and 4 percent did not complete this kind of degree. Of the rest of the entrepreneurs, 3 percent completed their 12 years of education, including secondary education, but 12 percent never completed it; 5 percent of entrepreneurs finished primary school and 4 percent did not.

In established entrepreneurial activities, the percentages are similar but with smaller gaps between people who have an incomplete technical education and an incomplete university education (GEM 2009).

- **Income:**
The income level of entrepreneurs' households is a significant variable to analyze their quality of life. GEM distributes income in thirds, according to the per capita income of the country.

If we consider entrepreneurs in the early stages, only 15.8 percent of the total adult population in the highest-third income bracket of the country are entrepreneurs, in the medium-third income group only 11.4 percent are entrepreneurs, and in the lowest-third only 9.4 percent are entrepreneurs. Following the same decreasing pattern, in the top-third of income 8.2 percent are established entrepreneurs, in the middle-third there are 4.6 percent established entrepreneurs and in the lowest-third only 3.0 percent fall in that category. The rest of the adult population are not involved in any entrepreneurial activity. Most entrepreneurs belong to the middle class, especially the C3 and D socioeconomic groups (GEM 2009).

Industrial sectors

Entrepreneurial activity varies among the different industrial sectors, depending on the economy of the country and the demand for each

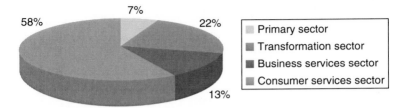

Figure 4.7 Early-stage entrepreneurial activity by sector
Source: GEM (2009: 42 (Chile)).

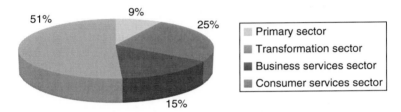

Figure 4.8 Established entrepreneurial activity by sector
Source: GEM (2009: 42 (Chile)).

sector. In Chile, both in early-stage and established businesses, the consumer-oriented service sector dominates with 58 percent in start-up businesses and 51 percent in established ones. The next most exploited sector is the manufacturing sector, with 22 percent of early-stage and 25 percent of established businesses as shown in Figures 4.7 and 4.8 (GEM 2009).

Legal framework

The regulatory framework in Chile is slightly more efficient compared to the rest of the region. According to the World Bank, starting a business requires nine phases. The process takes approximately 27 days and its cost is 10 percent of per capita income. The situation in other LA countries is even worse. It consists of approximately 11 phases, 70 days and 60.4 percent of income (World Bank 2009).

Legal regulations historically tended to be detrimental to small companies because there were no criteria of differentiation between a large and a small company. The legal regulations created in later years include the MEF (Micro Empresa Familiar) law, which aimed to decrease the cost of fulfilling the regulations needed for small family businesses. This law was not as

Table 4.4   Small family businesses in selected cities

City	Population	Small family business registered (number)	Small family businesses registered (per thousand inhabitants)
El Bosque	175594	180	1.03
Renca	133518	7	0.05
Recoleta	148220	169	1.14
Concepcion	216061	32	0.15
Talcahuano	250000	317	1.27
Chillan	161953	2	0.01

Source: Benavente (2008).

beneficial as intended since it depended on the different local municipalities of each city and their particular disposition to assist entrepreneurs.

Table 4.4 illustrates the number of family businesses in different cities of Chile, showing visible differences among them.

Funding

There are several entities responsible for providing financing to entrepreneurs. The main one is CORFO, an agency of the Chilean government in charge of executing policies related to entrepreneurship and innovation. It aims at developing a society with more opportunities and competition, thus contributing to the progress of the country.

CORFO's main clients are small to medium-sized businesses, especially in sectors with high growth potential. CORFO's main function is to help those businesses create value by gaining knowledge, by improving the quality of their goods or services and by accessing international markets. It offers incentives during the preinvestment, setup and development stages of each project. First of all, when businesses are created, CORFO provides support by means of credits, incubators, and investor networking. Companies can apply for funding depending on the type and size of business. Owners of small businesses (annual revenue of 320 million Chilean pesos, around US$640,000), for example, can access up to 32 million Chilean pesos during their first year, approximately 10 percent of annual revenue (InvestChile, incentives and services 2010).

Since 2007, there has been a new stimulus program called "Chile Emprende Contigo," designed by the government to foster the development of small businesses. An amount of US$620 million was set aside to assist entrepreneurs, increasing the amount of money available for CORFO to finance new business projects, coaching programs and access to technology.

Challenges

As shown in Figure 4.9, the main challenge Chile faces in order to improve the quality of entrepreneurship is the application of research and technology, being the worst-ranked condition according to GEM. This unsatisfactory situation can be explained by a poor relationship between universities and businesses – research developed by universities does not reach and/or is not implemented by companies.

The Chilean government invests approximately 0.79 percent of GDP in R&D, but there are no perceived positive effects. However, studies show that companies are not making an equivalent effort, and government investment is not enough to make real progress in this area. It is not clear whether the funds invested by the government in R&D are well focused, since universities have not had a real impact in business innovation.

Moreover, entrepreneurship education is still a challenge for the country; it first needs to prepare students and introduce them to the topic:

> The entrepreneurial process involves identifying an opportunity for an entrepreneurial venture, building a team capable of executing the opportunity, and obtaining the resources necessary to carry forth the venture.

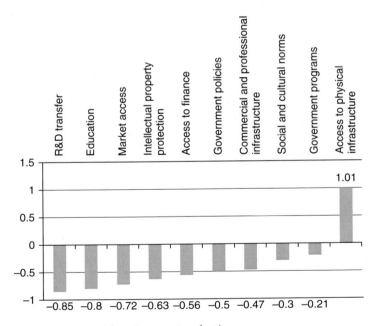

Figure 4.9 Entrepreneurial environment evaluation
Source: GEM (2009: 70 (Chile)).

The proper shaping of the opportunity by the team requires creativity in envisioning a new product, new market or a new distribution channel for an old product. Obtaining the resources for the venture, which usually come from external sources, requires strong skills in communicating the potential of the opportunity to those in control of the resources. Building the team and uniting it with the resources require leadership skills on the part of the entrepreneur. Finally, at the core of the whole process is the business plan: the conceptual model for the production, marketing, distribution, alliances, funding and other requirements to drive the venture forward. (Cale 2004: 136)

Another low-ranked factor is access to the market, which is understood as the ease with which new businesses enter the internal market. The markets do not seem very dynamic and existing important companies present a big obstacle for newcomers (GEM 2009). In addition, it is well known that the top two or three large businesses are dominant in most industrial sectors.

Intellectual property does not have a positive perception either. Chile is considered to have little respect for it, especially in technology products. This is very harmful for promotion of innovation, because it does not inspire confidence in entrepreneurs.

Projections of entrepreneurship in Chile

In September 2010, President Sebastián Piñera stated that in 2011 Chile would be the second-fastest-growing economy in Latin America.

The International Monetary Fund also declared that Chile is the best example of a country that has combined all three factors necessary to achieve the highest per capita income growth in the region in the past 25 years. Those factors are: boosting productivity, achieving macroeconomic stability, and keeping markets open to foreign trade.

Former finance minister and Harvard professor, Andrés Velasco, has said that after reforming capital markets, ensuring that the banking system is sound, bringing interest rates down, and promoting innovation and venture capital, the country would be ready for another period of a high growth, adding: "If we accept the idea that growing means to innovate, then to innovate means to be daring and to do something different."

Another complementary vision was expressed by a JP Morgan Report (October 6, 2010), which predicted that Chile's economy would be in the top three of GDP growth in the world. It was forecasted that in 2011 most economies in the world would have a slowdown in growth, while Chile was expected to show the opposite behavior.

In that context, according to recent JP Morgan projections for the 40 most important economies in the world, Chile's projected growth of close to 6 percent would be surpassed only by China (8.6 percent) and India (8.5 percent), and matched by Peru (6 percent).

Investment appears to be the key factor. According to the experts, the horsepower that would pull the wagon of the economy in 2011 would be investment. In Chile the investment rate would reach about 30 percent of GDP, in the framework of the reconstruction program after the 2010 earthquake that would focus on transportation, construction, and communications. "Chile has one of the fundamental sources for growth (...), with an investment coefficient of one third of the GDP; it has the capability of an uninterrupted sustained growth of 6 percent (JP Morgan, 2010)."

Conclusions

Many important sources define Chile as an ideal place to invest and to develop as an entrepreneur because of all the positive conditions that support and motivate people. With good indicators in macroeconomics and governability, and the predicted improvement of many of the poorly evaluated factors like access, Chile should become a more favorable environment in the next few years. There are still many aspects that need improvement in order to promote a more efficient entrepreneurial environment and the growth and development of Chile. There are crucial challenges such as research and technology transfer, which is an important resource in developed countries but is overlooked in Chile, and also better government assistance to small business.

However, as the next three cases show, enterprising opportunities for educated professionals are everywhere: In these cases we meet Ismael, a civil engineer with a master's degree from Stanford who was first a senior executive and later found a niche business in a son's outdoor hobby, and financial support from another family member. Then we will meet Francisco, a highflying architect, orchestrating a prestigious set of global professionals to bring the global trend of mixed-use complexes into Chile; when challenged by big players, he found himself turning to some friends at traditional business groups to finance his daring new venture. Finally we encounter Edmundo, an extraordinary engineer, a real serial entrepreneur creating a midsize business group out of engineering successes during the period between just after World War Two and the dot.com bubble; he also was joined by his family, experienced failure in the new economy and recovered by professionalizing the traditional businesses. The second generation led by his son Raúl has the vision of building the family business so that eventually an external CEO is needed.

These cases duly reflect what being enterprising means in Chile: technical abilities, family and friends' support and financing, private effort, opportunities to bridge the gap of development in consumer goods, services, engineering, mining, and agriculture.

What is missing in all these accounts of the practice of entrepreneurship? Government financial support and streamlining of bureaucracy. Chilean entrepreneurship is all about entrepreneurs, families, and the market. Government is normally not welcomed by these educated entrepreneurs, and its real role is to make entrepreneurship flourish by avoiding putting hurdles in the way.

Where is government failing? It needs to provide a level playing field for those who are not blessed with such knowledge, networks, and prestigious personal or family identities. This is where Chile requires an innovative, highly professionalized, and effective government.

Case studies

Case 1: Andesgear[1]

On December 31, 1999, Ismael Mena was finishing his career as an employee, after 20 years in senior management positions in different economic sectors. For about three months he had sensed that the company's situation did not provide interesting opportunities for him and he wanted to realize a long-cherished desire to become independent.

He studied hydraulic engineering at the Catholic University. After he graduated he worked for seven years as an engineer, until he lost his job in 1982 during the economic crisis that hit Latin America. In these circumstances, he got a scholarship to study business at Stanford University and later returned to Chile as a brand manager with Procter & Gamble. A year later, he switched to software and services house SONDA where he stayed until 1992, and attained the position of Commercial VP. After that he was VP for regional newspapers at *El Mercurio* (the best-known local paper), and finally he was hired by the Hendaya Group as Senior VP for their Communications Division. This position involved responsibility for a cable communications operator, Metropolis Intercom, and for a financial daily newspaper, *Diario Financiero*. At the end of his term in this position he was considering the idea of an independent venture.

In the early part of 2000 he started to work part-time in a real estate firm, while he developed his personal project. He decided it must meet four criteria:

(a) The business must be suitable to the scale of his economic resources.
(b) The business ought to be in a growth market niche.

(c) The market should not be clearly dominated by one player ("I want to win markets without having to do anything extraordinary").
(d) The chosen business must be structurally sound: "in other words, at the current state, it must make economic sense, be profitable, without depending on uncontrollable external factors."

Ismael's eldest son was a keen mountaineer, and he suggested selling equipment and accessories for mountaineers. They gathered information on how the number of students taking mountaineering courses at the main universities was evolving, and concluded that there was a growing market with increasing purchasing power. They discovered that there were only two relevant competitors at the time, who sold at high prices, in their own stores and through smaller retailers in Santiago and the regions.

Ismael decided that he could risk US$20,000 on this venture. A well-located physical store would have involved an outlay of some US$50,000, without considering inventories. This limitation was the first reason for considering a website. This planning stage was completed between January and February 2000.

In March he started the venture, under the name Andesgear. His eldest son and his brother designed, developed, and managed the website. They also set up links to climbing instruction centers, thus generating traffic to their site.

He focused his efforts on trying to get the support of potential suppliers. Finally Mamut, an important supplier unhappy with its Chilean sales, decided to trust this new channel. Other suppliers copied this player and decided to work with Andesgear. This allowed Ismael to secure exclusivity agreements with several top international brands.

Another complexity was setting up a product mix that would go with the business objective, and this was done by trial and error. There was also some trial and error in the payments system, because at the time, there was no online payments system in Chile.

Ismael believes that the website was and still is a differentiating factor:

> We were not only the first, but the website was put together with so much loving care and effort, dedication, and talent. It was a real success. Our competitors took a year to understand the use of a website, and we think they still haven't got over that. They took even longer to understand how to use databases for one-on-one marketing, and that allowed us to get a real head-start.

That first year the total sales were 36 million pesos (US$72,000). Their home served as warehouse and sales office, turning it into a business: "all the products were stored around the house; orders were put together and picked up from home, often dinner conversations revolved around Andesgear ... it was 24 hours of Andesgear."

He then decided to open a physical store, which was opened in October 2001, and sales climbed 50 percent the following month, which was a great success. So after this, in 2004, he decided to open a second store in the new sports shopping mall opening later that year. To fund this expansion, he considered an offer he had received for 10 percent of the company, which paid for the whole investment in the new store. Several offers had come his way, but Ismael decided on someone he felt especially close to: his father. "I wanted someone I trusted as a partner," said Ismael.

Case 2: Territoria, the Isidora 3000 development[2]

This is the story of a multimillion-dollar, mixed-use development in Santiago, Chile. It all started one winter afternoon in 2002 when Francisco Rencoret received a phone call from a friend who had gone bankrupt in the 1997 Asian financial crisis. He mentioned that he knew of a site in Santiago that was going to be available shortly. Not just any site, but one on the most expensive avenue in midtown. One could argue that it is the most distinguished location in the city. At the time three nondescript apartment buildings – divided into 100 property rights – stood on the site. His friend's contact owned half of a right. In other words, 0.5 percent of the property was in the hands of his friend's friend. Just enough to get him thinking ...

The acquisition

In Chile, one cannot develop a property unless one owns 100 percent of the rights. Therefore, Francisco's small architecture company in Santiago had to buy the remaining 99.5 percent of the development rights one by one before they could do anything. This was the challenge of the acquisition. Many big groups, recognizing the potential of the site, had tried before. All previous attempts up to that point had failed.

During 2002 Francisco was developing a number of small-scale projects, buildings worth up to US$25 million. He and his partners would organize the sites, develop the architecture, and then take a stake in the deal. Their exposure never exceeded 50 percent of the overall business. They used simple structures; the partnership financed 50 percent of the equity required, and a construction loan covered 50 percent of the overall cost. In simple terms: 50 percent equity and 50 percent construction loans from the banks. They guaranteed the loan with the site mortgage and the equity of the deal. The duration of each development was approximately 30 months.

After giving some thought to that fateful call, Francisco realized that the magnitude of this site was different: this could be his ticket to the big league.

Key decisions had to be taken in order to capitalize on this opportunity. First, Francisco realized that his existing organization was not going to work in such a venture. Second, he figured that the scope of this endeavor would require wisdom, skill, and aptitude at a magnitude of, say, six times that of his prior experience. Third, he was going to need an extremely sophisticated group of professionals to acquire the site, develop the program, and find a strong financial partner. At that time his group consisted of four people working in development and about 25 architects.

They took that first step in spring 2002. After about a day of reflection, Francisco told his friend that they wanted to go for the site. This project, for the record, was estimated to be a US$150-million proposition. Francisco's corporation at that time was worth – maybe – US$500,000. They brought on board a highly reputable law firm. Its senior partner, who had extensive experience in real estate and had worked with Francisco on prior deals, committed himself to organizing the acquisition process. Then as a team they nominated a person to be in charge of purchasing and to bring acquisitions experience to their staff. By the end of the year, they had a program in place complete with a law firm to handle legalities, strategies, and contracts, and a purchaser.

The site spanned an entire square block. Early on they were thinking this could be the spot for an iconic new building for Santiago. They envisioned a modern spin on New York City's Plaza Hotel. Avenida Isidora Goyenechea, a boulevard lined with offices, boutiques, and restaurants, cuts a ten-block slice through the heart of Santiago's midtown and El Golf, a high-end office-heavy neighborhood studded with regal twentieth-century palaces. The site is on Isidora Goyenechea opposite Plaza Peru, an immaculately maintained park with a parking lot (capacity 400) hidden beneath it. Back in 2002, the site held three-, four-, and six-story apartment buildings, all built during the 1960s. Tenants occupied each apartment. The market price was approximately US$50,000 per unit, but no one would buy or sell because the price of the land was five times the value of the price of the units.

Initially they used in-house architects for the analysis phase. Then they realized that the site was suitable for a mixed-use project and that an internationally known architect was required. The floor area ratio (FAR) was 6.7 times the site, and there were no height restrictions. It would be the first building of this nature in Latin America, and if all went as planned, it would put Santiago on the real estate map. Nothing had been built in this part of the world with this kind of program before.

After a few months of work on the boards, they decided to hire Handel Architects, a medium-sized architectural firm in New York with extensive experience in mixed-use projects. Francisco had seen their work with developer Chris Jeffries at Millennium Partners, and had worked with Handel during his six years at KPF Architects in New York, a professional experience, incidentally, that was instrumental in taking on this project. Naturally, hiring an architect without having acquired the site is not easy. On one hand, they wanted to keep the project going; on the other, they could not risk a lot of capital. They were very limited in terms of architecture budget. Handel personally agreed to develop schematics and a marketing package at no real cost.

Meanwhile, they started to sign up owners' titles one by one. The strategy was to pay everyone the same price and, as far as possible, at the same time. To start, the lawyers organized all the sellers into one small committee and hired a law firm to interact professionally with them. The key aspect of the process was to keep the sellers together. Many of the sellers wanted to negotiate in parallel to get additional money, but this could not be allowed. Their lawyer was very good, and the committee had to show extraordinary strength to keep everyone on the same page.

The real challenge was a unit that had been bought recently by a giant real estate group for speculation. Their intention was to acquire the other 99 rights and take the site. They only had one unit, but they were waiting until the other 99 units were secure to take them away. They did not know how, but time was on their side. And resources: they were a US$4 billion enterprise, Francisco's was a US$500,000 organization. At this moment, Francisco made another key decision; he decided to obtain world-class financial support and create a partnership that could stand up to the opposition on the other side of the table. The big lesson gleaned from this case: every fight needs to be fought correctly. As the big real estate group was going to go for the site, Francisco saw three options:

1. Sell them the site and make a profit;
2. Develop the site with them, 50–50 at proper valuation;
3. Acquire the unit and develop the project by themselves.

Of course, Francisco wanted option number 3. In order to achieve this, they had to start with option 1. Since they had a unit, the price of the site for them was going to be their unit asking price multiplied by 99 (the other units). Francisco opened fire and stated that they would like to acquire their unit as a first option. After some discussion, Francisco requested that they come up with a number for their unit. So they did – and they made a mistake. They asked US$1 million for the unit with area restrictions. As a result, their acquisition price of the site, which had been in the ballpark of US$21 million, shot up to US$99 million. Immediately they realized they could not buy it, and at that very instant, option 1 was off the table. After a week Francisco was notified that they would not enter a joint venture.

They settled for US$1 million and a restriction that not more than 120,000 square feet of office space could be built on-site. The covenant, however, was against the country's Constitution but they signed anyway, hoping that the authorities would eventually pick it up and void the restriction in court. And that is exactly what happened six months later.

The acquisition process lasted two years. By the end of 2004, the site was in Francisco's hands.

The project

Once the site was secure, they immediately moved on to the next phase. Francisco needed a structure that could provide all services to produce the project, so after a few meetings in spring 2004, Francisco and his three partners founded Territoria, a corporation that would undertake developments currently under construction, in particular Isidora 3000. They put together the best professional team available at that time. They hired both the New York and San Francisco offices of GEHA. Originally schematics were produced in New York and design development and programming in San Francisco, simply because they needed a team with experience working in the same seismic zone. Territoria sent six of its own architects to support and expedite the design process. Meanwhile, executives from Territoria were flying around the world meeting still more architects and engineers. Once the basics were developed, they broke the project down into five parts: hotel and convention center, retail, offices, residences and parking.

At this point, Gary Handel advised them to expand the site by buying more property. This sounds easy, but imagine how much a few houses next to the site might be worth? Adjacent to the site on the north side were four houses that were needed in order to properly develop the towers and, more specifically, the car ramp. The team of land acquisitions moved forward and acquired the four sites in six months.

Territoria knew that a hotel chain had to be the first player to come on board. They needed a company that not only had an interest in Chile but also had deep pockets to contribute substantially in terms of equity. Chilean banks were hesitant to finance hotels. Banks in general do not like hotels because of their residual value and limited guarantee.

They had conversations with a number of prospective hotel chains. Some of them were actually willing to invest in the project, but none of them would ante up the amount they needed. By chance at a dinner in San Francisco, Francisco met executives from Starwood Hotels. They expressed interest in both Chile and the project, potentially as an equity partner. They thought their W brand, which had proved extremely successful in Mexico City, would be a good fit. The following weeks were spent organizing the deal at their corporate headquarters in Miami, and by late 2006 they signed a letter of intent (LOI) to build the first W Hotel in Latin America. Starwood would invest 40 percent equity in the hotel, and Territoria would handle the remaining 60 percent.

Naturally, when one is planning a development, one has to pay special attention to design as it is the single most distinctive element in a project. People like and appreciate ingenious design, but the developer's real challenge is managing that ideal with the constraints and realities of construction. For instance, W Santiago, as the first in Latin America, was set up to be quite different in concept and design not only from all other W Hotels but also from all traditional Chilean hotels. They set out to make its food and beverage program the best in Latin America. To achieve that, they not only thought through and designed all restaurants, kitchens, and service areas, but they hired chef Jean Paul Bondoux, arguably the best chef in the region with his award-winning La Bourgogne at the Alvear Palace Hotel in Buenos Aires. After that, Osaka, the ultra-hip Asian-Peruvian fusion restaurant in Lima, signed up to open a sushi bar. Then the Gerber Group, the American company famous for seductive bars and lounges around the world, came aboard. As for room design, think of a mix of the unexpected, fancy and edgy with nothing less than the highest of standards. Every aspect of every part ...

After the concept of the hotel was complete, they turned their focus to retail. The challenge here was to build something that would draw people to it. Tourism potential is high in Chile, and these tourists spend on average US$200 million a year. That is what they were thinking when they began developing the retail component. What would be attractive, exciting, and useful for visitors to Chile? With this in mind, they determined that Chilean wine had to be at the heart of retail. Because Chile's wine is known around the world, it would in itself attract international travelers. But in order to create value, it had to be a destination in itself. Around the wine boutique, they positioned an enticing bistro, and next to it, straight from Colombia, Juan Valdez Café, the coffee sophisticate's coffeehouse.

They slotted Bang & Olufsen, the Bauhaus-inspired music store, on the other side at the same level. Underneath they tucked Coquinaria, a stylish gourmet market to provide luxury complements to the wines upstairs, and a space dedicated to cars and technology. Above ground, they put Brooks Brothers and The North Face, both of which would be appreciated by the locals working in the many offices in and near Isidora 3000. On the second floor they developed a house-and-office retail project. And the entire third level, which connects to the hotel and public areas, was dedicated to a spa and wellness shop.

With regard to the office portion of the project, they wanted to be market leaders, so they needed to produce a state-of-the-art product. The orientation and interior standards had to be spot-on. There could be no compromise on details because this industry is extremely competitive – both in terms of price and standards.

The residences also needed to be unique in design, orientation, and services. The market in Chile is quite unsophisticated in terms of standards, and it is limited in its range of products. A radical approach was needed to create a brand with the residences and also to hit their high target price.

The business

Originally, Territoria was going to build and sell the entire development as a condominium scheme. They had done it before, and it was going to be a straightforward business model. In terms of numbers, the project had to sell with a 30 percent return on investment for a four-year development. But since the project had changed quite a bit, there was a need to change the business model as well. Remember that they bought more land, added to the site, and substantially modified the program with the hotel's horizontal shift.

At that time it was a buyer's market in Chile and there was a forecast of zero vacancies in the office market in 2007–8. On the other hand, there was an emerging market of real estate funds around the world looking for international portfolios. During 2007, Territoria was approached by several funds interested in buying the building once rented. They were looking for a lease building and their intentions were to buy the cash flow at a certain cap rate. In the United States, cap rates were between 4 and 5 percent. In Chile their aim was 7 to 8 percent. Francisco decided to explore this kind of transaction since insurance companies discount 10 percent in local markets. They changed the business model from sale to lease in order to pursue this opportunity. They started to lease the building and implemented a commercial division at Territoria. The lease was going to be developed in-house because innovative products seemed difficult to sell in traditional markets. For most of the year they studied the mix of tenants in depth, and in 2008 they started the leasing program. The rents of the office building would be 15 percent higher than the market in Santiago, and retail was about 10 percent higher than urban retail. As for the hotel, the joint venture stipulated at least US$175 per night but with a new concept, it was going to open at US$220 per night. The prospects were auspicious. However, part of this value was already absorbed by the increase in construction costs.

In 2008, Territoria rented 50 percent of the office tower and 75 percent of the retail. The hotel was sold to the joint venture and long-term financing was available in Chile for the hotel portion to recuperate capital. Residences were going to be sold after the hotel was opened. Meanwhile Territoria organized the interest of real estate funds in order to create a bid process to formally sell the retail and office portions. Territoria hired an investment bank to organize the process and selected Kan Am Grund, a German real estate fund, as the formal buyer of both retail and office. At the moment of transition, the cap rate was near 7 percent with a price around US$120 million. They signed an agreement in August 2008, and a deposit of US$20 million was provided by Kan Am to guarantee the transaction until the building was built and completely leased. In March 2009, the transaction needed to be executed and Kan Am defaulted on the operation since they had temporarily suspended the redemption of funds. By April 2009, Territoria decided to take legal action against Kan Am and proceeded to finance the project in the long term and keep the assets since the cash flow allowed them to refinance properly and meet their financial commitments.

In conclusion, Territoria ended up owning the entire development and keeping the building until the real value in rents and hotel fees was stabilized. The cash flow of the hotel is approximately US$20 million and the retail and office portions are US$7 million as a base lease plus variable rent on sales. The variable rents might increase overall performance by another US$2 million. With a cash flow of US$27-plus million in stabilization, Territoria approached the financial system of Chile to seek long-term financing of the building. They estimated that part of the initial investment in the deal for the next two years would stay on the project. However, with the sale of the residences, the investors would get their capital back during 2009. If cap rates came back to 7 percent, the project might be worth more because the rents would be stable and there would be no real estate risk once the property was operating properly. After a couple of years, there might be damages arising from the Kan Am lawsuit and some additional compensation might come forward. If everything happened as planned, there might be an additional US$30 million worth of returns coming into the project, and this would make Isidora 3000 their most successful real estate project to date.

The residences went on sale in late 2009, at US$450–600 per square foot. They received at least two calls a week from every real estate company in the world looking for a distressed-asset opportunity since the contract default of Kan Am.

Francisco is sure that Isidora 3000 will be known around the world as a unique real estate story and a great financial success. In addition, by bringing the W brand to Santiago and building a state-of the-art mixed-use building with international-caliber professionals, they have made a significant cultural contribution to the city. They started with a small company, a big idea, and a fraction of a crummy 1960s apartment in a stellar location in Santiago. But they believed. After seven years of challenges, setbacks, meetings, flights, decisions, problems, and priceless lessons only learned with experience, they built their trophy building. They moved up to the big league.

Case 3: The Kayser family transgenerational intent[3]

Edmundo Kayser was born in Chile in 1920. His father was a German farmer who arrived in Chile in 1912. Being a second child, he wanted to free himself from his family's primogeniture tradition, and driven by a desire to find new horizons, followed his uncle. Edmundo, the first professional in his family, graduated in 1945 as a civil engineer at the prestigious Universidad de Chile, with a special mention in building engineering.

Though he did not inherit any special assets or means to start his own business, he had a technical genius that made him not only one of the most respected engineers in the country, but allowed him to start up a series of new businesses and to excel in both social and public service in Chile, gaining international recognition.

Edmundo Kayser married Nora Gatica and had three children: Raúl, Lidia, and Gabriel. Raúl, the eldest son, was an engineer like his father; Lidia, the only daughter, a textile designer and infant-school teacher; and Gabriel, an architect.

"Eddy," as Edmundo was called by his friends, was well known for his great ability to build up friendships; according to his grandsons, "our grandfather would turn over a stone and one of his friends would come out." He was also admired because of his public service spirit, which was beyond comparison, and he served in both non-profit and state service areas. He was recognized by France as an *Officier de la Légion d'Honneur*, as well as by Germany's merit order *Verdienstkreuz 1. Klasse* (1996) and by the Instituto de Ingenieros de Chile, his Chilean engineer peers, who admired his resourcefulness and wit, as well as his transparency and righteousness, which contributed to his own style of doing business.

Edmundo Kayser in business

Once Edmundo graduated from university, he began working in the construction business, at the invitation of his brother-in-law. Together they established a firm called Víctor Kayser (V-K). While working on serial construction projects, they were invited by a larger building company Tekra to join them as partners. Tekra had recently won a contract to build a sugar beet mill in Chile, and they needed Edmundo to build it. But the real challenge was to meet a building deadline almost impossible to fulfill. Edmundo therefore began a true "war against time" with creativity, invention, and enthusiasm; sacrifice and devotion were also displayed as he had to stay away from his family for long periods of time. His partners thought he would miss the tight deadlines but he did not.

Later, during the 1960s, Edmundo was invited to join a new consortium to lead the construction of Santiago's international airport, which demanded new and complex technology, unknown in Chile at the time. Edmundo led the project with forcefulness; he was very enthusiastic in overcoming tough regulations and standards and adopting new technologies and enjoyed solving engineering problems. Thus Edmundo kept acquiring new partners who invited or followed him into several new ventures in different industries.

At the same time, Edmundo entered the agricultural industry, forced by a family obligation. Twenty years later, in 1988, after a few failed experiences, Edmundo built new facilities, and implemented top technology that finally rendered results. By the end of the century, Las Martas was one of the most efficient milk producers in the country, and the main supplier and one of the major cooperative shareholders of Colun, a top-three player in the lucrative Chilean dairy business.

The 1960s were a productive decade for Edmundo. He also became involved in retail. Working in construction, his partners visualized the opportunity to develop a construction machinery distribution company that would deal with the importing and marketing of spare parts for cars, special machines, and electrical appliances. They asked Edmundo to help with the selection of machinery, and they finally established a new company representing and distributing Bosch products in Chile and later in Peru. Twenty years later, when planning to extend the list of products, they created a new firm, adding new products such as construction and forestry machinery, representing and distributing Stihl products in Chile. Both companies had satisfactory results for many years.

During the next two decades, Edmundo felt motivated to share his knowledge and know-how in other ways. In 1975, at the request of the government, Edmundo left his firm and took over as CEO of Santiago's Metro, to fulfill "my social service" for six years almost ad honorem. His achievements improved his reputation, especially for his capacity to complete the construction of the Metro, overcoming enormous difficulties deriving from international recession, lack of financial resources, domestic problems, and political isolation of the government's regime.

After Santiago's subway construction was finally finished, Edmundo accepted an invitation to become the chairman of the board of one of Chile's premier corporations, focusing on two major areas: energy and natural resources. During the next three years he remained a passive minority (although relevant) shareholder in his own companies, which were managed by his partners as well as by external managers, enjoying market success and attractive profits. Later, Edmundo was also invited to have a seat on the board of a Chilean–German health and charity non-profit corporation, and was later elected chairman.

Seeing a business opportunity, some of his old partners invited Edmundo, with his vast experience in tunnels and industrial assembly, to create a new construction company. This new business continued to develop successfully, executing many construction contracts. In the 1990s, the construction business was rapidly becoming overcrowded due to foreign competition. Edmundo, at that time supported by his son Raúl, decided to take advantage of their experience in tunnel construction to enter a new industry where those skills were key: mining. He bid for mining property in association with other partners. This company played an important role in the gold and silver underground mining business in Chile.

During the late 1990s several new firms were established. Encouraged by Raúl, they entered real estate and technology. As there was cash flow available from the established companies and easy access to bank loans, and Edmundo was enthusiastic about new projects, he supported them. He had already delegated the day-to-day management of his minority shareholdings to professional managers and could relax whilst his businesses were mature and profitable. Raúl was leading the new ventures, and Edmundo was not very involved with the technological and real estate companies.

Entry of the second generation

Raúl, on his own initiative, entered one of his father's construction companies as a field engineer, in charge of some projects over two years, when he learned a lot about tunnel construction techniques. "I had studied the same career as my father, he was one of the owners of the company, there was a job to be done, and he had an amazing know-how: for me it was a safe and excellent place to work."

After a few years, Raúl left the company because of differences with one of his father's partners. Soon after, together with two engineer friends, he established in 1993 the construction firm El Pastor operating in the low-segment market in small constructions, but the venture was neither successful nor profitable.

His brother Gabriel, after graduating, worked in architects' firms before setting up on his own with his wife, a project they had dreamt of while they were still students. Gabriel and his team undertook large projects in Chilean Patagonia, such as big hotels, avant-garde concert halls, theaters, and embassies, and also other projects in Santiago, and Gabriel was passionate about them. He also had the chance to work with world-renowned German architects.

Lidia, after marrying Ernesto Frías, traveled to many countries with her husband who was a high-potential executive with a promising career at a German MNC. When Ernesto accepted his in-law's invitation to join their businesses, they finally settled in Chile. Then she was finally able to combine her two passions and began teaching textile design to poor people who were in drug rehabilitation. She was always investigating and searching for new advances and innovations in textiles, in order to improve her performance and teach her students. Ernesto slowly began to become involved in the Kayser business, starting in agriculture and then expanding his knowledge of the other businesses, during the late 1990s.

Diversification and crisis

During 1998, the situation for the real estate business was becoming complicated, and operations were halted. Raúl, seeing that one of the construction companies had developed software useful for other industries, saw in this a growth opportunity to make up for the decline in the real estate business: to improve that software and market it. His first attempts did not prosper, but he recognized the great growth opportunities in the high-tech arena. About nine new start-ups were created, ranging from Linux software and service, to electronic security services, to brand new car- and people-searching technologies, to automatic teller machines, among others. Edmundo enthusiastically supported these new "engineering inventions" and shared his son's great expectations. However, they had lots of difficulties due to a lack of technological support; financing from their foreign partners was not forthcoming, and managing high-tech ventures was not among Raúl's skills. The technology business, a source of satisfaction in the beginning, soon turned into their main source of concern.

As the real estate and technological businesses outcomes were disappointing, Raúl asked Edmundo for funds to finance the firm's projects, money that came from the mature successful old-economy companies. At this point, due to the Asian crisis followed by the "Tequila effect," real estate collapsed, and sometime after came the bursting of the dot com bubble. The situation was critical by the end of 1999, getting worse year after year, and the banks began to ask questions of Raúl.

It was September 2001, and away from his cherished engineering challenges, Raúl did not feel he fitted in the day-to-day company management, believing that all his efforts had not accomplished much, and lacking adequate technology knowledge, financial expertise, and management skills, he felt the business was slipping out of his control.

Each new separate company had cash shortages and none was credit grade, so Raúl began to mortgage part of his personal patrimony and indebted the group. His family followed his example and they also put up their possessions as collateral for old and new debts, although they stood back from business and never quite understood the family businesses nor the fragile situation of the group. His family just "trusted" Raúl, and did not take the time, nor had the interest, to get involved.

Raúl felt stressed, tired, and anguished to carry this all by himself, and was falling into a deep depression. He felt alone, and was completely unable to communicate the situation to his family. When he finally decided to call a meeting with his relatives and inform them about the situation, he realized that there was no information about financial statements and that it was impossible to understand what was going on in the companies.

In this scenario, Raúl called for a family meeting, which took place with Lidia and her husband Ernesto. This time Raúl was convincing enough, and for the first time they were able to understand in a clear way one single idea: the businesses were completely out of control, chaos had ensued. Years later, Ernesto could still remember Lidia looking at him with anguish, saying with a guilty expression: "Year after year and so many times we heard Raúl asking, requesting, begging us to participate in our businesses; in different ways he tried to get us involved, we couldn't understand that those were cries for help."

They agreed that there were only two alternatives left: to continue being indifferent and observe from a distance as their father's effort and work disappeared under their noses; or get involved and begin to make informed and responsible decisions as a family team. They were well aware of their lack of professional qualifications to manage the situation; their careers, experience, and knowledge were far from those required, and their father was enjoying his golden years and out of sync with new business practices.

Post-crisis

The first day of October 2001 was when they decided to bring on board a management consultancy to diagnose the problems, reorganize, establish order, and set up guidelines to develop and control their firms and search for options to revitalize the technology companies.

The consultants found a mix of internal (managerial) and external (national and industrial crisis) causes. Among the managerial mistakes were running a business based on pure intuition and trial and error, permanent cross-subsidies, good businesses financing bad ones, dishonest and incompetent managers being uncontrolled, companies lacking information systems, and lack of follow-up and accountability.

In order to survive, in March 2002 the group created a formal holding company, Quintil; an external CEO was hired; family and external directors were required both at the holding and at the business unit levels; and consultants were enlisted to help.

In November 2002, Eugenio Rojas, project leader of the consultants engaged by the Kayser family, took over as CEO. As a civil engineer, with a sound commercial, financial, and management background, and having previously worked both as director of finance and director of development for a leading shopping center chain, as well as having managed a portfolio of funds involved in investment and real estate, he seemed to have the necessary business acumen to tackle Quintil Holding's daunting challenges.

Eugenio's first move was to be informed about all of the companies' activities and performance, rapidly becoming aware that he lacked resources due to Quintil's illiquid financial position. He realized that the reports presented by the portfolio firms were incongruent, outdated, incomplete, or plain wrong. Eugenio Rojas, working closely with Gabriel, reconstructed all the missing information and began clearing up the confusing scenario in which they had found themselves. In Eugenio's words: "After the autopsy, the reactions of executives were quite polarized: those who were in shady personal businesses, resigned; those who worked carelessly, quarreled; and good executives applauded the new management and remained with us."

What came next was a never-ending round of negotiation with banks, a process effectively led by Eugenio. Executive layoffs, rationalization, company closures, legal diligences, scenario building and rebuilding, as well as long nights of worry followed by sweaty days of number crunching, were day-to-day routine. Internally, Quintil went through a re-engineering of its processes, acquired sound managerial business practices, and developed up-to-date management report systems. As a result of this process, important changes were achieved.

In parallel, Eugenio began focusing his attention on where the money was: profitable companies.

> I quickly found out that those successful companies were not so professionally run, boards were accommodating, and powerful CEOs had won the right to get their own way. We desperately needed them to release cash and be predictable, but management were not used to tight budgets and having their assumptions challenged, and were unwilling to pay generous dividends, preferring instead to reinvest surplus cash in pet projects. The trouble was that Quintil's shareholdings in those companies were in a minority, mostly about 14% or 49% at most, and just one or two board seats were available to push through unpopular and misunderstood measures, so we had a tough time getting our hands on the money. Even worse, I had to act indirectly through the Kaysers, as I was not a board member in those companies.

The recovery

Eugenio Rojas's annual report presented in April 2004 reflected a new chapter in the family's history: "Finally... with pride, joy and satisfaction, I can mention that in these 3 and a half years of management in charge of the Holding ... we were able to preserve half of the initial Group's wealth after fearing that we would lose it all."

Consolidated liabilities were reduced 15-fold, and paid in six years, personal collateral was replaced with Quintil's, foundations were established to concentrate the property of all the group's assets under Quintil and the group was repositioned in the market, again becoming attractive, now as a professionalized holding. As a consequence of the corporate strategy chosen and much effort, and the addition of two external directors, the crisis was left behind and a new stage in the Kayser family story was heralded: "Creating value in the Holding."

The Quintil Holding Annual Report (2003) established a new mission: "To be a professional holding and a proactive investor, looking forward to add value to its companies, contributing through strategic planning, the development of new ventures and management and business control systems, in order to obtain positive financial results". Consequently, Quintil's results began to follow a new and positive trend.

Notes

1. Alfredo Barriga C. prepared this case study under the supervision of Professor Germán Echecopar as the basis for class discussion and not to illustrate the efficient or inefficient management of a business situation. Latest revision: December 30, 2004.
2. Case written by Francisco Rencoret and abridged by Professor Gonzalo Jiménez as the basis for class discussion and not to illustrate the efficient or inefficient management of a business situation. Latest revision: May, 2009.
3. Pía Bartolomé prepared this case study under the supervision of Professor Gonzalo Jiménez as the basis for class discussion and not to illustrate the efficient or inefficient management of a business situation. Latest revision: November 2007.

Bibliography

Agosin, M. and C. Ortega. 2009. "The Emergence of New Successful Export Activities in Latin America: the Case of Chile." Universidad de Chile, Red de Centros de Investigación del Banco Inter-Americano del Desarrollo, Paper #R-552.

Benavente, J. 2008. "Dinámica Empresarial en Chile 1999–2006." Gobierno de Chile.

Cale, E. 2004. "Educating Entrepreneurs." In S. Tiffin (Ed.), *Entrepreneurship in Latin America* (p. 136). Westport, Conn.: Praeger.

Chile Emprende Contigo. Pdf presentation.

DataGov, Governance Indicators Database. Inter-American Development Bank platform available from: http://www.iadb.org/datagob/.

GEM 2009 Global Report. Available at: http://www.gemconsortium.org/.

Henriquez, L. and L. Deelen. 2010. "La situación de la Micro y Pequeña Empresa en Chile." International Labour Organization.

InvestChile, CORFO. 2010. "Incentives and Services." Gobierno de Chile. Available at: http://www.investchile.com.

InvestChile, CORFO. 2007. "Wines of Chile." Gobierno de Chile. Available at: http://www.investchile.com.

JP Morgan. 2010. Article published by *La Tercera*, September 2010. Available at: http://www.latercera.com/noticia/negocios/2010/09/655-291323-9-jp-morgan-chile-estara-entre-las-tres-economias-del-mundo-con-mayor-crecimiento.shtml.

Lewis, G. 2007. "Who in the World Is Entrepreneurial?" *Fortune Small Business*, June. Available at: http://money.cnn.com/magazines/fsb/fsb_archive/2007/06/01/100049637/index.htm.

Mia, I., J. Estrada, and T. Gieger. 2007. "Benchmarking National Attractiveness for Private Investment in Latin American Infrastructure." Published by the World Economic Forum within the framework of the Global Competitiveness Network. Available from: http://www.weforum.org/reports/benchmarking-national-attractiveness-private-investment-latin-american-infrastructure-0?fo=1.

World Bank. 2009. "Ease of Doing Business, Doing Business in Chile." www.investchile.com.

5
The Emergence of an Entrepreneurial World: The Colombian Case

Rafael Vesga and Ana Cristina Gonzalez
Universidad de los Andes School of Management

Colombia appears to be at a defining moment in its trajectory towards becoming an entrepreneurial economy, that is, one where entrepreneurial initiatives are a major engine of growth. Entrepreneurship was a major policy issue for the national government over the first decade of the century, and there is evidence that it will continue to be so over the next one. The country shows a high prevalence of both opportunity and necessity entrepreneurship. However, there are as yet few results in terms of the presence of high-potential entrepreneurial ventures, of the kind that could lead the country into a new stage of economic development. While awareness of the importance of this kind of entrepreneurship is high in the country and there are several policy initiatives in place on this issue, Colombia appears to be in an incipient stage of development on this front. From an optimistic perspective, this means that the present state of affairs offers a rare opportunity for decisive policy interventions that could frame the high-impact entrepreneurship development model for many years to come.

Entrepreneurship has become increasingly important in the policy agenda in Colombia over the last decade and there is a growing debate in the country regarding the specific kind of entrepreneurship Colombia wants to stimulate, and which are the most effective policies and instruments that should be used to attain the desired objectives.

This chapter presents first an overview of the state of entrepreneurship and the entrepreneurial ecosystem in Colombia, and identifies how this ecosystem is responding to the challenge of fostering the creation of high-growth and high-potential business ventures. The chapter also presents the case of a Colombian entrepreneurial firm that has grown by using the mechanisms that this entrepreneurial ecosystem offers. This case illustrates some of the strong and weak points of this ecosystem. Finally, the chapter offers recommendations for strengthening the entrepreneurial ecosystem in Colombia and the development of Colombia as an entrepreneurial economy.

Increasingly, the policy debate in Colombia is moving towards recognizing the differences between necessity and opportunity entrepreneurship, and developing separate mechanisms for promoting each of these types of entrepreneurship as differentiated phenomena. Policymakers are trying to create an environment that is more favorable for the development of high-potential new ventures.

A profile of entrepreneurship in Colombia

Data from official statistics provided by the National Registry of Businesses shows that 636,665 new firms were created and registered in their local Chamber of Commerce in the three years between 2007 and 2009; 99.9 percent of these businesses can be classified as either small or microenterprises (Ministerio de Comercio, Industria y Turismo 2009). This registration is mandatory by law in Colombia and can be regarded as a birth certificate for a business venture. This is a necessary step if a business owner wishes to have access to credit from the banking system, or to register workers in the social security system. Many other businesses are created every year but never registered, which means that their owners have decided to remain in the informal sector and do not expect to pay taxes or comply with legislation regarding social security, pensions, and health benefits for workers.

Beyond the National Registry, there is little hard data in Colombia that captures the moment of creation of new businesses. Perhaps the best available source of information on this topic is the GEM study, which does a survey of the general population every year in Colombia, seeking to obtain information about how individuals engage in the creation of new businesses. The GEM study allows us to make comparisons between different countries and regions in the world and gathers information about the different stages of entrepreneurship, from the moment when individuals perceive the possibility of a business opportunity, to the time when actual actions are taken to create the business, the launch of the business, and its early stages of growth (Kelley et al. 2011).

The GEM survey is today the most important benchmark of entrepreneurial activity in the world and was carried out in 59 countries in 2010. The basic information is collected through interviews with entrepreneurs in each country, with a minimum sample size per country of 2000 respondents every year. The sample design reflects the structure and distribution of the general population in each country.

According to the GEM report, Colombia shows one of the highest rates of involvement of the population in entrepreneurial activities that can be found in the world. Entrepreneurial involvement refers to the percentage of the population who is engaged in some kind of entrepreneurial activity. The key indicator of the GEM is the TEA rate, which calculates the percentage of the population of a country that is actively engaged in the creation of a business. According to the GEM methodology, this period begins when real actions are first taken to initiate the business, and ends when the business is 3.5 years old.

Colombia has one of the highest TEA rates among the participating nations. The TEA for Colombia in 2010 was 20.6 percent, which means that one out of every five citizens between ages 16 and 64 were engaged in some activity related to the creation of a business (Kelley et al. 2011). This indicator has declined somewhat – in 2007 the TEA in Colombia was 22.7 percent. This decline may have a number of causes. On the negative side, it may be related to the slower rates of economic growth that the country has registered since 2009. On the positive side, the data shows that this has happened simultaneously with an increase in some indicators related to the robustness of entrepreneurial opportunity.

The complexity of the phenomenon of entrepreneurship cannot be captured in a single number. The GEM includes several other indicators besides the TEA, which allow for a more complete characterization of entrepreneurship in the country.

The GEM divides the nations of the world into three major groups, following the same methodology used by the *World Competitiveness Report* (World Economic Forum 2011), which correspond to three different levels of economic development. These three groups are factor-driven economies, efficiency-driven economies (Colombia belongs to this group), and innovation-driven economies.

Comparisons among countries using GEM indicators should be restricted to within-group evaluations. Similar levels of the variables captured by the GEM survey can have different implications in countries that are distant in terms of economic development, because the role of entrepreneurship in an economy is different at each level of economic development. Entrepreneurship tends to be the occupation for large portions of the population in factor-based economies because, since the supply of jobs is low, people begin early in life to consider starting a business to make a living as a key alternative for survival. In efficiency-driven economies, participation of the population in entrepreneurial ventures is somewhat lower because, as companies grow, sources of jobs become more abundant. In highly developed economies TEA rates are lowest, because these economies can offer their populations large numbers of jobs and substantial levels of support for the unemployed. However, as developed economies become more innovation-driven, entrepreneurship grows in importance again. Growing percentages of the population wish to try their luck and create new businesses, in high-quality areas, with high expectations of growth.

Therefore, entrepreneurship configures a "U" pattern relationship with levels of economic development. Entrepreneurship prevalence is high in underdeveloped economies, low in those in the middle of the range, and starts growing again as economies arrive at higher stages of development.

As Colombia is classified as an efficiency-driven economy, the intermediate level of development, this adds some complexity to the analysis of its situation. Variations in the basic GEM indicators may reflect conditions that are more related to the patterns that are usual in poor countries, but also may reflect patterns of behavior that are more common in richer countries. The coexistence of different types of entrepreneurship in the country adds to the difficulties in interpretation.

Colombia seems to be a fertile ground for very different kinds of entrepreneurship. A large part of entrepreneurial energy is dedicated to the development of necessity entrepreneurship, where individuals are motivated by the absence of viable alternatives for making a living in the job market. At the same time, a significant percentage of the population focus their energies on opportunity entrepreneurship, where individuals are motivated by the desire to improve their livelihoods and make more money than in their previous jobs. Colombia has a strong presence of both types of entrepreneurship (necessity and opportunity) in comparison to other nations.

The GEM methodology has developed an indicator of improvement-driven entrepreneurship that considers the aspirations for growth of the business, based on the type of motivation stated by the entrepreneur, the number of employees that the entrepreneur expects to hire within five years, and the degree to which the venture produces a product that is new to the market (even if it is the local market) and has little direct competition.

In Colombia, it seems that necessity-driven and improvement-driven entrepreneurship attract similar percentages of the population, with 40 percent in the first case and 41 percent in the second in 2010 (Kelley et al. 2011). Both values appear to be fairly high in comparison to other efficiency-driven economies in Latin America. This pattern is not common in the world, since countries tend to have a stronger inclination towards one type of entrepreneurship rather than another. It is unusual to have a country where the prevalence of these two distinct types of entrepreneurship is equally intense.

Beyond the brief birth period defined by GEM as the early stages of venture creation, Colombia also shows high rates of entrepreneurship. According to the 2010 GEM survey, 12.2 percent of the population owns an established business (firms that were created more than 3.5 years before the date of the survey), which is also a high rate among the group of efficiency-driven economies. Unfortunately, Colombia also ranks among the countries with the highest rates of business failures in the group of efficiency-driven economies, at 5.1 percent.

One troubling aspect regarding the quality of entrepreneurship in the country is the high rate of informal entrepreneurship in Colombia. It can be assumed that if a business is not registered at the National Registry it belongs to the informal economy, because it will not have access to financing from the banking system and will not be able to register its workers with the social security institutions. The percentage of new entrepreneurs who decide to remain in the informal economy is quite large, as only 16 percent of entrepreneurs registered their businesses with the National Registry at the moment of birth, and close to 47.6 percent are registered after three years in existence. Thus, more than half of the entrepreneurs in the country remained in the informal sector in 2009 (GEM Colombia 2010).

Other important characteristics of entrepreneurship in Colombia emerge from the GEM study. There appears to be a large gap between the basic propensity towards entrepreneurship in the population and the number of people who actually engage in it.

Over 68 percent of Colombians believe that they have identified an interesting opportunity in their immediate environment for starting a business. More than 65 percent of the population believe that they have the skills and capabilities needed to start a business. Both of these indicators are among the highest in the world. Just over 27 percent of the population believe that fear of failure would stop them in their efforts to start a new business, which is one of the lowest rates in the world for this question (Kelley et al. 2011).

However, these perceptions of opportunity and self-efficacy only lead to the creation of an actual business in the minority of the cases. Less than one in three of the people who perceive that there are opportunities for entrepreneurship in their immediate surroundings ever take any concrete step towards creating an actual business. Additionally, the fact that the discontinuation rate is among the highest in the world suggests that the perceptions of opportunity and self-efficacy may not be quite well-grounded in reality, or that unexpected factors that appear later in the process lead entrepreneurs to succumb to the competition.

There appears to be a misperception regarding the true demands that an entrepreneurial project entails. This suggests that there is an important issue for entrepreneurship policy that needs to be solved in order to achieve higher growth of entrepreneurship ventures of all kinds. The culture of entrepreneurship still needs to go deeper into the lives and routines of the population. Despite the general perception that entrepreneurship is an important issue in the country, only 36.3 percent of the population in 2009 said that they knew an entrepreneur personally (Levie and Bosma 2010). Colombia was in 41st place in the list of the 55 countries that did the GEM survey in 2009 for that question. Individuals may have the intention and willingness to become entrepreneurs, but they do not belong to the right networks, where they could learn from other entrepreneurs.

The quality of the entrepreneurial ecosystem in Colombia

From the perspective of entrepreneurship policy, this panorama raises several relevant issues. The country needs more individuals motivated by opportunity and improvement to move from the stage of considering the creation of a new business to actually doing it. The country also needs to have more entrepreneurs who are successful over the long term, in order to reduce failure rates.

The question leads to the consideration of the entrepreneurial ecosystem in the country. The term "entrepreneurial ecosystem" is increasingly used both in the practitioner and academic literatures (Isenberg 2010; Wessner 2004; Roland Berger Strategy Consultants and IESE 2009) to describe the set of institutions that surround the entrepreneur along the process that goes from venture idea to launch of the business and beyond.

The term is derived from the evolutionary biology construct that describes the development of a species in a geographical space. Survival of a species is subject to a myriad of intervening phenomena, such as competition, cooperation, specialization, learning, and others (Breslin 2008). A species may survive and thrive, while others may disappear, depending on the qualities of the ecosystem and the fit to these conditions. Similarly, business survival not only depends on the decisions of the entrepreneur, but also on the quality of the institutions that surround his/her action: financiers, governmental offices, trade associations, universities, incubators, etc. The fit between the entrepreneurs and these institutions is a critical point. The key objective of this ecosystem is to offer support to entrepreneurs as they move their ventures along the process.

The discussion about entrepreneurial ecosystems has many points in common with the concept of clusters (Porter 1998). In both cases, geographical location is a source of competitive advantage for entrepreneurs, because agglomeration produces external economies that benefit nascent businesses. Both in clusters and in ecosystems, there are key institutional actors that need to be present for these benefits to materialize. The presence of effective governmental units, trade associations, and other actors is necessary to achieve the potential advantages. However, an entrepreneurial ecosystem as a policy concept goes further than the idea of clusters, because (1) entrepreneurial ecosystems deal simultaneously with the levels of the institutional environment, the firm, and the individual, and considers the fit among these three levels; (2) an entrepreneurial ecosystem focuses on the entrepreneur and the entrepreneurial process, considering in an explicit way the characteristics of the individual; and (3) it focuses on designing the best possible arrangements for providing support for the entrepreneur in this development path.

In other words, when a country, a region, or a city decides to move from the idea of clusters to that of entrepreneurial ecosystems as the general framework for defining entrepreneurship policy, it takes the crucial step of putting the entrepreneur at the center of a system of service and support (Hsu et al. 2007, Roberts and Eesley 2009). In this mindset, considerable attention needs to be given to understanding in detail the characteristics of the entrepreneur as an individual and the key factors for success at each stage.

Figure 5.1 depicts a general framework for understanding an entrepreneurial ecosystem (Universidad de los Andes 2010). The well-being of each actor in the ecosystem depends on that of the whole system. The entrepreneur and his/her process are at the center of the ecosystem. The quality and the value of the ecosystem are directly proportional to the success of the entrepreneurs that are served by the system.

Figure 5.1 presents the entrepreneurial process, at the center of the graph, as a series of steps that start with the perception of an opportunity and ends

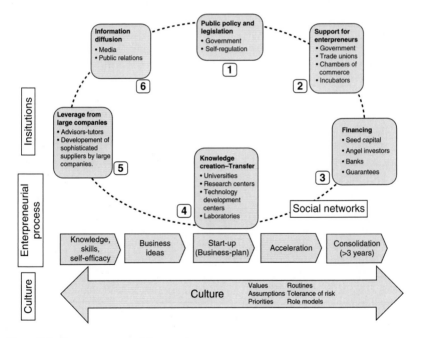

Figure 5.1   An entrepreneurial ecosystem
Source: Universidad de los Andes (2010).

when the venture has entered a stage of growth. The upper part of the figure presents the key institutional actors of the ecosystem. These include:

1. The government at the national and local levels;
2. Providers of support for entrepreneurs (such as chambers of commerce, in the case of Colombia);
3. Providers of financing (from angel investors to finance institutions such as banks and venture capital funds);
4. Universities and research centers, which create and transfer knowledge that can be used for the creation of value by new business ventures;
5. Large companies that promote the creation of new ventures; and
6. The media, which serve as a vehicle for enhancing cultural values around entrepreneurship and helping potential entrepreneurs to access resources quickly.

Finally, at the bottom of Figure 5.1 a horizontal line illustrates the importance of developing a strong entrepreneurial culture in the city, region, or country.

The framework in Figure 5.1 is a useful instrument for analyzing the Colombian entrepreneurial ecosystem. A brief overview of the available information on the components of the ecosystem provides a general perspective of the quality of the entrepreneurial ecosystem in Colombia.

The public policy and regulation component of the ecosystem (box 1 in Figure 5.1) has been the most active in recent times. Under the presidency of Alvaro Uribe (2002–10), the promotion of entrepreneurship was accorded an unprecedented degree of importance in the policy agenda, and the government of Juan Manuel Santos (elected to the presidency in 2010) has declared that entrepreneurship and innovation will also be policy priorities (Departamento Nacional de Planeación 2010). The advancement of entrepreneurship is a responsibility of the Ministry of Industry and Trade, which has defined an explicit agenda for the topic.

A law for the promotion of entrepreneurship was passed, Law 1014 of 2006, which created an institutional framework for the promotion of entrepreneurship at different levels in the executive branch of the Colombian government. The law decreed the creation of a national network for the development of entrepreneurship, with the participation of a variety of institutions from the public sector, chambers of commerce, and trade associations from the private sector. The national network is replicated at regional level in each of the departments of the country. Each of the regional networks is responsible for creating a monitoring center to follow the development of entrepreneurship in the region, and to propose initiatives that can have an impact on the creation of a fertile regional environment for entrepreneurship. The law also mandates a framework for the teaching of entrepreneurship in educational institutions at all levels, from primary to university education.

Another piece of legislation, Law 1286 of 2009, raised the status of the national science and technology agency, Colciencias, turning it into a cabinet-level agency and creating a mandate for supporting the development of high-technology, high-impact entrepreneurship.

The institutional changes needed to comply with the laws are happening slowly. The creation of the regional nodes of the national entrepreneurial network advanced in 2009 and 2010, but not all the nodes have been created yet. One important sign of advancement has been the decision to adopt the GEM study as the official instrument for measuring entrepreneurship in several of the regions. As a consequence, in 2011 the GEM study is being carried out at regional level in four regions in Colombia, and it is expected that there will be more regions doing this entrepreneurship survey in the future. Since the regional GEM studies have to be funded by the regions (no money from the central government is supplied for this purpose), the fact that this effort is taking place reveals that there is a growing awareness of the importance of the issue at the regional level.

The national government is also engaged in a sustained push to have the regions reduce the requirements and permits needed for the creation and routine administration of a business. Colombia participates in the *Doing Business* study, sponsored by the International Financial Corporation and the World Bank. This initiative measures and compares a series of conditions that mediate the relationship between businesses and their institutional environment. The variables that are measured include the difficulty in obtaining permits for starting a new business; the difficulties associated to complying with requirements and permits for the routine administration of a businesses; the ease of obtaining credit; and the conditions for enforcing contracts. In 2011, the *Doing Business* study covered 183 countries and Colombia is in 39th position. The country has moved up in the rankings in recent years, up almost 30 places in the ranking since it started participating in this international initiative and moving from 49th to 39th between 2009 and 2010. In 2011 Colombia was the third country in Latin America in the ranking, after Mexico and Peru (IFC 2010). Observers concur, however, on the perception that it will be difficult to maintain this upward trajectory in the ranking, because the easier measures have been taken and now the country will have to change more structural conditions, such as the ease of access to credit or to international markets. Despite recent progress, there is a long road ahead.

Other sources of information confirm this view on the relationship of entrepreneurs with the institutional environment. The GEM study includes

a survey with experts, in which they are asked to grade the quality of entrepreneurship support activities on a scale from 1 to 5 (with a score of 5 meaning that the burden is low). The average grade given by the experts on the
issue of bureaucratic requirements and permits as an important burden on
entrepreneurs was 2.4 in 2009, while in 2006 it had been 1.8. Progress has
been made, but the level of performance is not yet acceptable.

There is one institution within the government that has taken a special
role in the promotion of entrepreneurship. This is the Servicio Nacional de
Aprendizaje (SENA), a large entity founded in 1957. The mandate of SENA is
the provision of technical education for students who have a secondary education diploma but are not attending a university. Traditionally, graduates
from SENA educational programs have looked for employment in positions
requiring technical skills in Colombian companies. During the past decade,
however, the SENA was also given the task of promoting entrepreneurship
among its own graduates and also among students in all forms of post-
secondary education in Colombia.

Following this mandate, SENA created a seed capital fund, called the Fondo
Emprender, for financing venture initiatives by students of post-secondary
educational institutions. Students receive credits for a sum of approximately US$30,000 as seed capital for starting their companies. Payment of
these credits is forgone once the students have proven that their business
is operating. From 2004 to 2010 the Fondo Emprender financed 2104 new
ventures by students. SENA estimates that these firms created 8565 new jobs
(SENA 2010). The Fondo Emprender program has been a laboratory for the
development of entrepreneurial ventures among the young. However, critics
point to the fact that the amount of seed money given to each project is very
low, and, therefore, the result of the program is a large number of very small
businesses with low aspirations. This has not been, yet, a fertile ground for
the creation of high-impact businesses. Nonetheless, the Fondo Emprender
has important lessons for the development of the entrepreneurial ecosystem
in the country.

Despite increased governmental activity in this area, indicators of the general perception of the quality of support for entrepreneurship in Colombia
do not reflect high appreciation for the achievements to date. In the Expert
Survey of the GEM study, respondents report their opinions about the priority that support for new firms has in national government policies. The average response is a grade of 2.9 out a possible 5 points. Regional governments
received an average grade of 2.5 on this question (GEM Colombia 2010).

There are other institutions in Colombia that provide support services
for entrepreneurs. The importance of the national entrepreneurship policy
and the existence of an entrepreneurship law have resulted in an increased
awareness of the issue on the part of institutions that have been given

responsibilities in this area (box 2 on Figure 5.1). Chambers of commerce and some trade unions have been required by the law to become members of each regional entrepreneurship network node and have been summoned to sign up and become official members of these networks.

The chambers of commerce play a particularly important role. First, as mentioned above, all private firms are mandated by law to register at the local chamber of commerce and pay a fee for this service. These resources are considered public funds and, therefore, the chambers of commerce are given a number of responsibilities as agents in the interest of public policy towards business development. One of these responsibilities is the promotion of entrepreneurship. As a consequence, the chambers of commerce have created programs for support of entrepreneurial initiatives. These programs have achieved a high public profile in some of the cities. In Bogotá, for example, the GEM study for the city identified that 30 percent of the adult population of the city (approximately 940,000 people) know about the existence of at least one of the programs for the promotion of entrepreneurship that the Bogota Chamber of Commerce (CCB) has created (GEM Bogotá 2010). According to a report published by this institution, the entrepreneurial support programs by the CCB served 630,000 entrepreneurs between 2006 and 2008 (Cámara de Comercio de Bogotá 2009). This makes the chamber of commerce the institution with the highest recognition from the citizenry among public or private agents that support entrepreneurship.

The next element in Figure 5.1 is financing (box 3). This is generally regarded as one of the bigger obstacles (probably the biggest) for the development of entrepreneurial ventures in Colombia, and especially high-potential ventures that require larger sums of start-up capital. The expert survey in GEM gives a 2.1 average grade out of 5 possible points to the state of affairs of the country in this area (GEM Colombia 2010). The *Doing Business* report ranks Colombia in 65th position in the world, although the general ranking of the country is 39th (IFC 2010). Banks have no credit lines for the creation of new businesses. Activity by angel investors and venture capital funds is only just beginning in the country.

However, there are some positive signs. By 2010, the Ministry of Commerce estimated that the accumulated capital of the investment funds that were active in Colombia in the seed money stage was US$28 million (Ministerio de Comercio, Industria y Turismo 2010). This is far too low for the needs of the country, but it is a promising development because until recently the figure was zero. The country has also moved forward in improving the institutional conditions for the attraction of international capital. According to LAVCA, in 2010 Colombia was the fourth country in Latin America in terms of the conditions for attracting international risk capital. The strongest features of the country, according to LAVCA, are the laws on private equity and venture capital fund formation and operation. The weakest point is the lack of an efficient mechanism for exit by the funds, due to capital market restrictions in terms of size and liquidity (LAVCA 2010).

The role of universities and research institutions as agents for the creation and transfer of knowledge leading to high-impact entrepreneurship (box 4 in Figure 5.1) has also been limited. There is little activity in terms of entrepreneurial ventures that emerge from scientific research projects at universities. Colombia shows very low levels of activity in patent registration. According to the Departamento Nacional de Planeación,[1] between 2002 and 2004 Colombia registered 0.03 patents per 100,000 inhabitants, while the corresponding indicator for Chile was 0.13 and in Argentina 0.53. Total expenditures in research and development as a percentage of GDP in Colombia were 0.37 percent for the same period, while it was 0.93 percent in Brazil and 4.55 percent in Israel. The number of researchers per 100,000 inhabitants in Colombia was 109; while the indicator for Chile was 444; for Brazil, 323; and for South Korea, 3187 (Departamento Nacional de Planeación 2009).

Correspondingly, evaluation of the performance of the country in terms of technological innovation and knowledge-based business ventures is low. According to the *Global Competitiveness Report*, Colombia is in 68th position in the general ranking, out of 139 countries. However, when it comes to the indicators that are related to technology and innovation, Colombia's ranking is much lower. In terms of availability of the latest technologies, Colombia ranks in 87th place; in firm-level technology absorption, it is 85th; and in the quality of scientific research institutions, it is 81st. Technological innovation is an area that detracts from the general competitiveness situation of Colombia (World Economic Forum 2011).

Regarding support from large companies for the development of new ventures (box 5 in Figure 5.1), there is little documented evidence of this kind of activity, where large firms act as springboards for new ventures, either as investors or as supporters. This has been an important mechanism for supporting the expansion of new ventures in countries like Singapore and Brazil (Wong 1999). However, it does not yet appear to be a significant element in the Colombian entrepreneurial ecosystem, and there are no significant initiatives on this front.

Finally, the role of the media can be extremely important in fostering a culture of entrepreneurship, identifying role models, and helping entrepreneurs access information and resources (box 6 in Figure 5.1). Available information points in the direction that this is probably a strong factor in the Colombian environment. The GEM general survey asks respondents if they feel that entrepreneurship is a good career choice in their countries, if it is an activity that confers status, and if the media pay appropriate attention to entrepreneurs (GEM 2011). For the three answers, Colombia's percentages are high (88.6, 75.9, and 66.7, respectively). There is also anecdotal evidence available of the important role that the media have played in promoting a culture of entrepreneurship in the country over the last decade. There is a large business plan competition sponsored by *Dinero*, a business magazine, which has become a major annual event, with more than 1000 contestants entering the early stage every year. This competition was created in 2000 and is now a strong brand in the landscape of entrepreneurship in Colombia (*Dinero* 2010). It is sponsored by the Ministry of Industry and Trade and is promoted by government officials during their activities in the whole country all year round. The awards session is now a major event, where entrepreneurs and the major players who promote entrepreneurship meet. This is anecdotal evidence, but the perception is that the media today are a major ally in initiatives for the promotion of entrepreneurship in the country, and could possibly play an even larger role.

Finally, a culture of entrepreneurship (bottom of Figure 5.1) is a challenging topic. While the importance of culture is widely recognized as a major issue in initiatives towards achieving a more entrepreneurial economy (Czuchry and Yasin 2008, George and Zahra 2002, Thomas 2000), culture can be a fuzzy concept from the point of view of public policy. Culture involves shared ideas and values among a population, but it has to go beyond that, to the point where behavioral responses are shared by large groups of people as part of their daily routine. The information from the GEM survey offers some light on this issue of entrepreneurship culture. As was mentioned above, there appears to be a contradiction: while large numbers of Colombians engage in entrepreneurial activities and the general perception is that entrepreneurs are highly regarded in the country, the percentage who report that they actually know a real entrepreneur is low in comparison. A possible explanation is that even if the concept of entrepreneurship is widely known and is associated with positive values, it is not characterized by depth of content reflecting real experience in the minds of many Colombians. Policy initiatives oriented towards enhancing a culture of entrepreneurship should give more explicit importance to attaining objectives in terms of shared behavior.

This overview of the elements of the entrepreneurial ecosystem in Colombia shows that although interest in entrepreneurship in the country has risen quickly over the last decade, and it has become an important issue in the policy agenda, the impact, in terms of the creation of high-potential ventures, remains at present low.

Many of the actors in the ecosystem are only just beginning to understand and assume their roles in the general framework. A recent evaluation of the entrepreneurship ecosystem in Bogotá, which followed the framework presented in Figure 5.1 as a guideline (Universidad de los Andes 2010), found that this ecosystem provides highly uneven coverage in its services along the development paths that entrepreneurial ventures follow. Actors in the ecosystem tend to concentrate on certain stages of the process and have little awareness of other actors and also of their own roles in the ecosystem as a whole. Support activities for entrepreneurs tend to concentrate on the early stages of the entrepreneurial process, so that there are many institutions giving support in terms of motivating individuals to become entrepreneurs and helping them to create business plans. However, support becomes weak and scarce, and is perceived to be of low quality, when it comes to launching, financing, and maintaining the venture on a growth path.

The study analyzed the patterns of relationships among the network of actors in the entrepreneurial ecosystem of the city, and found that there are two central actors (the chambers of commerce and SENA) that concentrate the connections in the ecosystem. Other actors interact with these two, but they have few interactions with the rest. Universities tend to concentrate on the preparation of business plans and they act in an isolated fashion, maintaining relations with clusters of entrepreneurs but having little connection with each other, or with actors in other links of the entrepreneurial development process, such as financing agents. Trade unions and financing institutions operate on the periphery of the network and maintain few relationships with entrepreneurs or with institutions that specialize on the topics of entrepreneurship (Universidad de los Andes 2010).

In order to understand how these dynamics operate from the point of view of a firm, we consider the case of an entrepreneurial venture in the cosmetics sector, which had an intense interaction with actors in the ecosystem during its development process. The case shows some of the strengths and weaknesses of the entrepreneurial ecosystem in Colombia.

A case study in the cosmetics sector: CB Group[2]

The cosmetics industry has been recognized as a sector with high potential for future growth in Colombia. The country has an advantage in this industry in terms of natural resources, given its large biodiversity, where abundant rare materials can be found and used as components in cosmetic products. Domestic consumers are sophisticated and internal demand is strong. Latin America is well-known in the world cosmetics market because of the preference that consumers give to local brands, to the point that this is the only major region where local mass fragrances dominate over international brands, accounting for close to 85 percent of total sales (Pitman 2007). Companies are used to short product cycles and frequent product launches. These are all factors that favor strong innovation.

The sector has a few large players and a lot of small, specialized ones. Smaller companies do not have the resources of large firms for branding and distribution, thus they need to concentrate on innovation, in order to take advantage of the country's biodiversity. Only if Colombian companies can launch new-to-the world products on the international market, based on components extracted from this biodiversity, will the country be able to carve a truly differentiated niche in the global market. However, despite the fact that there are many firms that are active in the sector in Colombia, only a handful have the size and managerial capabilities that the task demands. Most of the firms are small and lack critical capabilities in marketing and other areas. There is an absence of producers of raw materials, which implies that the possibilities of developing new and high-impact products are low when compared to the biodiversity potential.

In this context, the Colombian Beauty Group (CB Group) appears as a small player that has managed to move with an innovative product to the international market. This firm is the result of an alliance of small cosmetics companies, which leverages the resources of all the partners and of the entrepreneurship ecosystem, and shows an important potential for product innovation.

CB Group's shareholders comprise nine small and medium-sized cosmetics firms. The objective of this firm is to develop new cosmetics products, leveraging the advantages of Colombian biodiversity, for the international markets. CB Group was founded in 2007, and it has already developed one line of products aimed at the male market, based on a natural ingredient that was identified by the company in the *Tibouchina lepidota* tree (known in Colombia as the *siete cueros* tree). CB Group has developed an extract from *T. lepidota* that has several properties, including hydrating the skin, re-establishing skin tension, and reducing the content of grease in the skin, among others.

The development of CB Group shows how associative mechanisms can be worked out to overcome the limitations of small firms' resources. It also illustrates the many difficulties that should be expected along the way, and the extensive learning processes that need to take place in Colombia if a cosmetics industry that is capable of having a sustainable competitive advantage in the international markets is to be developed.

The process started in 2004, when an initiative aimed at achieving an association of small and medium-sized firms in the cosmetics sector was started by the Ministry of Industry and Trade; Proexport (the state agency that is dedicated to the promotion of exports); ANDI (the National Business Association, an organization dedicated to the expansion and promotion of economic, social, and political principles within a free enterprise system); the Colombian Association of Science and Cosmetic Technology (ACCYT); the Corporación Andina de Fomento (CAF, a development bank in charge of promoting a model of sustainable development through credit operations, grants, and technical support for Latin America and the Caribbean countries); the universities El Rosario and Los Andes; and the Inter-American Development Bank. An open call was made to all companies in the sector, and the initiative started with almost 50 companies. A process of construction of trust and development of a common purpose started there, with activities that ranged from the construction of a common language (seeking consensual definitions of basic terms like "sales" and "shareholders") to sessions dedicated to exploring the importance of achieving concrete mechanisms for association.

Three years later, only 15 of the original firms remained. This group explored a wide variety of possible mechanisms for association and concluded that the best option would be the creation of a new firm, with its own administration, management, and charter set out by the shareholders. When the time came to put in the initial capital, however, five firms decided not to follow through. Therefore, an initial group of 10 founders was organized. Later, one firm dropped out from the group and the rest bought its share.

These are all small firms, with annual sales fluctuating between US$1 million and US$3 million. However, they have extensive experience in the Colombian market, with more than 20 years' history in some cases. It is worth noting that some of these firms are competitors in the local market, in some cases offering very similar products, although they compete using quite different strategies in terms of segmentation and distribution.

The first decision was that all partners would be owners of the new firm in equal proportion. Larger and smaller firms should make the same contribution to the initial capital. This was essential to maintain equality as partners along the way.

A very detailed process followed for defining what would be the product, or products, of the new firm. A set of criteria were approved for defining the product:

- All the shareholding companies should be able to produce the product at their own plants (the company uses the production facilities of the partners).
- Direct competition between the new product and the present product portfolios of the founding shareholders should be minimal.
- The product lines should be innovative and should leverage Colombian biodiversity and the traditional knowledge of the Colombian population. Technical criteria were agreed for this purpose.
- The target market should be international, not local, and this market should be new for all the partners. This was an important criterion from the standpoint of Proexport.
- Other criteria were set in the areas of finance and commercialization.

The search started for a natural ingredient in Colombian territory. The heads of three of the founder companies, all of them chemists and all women, took on the job of traveling around the country, going to small towns and taking the time to research local traditions and listen to the stories of the local people, seeking to understand how they used local plants and trees for healing purposes. The research not only covered the purposes for which the vegetation was used, but also how the specimens were treated, and manipulated.

Several possibilities were considered, but finally the group made a decision for Tibouchina, a component in the *Tibouchina lepidota* tree. This tree is common in the Andean countries, where people believe that it has curative powers and use it to heal scars. CB Group has established that the extract from the *T. lepidota* tree is rich in flavonoids, which makes it an excellent antioxidant and skin protector, with no potentially toxic components. The extract also increases tension on the skin surface and is good for helping the skin fight against the effects of aging. The extract has been certified by the Personal Care Council of the United States (formerly the Cosmetic, Toiletry, and Fragrance Association) as meeting the requisites to support the claim that this is a skin- and hair-conditioning, emollient, and antioxidant product.

The CB Group then started the search for a market niche that could be developed with a product based on Tibouchina. With support from CAF, a market study was undertaken. The study considered several markets (Mexico, Argentina, Brazil, and the United States) and concluded that the demand for cosmetics products for men was getting close to a point where consumption would accelerate due to changing customer tastes and increasing incomes in developing countries. This target market also fitted well with the criteria set by the partners for the development of their product. The initial market chosen for entry was Mexico, where CB Group's products compete in a high-end segment of the market.

The marketing study produced the basis for a name for the product: Thibou. It was also at this point that the group developed a technical study for the development of the product with the support of a center specializing in cosmetics. The next step was registering the product with the relevant authorities.

The company had to overcome several barriers at this stage. In the first place, it was necessary to obtain certification from laboratory studies to support the claims that the company was making for the Tibouchina extract, to show that it does not have adverse effects on humans, and to show that the properties were stable even when the extract was obtained at different times in different production plants. It was difficult to do the necessary studies in Colombia. The group sought quotes for the studies from laboratories in

Germany, Italy, Brazil, and Colombia. The Colombian laboratory's quotation was the most expensive of all, despite the fact that this laboratory had only a fraction of the experience and resources of the German laboratory, which was finally chosen.

Obtaining the official registers from INVIMA (the Colombian regulatory authority for drugs and cosmetics) also proved to be difficult. It turned out that it was the first time ever that a Colombian extract had been presented to INVIMA for approval and this institution wanted to be extremely careful with the precedents to be set with this case. Two months after the request had been submitted to INVIMA, the directors of CB Group went to present their case to the institution. After listening to the presentation, the INVIMA delegates said that although everything seemed to be in order, they needed to send the case to the Andean Community offices in Lima, since the case should conform to Decision 516 of the Community. The executives at CB Group were expecting to receive approval that very same day. Instead, they faced what amounted to a reinitiation of the process at the level of the Andean Community.

At that point, CB Group decided to obtain registration for its product at the Personal Care Council, which is the leading national trade association for the cosmetic and personal care products industry in the United States. This is a private organization that works to maintain consumer product safety standards in the cosmetics industry, from a perspective of self-regulation of the sector. In such a capacity, the Council produces evaluations on the safety of ingredients used in the production of cosmetics in the United States and has the support of the US Food and Drug Administration and the Consumer Federation of America. CB Group obtained a name for the Tibouchina extract under the International Nomenclature of Cosmetic Ingredients (INCI), through the Personal Care Council.

Once the company had this INCI register, it obtained the INVIMA registration within a few days. It seems that the international registration helped to solve the many doubts associated with having a Colombian extract being registered for the first time.

Given all the research and work that was involved in this development, it may be surprising to note that the Tibouchina extract cannot be patented. There is no way to protect this knowledge. After several consultations with specialized lawyers, CB Group established that a patent is not possible, because there is no novelty in the processes involved. In the end, the ingredient is produced by nature, the extraction process used in production is public knowledge, and the final result does not involve novelty, from the standpoint of patent law. The situation would be different if the production process involved a development that could be argued as novel, but that is not the case.

It is interesting to note how this result was received as a surprise by many actors involved in the process in Colombia, a fact due to the lack of experience in the sector regarding the development of new components and the intellectual property laws that support protection for the uses of new knowledge. The episode also serves as an eye-opener about what may happen with the exploitation of ingredients that come from Colombian biodiversity. The original ingredients are not patentable, because they are free in nature, but developments in the process or in the delivery vehicles are. It is quite possible, then, that foreign companies may come to Colombia, get access to the natural ingredients to be processed elsewhere, and then sell the final product back in the country, protected by patents.

Therefore, efforts to protect this development by CB Group must focus entirely on strengthening the brand in the eyes of its customers, not on patent protection.

CB Group is active in Mexico with its products for men, facing strong competing brands, such as Vichy, a niche brand from L'Óreal that is sold only in pharmacies. After evaluating its performance, the company now sees that CB Group needs to strengthen its marketing capabilities in order to succeed in the sophisticated international markets chosen for entry. In December 2010, CB Group held a board meeting where partners decided on their course of action to better deal with ongoing business challenges in Mexico, especially facing competition in a high-end segment like cosmetics products for men.

The firm is also expanding its activities beyond the initial scope. What started as a partnership to develop a new product is evolving into a service center for the members of the group and also other companies. CB Group has acquired a property in one of the Free Trade Zones in Bogotá, where it will be able to provide logistics services for the partners and also for third parties. It is expected that CB Group will be able to coordinate production in the different plants, set up registers for the different batches of production at each plant, and organize packaging and shipping in the Free Trade Zone. New alliances with other producers are being discussed, including with a laboratory in the pharmaceutical sector. The idea is to exploit the sum of capabilities that the firm has assembled, from logistics and production to reaching international markets.

The case illustrates the many potentials and pitfalls that are typical of entrepreneurial ecosystem. The potential gains for a new venture that derive from acting within an entrepreneurial ecosystem are clear. In this case, none of the individual partners could have developed the new firm on its own. Alliances can be quite difficult, particularly among competitors, but in this case it was possible to overcome doubts and mistrust because a long and well-structured process was adhered to, coordinated by a government agency and the universities. Out of this process came the realization that the very different competitive positions of the firms allowed the creation of an alliance where all could win without threatening their existing businesses, even if their products were technically similar.

Support from the ecosystem was also crucial in order to arrive at definitions regarding the international market to be targeted and to deploy a market-entry strategy. The resources required for international marketing studies were beyond the capabilities of any of the individual firms. The role of Proexport, a Colombian government agency, and CAF, a multilateral one, were key factors in these efforts.

The case also offers important lessons regarding the role of the ecosystem in terms of managing regulatory issues. Colombian companies have little experience in developing innovative products for international markets. In a sector like cosmetics, where seals of approval from regulators are of critical importance, this lack of experience in itself becomes an enemy of success; because it takes time for the different actors to learn the best way to solve problems and perform their roles. A successful entrepreneurial ecosystem should act as an flexible learning entity, where problems are quickly structured and lessons from experience integrated efficiently into routine procedures.

The most important lesson deals with the building of trust among all members in an ecosystem. Governments, universities, and entrepreneurs speak very different languages. Resources need to be assigned for the construction and administration of a process, and specific procedures and methodologies should be followed in order to build trust. The importance of this element cannot be underestimated.

Lessons learned and recommendations for future action

The Colombian case presents an example of a country where the promotion of entrepreneurship has had an important role in national public policy for several years. However, the country has not advanced substantially in the development of high-impact entrepreneurship. The case provides important lessons regarding the role of public policy in creating a large and steady flow of ambitious entrepreneurial ventures that could provide a key engine of growth for the economy. Some key lessons of this experience and recommendations for future action are presented below.

Commitment to measurement methodologies is essential

One of the most important initiatives that national policymakers adopted early in Colombia, as the push for entrepreneurship strengthened over the previous decade, was committing to a standard set of measurements for identifying a baseline and gauging the advancement of entrepreneurship in society. The decision was to follow standard international methodologies that permit a comparison of Colombia with other countries. Therefore, a strong feature of the Colombian environment for entrepreneurship at present is the existence of several standardized measurements of relevant variables that have been taken for a number of years. The state of entrepreneurship in Colombia is measured regularly by international instruments such as GEM, the *Doing Business* study, and the *Global Competitiveness Report*. This creates the conditions for an informed dialogue within society. Entrepreneurship is a complex phenomenon, and it will always be difficult to measure it. However, even if the measures have limitations, the systematic assessment of entrepreneurship from different perspectives and levels of analysis offers consistent results and greatly enhances the quality of dialogue. This is one of the important lessons that the Colombian experience may offer to other countries.

The entrepreneurial process should be at the center of policy objectives

The case shows that is not enough to define the achievement of higher rates of entrepreneurship activity as a policy objective. Policymakers need to define what kind of entrepreneurship is desired, consider the complete process entrepreneurs need to go through to develop the desired kind of ventures, and define policy actions to strengthen all the elements in that process.

Colombia has one of the highest rates of entrepreneurial activity in the world, but evidence shows that high-potential entrepreneurship is scarce. The government has worked for a decade on an intense campaign for promoting entrepreneurship. However, institutions that offer support for entrepreneurs have responded by offering solutions for ill-defined sorts of entrepreneurship, and concentrated on just a few stages of the entrepreneurial process. As a result, entrepreneurs find it difficult to reach solutions for the problems that they encounter along the way, and as a result many opportunities are never developed as new ventures.

National governments can have strong leverage in the development of local entrepreneurs

From a policy perspective, entrepreneurship is necessarily a local phenomenon. Support for entrepreneurs need to be given at the local level and an entrepreneurship culture also needs to be present at the local level. For this reason, it is difficult for national governments to be effective in the promotion of entrepreneurship. However, the Colombian case shows that national governments have considerable leverage when it comes to nudging local actors into supporting entrepreneurship initiatives.

After an entrepreneurship law was passed in Colombia in 2006, assigning responsibilities not only to the national government but also to local governments and to some private actors, a different dynamic started up in the process in Colombia. The national government has invested resources, time, and effort in motivating local actors to move forward as the law orders them. This has unleashed a process where cities and regions have started competing with each other in setting up better conditions for the development of entrepreneurship in their localities. The regional entrepreneurship networks ordered by the law are only just beginning to take shape, but already action is taking place at levels where it had not existed before. This initiative has engaged not only local government actors, but also the chambers of commerce, and universities. It is generating a process of emulation that shows promise.

The enhancement of the entrepreneurial ecosystem is a key policy objective

It is essential that key actors in society recognize that the advancement of entrepreneurship is not solely the responsibility of governments. Private actors need to understand that they do not act in a vacuum, and that collective action can greatly enhance the possibilities of success of new ventures.

In order for this to happen, a basic agreement around the key definitions of the problem needs to be achieved. It is important, for example, that public and private actors in regions and localities engage in a deep dialogue about the meaning and implications of the term "entrepreneurial ecosystem." As defined in our analysis, the entrepreneurial ecosystem is really a set of networked institutions that act under common definitions of the problem with the objective of aiding the entrepreneur to go through all the stages of the process of new venture development. It can be understood as a service network, where the entrepreneur is the focus of action and the measure of success. To do this, local actors need to reach an agreement regarding what kinds of entrepreneurship the region or city wants to promote; what the barriers and pitfalls are that threaten success at each stage of development of the entrepreneurial ventures; who the other actors are in the entrepreneurial ecosystem and how each can specialize and add value, offering truly competitive services to the entrepreneur and to other members of the entrepreneurial ecosystem. Learning to act as an ecosystem will enhance network effects and positive externalities, creating value for new entrepreneurial ventures at the local level.

The financing barrier needs intense treatment, including the development of exit strategies for investors

Just as happens in other countries in Latin America, lack of financing is a major hurdle and an important reason why many ventures never develop beyond the earliest stages. Colombia is making timid advances in the attraction of venture capital and the creation of angel investor networks.

These financing agents are indispensable elements in the ecosystem. Success in the task of attracting them should provide the country with important examples and role models that will serve to stimulate others into investing in high-growth entrepreneurial ventures.

However, it is necessary to devise ways to gather speed and scale up the effort at some point in the process. Policy efforts should be made to accelerate the creation of new angel networks and the arrival of venture funds. This effort should be accompanied by initiatives to accelerate the development of exit mechanisms for investors who enter in the successive stages of development of the projects. The development of exit mechanisms has not received explicit attention from policymakers in the past, and is an element of critical importance in the decision to enter this market by new investors. This is an area where successful international models are scarce, and it is necessary that policymakers in Colombia and other countries are bold enough to try and devise original solutions.

Universities need to commit to the objective of developing high-potential entrepreneurial ventures

Universities have shown scant enthusiasm for the idea of developing high-impact entrepreneurship ventures in Colombia. Their activity has been more directed at supporting the development of business plans by their students and, as a general rule, there is little commitment to the purpose of ensuring that these plans follow through the venture development stages and become real firms. Beyond this, there are few universities that have clear plans for turning the technologies developed at their science and engineering schools into entrepreneurial projects.

International experience shows that technologies coming out of universities and research laboratories are indispensable for developing a strong pipeline of high-impact entrepreneurial ventures in a country. The situation in the future should improve in this respect, since Colciencias has been given increased resources and has been assigned the mission to promote innovative entrepreneurship. Still, there are many cultural barriers that need to be reduced at universities. Among others, engaging in collaborative work between different disciplines and different universities, increasing the importance of the entrepreneur within the technical and scientific faculty, and creating incentives for efforts that turn research into entrepreneurial innovations, should be key objectives in the agenda for Colombian universities.

Large companies should be important actors in the drive towards the entrepreneurial economy

Large companies can act as strong levers for entrepreneurial initiatives. In Singapore, for example, large disk drive manufacturers were instrumental in supporting and fostering the development of a number of new firms that would become local suppliers of high-tech components (Wong 1999). These new companies eventually turned into strong specialized producers for the international markets. Large companies can be buyers of products and investors in new ventures, and executives from these corporations can act as board members and mentors of nascent entrepreneurs. These initiatives should not have to rely on luck as independent and isolated efforts, but should produce learning for the whole ecosystem. Actors in the ecosystem should be able to contribute and share knowledge on this issue as part of the established networking routines of the system.

The media can be a critical ally of entrepreneurship policy

The Colombian case presents a high-profile case of cooperation between one media outlet and governmental institutions for the promotion of entrepreneurial ventures. This collaboration has become a focal point of attraction for the community that is interested in the development of entrepreneurship in the country. This is a valuable experience that could be replicated in other countries, and could also be replicated at regional and city levels in Colombia.

Entrepreneurship culture is complex and its development needs to be considered as a specific policy objective

Although culture has been recognized as an important component of an entrepreneurial economy, there are few antecedents available regarding concrete steps that policymakers can take to enhance entrepreneurship culture in ways that go beyond obtaining a favorable attitude in the population towards the idea. It is necessary to move to a higher level, ensuring that entrepreneurship is assumed by society to be a set of individual and collective behavioral responses to the environment.

Usually, policy initiatives directed at enhancing a culture of entrepreneurship are limited to the promotion and diffusion of the concept of entrepreneurship and increasing the perception of self-efficacy in individuals regarding their ability to initiate their own businesses. However, self-efficacy is not necessarily followed by behavior.

It could be useful to look at other areas of public policy where substantial advancements have been made in terms of designing interventions that can change behavior in large groups of the population. For example, there is a lot of experience in the field of public health regarding the design of interventions with the objective of changing the behavior of entire populations on issues such as tobacco consumption, nutritional habits, or intrafamily violence. These interventions are based on specific methodologies that prescribe how to define the target population, how to identify influential individuals in that population, and how to induce behavioral change through staged, well-developed plans. We believe that the objective of promoting a culture of entrepreneurship could benefit from the adoption of similar practices and methodologies.

Patience and persistence are of the essence in entrepreneurship policy

Entrepreneurship is a complex and multifaceted phenomenon, where a few blockages can delay or cause the failure of otherwise excellent venture projects. Entrepreneurship policy has to reflect this complexity and has to work in many areas at the same time. Failure to develop one key area of an ecosystem may entail the failure of the whole system. Achievement of goals in one or several areas may not lead to the achievement of the larger policy goals, because blockages impede progress.

This seems to be the case of Colombia over the past decade. Despite achieving strong awareness of entrepreneurship in the population, advancing substantially in the construction of national and regional networks for the development of entrepreneurship, and raising its position in international rankings such as the *Doing Business* report, high-impact entrepreneurship remains in its early stages of development, because of large blockages in areas such as financing and the transfer of scientific knowledge to practical applications.

The worst mistake would be to decrease the effort and succumb to inertia. Colombia appears to have made substantial advances in many areas leading to the construction of a strong entrepreneurial ecosystem. The country now needs to focus on the few critical areas that have remained as laggards in the effort. The development of entrepreneurship policy needs to be understood as a long-term endeavor, where policymakers have to be permanently aware of changes in the system, correct problems as early in the process as possible, and share learning in an efficient manner across all actors of the ecosystem. The country appears to be poised for change, as lessons from the past are assimilated and the new government has given high priority to entrepreneurship development and has identified key components of the problem. If these policies are applied with focus and persistence, it is conceivable that the country will see results in terms of high-impact achievement for Colombian business ventures in the present decade.

Notes

1. This is the National Planning Department, a government agency in charge of both formulation and follow-up of the National Development Plan, designed by the national government for every presidential period.
2. This business case was originally developed as part of a larger research project on the competitiveness of the cosmetics value chain for the Inter-American Development Bank (Vesga 2009).

References

Breslin, D. 2008. "A Review of the Evolutionary Approach to the Study of Entrepreneurship." *International Journal of Management Reviews* 10, no. 4: 399–423.

Cámara de Comercio de Bogotá. 2009. *Informe de Gestión 2008*. http://www. empresario.com.co/recursos/page_flip/CCB/2010/informe_gestion_2008/index. html, date accessed January 14, 2011.

Czuchry, A. J. and M. M. Yasin. 2008. "International Entrepreneurship: the Influence of Culture on Teaching and Learning Styles." *Journal of Entrepreneurship Education* 11: 1–15.

Departamento Nacional de Planeación. 2009. *Política Nacional de Ciencia, Tecnología e Innovación*. Documento CONPES 3582. Bogotá, Colombia: Departamento Nacional de Planeación.

Departamento Nacional de Planeación. 2010. *Bases para el Plan Nacional de Desarrollo: Prosperidad para Todos*. Bogotá, Colombia: Departamento Nacional de Planeación.

Dinero. 2010. "Arranca el capital de riesgo." *Revista Dinero* Noviembre. Bogotá, Colombia.

GEM Bogotá. 2010. *GEM Bogotá Report, 2009–2010*. GEM Bogotá.

GEM Colombia. 2010. *GEM Colombia Report, 2009–2010*. GEM Colombia.

George, G. and S. A. Zahra. 2002. "Culture and its Consequences for Entrepreneurship." *Entrepreneurship: Theory & Practice* 26, no. 4: 5.

Hsu, D. H., E. B. Roberts et al. 2007. "Entrepreneurs from Technology-Based Universities: Evidence from MIT." *Research Policy* 36, no. 5: 768–88.

IFC. 2010. *Doing Business 2011*. Washington, DC: The International Bank for Reconstruction and Development – The World Bank. http://www.doingbusiness. org/reports/doing-business/doing-business-2011, date accessed January 14, 2011.

Isenberg, D. J. 2010. "How to Start an Entrepreneurial Revolution." *Harvard Business Review* 88, no. 6: 40–50.

Kelley, D. J., N. Bosma, and J. E. Amoros. 2011. *Global Entrepreneurship Monitor 2010 Global Report*. Global Entrepreneurship Research Association (GERA). http:// www.gemconsortium.org/about.aspx?page=pub_gem_global_reports, date accessed February 1, 2011.

LAVCA. 2010. *The 2010 Scorecard on the Private Equity and Venture Capital Environment in Latin America and the Caribbean*, in cooperation with the Economist Intelligence Unit. http://lavca.org/wp-content/uploads/2010/05/scorecard2010-updated-for-web-1.pdf, date accessed January 14, 2011.

Levie, J. and N. Bosma. 2010. *Global Entrepreneurship Monitor 2009 Global Report*. Global Entrepreneurship Research Association (GERA). http://www.gemconsortium. org/about.aspx?page=pub_gem_global_reports, date accessed December 10, 2010.

Ministerio de Comercio, Industria y Turismo. 2009. *Política Nacional de Emprendimiento*. http://www.mincomercio.gov.co/econtent/documentos/Emprendimiento/Politica Emprendimiento2009.pdf, date accessed January 14, 2011.

Ministerio de Comercio, Industria y Turismo. 2010. "Política Nacional de Emprendimiento: Avances y Retos." Presentation by Clementina Giraldo, Directora de Emprendimiento, at Universidad de los Andes, Bogotá, April 7, 2010.

Pitman, S. 2007. *Diversity and Globalisation Determine Fragrance Trends*. http:// www.cosmeticsdesign-europe.com/Products-Markets/Diversity-and-globalisation-determine-fragrance-trends, date accessed January 14, 2011.

Porter, M. E. 1998. "Clusters and the New Economics of Competition." *Harvard Business Review* 76, no. 6: 77–90.

Roberts, E. B. and C. Eesley. 2009. *Entrepreneurial Impact: the Role of MIT.* Kansas City, Mo.: Marion Kauffman Foundation.

Roland Berger Strategy Consultants and IESE Business School. 2009. *For Entrepreneurs, by Entrepreneurs.* Amsterdam/Barcelona: report available at http://www.iese.edu/research/pdfs/ESTUDIO-109.pdf.

SENA. 2010. *Informe de Gestión – Fondo Emprender,* Servicio Nacional de Aprendizaje, SENA. Bogotá, Colombia. http://www.sena.edu.co/downloads/2010/planeacion/octubre/informe_gest_OCT_2010_archivos/Page2920.htm, date accessed December 10, 2010.

Thomas, A. S. 2000. "A Case for Comparative Entrepreneurship: Assessing the Relevance of Culture." *Journal of International Business Studies* 31, no. 2: 287–301.

Universidad de los Andes. 2010. *Apoyar la Implementación de un Ecosistema de Emprendimiento en la Ciudad, sus Actores y Mecanismos de Operación.* Report for the Secretaría de Desarrollo de Bogotá.

Wessner, C. 2004. "Entrepreneurship and the Innovation Ecosystem Policy Lessons from the United States." Working paper. Jena, Germany: Max Planck Institute for Research into Economic Systems.

Wong, P. K. 1999. "The Dynamics of HDD Industry Development in Singapore." Working paper, Centre for Management of Innovation and Technopreneurship. Singapore: National University of Singapore.

World Economic Forum. 2011. *The Global Competitiveness Report 2010–2011.* Geneva, Switzerland. http://www3.weforum.org/docs/WEF_GlobalCompetitivenessReport_2010-11.pdf, date accessed January 14, 2011.

6
Costa Rica: IT Entrepreneurs Leapfrogging for Innovations

Luis J. Sanz and Román E. Porras
INCAE Business School

Costa Rica shows all the characteristics of an efficiency-driven economy. According to the last report of the GEM, we could not expect much entrepreneurial activity in the country, as it completes its transition to an innovation-driven economy (Kelley et al. 2010). Hence, the lack of supporting institutions and policies is not surprising, with the exception of long-standing solutions for SMEs, which are really not tailored to satisfy the needs of dynamic new ventures. But in spite of all that, we are seeing a new class of enterprising *ticos* or Costa Ricans pursuing innovating opportunities, particularly in the IT sector. To paraphrase one of the leading businessmen in the country (and the subject of one of our examples), Costa Rica is starting to transform itself from a knowledge society into a knowledge-based economy.

The country has the strongest economy in Central America, and is supported by a solid and stable democracy and strong institutions and regulations. Costa Rica had experienced a significant inflow of FDI in past years, mainly concentrated in the export sector due to the small size of the local market but given its free access to the markets of Central America, the United States, and more recently, the European Union. The exported goods are well known for having a high level of sophistication but at the same time a lack of differentiation. Costa Rica also has a banking sector at an intermediate stage of development, dominated by state-owned institutions, and infant capital markets not really used to the particularities of variable-return investments.

While, in general, the country seems to have multiple benign conditions for enterprise development and new ventures, in reality entrepreneurial activity seems to be growing very slowly. There are a few factors that are often identified as the main ones responsible for this poor performance. The most frequently mentioned factor is lack of financing; since there are not many options for angel or venture capital, the stock market is too thin, and the banking sector does not offer adequate products for dynamic new ventures (although strong development banking programs offer financial solutions to small and medium-sized enterprises (SMEs) with a track record. However, there are other related factors. For instance, employees are well trained but lack entrepreneurial drive; and bureaucratic inefficiencies undermine the formation of new enterprises.

In this chapter we explore the economic conditions that characterize Costa Rica's efficiency-driven economy, starting by looking at the economy and its competitiveness. We then show that notwithstanding all the barriers, the IT sector is burgeoning with entrepreneurial activity, presenting some brief case studies as examples. We finish by considering some recent trends as we offer some perspectives on entrepreneurship in the country.

Economic overview

Costa Rica has a market economy supported by one of the most peaceful and steady democracies in Latin America. Its stable economy is based on tourism, agriculture, and electronics exports. Traditionally dependent on coffee, banana, and beef exports, Costa Rica turned its economy around during the 1980s and the 1990s. Costa Rica's development program focused on integrating national industries with world markets and promoting a healthy flow of foreign private direct investment into the country. In particular, Costa Rica has recently attracted important FDIs in the electronics industry.

Costa Rica enjoyed robust economic growth from 2003 to 2007, with an annual average growth rate of 6.6 percent. It was supported by strong global expansion, sound economic policies, and strong business and consumer confidence. But economic growth slowed sharply (to 2.6 percent) in 2008 and turned negative (1.5 percent) in 2009, reflecting weakening activity in the construction, manufacturing, and tourism industries as a result of the global economic crisis (ILO 2010). Nevertheless, economic activity began to pick up in mid-2009 and the recovery is now gradually taking hold. The government has provided significant support for domestic demand, and the banking sector has remained sound (Globserver.com 2010).

Exports have become more diversified in the past ten years due to the growth of the high-tech manufacturing sector, which is dominated by the microprocessor industry and the production of medical devices (ILO 2010). Tourism continues to bring in foreign currency, as Costa Rica's impressive biodiversity makes it a key destination for ecotourism (CIA 2010). The US–Central American and Dominican Republic Free Trade Agreement (CAFTA-DR) came into force on January 1, 2009, after significant delays within the Costa Rican legislature. And in 2010 the country, with the rest of Central America, signed an association agreement with the European Union. This is particularly important for Costa Rica, since the country is currently the principal Central American exporter to the European market.

On June 1, 2007 Costa Rica established diplomatic relations with China, aiming to increase its access to the Chinese market, which has been growing strongly. Between 2000 and 2006 China moved from being Costa Rica's 32nd largest export market to being its second-largest (China accounted for 15 percent of Costa Rican exports in 2007, up from less than 5 percent as recently as 2004) (EIU 2009a). Other countries that have bilateral FTAs with Costa Rica are: Germany, Argentina, Chile, China, Korea, Spain, France, the Netherlands, Paraguay, the Czech Republic, and Venezuela.

However, poverty has remained at around 20 percent for nearly 20 years, and the strong social safety net put into place by the government has eroded due to increased financial constraints on government expenditure. Reducing inflation remains a difficult problem because of rising commodity import prices and labor market rigidities (ILO 2010). However, recent developments have raised hopes of a one-digit inflation rate either for 2010 or 2011.

Openness to foreign investment

Costa Rica has an open international trade and investment regime. The government is trying to attract high-quality foreign investment to Costa Rica. Since mid-1982, it has placed considerable emphasis on improving the investment climate, exemplified by the creation of the Ministry of Foreign Trade (COMEX), which coordinates government efforts in trade and investment.

The Costa Rican Coalition for Development Initiatives (CINDE), a private non-profit association also originally created in 1982 under USAID sponsorship, operates a very active investment promotion program through its office in Costa Rica and regional offices in the United States, Europe, and the Far East. CINDE has been closely associated with the arrival of some of the largest foreign investment in Costa Rica, for example, Intel, Alcoa, and (in the near future) Abbott Laboratories. Industry surveys suggest that investors are most attracted by competitive labor costs, a well-educated workforce, and the country's economic and political stability. As a result, Costa Rica has attracted, per capita, one of the highest levels of FDI in Latin America.

Industries that are relatively labor intensive and require moderately or highly skilled workers are considered to have good development potential in Costa Rica. Some of those that have taken advantage of this potential include manufacturing or assembly of electronic components, telecommunications equipment, machinery, consumer goods, electrical appliances, upscale apparel products, toys, sporting goods, selected leather products, and health and natural resource-based products, including food processing and agribusiness products.

Costa Rica's recent economic growth is fueled by exports – as much of goods as of services (especially tourism). This is not surprising if we consider the size of the internal market and the difficulties associated with increasing economies of scale. In fact, the companies that export tend to be more productive (and pay higher wages), which suggests extending the exporting sector would accelerate economic growth (World Bank 2009).

Health and education

Rapid economic growth in the 1960s and 1970s brought impressive increases in living standards, as improvements in nutrition, healthcare, and education were spread through the majority of the population. Investment in education brought literacy to most, and fostered the development of a relatively sophisticated higher education system (EIU 2008).

Costa Rica enjoys some of Latin America's most impressive education indicators. Primary and secondary education is free and compulsory. Illiteracy has fallen sharply over the past two decades, from 10 percent of those aged over 15 in the 1980s to 5.1 percent in 2005. However, in 2005 some 16 percent of Costa Ricans over 12 years of age did not complete primary education. Since the 1980s more than one-half of all students have not finished high school. Between 2000 and 2004 this figure dropped slightly, but it still remains above 50 percent. During the administration of Miguel Angel Rodríguez (1998–2002) an effort was made to expand the coverage of the education system. New school premises were built, increasing the number of schools from 5275 in 1995 to 6884 in 2000. However, the quality of teaching remains a concern, given that as many as 20 percent of teachers lack formal qualifications. Raising standards in science and technology is seen as a priority to underpin the continued development of high-technology industries (EIU 2008).

Costa Rica's health indicators, including immunization levels, life expectancy, and infant and maternal mortality rates, are among the best in the Latin American region and well above the Central American average. Health indicators continue to improve, consistent with efforts made by successive governments to improve the provision of health services. According to latest World Health Organization data, spending on healthcare has risen from 6 percent of GDP in 1999 to 6.6 percent of GDP in 2004. Over the same period, spending per head increased from US$249 to US$290 (at average exchange rates).

Main economic sectors

Agriculture

Climatic diversity encourages the specialization of agriculture in different areas. The main products exported are coffee, bananas, citrus, and pineapples. Trade liberalization, the removal of subsidies on domestic farm products, and the drive to encourage nontraditional exports since the middle of the 1980s have all discouraged the production of staples. The contribution made by agriculture to GDP has declined from around 13 percent of GDP in the first half of the 1990s to below 10 percent since 2000, following the establishment of high-tech manufacturing clusters in the country. The main traditional agricultural exports are bananas, coffee, sugar, and beef. In particular, the last two now account for only a small share of overall earnings. The production of nontraditional products, such as fish and shellfish, cut flowers, ornamental plants, and tropical fruits now accounts for an increasing share of overall export earnings.

Manufacturing

Having suffered a major decline during the 1980s owing to the regional economic crisis and recession, in the early 1990s manufacturing once again became one of the fastest-developing sectors of the economy. Export demand has boosted certain niche activities. Some of these are related to the newly diversified agricultural sector, but others, such as the production of microprocessors, medical supplies, and rubber joints and seals, are the fruit of proactive export-promotion policies (EIU 2007a). After the first plant built in Costa Rica by a US microprocessor company, Intel, was inaugurated in April 1998, the production of microprocessors became the largest single area of manufacturing activity. Food-processing, medical supplies, chemical products, textiles, and metal-processing are also important. Intel's investment encouraged other foreign high-technology companies to locate in Costa Rica. Among the largest are Abbott Laboratories and Baxter Health Care, two US companies that produce medical equipment. The high-tech assembly operations located in the country will encourage the government to continue to upgrade scientific and technical educational standards. However, as long as the microprocessor business dominates manufacturing in Costa Rica, the country will be vulnerable to fluctuations in world market conditions, reflecting the cyclical nature of the semiconductor market.

Financial services

The state continues to play a dominant role in the banking sector and its role has become more relevant since the 2008–9 economic crises (EIU 2007b). State-owned banks accounted for 52.8 percent of assets in the national financial system in December 2008, but this figure increased to 54.8 percent in December 2009 (SIGEF 2010). Since 1998, private sector banks have experienced a consolidation process, declining in number of institutions but growing in assets. The number of private sector banks (including cooperatives of various kinds) decreased from 26 in 1998 to 15 in December 2009, but the latter accounted for 31.2 percent of total bank assets, in comparison with 22.8

percent in 1998. Private sector banking is dominated by three institutions, BAC, HSBC, and Scotia Bank, which control 68.35 percent of private assets. The remaining financial assets are held by mutual, cooperative, and other financial institutions. Three state-owned banks, Banco de Costa Rica (BCR), Banco Crédito Agrícola de Cartago (BCAC), and Banco Nacional de Costa Rica (BNCR), dominate the retail banking scene together with Banco Popular y Desarrollo Comunal (BPDC), a private bank of public interest. Government initiatives include plans to promote development banking and venture capital, but fail to include substantial reform of the state-owned banks.

Foreign investors from Central America, Mexico, and the US own one-half of the private sector banks. Since 1999 there have been many mergers, strategic alliances, and takeovers by regional financial groups and foreign banks. Banks that are now partly foreign-owned include Banco Cuscatlán, Banco de San José, and Banca Promérica (EIU 2009b). Several other international financial institutions have branches in Costa Rica. Most of these local branches carry out international financial operations only, but a few offer limited financial services, mainly related to long-term loans and deposits.

The concentrated nature of the banking sector is partly responsible for the high levels of intermediation costs and interest rates (which are also compounded by the huge public-sector domestic debt). Given the high level of dollarization of the economy, it is important to note that the spread between lending interest rates in the domestic currency and in US dollars has historically been wide (EIU 2007b). As a consequence of the economic crisis, the banking sector adopted a cautious position, reducing credit to the private sector but increasing it to the government by 37.5 percent in 2009 (CAMTIC 2009). During 2010, banks seemed to continue with this prudent position but it is expected that credit to the private sector will be re-established once the economic impulse is renewed. Another issue is the fact that the government probably needs to finance its deficit within the internal market, so banks will be tempted to direct their portfolios to a less risky public sector and will have no incentive to reduce lending rates.

In summary, we have an emerging economy that has successfully reinvented itself, from coffee- and banana-grower to a service-oriented economy based on tourism and technology. This was largely made possible with massive investments of human capital. And, as we shall see in the next section, it is precisely this human capital that could help to enable the next transition towards an innovation-driven economy.

Winds of change

In its path to development Costa Rica has focused on improvements in physical infrastructure and regulatory arrangements to allow the integration of the economy with global markets. The country centers its competitiveness strategy on efficiency in producing standard products and services. As we have seen in other developing economies, companies in Costa Rica often started by producing equipment under contract to foreign manufacturers, with the design and marketing still controlled by companies overseas. All in accordance with the country being an efficiency-driven economy, as we can see in Figure 6.1, based on the results from the 2010 Competitiveness Report.

But as we mentioned earlier, there are winds of change blowing in the country, winds that suggest that the transition to an innovation-driven economy might not be that far off. Those winds are particularly important in the IT sector, as this section discusses.

Costa Rica and its software industry

Costa Rica's software industry is quite young since it only began developing in the middle of the 1980s. In 2003 there were 105 companies dedicated to software development in operation. Industry sales totaled close to US$170 million in 2002, of which nearly US$70 million corresponded to exports. The main export destinations were to other Central American countries, accounting for 62.5 percent of foreign sales. The second- and third-place destinations for Costa Rican software products were the United States and Mexico, where 13 and 9.4 percent of exports arrived respectively (CAMTIC 2004).

Figure 6.1   Results from 2010 competitiveness report
Source: generated by the authors based on data from WEF (2010).

According to a study conducted in 2003 by Costa Rica's Chamber of Software Producers (Cámara de Productores de Software de Costa Rica), the main problems faced by firms in the sector were related to hiring and contracts (hiring bureaucracy, payment schedules, guarantees for work), marketing, merchandising processes, and a lack of transparency. In terms of sales to international markets, the main problems were lack of capital and aerial transportation costs. Experts also indicated that key aspects such as: financing, company and university collaboration, infrastructure, an adequate regulatory framework, and business and merchandising strategies, seemed to be the greatest weaknesses for companies in this sector (CAMTIC 2004).

While experts agreed that the quality of technical training in human resources was one of the country's main strengths, they considered that deficiencies did exist in nontechnical aspects related to soft skills, like English fluency and managerial skills (marketing, finance, strategy, teamwork, reporting, etc.). In addition, they pointed out that the number of graduates could be an important limitation for the country if it wanted to participate in international markets, especially in areas of outsourcing.

But five years later in 2008, opinions aside and regardless of all these obstacles, industry sales closed on US$221 million with 290 firms operating formally in the industry (CAMTIC 2009). How did the enterprising *ticos* find a way to circumvent all this? In the next four case studies we will see some of the pioneering work undertaken by this new breed of Costa Rican entrepreneurs. We start with the case of Mora and Beck, leading investors looking to develop nothing less than a whole IT cluster. We then explore in a little more detail the case of Lidersoft, one of the companies Mora and Beck invested in. This case illustrates the difficulties that can arise between investors and entrepreneurs in an emerging economy like Costa Rica. Next we look at how the Link Program tried to build on these experiences. It would be the culmination of the Mora and Beck dream: to jump-start a burgeoning IT cluster in the country. Although that did not exactly happen, there are some very important lessons that we can extract from this case. Finally, the case of Fair Play Labs, one of the success stories steaming out of Link Investments, shows us the possibility of starting world-class ventures in Costa Rica.

Mora and Beck[1]

Richard Beck and Carlos Mora had been trying for the past several years to transform Costa Rica's knowledge-based society into a knowledge-based economy. To achieve this goal, they decided to expand the scope of their investment banking company by creating an angel capital fund, Capital Empresarial en Centroamérica (CEC). Leveraging the infrastructure of their original investment fund, they started looking for investors, mainly among their friends, who would be willing to undertake the high-risk and potentially high-reward investments that start-ups represent. And they chose a niche – the IT sector – to take advantage of Costa Rica's obvious potential, even though neither of them nor any of the other investors who came on board had expertise in IT.

CEC invested in several Costa Rican IT-related new ventures. In 2004, however, the original investors decided to stop contributing to the fund, and financial turmoil in Costa Rica, prompted by a sharp decline in the value of government bonds in the local market, made it impossible to find new investors. CEC's latest investments (Lidersoft and Predisoft) were performing remarkably well, but the fund could not obtain new cash inflows to keep investing in their development. Investors decided to retrench and wait for the proper time to harvest. Currently, the fund does not have a professional manager and is not making any new investments.

Ever since coming to the country in 1999, Intel has invested in a wide range of activities in both public and private universities and elementary school systems. Laboratory equipment donations, a traveling technology bus, and close links with the Ministry of Education began to have an impact. Many school systems voluntarily undertook curriculum revisions to reflect the growing importance of IT. Intel assisted this process with its "Teach the Teachers" program, which transferred IT knowledge informally throughout the educational system. All of a sudden, close to 20 percent of first-year students were pursuing IT careers.

Intel's investments, as well as the success of small companies like Artinsoft, a firm working with artificial intelligence technologies, were the first signs that the Costa Rican IT industry could become a significant player in the international market. Together with the regional opportunities presented by CAFTA, they contributed to a positive buzz about the country's IT sector. Local firms already had a technology advantage, with 78 percent of Central American and Dominican software firms located in Costa Rica. Most of this business was conducted by small firms with fewer than ten employees. More than one-third of these companies were already exporting to the US and their Central American neighbors. The general consensus was that the inevitable integration of the Central American market would provide Costa Rican software firms with a distinct opportunity for further expansion.

First steps in angel investing.   It was in the midst of these promising developments that Mora and Beck decided to promote an angel investing fund. Born in Brooklyn, New York, Richard Beck found himself in Costa Rica at the age of 12 as his parents explored business opportunities there. He returned to the US to pursue his education and graduated from Michigan State University with an honors degree in business administration and economics. Soon afterwards he returned to Costa Rica to embark on a successful career in manufactured goods such as plastics, cement, and paint. His early success led him to found Atlas Eléctrica (electrical appliances) in 1961 and Polipak (plastics) in 1970, where he served as president of the board until 1996. During this time, he also served on the boards of several high-profile firms such as BANEX (Agro-industrial Bank of Exports), the largest private bank in the country at the time. At first glance, Richard Beck aptly fits the profile of a typical angel investor, who is a successful entrepreneur and corporate manager.

"Don Richard," as many Costa Ricans call him, has also participated in creating high-profile organizations in the national landscape. As co-founder and director of INCAE Business School since 1963, he has served as an industrial adviser to several Costa Rican presidents. Arguably his most influential role was as founder of CINDE, Costa Rica's FDI promotion agency, recognized for its successful effort to bring investment to a region (Central America) that had historically been unstable and mired in conflict. As an angel investor, Beck has not only the experience of a successful entrepreneur but also an inherent understanding of the country's capabilities. The latter would prove pivotal to his angel investing efforts.

He was well complemented by Carlos Mora, a financial-sector veteran from Venezuela. Mora studied management engineering at Rensselaer Polytechnic Institute in Troy, New York, earning both a bachelor's and a master's degree. He then specialized in portfolio management and mergers and acquisitions at the New York Institute of Finance. As a merchant banking manager for Corporación Privada de Inversiones in Central America, a Costa Rican investment bank, he structured the first underwriting of a preferred shares issue by Atlas Eléctrica. He also did the initial public offerings (IPOs) underwriting for several firms, including nontraditional sectors like macadamia production. Later he advised Costa Rica's Securities and Exchange Commission on the design of the regulatory framework that enabled the creation of investment funds. He then founded the first such fund. These business activities eventually led him to Richard Beck and to the creation of the first angel investment fund in the country.

The investment process. In the late 1990s, after several years of retirement, Richard Beck became restless. He began to formulate a strategy to invest in local technology companies. He found two things: a wealth of technology ideas and a dearth of IT companies. He had already experienced a taste of what could happen when capital was infused into an IT start-up with strong management. In 1997 he had invested in a small company called Artinsoft. The company's technology used artificial intelligence systems to automatically migrate data to various platforms. Although the founders and management team came from the academic world, they showed a natural ability to manage a successful enterprise. The technology was widely successful, leading Microsoft to make a direct investment in the company. As a member of Artinsoft's board, Beck watched his initial investment become profitable.

Spurred by his success, Mora and Beck launched CEC in 1999 after securing informal commitments for approximately US$3 million in capital. More than half of the funds were provided by Beck himself, with Mora and a few other investors contributing the rest. These investors were successful businessmen whom Mora and Beck knew socially. Their backgrounds were mostly in construction and real estate. The fund was managed by Mora, and the investment decisions were made jointly by him and Beck. All investors served on the board of directors and regularly reviewed the fund's performance. The amount invested per company varied, depending on the particularities and potential of each venture. CEC was very concerned with giving entrepreneurs appropriate coaching and the right incentives, and therefore never took a majority stake in any of the ventures. The idea was that each investor would become involved in the company best suited to his interests and abilities. But because the investors lacked experience in the IT sector, they only offered general managerial advice.

When asked whether CEC would consider investing in other sectors in Costa Rica or in the IT sector in other Central American countries, Mora and Beck's answer was straightforward:

> We believe that in our case, investing in more than one country can only increase risk instead of reducing it. The reason is very simple: we don't know the IT sector in the rest of the region as well as we know it in Costa Rica. Actually, given our knowledge of Costa Rica, we would consider investing in other sectors here, but the problem becomes the lack of resources. This is what prompted us to focus solely on the IT sector.

Rather than sitting around waiting for projects to come to them, CEC went looking for potential investments. Their extensive business experience gave them a good idea of what was out there and where to look. They invested in some companies on the basis of their potential to become global players. They believed that only ideas with such potential would yield the returns required to compensate not only for the risk of those businesses, but also for the losses from other ventures in the fund's portfolio. Mora knew pretty well that "out of five investments, you can expect two of them to be successful, one to achieve a decent performance, one to have a regular result, and one to fail."

And they certainly had their share of failures. A combination of a lack of managerial talent in the portfolio companies and market problems led to poor results in most of the initial investments. One example, which was one of the first projects that interested the investors, was Cenfotech, a start-up that would provide training and placement assistance for technology students. In a decision that would prove costly, both CEC and Cenfotech decided that it was not necessary to seek the sanction of the Ministry of Education, assuming that market recognition was more important than fulfilling legal requirements. Ultimately, Cenfotech found it hard to recruit students because most families wanted their children to earn a legally recognized diploma. CEC could not turn it around until it established an alliance with a local university (which provided the legal recognition).

After several individual failures, Mora and Beck figured that the best way to enter the IT market was to create it. According to Beck, they "concluded that entering the market on a grand scale was not just an opportunity, but a necessity for any player to survive." Many IT technologies are complementary in nature, which is why Silicon Valley, northern Virginia, and Boston have become IT hubs in the United States. By creating a critical mass of companies and encouraging interaction, these regions can frequently solve the IT needs of a corporation. With this in mind, Mora and Beck set about developing a mini-Silicon Valley in Costa Rica. The investment strategy of CEC was to create a critical mass of IT companies through investing in a group of companies with interrelated businesses.

To that end, they decided to focus the portfolio on five ventures. In addition to Beck's original stake in Artinsoft and CEC's investment in Cenfotech, they invested in:

- Interamerica: A data and hosting center for local firms.
- Lidersoft: An outsourcing software company capitalizing on the global outsourcing trend (see details about this company in the next case).
- Predisoft: A software company with powerful prediction algorithms suitable for use in many industries. Its first commercial application was directed to the financial sector: the company's software could predict the amount of cash needed for ATMs, as well as the money needed at individual bank branches and the occurrence of fraudulent activity.

Predisoft quickly became the crown jewel of the fund's portfolio. The fund's investment strategy proved valuable in more ways than originally planned because some of the firms shared key resources. Artinsoft, for instance, started using Lidersoft's services to improve its performance. Mora and Beck emphasized that "as a result of CEC's investment, the businesses will obtain not only financial resources but also aid consisting of strategic management, organizational development, and financial oversight."

Investors, however, grew weary of the managerial problems at some of the portfolio companies, and individual concerns for each company gradually replaced the portfolio approach. Moreover, the ventures that were showing the highest potential, Lidersoft and Predisoft, were still demanding frequent capital inflows, and the fund's investors eventually ran out of patience. They decided not to make new investments, taking advantage of the informality of their disbursement commitment to the fund, and CEC rapidly ran out of cash. The timing could not have been worse, since a financial crisis in Costa Rica prevented Mora and Beck from attracting new investors.

After a journey that proved to be very educational in many regards, the administrative staff of the fund was dismantled. Without funds to invest, CEC's focus shifted primarily to supervising the performance of those companies already in the portfolio while waiting for the harvest to arrive. And in the case of Interamerica it did, and CEC was able to sell its investment obtaining a good return on investment. It was an important milestone, because it meant they had closed the venture capital cycle: they fundraised, invested, and exited, in at least one of their investments, providing a road map both for future investors and for future entrepreneurs.

Lidersoft[2]

Founding partners. In 1998 Roy Vargas founded Vision Tecnológica with approximately US$50,000. He was accompanied by two IT professionals who had worked in the banking industry under his direction. The distribution of capital for Vision Tecnológica was 90 percent to Roy Vargas, and the other 10 percent to be divided equally between the two other partners. After finishing this first project, another business administrator with banking experience joined the venture. The new team member received company shares as part of his contract. Shortly, the company's name was changed to Lidersoft.

As Lidersoft grew, Roy and his partners distributed shares to trusted employees to the point that in 2001, Roy Vargas held 77 percent and the rest were split among 13 employees. That year, employees/shareholders holding 23 percent of Lidersoft's shares decided to create a firm called Corporación Digital (CD), transferring their shares of Lidersoft to this company, which in turn would act as one shareholder.

When CD was formed, given profits, cash availability, and Lidersoft's stable position in the local market, the company's shareholders received dividends annually for their participation in the business. In addition to receiving their salaries as employees, CD's partners were especially motivated since they had seen the fruit of their labors reflected in dividend payments.

Angel investors, nearshore, and IsThmus. As we mentioned earlier, the partnership of Mora and Beck chose Lidersoft as one of their investment targets. At the time, CEC's intention was to leverage Lidersoft core competences so that they could tap into the outsourcing market for the US which, given Costa Rica's proximity, could be termed nearshore. As Lidersoft started to develop this new market, it soon was evident that they needed a new brand, and so IsThmus was born.

But as both businesses continued to develop, two rifts appeared. The first was within the company itself, as the profile of employees working on IsThmus projects differed from those working for other Lidersoft projects. Eventually, the two different organizational cultures led to an IsThmus spin-off, while both companies maintained the same ownership structure and the same board of directors.

In this context, investors wanted to focus their resources and attention on IsThmus given its market potential, pushing constantly for growth. The second rift then arose as a difference of opinion between angel investors and CD about the growth options for both companies, the urgency to pursue them, and the priorities of the two firms. This problem was created because Roy and the other founders followed typical international practice in an industry intensive in human capital: use your shares to attract talent, instead of using your scarce cash to pay higher salaries.

The problem is, in developed markets when things go right, those shares can be monetized. But in emerging economies like Costa Rica, it is very likely that even if things turn out great, employees will have to keep their shares. This fosters an inclination to seek control, as opposed to viewing shares simply as part of their compensation package.

Eventually, the problem was solved with a swap of shares. The angels and Roy kept the shares in IsThmus, while CD and Roy became the sole shareholders of Lidersoft. This has allowed Lidersoft to improve its position in the local market, while IsThmus runs free in the US, attracting important customers, although its development was recently held back by the international recession.

As a result of experiences like this and the previous one, Costa Rica was the chosen site to test a new program funded by the Multilateral Investment Fund of the IADB (FOMIN) and CAF: Link.

Link investments: a nontraditional source of financing[3]

The main objective of the Link Program was to contribute to the economic development of Costa Rica by fostering the creation and sustainability of dynamic new ventures in the technology sector. This US$7.5-million program was designed to promote accessible solutions for the challenges faced by most entrepreneurs and SMEs. It was structured as an initiative from FOMIN and CAF jointly with local partners, who were in charge of its execution. The program had four components initially, but one of them was never implemented.

Link incubation.   This component was in charge of Parque Tec, one of the first incubators in the country, founded in 2004 and initially focused on the software industry. The goal was to strengthen and further develop Parque Tec's capabilities in order to generate a critical mass of new ventures for the other components of the program. In order to achieve sustainability and share the risks, Parque Tec requested a share of the new ventures. However, poor positioning and lack of recognition, plus its focus on the software industry, undermined this strategy and in turn did not allow the organization to meet the initial targets. In spite of this, Parque Tec achieved a greater understanding of the entrepreneur's training needs, and there are multiple projects for new incubators in different parts of the country that will benefit from this experience.

Link exports.   This component was in charge of the Costa Rican Chamber of Technology, Information, and Communication Firms, CAMTIC. This was by far the most successful component of the program, in part due to the nature of its activities: attending trade fairs, training, and dissemination forums. However, it quickly became very clear that exporting was a project that required between six months and two years in order to yield quantifiable results. Also, one of the main learning points from this component was the need to prepare the entrepreneurs before attending trade fairs and other activities, so that they could get the most out of their participation.

Link financing.   This component was in charge of Desyfin, a leading financial firm providing leasing services in Costa Rica. But for multiple reasons this component was never implemented, affecting in turn the relative success of other components.

Link investments.   This component was in charge of Fundación Mesoamérica, the philanthropic branch of one of the main consulting and investment banking firms in Central America. The goal was to create a network of angel investors that could provide much needed equity financing for dynamic new ventures. In turn, this investment could be complemented by "soft" debt from a co-investment fund financed by FOMIN and CAF.
   The specific objectives were:

- To create an active, dynamic network of angel investors with a critical mass of angels. The original target of 15 angels was amply exceeded, and the network was able to group 34 angels, 23 of which were active investors.
- To create a common base of knowledge among entrepreneurs and angels to facilitate investment. While the training of the angels was carried out

through lectures by international speakers like John May, most of the work with entrepreneurs was done through tailored coaching of each team. The focus of the latter was to prepare the entrepreneurs to present their business plan to investors; while the former aimed to introduce the angels to international best practice.

- To develop devices that could facilitate a high-quality pipeline of new ventures seeking investment. In the second half of the program a business plan competition called Yo Emprendedor (I Entrepreneur) was developed. It was a very successful effort that amalgamated the initiatives of different institutions, contributing to promote entrepreneurship and providing the network with new investment opportunities. Furthermore, it is expected to continue after the conclusion of the Link Program.
- To assist angels in accessing the co-investment fund. The terms of the fund were (a) a subordinated loan in dollars; (b) six-month variable LIBOR interest rate; (c) seven-year payment period; (d) three-year grace period; (e) increasing sales royalties (2–10 percent); and (f) no penalty for paying in advance. Most entrepreneurs and angels considered these conditions too onerous, so only two of the investments benefited from the co-financing. One of the investments is being liquidated while the other is still without sales.
- To achieve the network's self-sustainability after the end of the program. Currently, a group of angels is looking to maintain the network and its operation has been assured until the end of 2010.

In general, the network looked to recruit investors with a specific profile tailored to these specific objectives. The details of the profile were:

- Wealth level: personal wealth above US$1 million was desired to invest at least in two companies for the first four years.
- Members must have an unquestionable reputation.
- Former entrepreneurs: they must be experienced in starting businesses.
- Interest in the IT sector must be shown.
- There must be willingness, background, and availability to assume the role of coach/investor in companies where it is decided to invest.

Nevertheless, this initial profile was modified in order to adapt it to some local realities. For instance, there were few "cashed out" entrepreneurs, one of the main resources for angel networks in the US and abroad. For the same reason, few angels ventured coaching or business opinions on the firms in which they invested. On the other hand, social responsibility concerns and helping the country were important motivating factors, even if these could lead to the complete loss of the invested funds.

At the same time, Link Investments defined clear selection criteria that new ventures must fulfill in order to present their proposals to investors:

- Scalability: they must have a big growth potential.
- Differentiation/entrance barriers: the business model must have a clear differentiation component.
- Business plan: it must be clear and convincing.
- Management team: they must be experienced in the business industry.

A total of 353 business plans were received during the 4-year program. Of these, 37 entrepreneurial teams presented their ideas to the investors, who invested in 4 through the network and an additional 2 outside the main mechanism. Although these results were lower than the targets set for the program, they were more or less in line with international practice.

Overall, the results of the Link Program highlight both the obstacles and the possibilities of the country as a whole. The lack of an angel investing culture was evident for both sides: investors and entrepreneurs. In this context, Link Investments adopted a trial-and-error strategy until it was better equipped to assess the expectations of the two groups. One interesting development turned out to be the composition of the entrepreneurial teams that actually received an investment from the network: in all of them there was at least one member with international experience. It seems that those entrepreneurs that had either studied or worked abroad were better prepared to deal with the angels and to manage the pressures inherent in discussing a business idea with a group of seasoned businessmen. One could also conjecture that due to their international experience, these entrepreneurs had a better understanding of the cost and benefits of bringing the angels on board, as opposed to merely viewing them as the only viable financing option (which was the case for many entrepreneurs). The next case study presents us with one of the program's success stories.

Fair Play Labs[4]

Fair Play Labs (FPL) is a young company formed by experienced and creative professionals. FPL is over four years old; the team has grown quickly and it currently employs 24 members, roughly divided 50/50 between developers and artists.

The company began in 2003 when Claudio Pinto was enthused by his son Daniel to start a game development studio. He had almost 20 years of software development experience in the area of enterprise applications, as co-founder of Exactus Software, an enterprise resource planning (ERP) software and services company with over 500 customers in 12 countries in the Latin American region. And he had gradually grown very interested in the gaming industry, particularly serious games and their applications in education.

After lots of research and some proof-of-concept projects, he realized that there were a large number of young and talented engineers and artists with interest in this field in Costa Rica. As the team grew, they started to work on more ambitious projects, and by 2004 it was clear that it would be feasible to enter the gaming software industry, to offer services and develop their own titles. With this aim, he started Fair Play Labs with the following mission statement:

Vision
We will be recognized as one of the best companies in the digital interactive entertainment industry, combining creativity, innovation and fun.

Mission
Develop fun games for children 8 thru 80, which are innovative and non-violent, emphasizing mobile platforms, and have fun doing it! Become a great company to work for.

Values
In Fair Play Labs we hold in great regard the following values: Fairness, Creativity & Innovation, Fun & Quality, Enthusiasm & Commitment, Confidence & Perseverance, Learning & Humility, Recognition & Pride, Teamwork & Solidarity, and Integrity & Honesty.

The company works in three areas:

1. *Licensed developments*: it is developing a game named ECOVOUTION. This is a role play game, based on the story of a character that wants to find the balance between the use of natural resources and the survival of humankind. Nintendo has the license for this game and it is expected to reach millions of portable devices like Nintendo DS and Game Boy.
2. *Outsourcing*: the company offers services related to game development like art, music, and software development at a competitive price and guaranteed quality.
3. *Own development*: "As Majesty" is a strategy game similar to chess invented in Costa Rica and declared of cultural interest by the Costa Rican government. It is being developed for Xbox 360 and Nintendo DS, and the company expects that 280 million chess players in the world will play it.

In 2007 FPL was looking for US$350,000 to develop the company's expansion plans. Since the Costa Rican market was too small for IT companies,

FPL needed to penetrate the US market and a cash inflow was necessary for that purpose. After consultation with some experts, three alternatives were identified as the strongest based on FPL characteristics. These were: a loan from the traditional banking system, financing from a venture capital fund, or gathering the required funds from a group of angel investors. The company eventually decided on the latter, taking advantage of a new program aimed to foster the creation of technology-based new ventures in the country called Link, described earlier.

More recently they have been working on Rushville – an extensible collection of mini-games for the Apple's iPhone and iPod Touch. FPL was recently accepted into the Sony Computer Entertainment America Inc. Incubation Program for developers in Latin America, as a first step towards becoming a PlayStation Portable (PSP) Licensed Developer.

We believe that these four cases are examples of the entrepreneurial potential of the country, but they also present us with some of the main obstacles. The next section discusses in more detail what we think these obstacles are, and offers some insights into what could be required for these examples to multiply and catapult the Costa Rican economy into the realm of innovation-driven economies.

Challenges in a transition economy

Perhaps the hardest transition in an economy is the transition from an efficiency-driven economy to an innovation-driven economy. This requires a direct government role in fostering a high rate of innovation, through public as well as private investment in research and development, higher education, and improved capital markets, and regulatory systems that support the start-up of high-technology enterprises. The shift from one phase of development to the next often requires new ways of organizing governments, markets, and enterprises, so it is not altogether surprising therefore that many countries fail at making the appropriate transitions, or even fail to recognize that such a transition is needed. While we have shown how entrepreneurs and investors are generating innovations to take advantage of market opportunities, it is clear that there are some critical factors that could undermine such transition.

Enterprise regulations

According to the World Bank *Doing Business* Report Costa Rica was ranked at 117 in 2009, a marginal improvement with respect to the 118 position held in 2008 (World Bank 2010). It is clear that a deeper improvement is required for the country to foster value creation from innovation. In particular, the following areas look like the most critical (ranking within parentheses): the process of opening and legalizing a start-up business (123); dealing with construction permits (123); protecting investors (164); paying taxes (152); and enforcing contracts (132). There are also some concerns about property registering, commerce across borders, and access to credit (World Bank 2010).

Human capital and the IT sector[5]

Costa Rica presents important achievements in human capital development with great accomplishments in its educational system, and its literacy rate is one of the highest in the region. But, according to a World Bank competitiveness assessment, the country still faces meaningful challenges in secondary education related to quality and promotion rates. Only one-third of students entering seventh grade attain a high school diploma. One of the main failures in the academic component seems to be a lack of quality and relevance associated with obsolete academic programs and evaluation systems, and poor teacher training. Another issue is that there are not enough students being trained in fields that could be important for the competitiveness of the country, such as math, science, and technical programs.

Nevertheless, there seems to be light ahead. Technical programs appear to be aligned to the needs of the job market, including practical courses in fields like informatics and electronics. However, this potential is still underused: in Costa Rica only 19 percent of high school students choose a technical/vocational field, compared with 43, 55, 72, and 35 percent in Chile, Panama, Austria, or Israel respectively.

The country produces relatively few graduates in science and engineering, constraining the competitiveness of the nation and hampering the quest for innovation. College students are concentrated in fields like education, social sciences, law, economy, and administration. Only 13 percent of graduates have studied engineering and basic sciences, compared to 20–25percent in Chile, Colombia, Mexico, Spain, Germany, and Australia, and 40 percent in Korea. Nevertheless, students with degrees related to informatics and engineering seem to be in high demand.

The small size of the specialized workforce supply and a growing demand from the software industry compel existing companies to compete fiercely for qualified collaborators, pushing sector wages above the national average. Interesting, this salary structure is still below the level of developed economies, allowing Costa Rica to compete in the nearshore outsourcing market, as we described in the Lidersoft case. The latter also highlights a potential conflict of interest (or perhaps it is just about timing) between outside investors and employees/shareholders that might not occur in more developed economies and should warn new ventures in emerging markets against blindly following international practices, and disregarding local conditions.

R&D in Costa Rica[6]

In spite of the country's success in attracting MNCs looking for locations for some of their R&D facilities, such as HP, there are areas where major improvements are needed. R&D expenses are low (0.32 percent of GDP) if we compare it to the Latin American average (0.6 percent), as well as to fast-growing economies like Korea (3.2 percent), the Czech Republic (1.5 percent), and Ireland (1.3 percent). Only 34 percent of these expenses come from private companies, compared with 65 percent in the US. As a percentage of total population, Costa Rica has only one-fourth of the researchers that Mexico has, and 15 percent of Chile's. Patent generation is also low compared with countries like Panama, Mexico, Chile, and Uruguay. R&D expenditure in private companies is more related to processes and new technologies in production processes, but only 29 percent of companies report investing in new technologies from 2006–8.

Collaboration between universities and the private sector is another concern. According to an innovation survey published by MICIT (the Costa Rican Ministry of Science and Technology), only 24 percent of R&D projects from the academic community, the public sector, or NGOs were connected to the private sector. Furthermore, only 6 percent of companies stated that they had links with universities for R&D purposes. It seems the university–company relationship is limited to the search for talent, wasting some of the human capital available at universities.

Additionally, there is an important lack of finance for innovation among local companies. While their multinational counterparts come to the country looking for human capital, local firms cannot leverage their talent due to the lack of financial capital. In the IT sector, the main source of funding for new ventures and innovation is the entrepreneur's own funds, and this is becoming one of the main constraints for the sector. On the bright side for IT firms, the few resources available through these mechanisms seem to focus on their sector. FPL clearly took advantage of this trend.

But looking at the problem from a different perspective, perhaps it is the lack of a whole ecosystem that limits the development of more comprehensive financial solutions. In any case, what is clear is that the traditional products developed for SMEs are not suited to the idiosyncratic needs of a new venture, and it is even worse in the case of the IT sector. That is why the lessons from Mora and Beck and Link Investments are important: we must learn from these experiences in order to continue improving financial solutions capable of fueling the next line of innovations.

Perspectives for innovation and entrepreneurship in Costa Rica

One of the main lessons from the Link Program was that improved coordination was required, among the different institutions supporting entrepreneurship in the country. Initiatives like Yo Emprendedor are contributing to improve such coordination and collaboration, and have become important beacons for the future of entrepreneurship in Costa Rica. As we have seen, in spite of still being an efficiency-driven economy, there are promising signs that Costa Rica could be on the verge of developing innovation-driven sectors that could boost its economy.

But in order to do so, it is clear that the country needs to streamline its policies. The starting point has to be the recognition that dynamic new ventures and SMEs are not necessarily the same thing, and hence each requires a different set of policies and solutions. For instance, consider the development banking approach. With the most important financial institutions in the country being state-owned, these banks offer a vast array of financial solutions to micro, small, and medium-sized companies. But these offers usually take the form of loans and other kinds of debt, imposing on the company a fixed payment schedule. While this could be a suitable financing option for an already established SME, three years old or more, a dynamic new venture in the service sector, like an IT company, could find it really hard to match this payment schedule with a very irregular cash flow from operations. That is why in more developed economies alternatives like angel investing and venture capital have been developed, together with grants and other programs aimed to foster innovation and new venture creation. We should look to these experiences, but if anything, we also need to adapt solutions to the local context.

Finally, it is important to work on the dissemination of success stories and previous experiences to motivate future entrepreneurs, while at the same time working in high schools and colleges across the country to foster an entrepreneurship culture among the young. It is time that we separate the discussion and set up specific solutions for dynamic new ventures. The experience of the Link Program, and the seeds that it planted, could flourish if we manage to build new programs, accords, and relationships based on the lessons learned.

Notes

1. This section and all the data cited in it are drawn from Condo et al. (2005).
2. The information in this section was taken from Sanz and Lesizza (2006).
3. This section is based on Camacho and Altamirano (2007b) and Loría (2010).
4. The information presented in this section was taken from Camacho and Altamirano (2007a).
5. The data in this section was taken from World Bank (2009).
6. The information in this section was taken from World Bank (2009) and Monge-Gonzalez and Hewitt (2008).

References

Camacho, A. and A. Altamirano. 2007a. *Fair Play Labs: Un Caso de Éxito*. INCAE Business School Case # 28898. INCAE Business School. Costa Rica.

Camacho, A. and A. Altamirano. 2007b. *Link Inversiones: Alternativa de Financiamiento no Tradicional para Empresas*. INCAE Business School Case # 28900. INCAE Business School. Costa Rica.

Cámara Costarricense de Tecnologías de Información y Comunicación (CAMTIC). 2004. *Costa Rica: Verde e Inteligente, Estrategia Nacional de Tecnologías de Información y Comunicación*. Cámara Costarricense de Tecnologías de Información y Comunicación. Costa Rica.

Cámara Costarricense de Tecnologías de Información y Comunicación (CAMTIC). 2009. *Costa Rica: Verde e Inteligente, Estrategia Nacional de Tecnologías de Información y Comunicación*. Cámara Costarricense de Tecnologías de Información y Comunicación. Costa Rica.

Central Intelligence Agency (CIA). 2010. *The World Fact Book: Costa Rica*. Central Intelligence Agency. https://www.cia.gov/library/publications/the-world-factbook/#.

Condo, A. et al. 2005. "Mora and Beck: Lessons from Investors in Costa Rica's Knowledge Economy." In E. O'Halloran, P. Rodriguez, and F. Vergara (eds), *An Executive Briefing on Angel Investing in Latin America*. Charlottesville: Batten Institute at the Darden Graduate School of Business Administration, University of Virginia. United States of America.

Economist Intelligence Unit (EIU) ViewsWire. 2007a. "Country Background. Costa Rica: Manufacturing." Retrieved online in November 2010. http://www.eiu.com/index.asp?layout=VWPrintVW3&article_id=33696788&printer=printer&rf=0.

Economist Intelligence Unit (EIU) ViewsWire. 2007b. "Country Background. Costa Rica: Financial Services." Retrieved online in November 2010. http://www.eiu.com/index.asp?layout=VWArticleVW3&article_id=1012415286&region_id=4...&country_id=190000019&channel_id=180004018&category_id=410004041&refm=vwCat&page_title=Article.

Economist Intelligence Unit (EIU) ViewsWire. 2008. "Country Background. Costa Rica: Education." Retrieved online in November 2010. http://www.eiu.com/index.asp?layout=VWPrintVW3&article_id=33696788&printer=printer&rf=0.

Economist Intelligence Unit (EIU). 2009a. *Country Report: Costa Rica*. Economist Intelligence Unit.

Economist Intelligence Unit (EIU). 2009b. "Risk Briefing. Costa Rica Risk: Financial Risk." Retrieved online in November 2010. http://www.eiu.com/index.asp?layout=RKArticleVW3&article_id=224173607&page_title=Article.

Globserver. 2010. "Costa Rica and the Financial Crisis." Retrieved online in November 2010. http://www.globserver.com/en/press/costa-rica-and-financial-crisis.

International Labor Organization (ILO). 2010. "Employers' Organisations Responding to the Impact of the Crisis". Working Paper No. 2. Bureau for Employers' Activities. Retrieved online in November 2010. http://www.ilo.org/public/english/dialogue/actemp/downloads/publications/working_paper_n2.pdf.

Kelley, D., N. Bosma, and J. Amorós. 2010. *2010 Global Report*. Global Entrepreneurship Monitor. Babson College, Universidad del Desarrollo and London Business School. Retrieved from http://www.gemconsortium.org/.

Loría, L. 2010. *Programa de promoción de la empresarialidad dinámica*. *"Evaluación Final"*. Banco Interamericano de Desarrollo (BID) and el Fondo Multilateral de Inversiones (FOMIN). Costa Rica.

Monge-Gonzalez, R., and J. Hewitt. 2008. *Innovación, Competitividad y Crecimiento, Desempeño de Costa Rica y de su Sector de las TICs*. Cartago, Ediciones el Castillo. Costa Rica.

Sanz, L. and M. Lesizza. 2006. *Lidersoft*. INCAE Business School Case # 11535. INCAE Business School. Costa Rica.

Superintendencia General de Entidades Financieras de Costa Rica (SIGEF). 2010. http://www.sugef.fi.cr/.

World Bank. 2009. *Costa Rica Competitiveness Diagnostic and Recommendations Volume 1*. Retrieved online in November 2010. http://siteresources.worldbank.org/ INTCOSTARICA/Resources/CR_Competitiveness_Vol1.pdf.

World Bank. 2010. *Doing Business 2010: Reforming through Difficult Times, Comparing Regulations in 183 Economies*. A co-publication of Palgrave Macmillan, IFC, and The World Bank. Washington, DC.

World Economic Forum (WEF). 2010. *Global Competitiveness Report 2009–2010*. Retrieved online in November 2010. https://members.weforum.org/pdf/GCR09/ GCR20092010fullreport.pdf.

7
Entrepreneurship in Mexico

Victoria Jones
University of Seattle

Introduction

Mexico came into the twenty-first century with one of the world's most open economies and trade agreements that include 44 nations (Villarreal 2010). Mexico's powerful economy consistently places it in the top 20 world ranking for largest gross domestic product. The population is about 110 million yet about half of Mexico's people live in extreme poverty, not even participating in the formal economy. The ranking for entrepreneurial activities is high (www.gemconsortium.org), while the ranking for ease of doing business is steadily improving (Doing Business in Mexico 2011). What drives entrepreneurship in these conditions? What are the resources entrepreneurs leverage to succeed here?

This chapter focuses on the dynamics of entrepreneurship in Mexico with extensive use of cases to illustrate the experiences of entrepreneurs in this country. First we review the context in which entrepreneurs in Mexico operate, and then we compare the two types of entrepreneurs identified by GEM – opportunity and necessity. We grapple with the pressures of, and responses to, infrastructural issues and the question of optimal size in Mexico's business environment. Finally we look at the role of entrepreneurship in Mexico's economic development and explore the international reach of Mexican entrepreneurs. Brief cases are scattered throughout this chapter, culminating with the story of Ricardo Salinas and how he built an entrepreneurial culture in Grupo Azteca.

The context and adaptive nature of Mexican entrepreneurship

Mexico's history is one of rich and beautiful cultural traditions sometimes convulsed by dramatic political and economic upheaval. Both creative traditions and disruptive transitions provide the context for Mexico's business enterprises and especially for its risk-taking entrepreneurs. A brief history of the country begins with the spectacular indigenous cultures that developed sophisticated technologies, intricate cosmologies, and extensive geographic trade networks.

The great ancient civilizations of Mexico exhibit the hallmarks of entrepreneurship – innovation, assumption of risk, new business models, new markets, and new products. Before the Spaniards arrived in the Americas, the Aztecs, Mayans, and other cultures had developed sophisticated methods of agricultural production, metalworking, and other artisan crafts such as weaving and pottery making. The maturity of these skills indicates progressive experimentation and development. Additionally the extensive trade routes suggest that business models were also developed over time, and by individuals willing to assume the risks of travel, transport, and exchange.

The Spanish conquistadors, in their search for gold and religious dominance, brought violent suppression of these peoples. This period of colonization that began in the 1500s ended with Mexico's independence in 1821 after a ten-year war. Mexico fought for its territory with both the US and France, and the young country suffered several military coups and political revolutions. Concentrations of wealth and bad economic times led to the Mexican revolution of 1910–21 that overthrew an elite dictator, Porfirio Diaz, whose 30 years of power brought impressive industrial progress to Mexico. In the relative political stability of the twentieth century, Mexico was rocked by extremes of economic expansion and collapse. The division between the wealthy and poor has been systemic and chronic. While NAFTA and other trade agreements have leveraged Mexico's innovative strengths to make many Mexicans wealthy, many others feel excluded. Corruption, drug trafficking, and gang violence are the most recent disruptions faced by the country.

Against this backdrop of drama and progress, Mexico has nurtured successful entrepreneurs throughout its history. It seems that the hazards of uncertainty and the opportunities of rapid change drive people to build their own routes to security while also giving them the strength they need to succeed in the tough business of building a new venture. Entrepreneurs thrive through skillful adaptation to Mexico's economy, politics, and culture.

Informality is an opportunity

Mexico's unemployment rate is remarkably low compared to other OECD countries (OECD Employment Outlook 2010, Fleck and Sorrentino 1994). Some factors that keep this number small in spite of relatively low education and a large percentage of the population that is poor include the way Mexico defines unemployment, *maquiladora* manufacturing, the escape valve of undocumented workers who find employment in the US, and lack of unemployment insurance (Maloney 2002, Fleck and Sorrentino 1994). In Mexico, unemployment is a luxury most cannot afford.

The GEM, an annual survey of entrepreneurial activity in more than 50 countries, identifies two main types of entrepreneurial motivation – necessity-driven and opportunity-driven (gemconsortium.org). Necessity entrepreneurship is defined by GEM as entrepreneurs who start businesses because they cannot find wage-paying jobs. But the 2006 GEM data shows that the majority of entrepreneurs in Mexico are those driven by opportunity, with 39 percent of entrepreneurs saying they sought a higher income and 49 percent saying they sought greater independence (Mares and Gómez 2006). Mexico's low wages and precarious economic conditions may make salaried jobs unattractive even when they are available (Maloney 1999), though Mexico has more high-performing salaried workers entering self-employment compared to more poor wageworkers in the US (Fajnzylber et al. 2006).

The relative ease of starting a business may lead to opportunity entrepreneurship among those of the lower classes who are not the typical opportunity-driven entrepreneurs of developing nations. While informality is often associated with necessity-driven entrepreneurship, in Mexico informality may provide a propitious business environment in which even people in the lower socioeconomic classes can open new businesses not because they do not have any wage-based options, but because self-employment is a better opportunity.

One striking feature of Mexican entrepreneurship is the low barrier to entry. In an analysis of Mexican business owners published in 2006, 24 percent of construction businesses and 47 percent of personal services businesses reported absolutely no financial investment to start. A full 25 percent of the sample reported having total capital stock of less than US$47. Transportation was the most expensive start-up in the survey, and a quarter of respondents in this industry reported that their initial investment was only US$2070. Even considering that Mexico is a relatively low-wage economy, these are low costs for a business start-up. Using the median initial investment across industries and the median earnings, an entrepreneur would need to save his income for less than one month in order to accrue the necessary start-up capital for a new venture (McKenzie and Woodruff 2006). In national rankings of business practices, Mexico ranks 35th of 183 economies for ease of doing business and 67th for ease of starting a business (Doing Business in Mexico 2011).

Besides the financial costs of starting a business, the regulatory costs must also be considered. The bureaucratic burden of opening a business in Mexico has decreased dramatically in recent years (World Bank, *Doing Business* report). However, many businesses continue to operate informally. A 2010 study estimated the level of informality to be about 30–40 percent of GDP and further determined that the rate has remained relatively stable since the 1980s (Macias and Cazzavillan 2010). Definitions of the informal economy vary, and the figures vary widely depending on the definition used. Based on the 1988 National Employment Survey, those employed in the non-agricultural informal sector could be 26.1 percent (the sum of those employed in domestic services, the self-employed, and unpaid workers), 33.6 percent (workers with no reported earnings and those with earnings under the legal minimum wage) or 38.5 percent (those working in enterprises with five or fewer workers) (Fleck and Sorrentino 1994).

Mexico's long history of doing business "under the radar" has made unregistered businesses culturally acceptable and very difficult to monitor. Many Mexicans operate with cash only and have no expectation of receiving a receipt for a transaction. And, while the huge number of informal businesses results in significant loss of tax revenue for the government, the cost of finding and penalizing tens of thousands of tiny business operators is prohibitive. In Mexico it is very easy to open an informal business with little cash and no paperwork.

While a premise of necessity entrepreneurship is that a formal job would normally be preferred to an informal one, William F. Maloney of the World Bank has proposed an alternative explanation for Mexican entrepreneurs. He found that fully 70 percent of workers transitioning from formal sector firms to self-employment did so voluntarily (Maloney 1999). He argues that one explanation for microentrepreneurial activity in Mexico is that the benefits of informal self-employment are actually greater than those of wage-earning jobs. A variety of examples are offered, including the relatively high taxes on workers who perceive relatively little benefit these taxes provide through government programs, the improved job status of being an *empresario* over being an employee, medical benefits that extend to the entire family when only one member is formally employed (Maloney 2002).

Maloney (2002) states, "The patterns we see are consistent with most micro-entrepreneurs voluntarily joining the sector and trying their luck running their own business, some successfully, some less so." Using Mexico's National Microenterprise Survey of 1992, Cunningham and Maloney identified six clusters of microenterprise entrepreneurs: very prosperous low-intensity firms (14 percent), highly capitalized firms with young and aspiring owners (7 percent), highly capitalized firms with older owners motivated by independence (4 percent), younger entrepreneurs and start-ups (32 percent), older entrepreneurs who have retired or been laid off (25 percent), and older owners of established, stabilized firms making up the balance (Cunningham and Maloney 2001).

More typical of opportunity-driven entrepreneurs in Mexico is a 1993 survey of a sample skewed to wealthier entrepreneurs. The average education level of respondents was the equivalent of a high school education, which represented only about 8 percent of the Mexican population in the same period (INEGI.org.mx). For this group, the main perceived obstacle to start-up was the financial cost – bearing the risk, obtaining a loan, credit from suppliers (Young and Welsch 1993). Additional concerns were finding a good location and the need for training and guidance. The barriers to entry in this group were not even considerations for the lowest sectors in the 2006 national survey cited previously. The majority started with no capital, no location, and no training (McKenzie and Woodruff 2006). Another indicator of the difference in this more expensive model of start-up is the frequency of finance-related problems once the business is underway – inflation, recession, seasonal cash flow changes, high interest rates (Young and Welsch 1993). These factors still exist but were not mentioned by the national sample.

Role models are a strong feature in the story of Mexican entrepreneurship. In a sample of university graduates enrolled in a course about starting a business, fully 87 percent of them said they wanted to be like a business owner they knew personally. More than half of them had relatives who were business owners – 50 percent had parents who were *empresarios*, 37 percent siblings and 47 percent grandparents (Bolaños 2006).

One of the most consistent and distinctive characteristics of entrepreneurship in Mexico is the connection with family business. The common term *empresario* in Mexico refers to the head of a business who has assumed the financial risk for that business – usually on behalf of the family (Martinez and Dorfman 1998). Start-up capital most often comes from family. The staff, or at least executives or managers, are usually members of the family. And one of the primary reasons for opening a new venture is to provide an independent living for one's children (Young and Welsch 1993). Themes of the *empresario* management culture include pride in craftsmanship (*artesanía*), a high priority on family, and efficiency that is characterized by effectively using personal relationships (Martinez and Dorfman 1998).

While the *empresario* culture includes a patriarchal model of caring for one's subordinates, the *empresario* is far removed from those who are dependent on his decisions for all aspects of company strategy, identity, alliances, and information flows. In this context of high power distance between the boss and subordinate, weak social services, and low barriers to entry for new start-ups, it is not surprising that many entrepreneurs have left the formal sector in search of the independence and status that come from being in business for oneself.

Microenterprise cases

Changarros or *abarrotes* are an example of Mexican microenterprise. In an exploratory survey (Jones, unpublished manuscript) of these family-run markets in one neighborhood of Mexico City, the businesses reported average sales of US$20–US$200/day. The US$200 peak for sales was payday for the neighborhood customers. The number of stock-keeping units (SKUs) was estimated to be in the low hundreds and the entire stock was displayed in the storefronts, which averaged about 40 square feet. The author's confidence in the income data provided by the respondents is not high as they demonstrated concern about the true strength of their business being discovered by government authorities. While prices in the larger formal stores are often lower than those of the *abarrotes*, neighborhood customers use the local shops because they can purchase very small quantities and can buy on credit based on their relationship with the owner.

One form of innovation among microenterprise entrepreneurs is in identifying ways to meet the particular needs of Mexico's poor. Shopkeepers purchase in quantities prepared for a typical middle-class household and divide the package into smaller portions. For example, a package of hard candies that contains 30 pieces for US$1 may be sold individually for 5 cents each. This allows people to buy just one candy when they want it and not have to pay for candy they will not eat until later with money they need immediately for something else. It also provides a small but nonetheless significant return on investment for the shopkeeper. The same is done for packages of cigarettes, which are sold individually from a standard pack. In the 1990s entrepreneurs began selling phone time in small increments. The entrepreneur owned the phone and purchased a bundle of minutes at a reduced bulk rate, which she resold to people without phones of their own (or those who had exhausted their minutes) for a premium by the minute. The phone itself provided the technology to verify the amount of time spent on each call. Start-up costs included the phone bundled with the prepaid phone card, a booth or table, and a chain to hold the phone to the booth.

One entrepreneurial store owner devised an entertainment option for his young clients. He had a foosball table chained to a telephone pole in front of his store. For a five-cent fee for a ten-minute game, he would take off the plywood top and let the local children play.

Pink taxis

Puebla was the first city in Mexico to launch women-only taxis in October 2009. According to the State Secretary of Communication and Transportation, Valentín Meneses Rojas, the dual motive of the service was to provide job opportunities for female workers and to provide secure and comfortable transportation for female passengers. Mexico City put its own "pink taxis" on the streets a year later. The Pink Taxi service provides 80 hours of training for the drivers who are all women in what had been a predominately male profession. Training includes information about security and women's rights. The bright pink Chevy compacts also provide mirrors, GPS tracking, and panic buttons to call for aid in case of an assault. The fees for passengers are the same as for ordinary city cabs. Complaints about the service are that it does not address the root cause of the problems of security and sexual harassment on one hand, and on the other that there are not enough pink taxis to meet demand. Pink Taxi de Puebla is a public–private venture, with US$440,000 in private investment and the state providing licensing and training (Noticiarias 2009, *The Economist* 2010, MSNBC 2009).

Is small an optimal size?

While low barriers to entry in Mexico make the start-up phase for entrepreneurs relatively easy, even the most ambitious will soon lose momentum when they run up against a regulatory environment that is both burdensome and inefficient. Although most entrepreneurs in Mexico, even those from the lower socio-economic sphere, claim to launch their ventures for opportunity motives, the opportunities are limited and the benefits accrue primarily to their immediate families rather than fueling economic growth for the nation. There is a significant divide between formal and informal businesses in Mexico.

Mexican businesses with low start-up costs provide excellent rates of return, but greater initial investments actually provide lower returns according to a 2006 report of Mexican microenterprises. Firms with invested capital of less than US$200 garnered returns of about 15 percent per month. The rates of return on investments over US$1000 were only about 3 percent per month. Low-investment low-income companies can grow steadily with reinvestment of profits; however, most remain small. In this comprehensive survey of Mexican microenterprises, 82 percent had no paid workers, 68 percent had no formal premises, and 59 percent had no inventory (McKenzie and Woodruff 2006). Only 3.5 percent of the manufacturing enterprises in one study had more than six workers (Fleck and Sorrentino 1994).

Through Mexico's National Statistical Institute's 1992 survey it was found that about 55 percent of the businesses had not registered with the Tax Bureau, but larger businesses were more likely to be registered. Some 66 percent of the one-person enterprises were not registered, but only 5 percent of the firms with at least six workers were unregistered. More than 80 percent of the businesses with no fixed address were not registered, while only 14 percent of those with a fixed location were unregistered (Fleck and Sorrentino 1994). In the ease of doing business rankings, Mexico is 107th of 183 economies for taxation, with a total corporate burden of 50.5 percent of profits (*see* Table 7.1). The country ranks 105th for registering property and title protection (Doing Business in Mexico 2011).

Table 7.1 Statistical rankings for Mexico

GDP	12 of 228 countries
Ease of starting a business	67 of 182
Ease of registering property	105 of 182
Ease of getting credit	46 of 182
Participation in paying taxes	107 of 182
Ease of enforcing contracts	81 of 182
Overall doing business rank	35 of 182
Number of mobile phones	11 of 220
Size of labor force	13 of 230

Sources: Doing Business 2011 (http://www.doingbusiness.org/data/exploreeconomies/mexico); CIA World Factbook 2010 (https://www.cia.gov/library/publications/the-world-factbook/rankorder/2001rank.html).

Studies of Mexican businesses find that as companies hire employees, acquire fixed locations, and otherwise increase the scale of their businesses, profits do not rise proportionally. The jump from informal to formal is especially costly, with payments for registering, taxes, employee benefits, etc., eating into the high profit margins enjoyed when companies operate without registering officially (McKenzie and Woodruff 2006). Motivation for businesses to operate informally includes high taxation, high wage rates for employees, insurance costs, and excessive regulation (Young and Welsch 1993, Macias and Cazzavillan 2010). Firms that stay small and informal do not face these issues (McKenzie and Woodruff 2006).

However, informality may bring costs as well as benefits. The divide between formal and informal businesses in Mexico correlates with a large gap in firm performance. It is formal businesses that enjoy greater longevity and overall profitability. Other factors that improve profitability include access to credit, association memberships, and participation in training programs (Fajnzylber et al. 2009). Benefits of registering a business include enforceable contracts, the perception of credibility, access to capital, and training programs (Maloney 2002). Entrepreneurs who choose to operate in the informal sector have lower costs but limited opportunities for improving their success.

One interesting finding is that firms that receive external support such as credit and training tend to grow less than firms that do not receive these services. The authors speculate that firms with access to these supports have already reached their optimal size (Fajnzylber et al. 2009). Business profitability improves with assistance, but owners do not continue to expand their businesses. Ironically, owners of the firms in this study said they did not take advantage of external supports because they felt their businesses were too small to benefit from them (Fajnzylber et al. 2009). Another study of microenterprises in Baja California found that owners do not seek business development services because they do not think general training will be useful and do not have time for these programs (Mungaray et al. 2007).

Yet firms that do not have access to formal services report receiving similar benefits through informal channels. Loans may be acquired through interpersonal credit networks such as from friends and family. Training comes from successful mentors and relatives. And these are not necessarily inferior to formal institutions (Fajnzylber et al. 2009). It may be a factor of Mexico's collectivist culture that interpersonal support is so strong. In a study of six countries, including Mexico, it was found that those with a higher ranking on Hofstede's scales of collectivism and femininity (quality-of-life orientation) were more likely to pursue strategic alliances for entrepreneurial ventures. Mexico fits both of these characteristics (Marino et al. 2002).

In an ethnographic study of Mexican *empresarios* five of six roles identified for the head of family firms were about establishing the nature of business relationships both internally and externally – building alliances, patriarchy, judgments about *confianza* or trust, information sharing, and how the firm practices its social responsibility (Martinez and Dorfman 1998). Business owners in Mexico do not focus on being financiers or strategists but accomplish these and all functions of management by building and maintaining effective relationships.

But relationship networks are also a way of compensating for weak infrastructure. Mexican firms tend to stay small in states with a weaker legal environment, strength being a factor of the quality of enforcement rather than the existence of the laws themselves. This is especially true for firms that are individually owned. Indeed, forming a corporation is a form of legal protection that separates the individual from the business. Self-owned firms in weaker legal environments may stay small to minimize personal risk. In Mexico legal systems are weakest in agricultural states and those with historically larger indigenous populations (Laeven and Woodruff 2007). In the ease of doing business rankings Mexico is 81st of 183 countries for enforcing contracts and 44th for protecting investors (Doing Business in Mexico 2011).

One historical study comparing Brazil and Mexico during the period of industrialization found that in Brazil infrastructure was stronger while in Mexico business networks were stronger. Both nations achieved similar rates of economic growth in this period. However, with little public infrastructure and extremely close relationships between politicians and executives, the reliance on networks may have contributed to the populist uprising that became the Mexican Revolution (Musacchio and Read 2007). The strength and importance of networks for entrepreneurs in Mexico have been hypothesized to be a way of overcoming the uncertainties of a weak institutional framework. Staying small and informal and working together is a strategy that leads to just enough success for many Mexican entrepreneurs.

But there are also many large entrepreneurial ventures in Mexico. Some start small and work their way to a larger scale organically, while others have been able to leverage opportunities in Mexico's various economic transitions.

One successful chain of taco restaurants was started in Mexico City by a woman whose purpose was to support her family through extra income. Her entrepreneurial son sought ways to innovate and improve and eventually grew the business to 17 El Fogoncito restaurants in Mexico. Carlos Roberto explains that he financed the growth of the business through family and friends in the same way that smaller enterprises do. He claims his success came through the innovations he implemented in all areas of his operations and especially in innovative investments he made in his employees. The company makes up for the lack of good public education in Mexico by providing it themselves. They not only teach employees how to do their jobs but also partner with the National Institute of Adult Education to facilitate the acquisition of primary and middle school certificates. They also assist with social basics such as how to open a checking account and how to access the public health system. Roberto believes these innovations in managing and investing in people are responsible for the company's low turnover rate of 35 percent compared the Mexican average in the restaurant industry of 162 percent (Saliba and Nava 2004). See the development indicators for Mexico in Table 7.2.

Table 7.2 Development indicators for Mexico

Total adult literacy rate (2003–8)	92%
Primary school net enrolment/attendance, 2003–8	98%
Share of total household income to the lowest 40%, 2000–7	13%
Share of total household income to the highest 20%, 2000–7	53%
Life expectancy, 2008	78 years
Internet users, 2010	29.4%
Households with electricity	97.8%
Total homes with dirt floor	6.2%
Rural homes with dirt floor	15.1%
GDP per capita (purchasing power parity)	US$13,900

Sources: UNICEF (http://www.unicef.org/infobycountry/mexico_statistics.html); Internet World Stats (http://www.internetworldstats.com/am/mx.htm); Geo-Mexico (http://geo-mexico.com/?p=4052); CIA World Factbook 2010 (https://www.cia.gov/library/publications/the-world-factbook/rankorder/2001rank.html).

When the government of Mexico began to privatize the more than 1000 ventures it owned on behalf of the public, individual investors and entrepreneurial groups were able to take advantage of the opportunity. Three of Mexico's public banks were first purchased by Mexican investors and then later all three were forced to accept foreign investment due to Mexico's weak economy. Carlos Slim with AT&T and France Telecom bought 20 percent of the phone company Telmex. These opportunistic entrepreneurs have been criticized for reproducing the noncompetitive market conditions of the state-owned companies they purchased. For example, Telmex was sold with a seven-year guarantee of monopoly status in 1990 and in 2010 the new company controls 92 percent of Mexico's phone lines. Because economic control remains concentrated among several strong individuals and *grupos*, Mexico's privatization has been accused of replacing "public monopolies with private monopolies" (Vargas-Hernández and Noruzi 2010). The economic impact of these powerful conglomerates is significant and can make a positive impact in employment and provision of services. A World Bank study of Banco Azteca, which is part of the Grupo Elektra, found that in communities where the bank operates it increased the number of businesses by 7.6 percent and increased incomes by 7 percent (Bruhn and Love 2009). However, there is little doubt more can be done to improve income distribution and free market competition through policy reform by state and federal government in Mexico. These reforms will likely also improve the competitive prospects of small and medium-sized entrepreneurs.

Working together – the entrepreneurship of the Zapatistas

Mexico is characterized by extreme regional differences in wealth and economic production (West et al. 2008, Laeven and Woodruff 2007). The northern states have prospered more than the southern ones. In 1994 when the North American FTA opened up trade between Mexico and the US, it provided greater opportunities for the states closest to the US compared to those of the south. Simmering tensions in the poor southern state of Chiapas erupted in a violent protest by the Zapatistas (Ejército Zapatista de Liberación Nacional). As peace was restored through military intervention and negotiations, the region developed several successful entrepreneurial ventures.

The Zapatistas are a political movement that has experimented with an alternative sociopolitical order. As defenders of the rights of the poor and of indigenous peoples, they have established solidarity with other movements around the world. In the negotiations that followed the violence, the Zapatistas received support from NGOs sympathetic to their cause. The small grants and guidance the NGOs provided were the tangible resources that propelled entrepreneurial ventures. These tangible resources were small but significant in a subsistence economy where there is no margin for error in which to risk innovation, and no resources to experiment with anything that does not meet one's immediate needs for survival (West et al. 2008).

The speedy and stellar success of the start-up enterprises suggests that the necessary intangible resources were latent in the population – entrepreneurial orientation, social networks, and local knowledge. Beekeeping was one of the first industries that launched in the entrepreneurial period. With help from an NGO, a beekeeping operation was set up in Miguel Hidalgo. The locals experimented with techniques and learned, for instance, that both honey and harvests improved with increased cross-fertilization after moving the hives into orange groves. Returns were reinvested into the business with a 50 percent increase in production from 20–30 hives in just three months. Innovation spread to the business model when there was more than enough honey for local consumption. The beekeepers opened trade with non-Zapatista communities. They continued to invest in the business, eventually buying trucks for transporting the product to neighboring towns (West et al. 2008).

As one tenet of the Zapatista philosophy is the injustice of the neo-liberal economic model, a contrast with the motivation of other entrepreneurs is important. The Zapatistas returned profits to their communities. They made investments in education and skills training. Indigenous knowledge about plants informed a new service sector in pharmacies, midwifery, and dentistry. And when schoolchildren needed desks and chairs, a local furniture start-up met that need. What the researchers who studied this community convey convincingly in their publication is the contagious spread of entrepreneurial activity. Activities started in a broad range of sectors. Innovation was encouraged. The fear of starting new ventures was replaced with confidence and eagerness. The influx of a relatively small amount of tangible resources provided enough momentum for this community to break free of its subsistence-only cycle and to develop profitable new ventures and a virtuous cycle of investment in the community (West et al. 2008).

The Barcelonnetes – an early relationship network

An interesting case study of entrepreneurship in the 1800s highlights some of the protracted challenges facing entrepreneurs in Mexico and some effective ways that have been employed to overcome these challenges. The Porfiriato period (1876–1910) was Mexico's period of industrial revolution with huge expansion of the railroad system, mining operations, and mechanical advances in agricultural production. During this period of rapid change, a group of immigrants from the Barcelonnete Valley in France formed a network of trust and collaboration that allowed them to prosper in spite of lagging socioeconomic institutions. The first immigrants from the Barcelonnete Valley arrived in Mexico in the early 1800s and by 1955 some 7000 men from this region had made the journey across the Atlantic. They opened dry goods stores and later textile mills. Because property rights in Mexico were weak, they developed networks among themselves and conducted business according to a code of trust rather than law (Gómez-Galvarriato 2008).

The Barcelonnetes maintained close ties with family and colleagues in Europe, with many corporate board members living in France. The flow of ideas between France and Mexico is doubtless the reason that these Mexican dry goods stores evolved to be department stores that looked identical to those operated in Paris at the same time (Gómez-Galvarriato 2008). Access to capital markets was a challenge in Mexico and eventually, these entrepreneurs reinvested their profits into ownership of some of Mexico's largest banks – Banco Mercantil Mexicano and Banco Nacional de México. The success of this entrepreneurial family network is still felt in Mexico today. One of the Barcelonetes founded his store in 1847 using the name The Cloth Case. Today that store is one of Mexico's largest retail establishments with 76 stores, 11 commercial centers and 33,000 employees. The founder's name was Jean Baptiste Ebrard and today that business is named Grupo Liverpool.

Economic development and international expansion

Mexico's entrepreneurship among the poor is a release valve for the pressures of unemployment, providing income that is not dependent on the state (Musacchio and Read 2007, Fleck and Sorrentino 1994). Additionally, the relative ease of starting an informal business gives people the hope of better opportunity (McKenzie and Woodruff 2006). However, with the informal sector estimated to be about 30–34 percent of GDP, the loss of tax revenue to the government of Mexico is significant (Macias and Cazzavillan 2010). Yet onerous government burdens are the primary reason entrepreneurs give for not registering their businesses (Young and Welsch 1993, Macias and Cazzavillan 2010). Is the economic impact of informal entrepreneurship a justifiable trade-off to overhauling the regulatory system? Is Mexico's style of entrepreneurship through informal microenterprise good for the nation's economy? (*See* Table 7.3 for Mexico's world rankings.)

A Bank of Mexico study of 22 OECD countries found that innovation is a better contributor to economic growth than business ownership. In fact, economic growth as defined by gross domestic product per capita is actually inversely related to the percentage of self-employed relative to the entire

Table 7.3 Mexico by world rankings

Largest population	11
GDP (adjusted for PPP)	11
GDP per capita (adjusted for PPP)	78
Oil production	5
Oil consumption	10
Population below the poverty line	122
Diversity of flora and fauna	4
Economic Freedom	48
Democracy	65

Sources: indexmundi.com (data collected from CIA World Factbook 2009); UNESCO (http://www.unesco.org/water/wwap/wwdr/wwdr2/case_studies/pdf/mexico.pdf); Heritage Foundation (http://www.heritage.org/index/country/mexico); World Audit (http://worldaudit.org/countries/mexico.htm).

workforce (Salgado-Banda 2007). The implication for Mexican economic policy is that the focus should not be on formalizing the informal sector but on stimulating innovation in all sectors.

The city of Monterrey is actively pursuing this strategy for economic growth through a public–private partnership designed to transform it to "an international city of knowledge." The city that profited from its manufacturing base is shifting to "mindfacturing" (Engardio 2009). One action in this transformation is a technology park planned for almost 200 acres and 3500 people. Tenants include PepsiCo research, a Motorola design center, smaller technology start-ups, and commercialization operations of the region's major universities including the IC2 Institute of the University of Texas at Austin (http://www.piit.com.mx; Echeverri-Carroll 2008).

Any discussion of Mexican entrepreneurship must include cross-border activities, especially those linked to the dominant US economy. The US affects Mexican entrepreneurship in at least three significant ways: the *maquiladora* program, Mexican entrepreneurs in the US, and the effect of US-earned dollars on entrepreneurship in Mexico. The *maquiladora* program has passed the quarter-century mark and is still a strong driver of Mexican business. It provides special cross-border privileges designed to increase employment opportunities for Mexico's relatively young and poorly educated labor force. As long as they are used for products that will leave Mexico, machinery and equipment, parts and raw materials can be imported into the country without customs duties. Although the *maquiladora* sector has suffered from Chinese price competition, concerns about gang violence, and economic downturns, Mexico still offers strong advantages for cross-border business such as quick turnaround times and low transportation costs (Power 2010, Sargent and Matthews 2009).

Many Mexican nationals have also found work and entrepreneurship opportunities in the US. From 1970 to 2008 the number of Mexican immigrants in the US increased 17-fold to almost 13 million people. Fully a third of all immigrants in the US are from Mexico. While this percentage is large, two other nations each accounted for 30 percent of the US immigrant population in the 1800s – Ireland and Germany. Mexican immigrants are the largest share of immigrant business owners in the US, accounting for almost 3.5 percent of all businesses in the US and producing 1 percent of all business income in the country (Hull 2010).

Many Mexican immigrants who start entrepreneurial ventures in the US do so because they face barriers to mainstream employment in the US. Weak English language skills, cultural issues including discrimination, and immigration status (about half of Mexican immigrants in the US are unauthorized) are all obstacles to employment. Other reasons why Mexican immigrants in the US open entrepreneurial ventures include family flexibility and better opportunities than salaried work given their relatively low education and the low wages available to them (DelCampo and Thomas 2009). With entrepreneurs who stay in Mexico, interpersonal networks are an important resource and opportunity. Many Mexicans open businesses especially designed to serve the needs of other Latinos (DelCampo and Thomas 2009). And Mexican women in the US are effective entrepreneurs, with almost half a million Latina-owned businesses in 2002 generating almost US$30 billion in receipts and employing some 200,000 workers (Robles 2004).

One study of entrepreneurship on the US–Mexico border found that Mexican immigrants in the border states were more likely to be self-employed. All other factors being equal, living in a border state accounted for 30 percent more self-employment among Mexican immigrants than in non-border states. Being on the physical border between inexpensive production and copious consumption provides unique trade opportunities for entrepreneurs. Some immigrants in the US moved specifically to take advantage of these opportunities. Mexican entrepreneurs in the US have an advantage in serving Mexican consumers living in the US. They know their customers (Mora and Dávila 2006).

Many characteristics of Mexican entrepreneurs in Mexico describe Mexican immigrant entrepreneurs in the US. Both groups involve their families in the business, both to run the operation and for financing. In the US 75 percent of entrepreneurs from Mexico have family help to run their businesses and 44 percent borrow their start-up capital from family or friends or start with nothing more than personal savings. They also get their business advice and training from personal networks (Robles 2004).

What is different for Mexican entrepreneurs operating in the US is that their "cultural capital" provides advantages in the US. Being bilingual and bicultural allows them to do business with the large population of immigrants from Mexico and other Spanish-speaking countries (Robles 2004). Many Mexican entrepreneurs in the US are entrepreneurs of necessity who market their own labor or run small businesses with no employees. Many work in construction, including an increasing number of Mexican women (Robles 2004). But many Mexican entrepreneurs run professional services that target compatriots, for example legal services, real estate, insurance, PR, and marketing. Entertainment, restaurant, and retail businesses are also run by Mexican entrepreneurs for Mexican immigrants.

However, Mexican entrepreneurs in the US do not earn as much as their counterparts who are non-immigrants (Mora and Dávila 2006). In the US Mexican female entrepreneurs tend to be older, less educated, and have more dependent children than black and non-Hispanic white entrepreneurs (Robles 2004). Relative to non-Hispanic white and Asian entrepreneurs, more Mexican entrepreneurs in the US are engaged in manual labor such as security, crafts, and service rather than non-manual secretarial, professional, or management areas (Spener and Bean 1999).

Remittances sent to Mexico from workers in the US account for about 4 percent of Mexico's GDP and totaled about US$26 billion in 2007. In 2010 Mexico received the largest amount of remittances in Latin America and the third largest in the world, after India and China (http://www.cbsnews. com/stories/2010/01/27/world/main6148649.shtml). These "migradollars" impact Mexican entrepreneurship in two significant ways. Richer communities can afford to buy more products and services. More money flowing into the country from any source increases the market for entrepreneurs. The other way remittances affect entrepreneurship in Mexico is that they provide start-up capital for new businesses in Mexico. In fact, the absence of a male head of household, who is working in the US, may be offset by the influx of cash he sends back to the family. In Mexico, the amount of money provided to a family in remittances is strongly correlated to the likelihood of creating a new business enterprise (Massey and Parrado 1998).

Of course the US is not the only international destination for Mexican entrepreneurs. Proximity and the Spanish language are advantages Mexican entrepreneurs have leveraged throughout Central America, the Caribbean, and in South America. While the US embargoed businesses from operating in Cuba, some Mexican entrepreneurs saw this as an opportunity to enter before larger companies could compete (Sagebien and Tsoutouras 2000). Carlos Roberto opened the first international El Fogoncito restaurant, not in the US, but in Managua, Nicaragua (Saliba and Nava 2004).

Monterrey case

Mexico's wealthiest state is Nuevo Leon, where large family-owned conglomerates built great wealth by integrating production and supply in industries such as construction (cement and steel) and beer (glass bottles and distribution networks). They also formed universities to further provide for their needs in skilled human capital, principally engineering and management. Entrepreneurial innovation maintained the profitability of the large conglomerates and their community for many years. But a new model of economic development is shifting the focus from manufacturing to technology. Small-businesses and technological entrepreneurs are being vigorously supported by government policies and investments (Echeverri-Carroll 2008).

Three sources of support are driving entrepreneurial activities in the high-tech industry in Monterrey. The large traditional firms have served as a training ground for innovators who "graduate" to starting their own companies, often as suppliers to the firms that gave them their start in business. The local universities are supporting high-tech entrepreneurship through degrees, executive education, and incubators. And centers for research and development have been established by the federal government as well as the universities. The secretary of the economy created a program to help Mexican entrepreneurs by providing on-the-ground support in important markets like the US, Canada, and Spain. The city of San Antonio and several NGOs have also developed an incubator program primarily to assist Mexican entrepreneurs successfully enter the US market (freetradealliance. org/ibdcprogram).

One success case of the intensive incubator–education–assistance model started as a student project at the Instituto Tecnológico de Estudios Superiores de Monterrey where they focus on high-technology and social responsibility. A team of business and engineering students developed a low-cost instrument (about US$1) that allows women to screen themselves for cervical cancer. It is moving from classroom to incubator to production supported at every stage by the new Monterrey infrastructure for high-tech entrepreneurship (personal conversation with Jaime Alonso Gomez, Dean of EGADE, 2006).

Another successful case came from the San Antonio incubator, the International Business Development Center (IBDC). The Carlos Costa company wanted to capture a piece of the huge US market for promotional items and corporate apparel. The business started with textile manufacturing in Mexico for the Mexican market. Taking advantage of the assistance provided in the city of San Antonio, one of the company's executives moved to the US and enrolled in the IBDC program. He attended classes about doing business in the US and used consulting services about how to adapt his product and marketing for the US market. He had an office space with secretarial support and a network of colleagues in the US. In a personal conversation, he remarked that developing a successful US operation was more difficult than he had expected, even with the extensive support of the IBDC. And while they have not yet replicated their success in Mexico, the US business is on its way to profitability after three years (personal conversation with the US director 2009).

The story of Ricardo Salinas and Grupo Azteca

"There is an expression that states 'all progress in the world is made by the dissatisfied. The secret is to always be dissatisfied.'" – Ricardo Salinas.

With the abundant flow of his entrepreneurial spirit, Ricardo Salinas nurtured a modest family business into a remarkable wellspring of successful ventures. Grupo Salinas employs more than 50,000 people in ten countries across nine independent business units. TV Azteca is the second-largest producer of Spanish-language television programming in the world. Half of all motorcycles sold in Mexico are Italika. Salinas supports a food bank through Fundación Azteca that provides daily meals for 98,000 people in 20 states. He set a world record by opening 800 bank branches in a single day. When he opened a music label, it took just 15 days for the pop sound to turn to a gold record. Annual sales across Grupo Salinas affiliates are equivalent to 1 percent of Mexico's GDP. The story of Ricardo Salinas is the story of a tireless innovator who leveraged every advantage possible from his Mexican roots with all its tangle of challenges and opportunities.

The family began its entrepreneurial investments in 1906 when Ricardo Salinas's grandfather and a partner opened a furniture-making business called Salinas y Rocha. Faded newsprint clippings from the era advertise a variety of products and marketing promotions. The store sold "American style" metal beds. And consumers could buy ovens with payment options. When Ricardo Salinas's father took charge of the company, he started door-to-door sales and offered consumer credit. Following the generation before him, financing purchases and door-to-door service would be pivotal strategies in Ricardo Salinas's success.

Salinas was groomed for business from an early age, but not necessarily with any intent on the part of his family. He simply and eagerly absorbed what was in the air around him. This is common for many entrepreneurs in Mexico. Their friends and family are both role models and mentors as they open and establish new business ventures. Ricardo Salinas has said, "In the house we always talked about business; with my father and my grandfather this was the subject. If my grandfather invites us to eat in his home, the conversation is about business; in my house too we speak of business" (Ricardosalinas.com). In fact, the entrepreneurial spirit is woven through generations and across branches of the Salinas family. Ricardo still considers his father to be a mentor in business. There is an uncle who also advises him. And Ricardo's three oldest children have all made innovative contributions through their careers. One launched his own advertising/marketing firm. Another broke away from the ordinary with innovative television productions. And the third is a business entrepreneur who has opened his own retail ventures.

It would not be fair to compare the Salinas family with the majority of Mexico's entrepreneurs who work for themselves primarily as a means of meeting their basic needs. At the time Ricardo Salinas was named CEO of Elektra, the retail chain had 60 stores. And his father took out a bank loan in 1963. Access to credit is one of the greatest challenges that keeps most Mexican entrepreneurs from growing in scale beyond employing the imme-diate family. But typical of the family conglomerates that are the powerful minority of Mexico's entrepreneurs, Ricardo Salinas found opportunity in the privatization of Mexico's state industries. For this group of elite entrepre-neurs, the combination of family wealth, relationship networks, and gov-ernment policies provided unique opportunities. While there is little doubt that the distribution of wealth in Mexico is extremely unequal, it must also be acknowledged that the large conglomerates have provided a huge number of jobs and fueled economic growth for the country. Whatever advantages brought them by the initial opportunities, Mexico's wealthy *empresarios* have launched innovations in products and operations that have made Mexico's economy stronger.

TV Azteca is one of these stories that combines privilege and challenge. Ricardo Salinas led a group of investors who bid US$623 million for Instituto Mexicana de la Televisión when it was sold by the Mexican government in 1993. At the time Imevisión, as the network of stations was known, had only 10 percent of the market. The privately owned Televisa had a near monopoly with 90 percent of the Mexican market. And while the govern-ment's decision to privatize opened the door for Salinas and his partners, federal regulatory policies did nothing to help them compete. The weak regulatory and legal environment that is a hindrance to many entrepreneurs today was a problem for TV Azteca when it was small and struggling.

It is not uncommon in Mexico for dominant market leaders to use intimi-dation tactics, to offer bribes, or to evade complying with certain regula-tions. There is a correlation between business registration and the strength of the legal infrastructure among Mexican states. For start-ups and new entrants this is a serious barrier to growth.

Ricardo Salinas decided he had to compete by being better. He invested in the quality of his television programs. He opened a production business to produce high-quality programs with the stories and look that Mexican audiences would appreciate. *Nada Personal* was the first *telenovela* produced by the studio, soon followed by the breakaway hit *Mirada de Mujer* that has also been broadcast in Afghanistan, Israel, Eastern Europe, and India. Salinas made bold programming decisions such as launching his own news show *Noticiarias Hechos* and purchasing exclusive broadcast rights in Mexico for both the US National Basketball Association and Walt Disney. But perhaps his most daring innovation was to challenge the way television advertising was sold in Mexico. Confident of the superior quality of TV Azteca programming, Salinas charged his advertisers based on the actual number of viewers. Other television stations charged for the amount of time regardless of how many viewers were actually watching.

The success of TV Azteca is now media legend. The news program *Hechos* airs four times a day on weekdays, once at the weekend, and has several local versions. TV Azteca *telenovelas* have been shown in more than 100 countries. The broadcaster has expanded into Central America, and the US unit, AztecaAmerica, reaches 90 percent of Spanish-speaking households in the US. TV Azteca holdings now include a soccer team as well – Monarcas Morelia.

Another example of the privilege and challenge Ricardo Salinas faced doing business in Mexico's tumultuous economy is the near bankruptcy of the Elektra Group. Although he inherited responsibility for 60 stores, when the peso had devalued drastically, the entire business operation was put at risk, and business practices were altered in order to survive. For example, the company stopped offering credit for consumer purchases. Ricardo Salinas began the corporate recovery by focusing on the core business – providing access for lower- and middle-income consumers. The product lines, the financing, the service were all focused on the mass consumer market of Mexico. And Salinas innovated with more ways to serve these core consumers. He became the Western Union representative for wire transfers, which could be handled in Elektra stores. Today they handle 12 percent of all US–Mexico remittances. He bought an online retailer and applied the same successful formula of products and financing. Today TiendaElektra.com has more than 4 million visitors and sells 60 percent more than its nearest competitor. Grupo Elektra has expanded to more than 2000 sales locations in Mexico, Central America, and South America. Ricardo Salinas has accomplished this phenomenal success in just 25 years since taking over as the head of Grupo Elektra.

No one navigates this type of meteoric rise without attracting scandal and controversy. His was the first foreign company to be sued by the US Securities and Exchange Commission under the Sarbanes–Oxley Act. He settled in 2006 for US\$7.5 million without admitting guilt (Noon 2006). The business model of providing credit for the poor has also aroused severe criticism. The interest rates charged for purchases in Elektra stores or for loans made by Banco Azteca are very high by the standards of banks that serve wealthier populations. With little regulation or oversight, for-profit microlenders in Mexico provide loans that average US$257 with interest rates that range from 50 to 120 percent. The worldwide average for not-for-profit microlending is 31 percent (Bruhn and Love 2009, Epstein and Smith 2007).

Defenders of for-profit microlending point to the awful alternatives available to the poor. With no credit history, little collateral, and no proof of income, the poor are turned away from traditional lending institutions. Pawnshops and loan sharks charge up to 300 percent interest. And the rates charged by for-profit microlenders are fully legal in Mexico. In fact, there is no legal limit on interest rates in Mexico. One bank executive explained the market forces at work in the system, "We lend them as much as they can borrow, and they can borrow as much as they can pay" (Epstein and Smith 2007). Indeed the line between business and charity, profit and service is not entirely clear in the Mexican context where the government may not be up to the tremendous challenges of providing for the basic needs of its poor through social services or of protecting their rights through legislation and enforcement.

ASMAZ is an association founded by Ricardo Salinas to support entrepreneurs. The association provides three services to its members: financing, procurement of equipment and supplies, and business development services such as training courses and legal, financial, and accounting advice. The ASMAZ website states:

> The secret of success is to do what you love and love what you do. And if you decide to be an entrepreneur or if you already are, you should have vision, dedication, and a great capacity to reinvent yourself and your company. And most important, you should have the capacity to face and manage enormous risk, risk that can challenge your own well-being. (http://www.empresarioazteca.org/asmaz/principal/index.htmb)

ASMAZ and the Mexican Secretary of the Economy have produced a DVD called *My Own Business* to inform and provide step-by-step guidance about how to open a business. While many resources of the website are available free of charge, there are some services available only to members. Membership costs US$259 a year or is free for those who take out a loan. ASMAZ has about 100,000 members to date.

Ricardo Salinas speaks often about the problems of the Mexican government and economy. Serving the poor with his business, he also serves them with his charities. The Azteca Foundation raises US$10–20 million each year for designated charities. Plantel Azteca is a middle school for poor students with strong academic records. The program has provided almost 27,000 scholarships, and the school has graduated more than 6000 students. Fomento Cultural Grupo Salinas is dedicated to instilling pride in Mexico's rich artistic heritage. TV Azteca airs campaigns for social causes and several have won national recognition such as the prize awarded by the United Nations for the campaign "Live Without Drugs." Ricardo Salinas and the charitable organizations affiliated with Grupo Salinas are dedicated to the people of Mexico and to improving health, education, the environment, and to promoting culture.

Ricardo Salinas began 25 years ago with a family business of modest success and now heads one of the most successful business groups in the world. His success comes from his personal entrepreneurial spirit – his drive to learn and to overcome obstacles, to challenge the status quo and to improve meticulously, his balance of vision and attention to detail. And he has passed on these energies to his companies. Each unit is run independently and each employee is challenged to contribute. Innovation, transparency, and accountability are core values throughout Grupo Salinas. What he began in Mexico now extends throughout the Americas with an impact that reaches around the globe. Though his talents and drive would have made him a successful entrepreneur in any country, Ricardo Salinas was shaped by the challenges and opportunities of Mexico and he has in turn influenced the future of his country.

Conclusion

Mexico provides both opportunities and challenges for entrepreneurs. Periods of instability in politics, economics, and security are part of Mexico's business landscape. Government policies provide opportunities for those who can take advantage of them but may not adequately support and protect new ventures. The landscape is uneven, with oases of wealth, seas of poverty, strong physical infrastructure marooned in crumbling relics, and a regulatory environment that simply works better in some places than in others. Yet the nation fosters entrepreneurs in all of these conditions. Wealthy *empresarios* like Ricardo Salinas are drivers of innovation and wealth and jobs. Entrepreneurs of necessity find ways to provide for themselves and their immediate families. Both groups rely on networks of friends and family. The resources for financing and business development are available to entrepreneurs through formal or informal channels. Improvements to the business environment would undoubtedly improve the economic impact of small entrepreneurs, allowing them to formalize their businesses and grow enough to provide jobs and revenue. Mexico is breaking away from dependence on the US market and entrepreneurs are reaching throughout the Latin America for new opportunities. Because that is a strength of Mexican entrepreneurs – they seize every opportunity with creativity and passion.

References

Bolaños, R. 2006. "Impacto del Modelo a Imitar en la Intención de Crear una Empresa." *Estudios de Economía Aplicada* 24, no. 2: 491–508.

Bruhn, M. and I. Love. 2009. "The Economic Impact of Banking the Unbanked: Evidence from Mexico." World Bank Policy Research Working Paper 4981.

CBS News. "Mexico Sees Record Drop in Remittances." January 27 www.cbsnews.com/stories/2010/01/27/world/main6148649.shtml.

Cunningham, W. V. and W. F. Maloney. 2001. "Heterogeneity among Mexico's Microenterprises: an Application of Factor and Cluster Analysis." *Economic Development & Cultural Change* 50, no. 1: 131–56.

DelCampo, R. G., and D. E. Thomas. 2009. "Mexican–American Entrepreneurship and Social Networks: a Review and Vision for the Future." *International Journal of Business Research* 9, no. 6: 120–7.

Doing Business in Mexico 2011. http://www.doingbusiness.org/data/explore economies/mexico.

Echeverri-Carroll, R. 2008. "The Growth of Knowledge-Based Small Firm in Monterrey, Mexico." *Texas Business Review* February: 2–6.

Economist, The. 2010. "Pink Cabs Rev Up." August 28: 30.

Engardio, P. 2009. "A Mexican Technology Park in Monterrey." *Business Week Online,* June: 16. http://www.businessweek.com/innovate/content/jun2009/id2009061_243746.htm.

Epstein, K. and G. Smith. 2007. "The Ugly Side of Microlending: How Big Mexican Banks Profit as Many Poor Borrowers Get Trapped in a Maze of Debt." *Business Week* 13 December. http://www.businessweek.com/magazine/content/07_52/b4064038915009.htm.

Fajnzylber, P., W. Maloney, and G. M. Rojas. 2006. "Microenterprise Dynamics in Developing Countries: How Similar Are They to Those in the Industrialized World? Evidence from Mexico." *The World Bank Economic Review* 20, no. 3: 389–419.

Fajnzylber, P., W. F. Maloney, and G. V. Montes-Rojas. 2009. "Releasing Constraints to Growth or Pushing on a String? Policies and Performance of Mexican Micro-Firms." *Journal of Development Studies* 45, no. 7: 1027–47.

Fleck, S. and C. Sorrentino. 1994. "Employment and Unemployment in Mexico's Labor Force." *Monthly Labor Review* 117, no. 11: 3–32.

Global Entrepreneurship Monitor. 2010. Global Report. http://www.gemconsortium.org.

Gómez-Galvarriato, A. 2008. "Networks and Entrepreneurship: the Modernization of the Textile Business in Porfirian Mexico." *Business History Review* 82: 475–502.

Hull, G. S. 2010. "Immigrant Entrepreneurs: the Face of the New Nashville." *iBusiness* 2: 1–18.

Instituto Nacional de Estadística y Geografía. Encuesta Nacional de Educación, Capacitación y Empleo. 1993. http://www.inegi.org.mx.

Instituto de Innovación y Transferencia de Tecnología. "Acerca del PIIT." http://www.piit.com.mx/parque/default.aspx.

Jones, V. (unpublished manuscript). "An Exploratory Study of Micro-Stores in Mexico City."

Laeven, L. and C. Woodruff. 2007. "The Quality of the Legal System, Firm Ownership, and Firm Size." *The Review of Economics and Statistics* 89, no. 4: 601–14.

Macias, J. B. and G. Cazzavillan. 2010. "Modeling the Informal Economy in Mexico: a Structural Equation Approach." *The Journal of Developing Areas* 44, no. 1: 345–66.

McKenzie, D. J. and C. Woodruff. 2006. "Do Entry Costs Provide an Empirical Basis for Poverty Traps? Evidence from Mexican Microenterprises." *Economic Development and Cultural Change* 55, no. 1: 3–42.

Maloney, W. F. 1999. "Does Informality Imply Segmentation in Urban Labor Markets? Evidence from Sectoral Transitions in Mexico." *World Bank Economic Review* 13: 275–302.

Maloney, W. F. 2002. "Distortion and Protection in the Mexican Labor Market." Center for Research on Economic Development and Policy Reform Working Paper no. 138.

Mares, A. I. and L. Gómez. 2006. "Hacia un dianóstico latinoamericano para la creación de empresas con la aplicación del Modelo GEM 2006." *Pensamiento y Gestión* 22: 85–142.

Marino, L., K. Strandholm, H. K. Steensma, and K. M. Weaver. 2002. "The Moderating Effect of National Culture on the Relationship between Entrepreneurial Orientation and Strategic Alliance Portfolio Extensiveness." *Entrepreneurship Theory and Practice* Summer: 145–60.

Martinez, S. M. and P. W. Dorfman. 1998. "The Mexican Entrepreneur: an Ethnographic Study of the Mexican Empresario." *International Studies of Management & Organization* 28, no. 2: 97–123.

Massey, D. S. and E. A. Parrado. 1998. "International Migration and Business Formation in Mexico." *Social Science Quarterly* 79, no. 1: 1–20.

Mora, M. T. and A. Dávila. 2006. "Mexican Immigrant Self-Employment along the U.S.–Mexico Border: an Analysis of 2000 Census Data." *Social Science Quarterly* 87, no. 1: 91–109.

MSNBC 2009. "Mexico's Pink Taxis Cater to Fed-Up Females." October 19. http://www.msnbc.msn.com/id/33385984/ns/world_news-americas.

Mungaray, A., M. Ramirez-Urquidy, M. Texis, D. Ledezma, and N. Ramirez. 2007. "Promoting Learning in Small Entrepreneurs and Higher Education Students through Service Learning Programs." *International Journal of Business Research* 7, no. 3: 10–13.

Musacchio, A. and I. Read. 2007. "Bankers, Industrialists, and their Cliques: Elite Networks in Mexico and Brazil during Early Industrialization. *Enterprise and Society* 8: 842–80.

Noon, C. 2006. "Mexico's Salinas Settles Sarbanes–Oxley Suit." Forbes.com. September 15. http://www.forbes.com/2006/09/15/salinas-azteca-sec-face-cx_cn_0915autofacescan03.html.

Noticiarias. 2009. "En Puebla ponon en marcha el Pink Taxi, exclusive para mujeres." Miércoles, 07 de Octubre. http://www.noticanarias.com/mexico/en-puebla-ponen-en-marcha-el-pink-taxi-exclusivo-para-mujeres-7874.

OECD Employment Outlook 2010. http://www.oecd.org/dataoecd/13/54/45604604.pdf.

Power, C. 2010. "U.S. Companies are Still Rushing to Juárez." *BusinessWeek* June 14: 1.

Robles, B. J. 2004. "Emergent Entrepreneurs: Latina-Owned Businesses in the Borderlands." *Texas Business Review* October: 1–2.

Sagebien, J. and D. Tsoutouras. 2000. "Solidarity, Entrepreneurship and Hard Times: the Political Economy of Mexico–Cuba Commercial Relations at the End of the Twentieth Century." *Latin American Business Review* 1, no. 4: 85–99.

Salgado-Banda, H. 2007. "Entrepreneurship and Economic Growth: an Empirical Analysis." *Journal of Developmental Entrepreneurship* 12, no. 1: 3–29.

Saliba, A. and A. Nava. 2004. "15 minutes with ... Carlos Roberts." *Business Mexico* March: 28–30.

Salinas, Ricardo. http://www.ricardosalinas.com/.

Sargent, J. and L. Matthews. 2009. "China versus Mexico in the Global EPZ Industry: Maquiladoras, FDI Quality, and Plant Mortality." *World Development* 37, no. 6: 1069–1082.

Spener, D. and F. D. Bean. 1999. "Self-Employment Concentration and Earnings among Mexican Immigrants in the U.S." *Social Forces* 77, no. 3: 1021–47.

Vargas-Hernández, J. and M. R. Noruzi. 2010. "A Chronological Study of Entrepreneurship and Ownership in Mexican Governance since 1982." *Journal of Politics and Law* 3, no. 2: 239–54.

Villarreal, M. A. 2010. *Mexico's Free Trade Agreements.* Congressional Research Service Report R40784: 1–19.

West, G. P. III, C.E. Bamford, and J.W. Marsden. 2008. "Contrasting Entrepreneurial Economic Development in Emerging Latin America Economies: Applications and Extensions of Resource-Based Theory." *Entrepreneurship Theory and Practice* January: 15–36.

Young, E. C. and H. P. Welsch. 1993. "Major Elements in Entrepreneurial Development in Central Mexico." *Journal of Small Business Management* October: 80–5.

8

The Emergence of an Entrepreneurial World: Peru

Keiko M. Nakamatsu, Oswaldo Morales-Tristán, and Jaime Serida-Nishimura
Universidad ESAN, Lima, Peru

Forces and factors shaping an entrepreneurial world

Economic outlook

After the internal economic crisis at the end of the 1980s, which spurred a drastic policy of neo-liberal openness and fiscal account correction in the 1990s, Peru took off economically. This change, which was particularly evident in the last decade, was attributable to the consistent application of economic measures to organize internal accounts and global economic expansion. As shown in Figure 8.1, Peru grew 6.8 percent per annum on average and in 2008, led growth in the region (International Monetary Fund [IMF] 2009).[1]

Nevertheless, in 2009 Peru faced the worst international economic crisis of the last 80 years. As a result, the country experienced an abrupt deceleration in economic growth, which went from 9.8 percent in 2008 to 1 percent in 2009. The impact of the crisis stemmed primarily from the decline in external demand for raw materials (prices and quantities) and metals in particular. This was further exacerbated by decreasing demand for nontraditional products. Additionally, Peruvians living abroad sent fewer remittances and direct foreign investment declined (Ministerio de Economía y Finanzas [MEF] 2010b: 4).

Fortunately, prudent economic policies during economic expansion ensured that Peru's fiscal platform was solid with low debt levels and strong external asset positions (net international reserves), which helped the country weather the impact of the economic crisis better than its Latin American neighbors. As such, GDP decelerated one quarter later. Recovery has been vigorous and Peru is one of the few countries in the world that has been able to maintain positive growth rates (MEF 2010b: 11, 12, and 103) (*see* Figure 8.2). In 2009, as the world was submerged in the worst of the crisis, Peru was awarded its third investment grade (Moody's Investor) after having received this distinction from Standard & Poor's and Fitch Ratings in 2008 (MEF 2008 and 2009, "Perú obtiene otro reconocimiento" 2008).

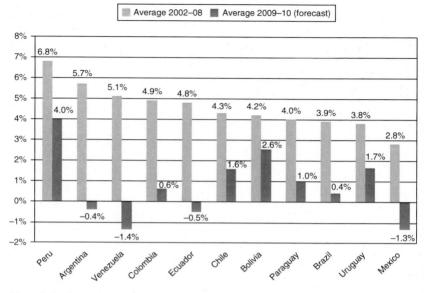

Figure 8.1 Gross domestic product (annual percentage variation) in the region
Source: IMF (2009).

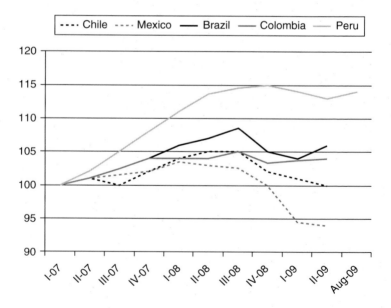

Figure 8.2 Deseasonalized GDP (IT 2007 = 100)
Source: IMF (2009).

To avoid a scenario of hyperinflation like that seen in the 1980s, the Central Reserve Bank of Peru (BCRP) opted to control inflation, proposing a target range between 1 and 3 percent (Armas and Grippa 2006). This has helped the country to maintain its average inflation rate among the three lowest in Latin America (*see* Figure 8.3).

The BCRP has maintained a flexible exchange rate policy but has intervened to head off significant and abrupt depreciations. Given the high level of loan dollarization in Peru (around 58 percent) – which generates currency mismatches – it is important to mitigate any abrupt and significant currency movement (Choy and Ayllón 2007). The potential for high volatility in exchange rates is less significant than in past crises, and in the last few years the country has accumulated a large amount of international reserves while reducing the number of loans denominated in dollars in the banks' portfolios.

The macroeconomic fundamentals, along with prudent regulation and risk oversight, have helped financial companies adequately manage the external negativity produced by the international crisis. As shown in Figure 8.4, although some of the financial indicators and banking businesses reported a slight deterioration as a result of the international crisis, they are recovering to adequate levels and further strengthening is expected in the coming years (Superintendencia de Banca, Seguros y AFP [SBS] 2010). In this scenario, many financial companies have shown interest in entering the Peruvian market or expanding existing operations.

According to World Bank (WB) data, there is a large margin for loan growth in Peru in terms of percentage of GDP in comparison to other countries in the region (*see* Figure 8.5).

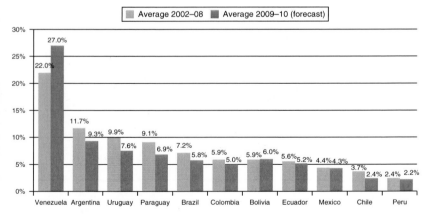

Figure 8.3 Inflation in countries in the region (annual % variation)
Source: IMF (2009).

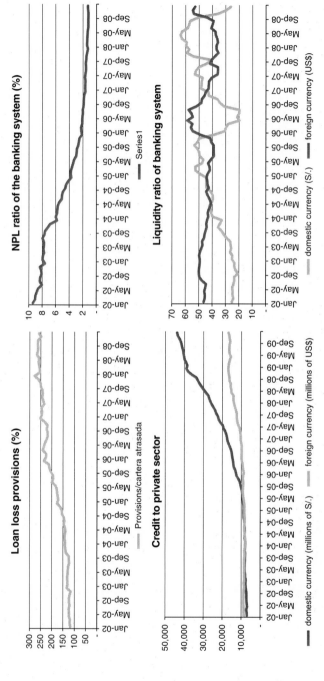

Figure 8.4 Peruvian financial system, liquidity indicators
Source: SBS (2010).

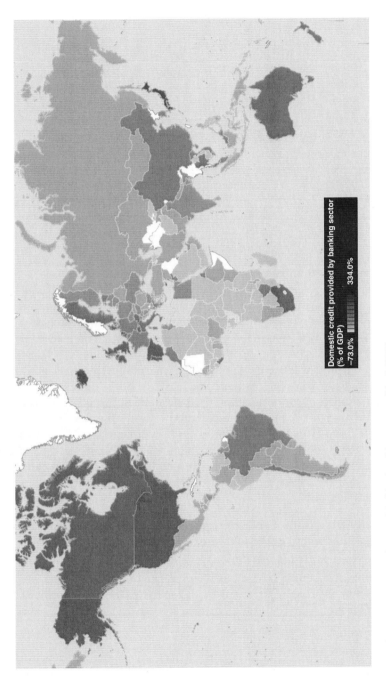

Figure 8.5 Domestic credit provided by banking sector (% of GDP)
Source: World Bank, World Development Indicators (2005–9).

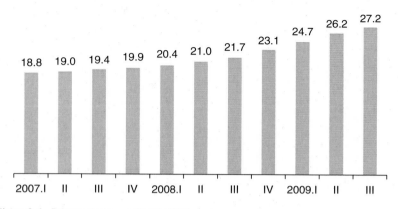

Figure 8.6   Private sector credit (% GDP)
Source: BCRP (2009).

Proof of this sector's potential can be found in the fact that loans to the private sector reported annual growth of 16 percent in June 2010 and 9.4 percent a year in the first half of 2010 after having fallen to the lowest rate recorded in five years at the end of 2009 (MEF 2010a: 5). According to BCRP (2009), private sector credit had an upward trend and reached 27.2 percent of GDP in the third quarter of 2009 (*see* Figure 8.6), showing that the economy is recovering and that Peru did not suffer restrictive loans even in its most acute financial international crisis.

In the context of the international financial crisis, the BCRP prioritized its efforts to provide liquidity to the domestic financial system in order to prevent a credit crunch in the country, and encouraged increased funding for long term from abroad. In this regard, private sector credit grew more in Peru during the first half of the year in 2010–11 compared to other countries in the region. Peru was the most dynamic country in Latin American credit after the crisis.

Economic Stimulus Plan (PEE)

Similar to other countries, the government implemented an Economic Stimulus Plan (PEE) in January 2009 (Carranza 2009b) to absorb the effects of external shock, minimize the impact on well-being, and protect the most vulnerable population by increasing social spending. The primary objectives of the PEE were:

– Convergence to a long-term growth rate.
– Maintain inflation within the Central Bank's target range and ensure that external accounts are sustainable.

– Preserve job creation through public investment (approximately 30 percent of job generation in 2009 had to be produced by the plan). Additionally, more than half of the spending is directed at public investment in infrastructure (*see* Figure 8.7) and of this amount, more than half is concentrated on the Southern Inter-Ocean Highway, road maintenance, construction, education, infrastructure maintenance, the Water for Everyone Program, and family housing bonuses.

In summary, in macroeconomic terms, Peru is situated in a privileged position on the international scene and is also one of Latin America's economic growth leaders. Some analysts (Santa María 2010) believe that four percent growth in 2010 is already assured. The possibility exists that growth may be even higher due to global economic growth and the results of the Economic Stimulus Program, which will be observable throughout the year. For the first semester of 2010, growth in GDP was 8.2 percent and projections for annual growth currently exceed the 5 percent initially forecast (MEF 2010b: 19).

The Business Confidence Index (BCRP 2010a) went from 32 points in December 2008 to 71 points in July 2010. A survey conducted with a group

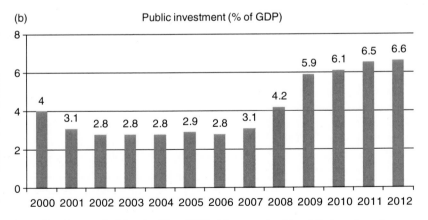

(a)

Concept	%	% of GDP
1. Impulse to economic activity	15.1	0.3
2. Infrastructure investment	65.2	2.2
3. Social protection	14.9	0.6
4. Other	4.9	0.5
Total PEE	100	3.6

(b) Public investment (% of GDP)

Figure 8.7 Economic Stimulus Plan (PEE): (a) concepts; (b) public investment
Sources: (a) Carranza (2009b); (b) MEF (2010c).

(a)
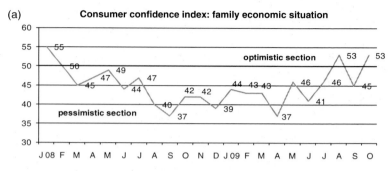

(b)

(c)

GDP growth forecast

	2009		2010	
Date of survey:	Sep-09	Nov-09	Sep-09	Nov-09
Economic analysts	1.8	1.0	4.0	4.0
Non-financial companies	2.5	1.5	4.0	4.0
Financial system	2.0	1.1	4.3	4.0

Figure 8.8   (a) The consumer confidence index, (b) business confidence index, and (c) expectations for GDP growth
Sources: (a) Apoyo Consultoría (2010a); (b) BCRP (2010a); (c) BCRP (2010a).

of businessmen in June indicated that 55 percent planned to accelerate their investment projects compared to 9 percent in 2009 (Apoyo Consultoría 2010b). The consumer confidence index returned to optimistic levels (Apoyo Consultoría 2010a) (*see* Figure 8.8).

Political framework

Peru's history has been marked by political instability and movements led by military and civil caudillos. After an extensive bout with terrorism, Peru has reached a milestone of 15 years of economic stability. Nevertheless, economic growth does not necessarily go hand in hand with political and legal stability. According to the WGI Project (Kaufmann et al. 2010) conducted in 215 countries, Peru's governability indicators fall below 50 percent, with the exception of regulatory quality (*see* Figure 8.9).

With regard to the regulatory quality to promote investment, the Peruvian government has made efforts to improve the business climate by improving the country's competitiveness. The goal is to go from position 62 in *Doing Business 2009* (WB 2008) to number 25 in *Doing Business 2012*.

The Constitution of Peru and the Legal Framework for Private Investment[2] allow the state to ensure that legal stability is in place for foreign investors and the companies they invest in. This is achieved through legal stability agreements (CEJ), which are governed by the Civil Code's guidelines for contracts. The state guarantees that the investor will experience stability with regard to labor contracts, export promotion, and the income tax regime. In general terms, CEJ guarantees:

- Equal treatment given that national legislation does not differentiate between national and foreign investors (equal terms for both).
- Stability of the income tax regime when the agreement is signed.
- Stability of the regime of free availability of currencies and remittance of earnings, dividends, and royalties in the case of foreign capital.

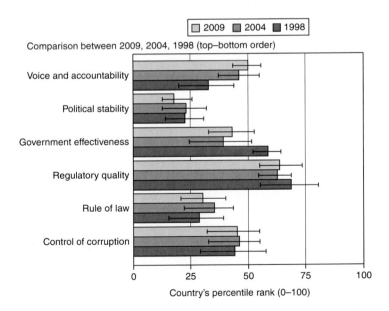

Figure 8.9 Governance indexes in Peru
Source: Kaufmann et al. (2010).

To consolidate the legal framework that guarantees and protects investment and generates an adequate climate for an increase in foreign investment in the country, Peru has been active in processes to negotiate bilateral, regional, and multilateral instruments to establish guarantees for treatment, protection, and access to conflict resolution mechanisms for investments (Projusticia 2007). In April 1991, the Peruvian Congress ratified the Constitutive Agreement with the Multilateral Investment Guarantee Agency (MIGA) of the World Bank.[3] To date, important investments have been made in the MIGA framework, particularly in the mining and financial sectors.

Peru has also ratified the Constitutive Agreement with a conflict resolution court used by the majority of countries for investment matters (International Center for the Settlement of Investment Disputes [ICSID] 2010).[4] The country has also adhered to the Agreement for Recognition and Execution of Foreign Arbitration Rulings (also called the New York Convention) (United Nations Commission on International Trade Law [UNCITRAL] 2010),[5] which means that differences that arise with the state in investment matters will be handled at this level.

At the bilateral level, Peru has signed 28 agreements for reciprocal investment promotion and protection with countries in the Pacific Basin, Europe, and Latin America and is currently conducting negotiations to sign these agreements with another 23 nations (Ministerio de Relaciones Exteriores del Perú [RREE] 2010a). For the same purpose, Peru signed the Financial Agreement for Investment Incentives in 1992. Under this agreement, the Overseas Private Investment Corporation (OPIC) has been issuing insurance, reinsurance, or guarantees to cover US investments in Peru (RREE 2010b).

As Moro has analyzed, another effort to generate a climate of credibility, transparency, predictability, and legal stability for national and foreign economic agents was consolidated with the implementation of sub-specialty Courts of Commercial Justice in 2005. These courts rule on matters related to partnerships, finance, and securities operations as well as those associated with mercantile and goods transportation contracts, among others. The results obtained from these courts and commercial arbitration instances in Peru constitute one of the state's primary transformations. This has consolidated legal security by cutting the time and money needed to conduct commercial processes (Moro 2010).

Concerns about economic and legal stability are no longer major obstacles for private investors. Private investors, however, are still worried about political stability – a recurring theme in pre-election periods. Thus, political and social investments are as important as public policies to attract investment. Given the political instability of years past, a deceleration in investment in a pre-electoral year is inevitable. This is particularly true in the case of private investors who have no experience in Peru. This group is particularly susceptible to the rhetoric of anti-system candidates, who are adverse to any kind of effort to modernize the country and create wealth in particular. Pre-electoral periods are also marked by an increase in social conflict due to the growing demands of different sectors of the population (*see* Figure 8.10), who have become increasingly aware that their rights have been affected or recognize an opportunity to make their complaints heard. Nevertheless, according to Althaus (2010), the current conflicts constitute a process to generate new social relations in Peru. These relations will be more modern and democratic given that they bring the population and companies together to learn from one another, listen, recognize their respective rights, and negotiate.

Another source of conflict, which also constitutes a source of concern for investors, is known as "obtaining social license" (Arienza and

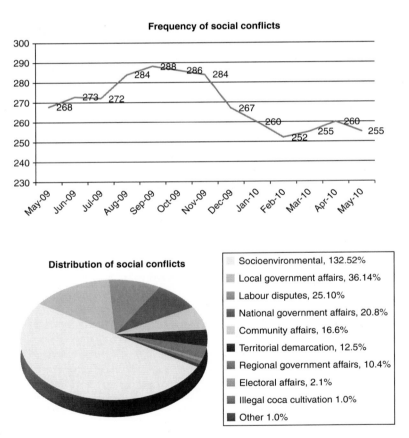

Figure 8.10 Frequency and distribution of social conflicts in Peru
Source: Defensoría del Pueblo (2010).

Mallmann 2010). This requires the government to take a much more active role (in coordination with investors) to adequately inform neighboring populations and communities about the projects planned for their areas. The objective is to avoid the social conflicts that have blocked investment projects.

Investors are also concerned that collective values have deteriorated as a result of corruption in public and private administration. Peru is currently ranked 75 out of 180 countries registered in the Corruption Perception Index 2009 of Transparency International (2009), which gathers survey participants' perceptions of the degree of corruption in the countries studied. Although Peru has risen three points in terms of corruption (in 2007 and 2008 it was ranked 72), a national study (Proética 2010) indicates that there has been an increase in the percentage of the population that perceives corruption as the country's main problem (*see* Figure 8.11); it is worrisome that 12 percent of the population approve of daily efforts to get ahead that

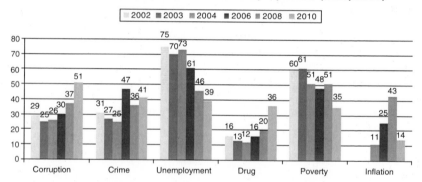

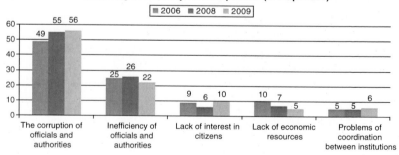

Figure 8.11   The problems that the country and Peruvian state face
Source: Proética (2010).

are actually acts of corruption in disguise. It is also a matter of concern that 91 percent of these acts are never denounced because people feel that complaints are futile and perceive that the state has little or no interest in combating this problem. Moreover, the population believes that 66 percent of businessmen and 77 percent of politicians are corrupt.

In its campaign against corruption (Olivera 2002), the state has implemented some measures, including presenting a National Anticorruption Plan and setting up a High Level Commission to Fight Corruption. The purpose was to coordinate the efforts of the three branches of state, like-minded institutions, businessmen, the press, and the National Agreement to prevent illegal acts in public entities. At a civil society level, some organizations have established strategies that focus on prevention and strengthening social institutions to develop local anticorruption initiatives.

Peru's commercial integration on the global scene

The country's central location on the western coast of South America has allowed it to project itself as a productive nucleus and hub for regional commercial activity. The port of Callao, which is currently being expanded, is one of the most dynamic ports on this coast. Twelve South American countries have joined forces in the Initiative to Integrate the Regional Infrastructure of South America (IIRSA),[6] whose purpose is to promote infrastructure development for transportation, energy, and communications within a regional focus. This will consolidate Peru's position as an efficient bridge between the markets of South America, Asia, and the United States. The Trade Promotion Agreement (TPA) with the United States, in effect since February 1, 2009 (Presidential Proclamation 8341, 2009),[7] consolidates the customs preferences that had been temporarily granted by the Andean Trade Promotion and Drug Eradication Act (ATPDEA). These preferences have been responsible for much of the dynamism in exports over the past few years and have consolidated the trade policy reforms that Peru implemented in the 1990s.

The TPA negotiation with the United States set new standards for the circulation of goods and services as well as investment protection, which were used as the basis for the process to negotiate FTAs with Singapore,[8] Canada,[9] China,[10] and the EFTA countries,[11] the Early Harvest Protocol with Thailand[12] and the FTAs with Chile.[13] Utilizing this same base, negotiations are underway to deepen the ACE with Mexico[14] and sign a FTA with Japan.[15] Peru has also concluded the Negotiation Agreement with the European Union (EU), which, through the General System of Andean Preferences, has eliminated customs tariffs for fishing, agricultural, and textile products (Perú y Unión Europea 2010).

At the Latin American level, Peru is a member of the free trade zone in the Andes, which includes Bolivia, Ecuador, and Colombia (Andean Community of Nations, CAN)[16] and covers a market of close to 100 million inhabitants. In the framework of the Latin American Association of Integration (ALADI), Peru has signed the Economic Complementation Agreement (ACE) with MERCOSUR.[17]

It is also important to point out that Peru has been a member of the Asian Pacific Cooperation Forum (APEC) since 1998, which comprises almost 50 percent of the world's population. This association will be a natural point of convergence between the industrialized countries of Asia and the emerging economies of Latin America.[18]

In summary, Peru's integration in global trade is the result of a clear openness policy (*see* Figure 8.12), which should allow the country, by 2012, to enter into trade agreements with countries that have 41 percent of the world's population and represent 69 percent of the world's product (MEF 2010b: 67).[19]

Commercial integration assures access to new markets and more possibilities for exports. The Agency for Promotion and Private Investment (Agencia de Promoción de la Inversión Privada 2010) points out that prior to the crisis, exports grew at an accelerated rate (annual average rate of 16.2 percent in 2000–9) to become a key variable in economic growth. In the first few months of 2010, this variable showed signs of recovery and reached 6.8 percent in February.

The same agency says that during 2009, 17 percent of Peruvian exports were shipped to the United States of America under the preferences established by the FTA. Other important markets are Asia and Europe, which received 27 and 31 percent of the country's exports respectively. In the case of Asia, exports to China, Japan, and South Korea were particularly significant. In Europe, the primary export destinations were Switzerland, Germany, Spain, and Italy. Within the South American bloc, Chile, Colombia, and Venezuela were the main destinations for Peruvian exports.

Telecommunications development

In Peru, the telecommunications sector is regulated by two institutions: (i) the Ministry of Transportation and Telecommunications (MTC), which is primarily in charge of developing policies and issuing licenses to operators; and (ii) the Supervisory Entity for Private Investment in Telecommunications (OSIPTEL), which has technical, economic, and financial autonomy, and is primarily in charge of regulating and supervising free competition in the sector.

As Bossio indicates, after the telecommunications companies were privatized in 1994, the Peruvian state guaranteed the company a five-year period during which market access to new competitors would be restricted for all services. This process was conducted parallel to basic telecommunications

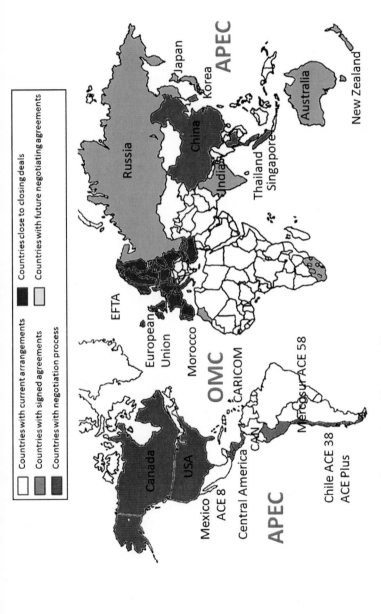

Legend:
- Countries with current arrangements
- Countries with signed agreements
- Countries with negotiation process
- Countries close to closing deals
- Countries with future negotiating agreements

Canada
USA
Mexico ACE 8
Central America
CARICOM
CAN
Chile ACE 38
ACE Plus
Mercosur ACE 58

EFTA
European Union
Morocco
Russia
Japan
Korea
China
India
Thailand
Singapore
Australia
New Zealand

APEC
OMC
APEC

Figure 8.12 Peru's commercial integration with the world
Source: Carranza (2010).

negotiations in the OMC, which were based on a reference document that favors openness and competition and which establishes criteria for new entrants' access to, and use of, telecommunications services. In 2007, various changes were produced in the regulatory framework to consolidate competition and expand telecommunications services in underserved areas. The Peruvian government added a new set of guidelines to (i) consolidate competition, (ii) reduce the infrastructure gap, and (iii) expand service to rural and low-income groups. As in the previous case, this situation occurred within the context of trade negotiations: Peru had just concluded negotiations for the Trade Promotion Agreement with the United States, whose telecommunications chapter is a GATS+ agreement given that it includes concepts such as numeric portability, resale, and co-location within the dominant operators' obligations. The policies introduced basically cover elements of rate policies, transparency, retail commercialization (resale), promoting formality, interconnection, spectrum administration, numerical portability, and universal service (Bossio 2008).

The most dynamic and competitive segments, such as long-distance carriers and cable providers, have had to invest less. In contrast, the services that require more investment in infrastructure (land lines, public lines, and mobile telephones) are concentrated in only a few operators. Recent data published by the National Institute of Statistics and Information (INEI 2010b) shows that Internet cafes continue to be the main point of access for more than 65 percent of the users at a national level, and more than 40 percent of Peruvian households own no technological devices beyond radio and television. Razo and Rojas (2007) contend that the changes introduced in the regulatory framework favor the development of convergent services, reduce the entry barriers, and facilitate the entry of new operators. According to them, whether new operators enter or not, the new framework creates more competition in the market, limiting the action of involved parties. In terms of demand, the guidelines give power to the consumer, allowing them to choose the company that provides their long-distance services and to change mobile providers while keeping the same number (as of 2010).

There is no doubt that the most obvious result of the aforementioned growth and the implementation of competition policies has been an expansion in mobile phone services (Gallardo et al. 2007). The results of the National Household Survey (INEI 2010a) confirm that mobile telephone coverage has grown considerably, going from 16.4 percent in 2004 to 67 percent in 2009, which represents more than 15 million mobile phones. Nevertheless, it is important to point out that having mobile phone equipment in rural areas does not mean that these areas have service coverage. In fact, individuals in these areas many only be able to use their phones when they are close to urban areas for commercial or personal reasons. The mobile phone network covered 1584 districts in June 2010, which indicates growth that is 3.5 times higher than that reported at the end of 2005. However, 13.4 percent of the country's districts do not have mobile telephone coverage. Growth in the public telephone segment appears to have stagnated, possibly due to informal alternatives that appeared in the country's main cities at telephone cafes and informal establishments that offered mobile telephone access. In 2008, OSIPTEL lowered the cost of calls from public telephones, which was followed by initiatives by providers to reverse this tendency.

In terms of broadband, March 2010 saw the creation of a Temporary Multi-Sector Commission in charge of developing a National Plan to Develop Broadband in Peru. This plan has ambitious goals prior to 2016, including 100 percent coverage for education and health institutions in the urban and rural ambit as well as 100 percent coverage for the main institutions in Peru's districts. The plan also contemplates increasing broadband connections to 4 million and high-speed connections to a half a million (Comisión Multisectorial Temporal encargada de elaborar el "Plan Nacional para el Desarrollo de la Banda Ancha en el Perú" 2010: 6–7).

Social growth in the country

In the Peruvian case, during 2003–9, there were significant changes in household income and the distribution of households. In this period, the national poverty level fell 17 percentage points, going from 52 to 34.8 percent (MEF 2010c). Likewise, according to a report of the United Nations and Presidency of the Council of Ministers of Peru (2009), extreme poverty fell from 24 percent of the population in 2002 to 12.6 percent in 2008.

With regard to income, per capita income has doubled in the last six years (*see* Figure 8.13). It has gone from 2200 dollars to 4600 dollars per capita (BCRP 2010b). This quantitative jump has had an important qualitative impact. The increase in income has allowed the population to improve their economic situation, which means they have more opportunities to do business and acquire a more varied gamut of products; consequently, this segment has the opportunity to rise from poverty to the middle class. The recent economic crisis showed the strength of this socio-economic segment, which reduced but did not withdraw its spending, maintaining internal consumption. According to the Peruvian Association of Market Research Companies (APEIM), the middle class in Lima increased two percentage points from 14.6 to 16.5 percent between 2003 and 2009 (APEIM 2008).

Nevertheless, social change is apparent in this segment. Prior to the 1990s, the traditional middle class defined itself by the type of work it did rather than its income. Typically, they had higher education and were on the payroll in private companies or worked in the state apparatus/public companies. In the 1990s, a new middle class emerged. This segment's

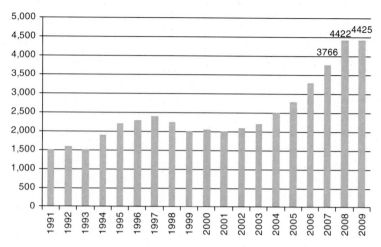

Figure 8.13   Evolution of per capita income in Peru, 1991–2009 (US$)
Source: BCRP (2010b).

income was the product of independent employment, business, or commercial activities. During this time, the traditional middle class's numbers began to fall. Between 2003 and 2008, which was marked by an increase in formal employment, the traditional middle class recovered but the new middle class found new business opportunities (Gilvonio 2010).

In a psychographic study, where participants are asked which class they belong to, 56 percent answered "middle class" (Arellano 2010). This new middle class consists of emerging sectors and has been growing for 30 years. The phenomenon began with the arrival of migrants, who accumulated properties and started small companies. This constituted one of the most noteworthy economic and social ascents in the last few years. The new middle class does not necessarily have the same habits as the traditional middle class, which is located in central districts of Lima, and instead has its own musical, artistic, cultural, and economic codes and resides primarily in the northern, southern, and eastern cones on the periphery of the capital.

An additional point of consideration is the redistributive aspect of income, or the gap between those that have more and less income in the country. Between 2003 and 2009, the poverty rate fell 17.42 percentage points; 79 percent of this decline was due to an increase in income (the impact of economic growth) while 21 percent is attributable to income redistribution. In other words, the effect of long-term growth (2003–9) has been greater than the redistribution (MEF 2010b: 64). This results show that the long-term redistribution effect in Peru has been slightly lower than the average (25 percent) reported in Latin America (Kacef and López-Monti 2010).

This situation is more evident if we look at the rural and urban ambits separately given that significant differences exist (*see* Figure 8.14). In the first group, household income has increased but the redistributive aspect has remained basically the same, while in urban areas improvements have been observed in both aspects of the analysis. In this scenario, poverty–growth elasticity has been higher than in urban areas, which has meant that poverty reduction in this ambit has occurred at a more accelerated pace.

The aforementioned makes it logical to conclude that although income has grown significantly in the poorest deciles, the increase has not been

	2003–6	2006–9	2003–9
I. National			
Point reduction	−7.48	−9.95	−17.42
Effect of growth	−6.18	−7.09	−13.27
Redistribution effect	−1.53	−2.61	−4.14
Remainder	0.24	−0.24	0
II. Rural			
Point reduction	−4.28	−10.02	−14.30
Effect of growth	−3.58	−10.91	−14.49
Redistribution effect	−0.28	−0.32	−0.61
Remainder	−0.42	−1.21	−1.63
III. Urban			
Point reduction	−9.13	−9.69	−18.83
Effect of growth	−6.71	−5.92	−12.63
Redistribution effect	−1.82	−3.19	−5.01
Remainder	−0.60	−0.58	−1.18

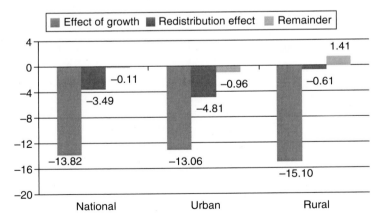

Figure 8.14 Breakdown of the variation in poverty rate (%)
Source: MEF (2010b).

sufficient to improve the distribution of wealth compared with the richest deciles. It is necessary to implement policy mechanisms that strengthen this effect, particularly in the rural ambit, where more than 50 percent of the population lives in poverty. It is important to emphasize the need to distribute wealth more effectively given that the redistributive component can impact directly on the increase in the poverty rate despite the fact that increases in household income are apparent, as Gasparini et al. (2007) indicated with regard to some countries such as Costa Rica (1997–2003), Colombia (1992–2000), Ecuador (1994–98), and Uruguay (1989–98).

Based on the above, the population's higher income and improvement in the distribution of the same will allow the middle class to keep growing, which will dynamize and expand the markets for financial and non-financial goods and services. This process is underway and is reflected in the increase in shopping centers across the country. Cities such as Piura, Trujillo, Chiclayo, Ica, Arequipa, Cajamarca, Huancayo, Cusco, and Juliaca now have at least one shopping center that has been completed or is under construction. This goes hand in hand with more expansion in financial services outside the capital as well as a larger presence of nonbanking microfinancial institutions throughout the country over the last few years. In this way, consumption and private investment will come together to drive growth in the next few years.

Forces and factors that challenge or threaten entrepreneurship

Opportunity versus necessity driven entrepreneurship

According to studies on entrepreneurship in the framework of the GEM, since its first participation in 2004, Peru has been one of the countries with the highest entrepreneurial activity (Serida et al. 2006, 2007, 2009, 2010). In the National Report GEM 2009 (Serida et al. in press), 21 out of 100 adults were involved in some type of entrepreneurial activity. Over time, the level of entrepreneurial activity (TEA) has fallen as the country has grown in terms of GDP (*see* Figure 8.15), which is consistent with the migration of necessity-based entrepreneurs to the labor force as the opportunities for employment improve.

Peru has demonstrated a level of opportunity-based entrepreneurship that is at least twice that of necessity-based entrepreneurship, and the nature of entrepreneurship tends to slowly exploit business opportunities (*see* Figure 8.16), driven by the fact that the population perceives that more business opportunities are available.

In all stages of entrepreneurship, opportunity-based entrepreneurship predominates, which indicates that the owners of established businesses are those who have most exploited opportunities, demonstrating the highest growth in this indicator (*see* Figure 8.17).

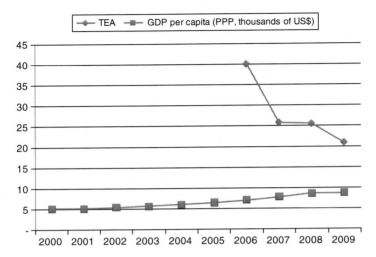

Figure 8.15   Peru: evolution of the GDP per capita (in thousands of US$) and TEA
Source: Serida et al. (2006, 2007, 2009, 2010) and INEI (2010a).

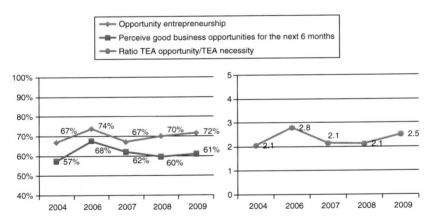

Figure 8.16   Indicators of opportunity-based entrepreneurship
Source: Serida et al. (2006, 2007, 2009, 2010).

Both men and women make up the group of entrepreneurs that set up businesses to exploit opportunities and tend to have higher levels of education. The majority of opportunity-based entrepreneurs have more faith in their ability and knowledge to engage in entrepreneurial activity than necessity-based entrepreneurs. Fear of failure is less prevalent among those that undertake opportunity-based entrepreneurial activities, while a larger percentage of necessity-based entrepreneurs think that everyone wants the same quality of life, which reflects the fact that their efforts are geared towards ensuring subsistence. If this were not necessary, they would probably have forgone their entrepreneurial aspirations. Nevertheless, both types of entrepreneurs show the same prevalence in indicating that society views entrepreneurs positively (*see* Figure 8.18).

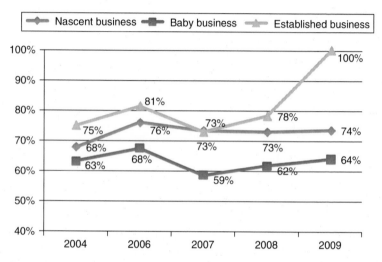

Figure 8.17   Percentage of opportunity-based entrepreneurs by stage of entrepreneurial process
Source: Serida et al. (2006, 2007, 2009, 2010).

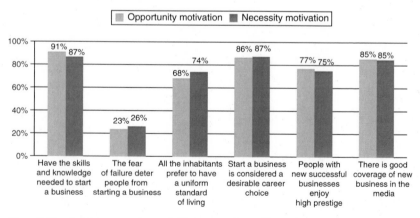

Figure 8.18   Average percentage of affirmative responses from entrepreneurs in the initial stages of activity according to motivation for engaging in entrepreneurial efforts
Source: Serida et al. (2009).

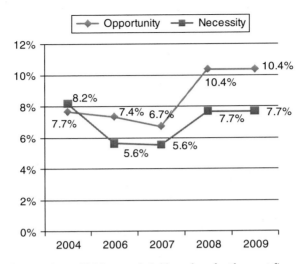

Figure 8.19 Expectations of high growth (>20 workers for the next five years) according to motivation to engage in entrepreneurial activity
Source: Serida et al. (2006, 2007, 2009, 2010).

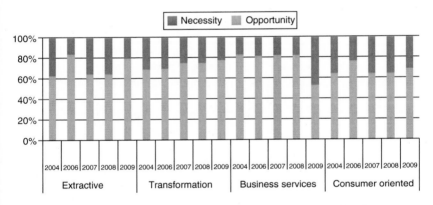

Figure 8.20 Percentage of the TEA according to motivation to undertake entrepreneurial action
Source: Serida et al. (2006, 2007, 2009, 2010).

The potential of opportunity-based entrepreneurs is evident in Figure 8.19, which shows that the expectations of growth of entrepreneurs motivated by opportunity are clearly higher than those motivated by necessity.

With regard to the structure of the sector of Peruvian entrepreneurs (*see* Figure 8.20), the GEM study currently shows that opportunity-based entrepreneurship predominates. An upward trend is evident in all sectors, with the exception of business services, which after representing more than

80 percent of entrepreneurial undertakings in the initial stages, fell in 2009 to slightly less than 50 percent. It is important to point out that this sector has experienced sustained growth, reporting 78 percent in 2009. The extractive sector has also recovered after two years of hovering at the 64 percent mark, and represented 80 percent of entrepreneurial undertakings in the initial stages in 2009.

Migration and entrepreneurship

In Peru, migratory phenomena have had an impact on the country's course. Two types of migration have occurred: from the countryside to the city and international migration.

The first occurred gradually and began in the mid-twentieth century. It was initially spurred by high poverty levels in rural areas and was later driven by terrorism. As a consequence, large cities, and Lima in particular, expanded unevenly and along the periphery. The majority of migrants could not find employment and had to generate opportunities. Although many did not initially set out to become businessmen, they eventually became successful entrepreneurs and escaped poverty.

Pinilla (2004) analyzed the factors that led these emerging entrepreneurs with migrant roots to success. Their social characteristics included strong ties to their birthplace and the tendency to seek out spouses from migrant backgrounds who were capable of better understanding and adapting to their personal and work styles. The majority come from families involved in productive labor. Although the education level of these entrepreneurs is not necessarily related to their business success (as it is to their attitude toward work and high self-esteem), it has an impact on the ability to have a wider vision of business to diversify markets and business lines.

The majority of the migrants' descendants (who today comprise the majority of the middle class) were born in the city. The main lessons that these individuals teach their children are the same ones that their parents taught them: work and study. This group also had a strong tendency to save to cover potential crises in the future.

These emerging businessmen are now challenged to work toward higher levels of professionalization, transparency, and formalization to ensure competitiveness. Emerging groups tend to be, like the majority of Peruvian businesses, family-owned firms. These operations are generally in the second generation of manager-owners and some have already passed to the third generation. Without a doubt, succession is a major issue, and ensuring the business's continuity becomes a challenge for the successors.

According to the International Organization for Migration (OIM), with collaboration of the INEI and General Directorate of Immigration and Naturalization (DIGEMIN), the other aspect of migration involves the population that emigrated to other countries in search of better development opportunities. It is estimated that more than 1,940,000 Peruvians emigrated between 1990 and 2007 (OIM, INEI and DIGEMIN 2008).

Another report (OIM and INEI 2009) indicated that more than 704,000 households reported having a member living abroad. This represents 10.4 percent of the total number of households in the country. The majority are concentrated in Lima and the Constitutional Province of Callao, constituting 50.6 percent of the national total. There is an association between migration and the socio-economic level of the household; 73.6 percent of the households that have experienced international migration are households with middle, low-middle and low incomes. The causes and consequences of migration are numerous in terms of the changes in the family makeup, the exodus of trained professionals, and the remittances that the migrants send, which constitute an important source of supplementary income that is second only to the profits obtained from mining exports.

The same source also notes that the substantial increase in number of citizens who have migrated abroad over the past 20 years has generated a significant increase in the remittances that ex-nationals send to Peru, which impacts on the economy of national households. In the last 19 years, the country has received US$16 billion in remittances. In terms of percentages, 40.7 percent come from the USA, followed by Spain with 15 percent, Japan with 9.4 percent, and Italy with 6 percent. The majority of the money received (75.3 percent) is used for household expenses and another 13 percent is destined for education.

Also, between 2006 and 2009, of the 80,000 people who returned to Peru, 53.6 percent were women. The majority of those who returned came from Chile (29 percent). Although 66.2 percent of the Peruvians who have returned belong to low-income households, the majority are university graduates. More than 9000 Peruvians have come home with a degree and many are teachers, engineers, and administrators. This data seems to indicate that international migration has allowed returning migrants to achieve higher levels of education. These individuals are well prepared academically and are capable of making significant contributions to the country's development.

As such, it is necessary to recognize the experience, skills, and knowledge that Peruvians have received abroad, which they can invest in the country and provide positive and productive options. This group can work side by side with the government to generate economic and social opportunities that contribute to national development. It is necessary to identify the population that wants to return to the country because of the renewed confidence generated by democratic security, separating them from those who have been forced to return due to the grave employment crisis generated by the global economic meltdown.

Economic stimulus and entrepreneurship

The current economic crisis has generated a new context, which is characterized by the loss of jobs in specific sectors. The decline in prices and the demand for metals, raw materials, and garments has had a negative impact on exporting companies in the main cities on the coast. Sectors such as construction, urban services, and commerce have experienced a sustained increase in employment. In response to this development and as part of the Economic Stimulus Plan, the Peruvian government created the Special Program for Job Reconversion (PERLAB), known as Revalora Perú, to promote employment and protect the employability of workers affected by the international crisis. This program uses an employment reconversion strategy that targets unemployed workers in affected sectors in order to reinsert or relocate them, after a period of qualification, training, and placement, in sectors that have not been affected by the crisis. In this manner, the program will help head off an increase in unemployment and facilitate job reinsertion for displaced workers while covering the demand for employment in emerging sectors (Verdera 2010).

Since its beginning in September 2010, the program has provided more than 37,000 Peruvian men and women with training in 14 regions across the country (more than half were young people). Nevertheless, many of these individuals will choose to start their own companies rather than take a job at another workplace. This attests to the population's entrepreneurial spirit and the fact that potential business opportunities exist. The program strengthens people's management capacities and provides technical support for their business plans. The goal is to help them choose an adequate business structure and set up operations as fast as possible (Barreda 2010).

Business informality and the new SME law

In Peru, a microbusiness is an economic unit with one to ten employees. Its sales volume does not exceed 150 tax units (UIT) or about US$190,000 a year. Small businesses can have between one and 100 workers and their sales volumes are below 1700 UIT, or about US$2 million a year.[20]

Peñaranda (2010) showed that this sector contributes approximately 42 percent of GDP and represents 98.5 percent of the total number of Peruvian companies. Also, of the more than 3 million microbusinesses that operate in the country, only 18 percent are in the Single Taxpayer Registry (RUC) and 75 percent lack an operating license and as such remain informal. Micro and small businesses at the national level are concentrated primarily in extractive activities, agriculture, and livestock and fishing, which represent approximately 1.9 million business units. This means that 59.8 percent of the SMEs are involved in these activities, which also report the highest numbers of informal businesses.

Also, in terms of management structures, 80 percent of these business units are family-owned subsistence operations (street vendors, microproducers, among others). The remaining 20 percent (around 600,000 microbusinesses) have an emerging business focus and just over 49,000 enterprises are in the small business category.

Recently, Vuletin (2008) found that the size of the informal economy in Peru is 38.1 per cent of GDP. With regard to the variables that explain the size of informality in the country, this study estimates that the tax burden is responsible for 31.9 percent of the problem, followed by job rigidity at 36.7 percent, the importance of the agriculture sector at 24.4 percent and inflation at 7 percent. According to Perry and Maloney (2007), the primary motivation for formalization seems to be the risk of being detected (particularly when the business grows) and second, the possibility of accessing other markets and services.

Micro and small businesses play a fundamental role in generating employment and in fact account for 88 percent of employment in the private sector. Fifty percent of the economically active population (PEA) work in a microbusiness, but only 9.2 percent work in formal companies. As such, the majority of workers in this sector have no social benefits (Instituto de Economía y Empresa 2008).

This state of informality hinders businesses from accessing training, public purchases, health protection, and pension funds. In this context, in 2008 the Peruvian government passed the Law to Promote Competitiveness, Formalization and Development of Micro and Small Businesses and Access to Decent Employment.[21] Its objective is to make microbusinesses more competitive, ensuring that they formalize, develop significantly, and provide access to decent jobs. First, the norm has five key points that consist in providing a new definition that differentiates the microbusiness from small businesses; second, it aims to facilitate instruments to promote competitiveness; third, it strives to offer promotional tax measures; fourth, it seeks to provide special labor regimes; and fifth, it aims to offer new systems for health and pensions.

By August 2010, more than 90,000 SMEs had adhered to the new law, putting their businesses in the respective registry (Remype). This represents a significant increase (50 percent) over the 60,000 that had registered at the beginning of this year and the 100,000 expected to register at the end of 2010 (Ministerio de la Producción 2010).

Those that are registered in Remype can participate in state purchases and access the 40 percent reserved for SMEs, receive training and financing, access reduced rates and be subjected to lower labor fines, access a special labor regime (which implies paying salaries and social benefits according to the company's size), access to a health system, pensions subsidized by the state, and a fund for invoice negotiation (which allows for the use of factoring).

Improving the business climate

In 2010, there was evidence of progress in policy reforms to improve the business climate, which allowed Peru to go from 46th to 36th place in the *Doing Business 2011* indicator (WB and IFC 2010). The reforms that drove this indicator include labor regulation for micro and small businesses, the implementation of new technological tools for income tax payments, business charters and property registration, as well as the acquisition of new infrastructure for ports. The plan (Carranza 2009a) contains a set of reforms that have generated reductions in time, the number of procedures, and costs of processes in problematic areas. The goal is to attract more investment and drive business development to ensure that Peru has the best climate in Latin America and is a front-runner in the global economy.

Growth in microfinance

Part of Peru's financial attractiveness is due to widespread development in microfinance. Emerging financial entities such as the Rural Savings and Municipal Savings Institutions, Edpymes (development companies for small and medium businesses) have driven this growth. These entities have expanded because they serve high-growth sectors of the economy, primarily microbusinessmen in sectors linked to services, commerce, and industry. Although these institutions assume more risk than the banking system, the sectors in which they invest have grown sustainably. As a result, they have stirred the interest of multiple banking institutions, which now have highly active microfinance divisions that will undoubtedly attract foreign capital that wants to redirect investments to highly specialized institutions which serve the various sectors of small and microbusinesses.

On the other side, Tam says that microfinance loans and deposits have grown in the past five years at average annual rates of 32 and 30 percent respectively. The number of microbusiness borrowers has increased by an annual average of 19 percent, which represents a 140 percent increase in new borrowers when compared to the figure reported five years ago. This growth has gone hand in hand with constant growth in equity levels, which is rooted primarily in earnings. As such, these businesses have proven to be solid and exceed international requirements for capital adequacy and local minimum regulatory levels. It is also important to point out that growth in the microfinance segment has been decentralized. Unlike other financial and productive activities, the microfinance sector has shown high growth in the provinces over the past few years and has surpassed levels recorded in the capital. This is clearly visible in areas that have recorded higher levels of economic dynamism due to mega mining projects and new agricultural export activities (Tam 2010).

Thanks to continuous improvements in the regulation and supervision ambit, the Global Microscopic Study, which included 55 countries in Latin America, Asia, Africa, Eastern Europe, and the Middle East and was conducted by the Economist Intelligence Unit of *The Economist* at the request of the Inter-American Development Bank, the Andean Development Corporation, and the International Financial Corporation of the World Bank, chose Peru as the best microfinance environment for a second consecutive year. This specialized study emphasized the importance of having an independent, informed, and autonomous regulatory entity (represented by the SBS) as well as the support of authorities, who are committed to promoting microfinance and ensuring the stability of the legal framework (Economist Intelligence Unit 2009). This formal recognition is very important for the microfinance system because it strengthens its capacity to attract new investment, which is necessary to consolidate development, increase the scale of operations, and achieve financial inclusion. Nevertheless, the SBS believes that although the country leads microfinance in the region, there is still considerable room for improvement, particularly in terms of strengthening the institutional structures of microbusinesses, their governability, and risk administration practices, consistent with the expansion in the number of operations assumed.[22]

Other specific conditions in the entrepreneurial context

These changes are the result of a positive evolution that most conditions in the entrepreneurial context have shown since the country began to participate in the GEM (Serida et al. 2006). One of the most important factors has been the evolution of social and cultural norms, which have become increasingly supportive of entrepreneurs and have stimulated more individuals to seek out and exploit business opportunities that go beyond ensuring subsistence. This allows entrepreneurs to increase their wealth and social status. The valuation of physical infrastructure conditions is also positive despite the fact that growth has been minimal. It is important to point out that these conditions are relative to access to financing and government policies despite the fact that the country is ranked somewhat lower in these indicators (*see* Figure 8.21). In fact, Peru ranks second and third respectively in terms of growth in these areas, which attests to the state's efforts and the ability of private businesses to promote opportunities and accompany entrepreneurial growth.

Figure 8.22 shows that the experts interviewed believe that the primary factor that is driving entrepreneurial activity in Peru is the economic climate, which offers a trustworthy and favorable environment for long-term investment. Free trade agreements have led to market openness that offers vast opportunities for countries like Peru, which have a wide range of resources. It should be no surprise that another driver of entrepreneurial growth in Peru has been the positive changes in social and cultural aspects. The media has stepped up its coverage of successful entrepreneurs and matters of

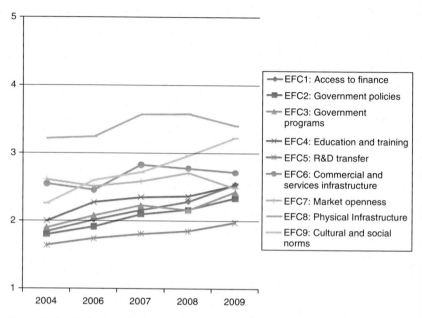

Figure 8.21 Evolution of experts' valuation of conditions in the entrepreneurial context (EFC)
Source: Serida et al. (2006, 2007, 2009, 2010).

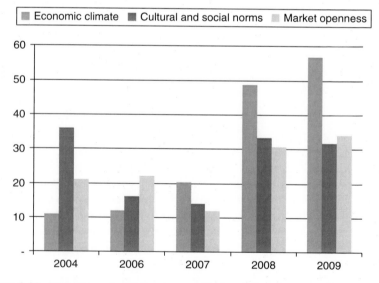

Figure 8.22 Percentage of experts who gave their opinion about specific conditions in the environment that support entrepreneurial activity
Source: Serida et al. (2006, 2007, 2009, 2010).

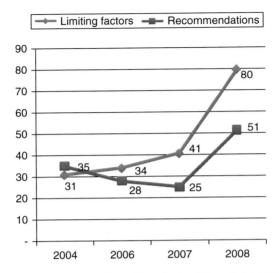

Figure 8.23 Percentage of experts who believe that public policies impede entrepreneurial activity and recommend actions in the same ambit to promote entrepreneurship
Source: Serida et al. (2006, 2007, 2009, 2010).

interest for business development. Over the past few years, advertising campaigns for products have become increasingly creative and Peruvians have made great strides in contributing to business initiatives.

Nevertheless, it is worrying that the experts believe that the state is the main impediment to entrepreneurial activity. Accordingly, this point received the highest number of recommendations (*see* Figure 8.23), including a call to make entrepreneurial activity a priority on the national and local agenda, and reduce the excessive tax burden and the number of procedures necessary to start up a business.

Outlook for entrepreneurship in the country over the next several years and recommendations for improving and fostering greater entrepreneurial activity in the country

The largest investment opportunities are associated with abundant natural resources and the infrastructure gap as well as the potential to generate high returns on productivity as the informal sector becomes part of the formal economy. This means that Peru is in a good position to develop more and better entrepreneurial offerings in the future.

The report on Peru in the GEM in 2009 (Serida et al. 2010) mentions the results of the panel of experts who were asked to give recommendations to promote entrepreneurship in the country. This report indicates that the main recommendations are related to government policies and education for entrepreneurs (mentioned by 70 and 58 percent of the experts respectively), followed by the transfer level in R&D (28 percent) and the financial environment (23 percent).

With regard to government policies, the majority of experts concur that promoting entrepreneurial activities should become a national strategic axis. In this scenario, the state would become the promoting entity for entrepreneurship and would create awareness of this sector's importance at all political levels. Entrepreneurship would be included in the objectives for all lines of action both nationally and locally, and the private sector and the principal actors in the field would be called on to participate. One of the priorities for government policies could be to offer preferential treatment for state purchases to businesses that have been set up recently and not just to the SMEs, which is currently the case.

Similar to the situation in 2008, the experts insist on the need to reduce the number of procedures to set up businesses as well as obtain municipal licenses and sector permits. Awareness needs to be created of the efforts to reduce the number of procedures to set up business and achieve greater impact among entrepreneurs and ensure more inclusion. The One-Stop Service Window should also provide licenses and operating or commercial permits to ensure that the business is operative in the shortest time possible. One alternative would be to provide temporary licenses for a specific duration to help new companies adapt their operating procedures to the regulations in the corresponding sector and cover the respective costs. The majority of experts concur that fiscal normativity needs to be reformulated to provide more benefits to business initiatives. There is a need to develop a system of incentives to promote business creation, including offering tax exemptions for reasonable periods of time as well differentiated taxes for the products or services produced by these endeavors, eliminating advance tax payments, among other efforts. In parallel, it is necessary to strictly enforce tax compliance for businesses that have reached the capacity to contribute. According to the experts, it would also be a good idea to create a collections entity that specializes in the SME sector and new businesses to establish tax regulations that are in line with the specific needs of this business sector, which will stimulate its growth and consolidation.

With regard to education, the experts recommend revolutionary action in terms of training and education. Changes must be made in the design of professional profiles and teachers require specific training with regard to entrepreneurship. Education must be linked to entrepreneurial production to ensure that theoretical knowledge is applicable to productive issues. It is important to introduce mechanisms to develop creativity as well as leadership and management capacities for entrepreneurs, beginning at the most basic levels of regular education. Efforts must be made to expand the sphere of action to provide technical and management assistance to productive units that have received no help thus far. It is necessary to create a current of knowledge to obtain better perspectives for growth. Similar to 2008, the experts recommended promoting teamwork and win–win negotiation so that people have a better attitude toward associative work schemes and benefit from models of productive chains and/or business networks. To ensure that education provides adequate training for entrepreneurs, it is necessary to train teachers in entrepreneurship. The state has become the main employer for educators, which has encouraged dependent employment. Education models are needed to promote public–private alliances that allow teachers to generate their own jobs. These models should encourage creating and experimenting with individual and associative activities. The experts believe that it is important to create a knowledge bank in entrepreneurship for education institutions that want to include this topic in their programs and participate in creating awareness. Ideally, this knowledge bank will become a valuable source of information for the institution and the small businessman, who will learn from the experience of other entrepreneurs.

In terms of technological transfer and research and development, there is a need for more and better business services at the advisory, consultancy, and training levels. Training should include technical instruction on "how to do things" and "how to do them better" and be linked to management knowledge so that businessmen realize that improving productivity, using business practices, and adhering to a quality culture lead to more competitiveness, lower costs, and higher earnings. This perspective should be accompanied by the development of technical norms and standardization projects that help develop internationally competitive products. Entrepreneurs should be encouraged to use new tools like the Internet to do business. This is necessary particularly in the provinces, where the state and universities play a fundamental role in promoting these services and access to this kind of knowledge.

In terms of the financial environment, the experts indicate that the state, given its capacity to access international funds, should develop financing models for entrepreneurs with low interest rates and grace periods. It would be a good idea to set up a competitive, rotating fund for each region in the country to provide start-up financing for entrepreneurs and working capital to businessmen who intend to expand their projects. It is also necessary to create awareness about the best financing tools and sources for each stage of business development and provide information on how to access both.

The experts believe that focusing on the aforementioned aspects will generate a greater impact on the growth of entrepreneurship. Nevertheless, in order to take the leap and emulate the most successful experiences, including those in Asia, it will be necessary to combine these measures with mechanisms to enhance competitiveness, human capital, research and development, productive diversification efforts, and plans to strengthen sectors that offer clear competitive advantages, etc. This goal is not in opposition to the intensive and sustainable use of natural resources, as has been proven in Australia, New Zealand, Canada, and other countries.

Although the economy has performed well over the last few years, ignoring the issues addressed above may compromise the sustainability of economic growth and the progress made thus far in reducing poverty. The current economic conditions offer a favorable opportunity to tackle these challenges.

A case of entrepreneurship: Roky's Chicken and Grill

The Peruvian gastronomic boom

Over the last few years Peru and the world have witnessed the revaluation and extraordinary growth of Peruvian gastronomy. Thanks to the country's mixture of races and cultures, unusual geography, and biodiversity, as well as local visionaries, Peruvian cuisine is now considered among the world's finest.

The Peruvian culinary tradition mixes the pre-Incan, Incan, and Spanish traditions (the latter was strongly influenced by the Muslims). Immigrants from Africa, France, China, Japan, Germany, Italy, and other countries have also contributed a great deal to the local flavors. Every region in Peru has preserved its ancestral culinary riches, which are highly colorful and use food products that reflect the fusion of native products and foreign offerings. Peru has a variety of soil types and geographic conditions, which helps provide a healthy supply of natural ingredients. Proof of this can be found in the fact that Peru has more than 2500 kinds of potato ("Día de la papa" 2008) and 650 varieties of native fruits, including *Chirimoya* and *Lucuma* (Ruiz 2010).

Many young chefs are currently redefining Peruvian cooking by creating fusion dishes, a number of which have won prizes at global gastronomic events. At the Fourth International Gastronomy Summit Madrid Fusion 2006, the city of Lima was declared the gastronomic capital of Latin America ("Lima, capital gastronómica" 2006). Once again, Peru achieved its rightful place among the world's best. In 2008, the recently formed Peruvian Association of Gastronomy (APEGA) organized the First International Gastronomy Fair of Lima (locally known as Mistura), which received more than 23,000 visitors. Its success has made it an annual event, and in 2010, attendance topped 200,000 (APEGA 2010).

Mario Vargas Llosa, who recently won the Nobel Prize for literature, wrote:

If anyone had told me a few years ago that they were going to organize "gastronomic tours" to Peru I wouldn't have believed it. But it has
happened and I suspect that our *chupes de camarones, piqueos, causa,
pachamancas, cebiches, lomito saltado, ají de gallina, picarones, suspiro a la
limeña*, etc. will bring as many tourists to the country as the colonial and
pre-Hispanic palaces of Cuzco and the rocks of Machu Picchu.

(Vargas Llosa 2009)

And he is right. Studies of foreign tourists show that 91 percent rate
Peruvian food as good or very good (Promperú 2006: 22). In terms of restaurants, patrons value the flavor of the food, the personalized service, and
variety of dishes. The quality of Peruvian food is highly valued by 97 percent
of foreign tourists (Promperú 2010b: 5), while 95 percent indicated that the
food met their expectations (Promperú 2010a: 16).

As we have already mentioned, one noteworthy aspect of Peruvian cuisine is the fact that it is open to innovation and constantly developing new
dishes; chefs are always on the cutting edge and willing to experiment. An
example of this is the contemporary reinvention of well-known dishes in
Peru, such as *pollo a la brasa*, or spit-roasted chicken.

Pollo a la brasa

Pollo a la brasa is a Peruvian variation of *pollo al spiedo*, which was developed
50 years ago by two Swiss residents in Peru, Roger Shuler and Franz Ulrich,
who invented a machine to cook chicken uniformly over coal or wood fires
(Angulo 2010). The dish is accompanied by French fries, salad, and different
creams and sauces.

Originally, it was consumed primarily by the upper classes. Over time,
consumption became so widespread that in 2004, the National Institute of
Culture included the dish in the country's cultural legacy;[23] in 2010, the
government declared the third Sunday of July as Pollo a la Brasa Day[24] and
has included this meal in the basic family basket used to determine the
country's monthly inflation rate (INEI 2010c).

Over time, specialist restaurant chains have made *pollo a la brasa* the
country's first choice in culinary fare. In fact, 98 percent of Peruvians, the
majority young people from middle-low and low-income brackets, prefer to
eat at restaurants specializing in chicken (MAXIMIXE 2009).

In Lima, the competition is concentrated in large chains such as Roky's,
Norky's, Pardo's Chicken, La Caravana, and Mediterráneo Chicken, among
others. *Pollo a la brasa's* internationalization began in the last decade of the
twentieth century, when Peruvian residents in different countries and cities

began to open restaurants specializing in this dish. Operating sites included Argentina, New York, San Francisco, Bolivia, Brazil, Canada, Ecuador, Spain, and even Japan and China. Some brands, such as Pardo's Chicken and La Caravana, have established their presence through franchises in Chile, Mexico, Colombia, and Miami, etc.

Armando Kiyán and his chicken restaurant

Roky's is a typical family business. It is led by its founder and general manager, Armando Kiyan, a 50-year-old Peruvian of Japanese descent.

Kiyán became involved in business at an early age, selling the fruit that his father produced on a small farm in the countryside. When the family moved to Lima, Kiyán continued to lean about business while helping his father in a small grocery store. He longed to open his own business and checked out any opportunity that came up in casual conversation. This constant search yielded fruit in 1985, when Kiyán opened his first chicken restaurant where his father's store had stood. Nevertheless, Kiyán was not new to the business: "My friends and I had been involved in chicken restaurants for a long time. I had observed customer turnover and came to realize how much I could earn from this business, which was not too hard to control" (Kiyán 2010). During this time, Armando Kiyán (2010) learned several key concepts of management: "resource administration, cash flow management and merchandise turnover management but mainly I learned that this business is based on customer relations, which is the business's main driver."

He was set on making Roky's the best chicken and meat restaurant in the country. Soon after, the public began to recognize Roky's for its cozy atmosphere and more importantly for its use of quality products that were exceptionally flavorful.

Roky's continues to maintain a philosophy directed at fully satisfying its clients with exquisite dishes based on chicken and grilled meats, which are complemented by desserts and drinks.

Commercial strategy at Roky's

Over the years, the company has identified some aspects to doing business – beyond its flavorful chicken and dedication to service – that have helped it earn customer preference:

• We do what others don't

Armando commented:

> The business strategy was simply to do what others do not. Over time, we
> saw that no one was concerned about meeting the needs of clients with

children so we equipped our locales with play areas for little ones and held children's shows on Sunday. Our competitors eventually followed suit. We also figured out that people wanted to eat and have fun at the weekends, so we provided live music. In the beginning, people asked "what is an orchestra doing in a chicken restaurant?" Now it's commonplace. (Kiyán 2010)

- A place to spend family time

Roky's target market is comprised of families that are looking for a place to eat and have fun. This is precisely the target market that has allowed the chain to obtain a 37 percent brand recognition rating as one of the most patronized establishments, with 56 percent share of consumer preferences (Ipsos Apoyo 2010).

- More quality at a lower price

High-quality products are used in Roky's dishes. The chicken comes from the best farms and clear standards have been set for the animals' weight and age. The vegetables, sauces, and beverages (to a lesser extent) have been standardized to ensure a uniform product. This is what differentiates Roky's from other chicken restaurants – whether chains or neighborhood operations – which do not apply these policies.

Roky's has introduced new products for the youngest members of the family, including boxes that contain special combos for children and toys.

Given that the stores are formally or intrinsically segmented by socioeconomic level, prices are not standardized in the chain's different locales in Lima or the provinces. Nevertheless, Roky's prices are considered fair because its products exceed the quality of the neighborhood restaurants at a price that is either similar or better.

- Good service in a good environment

Roky's service is better than that of neighborhood restaurants and a service standard has been set. Today, people measure a chicken restaurant's price and service by Roky's standards.

Roky's has at least one location in each district, located close to principal arteries to ensure easy access. Locales vary in design from small, one-floor establishments to modern, multi-floored structures. In some cases, the locale's distribution is a draw for customers who are either looking for something small and cozy or large enough to accommodate games for the youngest members of the family.

The main moments during the customer's service experience at Roky's include: waiting for service, obtaining information on the menu and suggestions, and waiting to receive an order. Roky's reduces any discomfort that may arise during these moments by offering additional services such as karaoke, live music, children's shows, face painting, and children's games. The last contact the customer has with the establishment is generally agreeable, which helps boost the perception of service and acts as an important element of customer fidelity.

Not just *pollo a la brasa*

The first store set itself apart by always exceeding expectations. This helped generate success beyond anyone's expectations, including Kiyán's. Roky's went from a five-table establishment to a four-story mega restaurant with room for 80 tables, which was inaugurated three years later. One year later, Kiyán, amidst many doubts, decided to open three more restaurants. With five locales in its portfolio, Roky's began to expand quickly throughout Lima (there are currently 44 establishments and the chain has a presence in almost all of Lima's districts). Eight years later, after closely observing economic trends and noting the increase in national consumption, Roky's extended its operations to the provinces (where it currently has 12 establishments) (Kiyán 2010) to become the country's largest national chain. In fact, Roky's has crossed borders and now operates restaurants in Bolivia and Brazil.

Kiyán also owns the Rodizio chain (grilled meats), the Soprano Karaoke chain, the Scencia Convention Center, and Villapan, an industrial bakery. According to our entrepreneur, all of these businesses were set up as complementary services of the chicken restaurant chain. But this is not all. A few years ago Kiyán decided to diversify the business at a market rather than product level. Taking advantage of the real estate boom, he founded a construction company and a pre-mixed concrete company.

Up-and-coming

According to Gomez de la Torre et al. (2007), the level of family involvement in operations of Kiyán's enterprises is considerable. Positions of trust are held by family members or people close to the family. The organization is vertical and has grown over the years along with the increase in establishments. There are large gaps of power between the top and bottom of the organization and significant communications problems exist, which is a reflection of a limited capacity for planning.

The founder and executive management are conscious of the importance of reorganizing to face a competitive and changing environment. They are aware of the fact that family businesses face continuity risks in the long term and the following challenges must be tackled:

- Planning for succession and guaranteeing that the new generation is professional and competent
- Include officers that are not direct family who possess the capacity to attract and retain directors and professionals that are not related to the family.

The country's good economic situation, the role that Peruvian cooking currently plays on the international scene, and other conditions have helped Roky's establish its competitive position and opportunities for growth at the international level. The questions are: "Can it maintain its family structure and face market challenges? Can it insert itself in the boom to internationalize Peruvian gastronomy?"

Notes

1. Report for Selected Countries and Subjects: Gross domestic product (constant prices, annual percent change) http://www.imf.org/external/pubs/ft/weo/2009/01/weodata/weorept.aspx?sy=2002&ey=2014&scsm=1&ssd=1&sort=country&ds=.&br=1&c=213%2C273%2C218%2C223%2C228%2C233%2C288%2C293%2C248%2C298%2C299&s=NGDP_RPCH&grp=0&a=&pr.x=51&pr.y=8 [Retrieved September 16, 2010].
2. Decreto Legislativo No. 757, No. 662, No. 668, Decreto Supremo 162-92-EF, and others.
3. Resolución Legislativa No. 25312.
4. Peru signed this convention on September 4, 1991, Deposit of Ratification: August 9, 1993, Entry into Force: September 8, 1993.
5. Perú ratified the convention on July 7, 1988, and Entry into Force on October 5, 1988.
6. The initiative emerged from the meeting of South American presidents held in August 2000 in Brasilia. Participating countries are Brazil, Argentina, Bolivia, Chile, Colombia, Ecuador, Guyana, Paraguay, Peru, Suriname, Uruguay, and Venezuela (http://www.iirsa.org//Index.asp?CodIdioma=ESP).
7. The USA–Peru Trade Promotion Agreement was signed on April 12, 2006; ratified by the Peruvian Congress on June 28, 2006; by the US House of Representatives on November 2, 2007 and by the US Senate on December 4, 2007. The agreement was implemented on February 1, 2009.
8. Peru–Singapore Free Trade Agreement, signed on May 29, 2008 and ratified by Decreto Supremo No. 043-2009-RE. Agreement entered into force on August 1, 2009.
9. Peru–Canada Free Trade Agreement, signed on May 29, 2008 and ratified by Decreto Supremo No. 044-2009-RE. Agreement entered into force on August 1, 2009.

10. Peru–China Free Trade Agreement, signed on April 28, 2009 and ratified by Decreto Supremo No. 092-2009-RE. Agreement entered into force on March 1, 2010.
11. Since April 2006, Peru has developed a process to prepare for the negotiation of an FTA with countries of the European Free Trade Association (EFTA) involving Switzerland, Iceland, Liechtenstein, and Norway. The agreement was signed on July 14, 2010.
12. Framework Agreement for a Closer Partnership between the Government of the Republic of Peru and the Government of Kingdom of Thailand was signed on October 17, 2003. Ratified by Decreto Supremo No. 010-2005-RE. The Thai government ratified it on October 18, 2005.
13. Peru–Chile Free Trade Agreement, signed on August 22, 2006 and ratified by Decreto Supremo No. 057-2006-RE.
14. The Economic Complementation Agreement No. 8 (ACE 8) was concluded between the Republic of Mexico and the Republic of Peru under the 1980 Montevideo Treaty. The ACE 8 was incorporated into national law by Decreto Supremo No. 054-87-PCM and it is in force until 31 December 2011.
15. April 14, 2010, saw the officially launched trade negotiations between Peru and Japan.
16. See http://www.comunidadandina.org/.
17. See http://www.mincetur.gob.pe/newweb/Default.aspx?tabid=1676.
18. Peru began to participate as a full member of APEC in November 1998 during the Tenth Ministerial Meeting in Kuala Lumpur, Malaysia. See http://www.mincetur.gob.pe/apec1/index.asp?cont=694993.
19. Calculated on the projected GDP and population from World Economic Outlook Database of the International Monetary Fund for 2012 and the list of countries with which Peru would have trade agreements in 2012.
20. Decreto Legislativo No. 1086.
21. Ibid.
22. Tam (2010).
23. Resolución Directoral No. 1066/INC.
24. Resolución Ministerial No. 0441-2010-AG.

References

Agencia de Promoción de la Inversión Privada. 2010. *Por qué invertir en el Perú: Exportaciones crecientes*. Available at: http://www.proinversion.gob.pe/0/0/modulos/JER/PlantillaStandardsinHijos.aspx?ARE=0&PFL=0&JER=68 [Retrieved on September 5, 2010].

Althaus, J. 2010, April 23. "La creación del 'otro'" *Diario El Comercio*. Available at: http://elcomercio.pe/impresa/notas/creacion-otro/20100423/465994 [Retrieved on September 13, 2010].

Angulo, W. 2010, July 16. "Jimmy Schuler: El pollo a la brasa es para todos y no distingue clases sociales." Retrieved September 10, 2010, from Peru.com: Available at: http://www.peru.com/noticias/portada20100716/108377/Jimmy-Schuler-El-pollo-a-la-brasa-es-para-todos-y-no-distingue-clases-sociales.

Apoyo Consultoría. 2010a. *Informe SAE. Setiembre 2010*. Servicio de asesoría Empresarial (SAE). Available at: http://www.apoyoconsultoria-sae.com/images/upload/informeportada/archivo/2010-068%20CONFIANZA%20DEL%20CONSUMIDOR%20EN%20MAYOR%20NIVEL%20EN%20TRES%20ANOS.pdf [Retrieved September 30, 2010].

Apoyo Consultoría. 2010b. *Sondeo SAE. Setiembre 2010.* Servicio de asesoría Empresarial (SAE). Available at: http://www.apoyoconsultoria-sae.com/images/upload/pagina/ archivo/Resultados%20-%20Sondeo%20SAE%20set%202010.pdf [Retrieved September 25, 2010].

Arellano, Rolando. 2010. *Al medio hay sitio. El crecimiento social según los estilos de vida.* Lima: Planeta.

Arienza, M. and D. Mallmann. 2010. "Licencia social, alcances y límites." *Gerencia ambiental.* [online] year XVII, March: 28–34. Available at: http://www.greencross.org. ar/downloads/RevistaGerenciaAmbiental.pdf [Retrieved on September 7, 2010].

Armas, A. and F. Grippa. 2006. "Metas de inflación en una economía dolarizada: La experiencia de Perú." In A. Armas, A. Ize, and E. Levy-Yeyati (Eds), *Dolarización Financiera. La agenda de política.* Lima: International Monetary Fund and Banco Central de reserva del Perú, Ch. 6.

Asociación Peruana de Empresas de Investigación de Mercados. 2008. Niveles socioeconómicos 2009, Lima. Available at: http://www.apeim.com.pe/images/ APEIMNSE2008_2009.pdf [Retrieved August 31, 2010].

Asociación Peruana de Gastronomía. 2010, September 14. "Todos reunidos en Mistura: Fiesta de la integración e identidad." [online] Available at: http://www. apega.pe/2010/09/todos-reunidos-en-mistura-fiesta-de-la-integracion-e-identidad/ [Retrieved September 26, 2010].

Banco Central de Reserva del Perú. 2009. *Nota informativa.* No. 085. [online] Available at: http://www.bcrp.gob.pe/docs/Transparencia/Notas-Informativas/2009/Nota-Informativa-085-2009-BCRP.pdf [Retrieved September 25, 2010].

Banco Central de Reserva del Perú. 2010a. *Encuesta de Expectativas Macroeconómicas. Agosto 2010.* Available at: http://www.bcrp.gob.pe/docs/Estadisticas/Encuestas/ Series-de-indices.xls [Retrieved September 3, 2010].

Banco Central de Reserva del Perú. 2010b. *Memoria 2009.* [online] Available at: http://www.bcrp.gob.pe/docs/Publicaciones/Memoria/2009/Memoria-BCRP-2009. pdf [Retrieved September 25, 2010].

Barreda, Javier. 2010, September 16. "Capacitación, emprendimiento y competitividad." *El Peruano.* [online] Available at: http://www.elperuano.com.pe/edicion/ noticia.aspx?key=XpTSf0a5ea4= [Retrieved on September 17, 2010].

Bossio, Jorge. 2008. "Acceso y uso de servicios de telecomunicaciones en el Perú." Peru GISWatch Report 2008. CONDESAN. In A. Finlay (Ed.). *GISWatch Report 2008, Access to Infrastructure.* APC, Hivos and ITeM, p. 162. Available at: http://www. giswatch.org/country-report/2008/peru [Retrieved on September 12, 2010].

Carranza, Luis. 2009a. *Competitividad: Plan de Mejora del Clima de Negocios.* Ministerio de Economía y Finanzas. [PDF slides]. Available at: http://www.incagro.gob.pe/ WebIncagro/userfiles/file/MEF%20Plan%20para%20la%20Mejora%20del%20Clima %20de%20Negocios%20-%2015JUL2009.pdf [Retrieved on August 23, 2010].

Carranza, Luis. 2009b. *El Perú frente a la crisis internacional.* Ministerio de Economía y Finanzas. [PDF slides]. Available at: http://as.americas-society.org/files/Luis% 20Carranza%20MEF.pdf [Retrieved June 29, 2010].

Carranza, Luis. 2010.*Perú: Una visión de largo plazo.* Ministerio de Economía y Finanzas. [PDF slides]. Available at: http://www.fiap.cl/prontus_fiap/site/artic/20100510/ asocfile/20100510132201/luis_carranza_ugarte___panel_de_analisis.pdf [Retrieved on June 13, 2010].

Choy, M. and R. Ayllón. 2007. *La liquidez intradiaria en el sistema de pagos en una economia dolarizada: la experiencia peruana.* Lima: Banco Central de Reserva del Perú, p. 19.

Comisión Multisectorial Temporal encargada de elaborar el "Plan Nacional para el Desarrollo de la Banda Ancha en el Perú." 2010. *Visión, metas y propuestas de políticas para el desarrollo de la banda ancha en el Perú.* (Informe No. 3, Julio). Available at: http://www.mtc.gob.pe/portal/proyecto_banda_ancha/INFORME_03_BANDA_ANCHA_.pdf [Retrieved on August 15, 2010].

Decreto Legislativo No. 662. "Aprueba régimen de estabilidad jurídica a la inversión extranjera." September 2, 1991. *El Peruano.* Available at: http://www.estudiorivarola.com/D.Leg.662_Regimen_Estabilidad_Juridica_Inversion_Extranjera.pdf [Retrieved September 25, 2010].

Decreto Legislativo No. 668. "Dictan medidas destinadas a garantizar la libertad de comercio exterior e interior como condición fundamental para el desarrollo del país." September 14, 1991. *El Peruano.* Available at: http://www.indecopi.gob.pe/repositorioaps/0/6/par/normalizacion/decreto%20legislativo%20n668.pdf [Retrieved September 25, 2010].

Decreto Legislativo No. 757. "Aprueban ley marco para el crecimiento de la inversión privada." November 13, 1991. *El Peruano.* Available at: http://www.proinversion.gob.pe/RepositorioAPS/0/0/JER/MARCOLEGALTRIBUTARIO/11-D_L_757.pdf [Retrieved September 25, 2010].

Decreto Legislativo No. 1086. "Ley de promoción de la competitividad, formalización y desarrollo de la micro y pequeña empresa y del acceso al empleo decente." 2008, June 28. *El Peruano, Boletín de Normas Legales* 25 (10276): 375103–09.

Decreto Supremo No. 010-2005-RE. "Ratifican el Acuerdo Marco para una Asociación Económica más Cercana entre el Gobierno de la República del Perú y el Gobierno del Reino de Tailandia." 2005, January 27. *El Peruano. Boletín de Normas Legales* 22 (8990): 285530.

Decreto Supremo No. 043-2009-RE. "Ratifican el Acuerdo de Libre Comercio entre el Gobierno de la República del Perú y el Gobierno de la República de Singapur." 2009, July 26. *El Peruano. Boletín de Normas Legales* 26 (10681): 399716.

Decreto Supremo No. 044-2009-RE. "Ratifican el Acuerdo de Libre Comercio entre el Gobierno de Canadá y la República del Perú." 2009, July 31. *El Peruano. Boletín de Normas Legales* 26 (10685): 399835–36.

Decreto Supremo No. 057-2006-RE. "Ratifican el Acuerdo de Libre Comercio entre el Gobierno de la República del Perú y el Gobierno de la República de Chile, que modifica y sustituye el ACE N° 38, sus Anexos, Apéndices, Protocolos y demás Instrumentos que hayan sido Suscritos a su Amparo. ACUERDO DE LIBRE COMERCIO PERU–CHILE." 2006, August 26. *El Peruano. Boletín de Normas Legales* 23 (9570): 326900–1.

Decreto Supremo No. 092-2009-RE. "Ratifican el Acuerdo de Libre Comercio entre el Gobierno de la República del Perú y el Gobierno de la República Popular China." 2009, December 6. *El Peruano. Boletín de Normas Legales* 26 (10816): 407395–96.

Decreto Supremo No. 162-92-EF. "Aprueba el reglamento de los regímenes de garantía a la inversión privada." October 12, 1992. *El Peruano.* Available at: http://www.proinversion.gob.pe/RepositorioAPS/0/0/JER/MARCOLEGALTRIBUTARIO/14-D_S_162-92-EF.pdf [Retrieved September 25, 2010].

Defensoría del Pueblo. 2010. *Reporte de conflictos sociales. Adjuntía para la prevención de conflictos sociales y la gobernabilidad.* Publication No. 75, May 2010. Available at: http://www.defensoria.gob.pe/modules/Downloads/conflictos/2010/reporte-75-2010.pdf [Retrieved on August 20, 2010].

Día de la papa revaloriza tubérculo e incentiva su consumo. 2008, May 30. *Andina.* [online] Available at: http://www.andina.com.pe/espanol/Noticia.aspx?id=PIgfPRkmv74= [Retrieved on September 10, 2010].

Economist Intelligence Unit. 2009. "Global Microscope on the Microfinance Business Environment." [online] *The Economist.* Available at: http://viewswire.eiu.com/report_dl.asp?mode=fi&fi=134884398.PDF&rf=0 [Retrieved on August 25, 2010].

Gallardo, J., K. Lopez, and C. González. 2007. *Perú: Evolución del Acceso, la cobertura y la penetración en los Servicios de Telefonía.* OSIPTEL. (Report No. 1 SGI-GPR 2007). Lima. [online] Available at: http://www.mtc.gob.pe/portal/consultas/cid/Boletines_CID/25_AGOSTO/ARCHIVO/Telecom/Osiptel.pdf [Retrieved on August 15, 2010].

Gasparini, L., F. Gutierrez, and L. Tornarolli. 2007. "Growth and Income Poverty in Latin America and the Caribbean: Evidence from Household Surveys." *Review of Income and Wealth* 53, no. 2: 209–45.

Gilvonio, Sonia. 2010, February 10. "El 16.5% de los limeños ya es de clase media." *Diario Gestión* pp. 16–17. Available at: http://gestion.pe/impresa/edicion/2010-02-10 [Retrieved August 23, 2010].

Gomez de la Torre, S., J. A. Irey, F. M. Silva, and G. Vacas. 2007. "Propuesta de un método de internacionalización para una cadena de restaurantes: El caso Roky's." Master's thesis. Lima: Universidad ESAN.

Instituto de Economía y Empresa. 2008. "Economía informal y Mypes en el Perú (I)." *Boletín Económico empresarial A–Z,* 01(36): 1. Available at: http://www.iee.edu.pe/doc/publicaciones/az/Boletin_36_IEE.pdf [Retrieved on August 23, 2010].

Instituto Nacional de Estadística e Informática. 2010a. *Encuesta Nacional de Hogares (ENAHO), Anual 2003–2009.* Available at: http://www1.inei.gob.pe [Retrieved on August 10, 2010].

Instituto Nacional de Estadística e Informática. 2010b. *Las Tecnologías de Información y Comunicación en los Hogares, Trimestre: Abril-Mayo-Junio 2010.* Informe Técnico No. 3. Available at: http://www1.inei.gob.pe/web/Biblioinei/BoletinFlotante.asp?file=11388.pdf [Retrieved on September 3, 2010].

Instituto Nacional de Estadística e Informática. 2010c. *Metodología del Cambio de Año Base 2009 del Índice de Precios al Consumidor de Lima Metropolitana.* [online] Available at: http://www1.inei.gob.pe/web/Metodologias/Attach/9944.pdf [Retrieved September 24, 2010].

International Centre for Settlement of Investment Disputes. 2010. *Lista de estados contratantes y signatarios del convenio(al 5 de mayo 2011).* Available at: http://icsid.worldbank.org/ICSID/FrontServlet?requestType=ICSIDDocRH&actionVal=ShowDocument&language=Spanish [Retrieved on June 13, 2011].

International Monetary Fund. 2009. *World Economic Outlook Database,* April 2009 edition. Available at: http://www.imf.org/external/pubs/ft/weo/2009/01/weodata/index.aspx [Retrieved September 16, 2010].

International Organization for Migration, Instituto Nacional de Estadística e Informática and Dirección General de Immigración y Naturalización. 2008. *PERÚ: Estadísticas de la Migración Internacional de Peruanos. 1990–2007.* Lima. [online]. Available at: http://www.inei.gob.pe/biblioineipub/bancopub/Est/Lib0758/Libro.pdf [Retrieved August 5, 2010].

Ipsos Apoyo. 2010. "Perfil del adolescente y el Joven 2010." *Informe Gerencial de Marketing* 10 (166).

Kacef, O. and R. Lopez-Monti. 2010. "América Latina, del auge a la crisis: desafíos de política macroeconómica." *Revista CEPAL* no. 100, April 2010. Available at: http://www.eclac.cl/publicaciones/xml/8/39118/RVE100Kacefetal.pdf [Retrieved September 3, 2010].

Kaufmann, D., A. Kraay, and M. Mastruzzi. 2010. *Peru: Governance Indicators 1996–2009.* [Data file]. The Worldwide Governance Indicators (WGI) project. The World

Bank. Available at: http://info.worldbank.org/governance/wgi/index.asp [Retrieved September 25, 2010].

Kiyán, A. 2010, September 20. Interviewed by J. A. Irey.

Lima, capital gastronómica. 2006, January 24. *La República*. [online] Available at: http://www.larepublica.pe/archive/all/larepublica/20060124/pasadas/13/83287 [Retrieved on September 10, 2010].

MAXIMIXE. 2009. *Servicios Gastronómicos del Perú*. Lima.

Ministerio de Economía y Finanzas. 2008. *Perú: rumbo al primer mundo Fitch otorga grado de inversión a la deuda peruana*. [Nota de prensa], April 2, 2008. Available at: http://www.mef.gob.pe/index.php?option=com_content&view=article&id=16 18%3Aperu-rumbo-al-primer-mundo-fitch-otorga-grado-de-inversion-a-la-deuda-peruana-&catid=100&Itemid=101108&lang=es [Retrieved September 10, 2010].

Ministerio de Economía y Finanzas. 2009. *Moody's otorga grado de inversión al Perú*. [Nota de prensa], December 16, 2009. Available at: http://www.mef.gob.pe/index. php?option=com_content&view=article&id=1343%3Amoodyas-otorga-grado-de-inversion-al-peru-&catid=100&Itemid=101108&lang=es [Retrieved August 29, 2010].

Ministerio de Economía y Finanzas. 2010a. *Informe de Seguimiento del Marco Macroeconómico Multianual 2010-2012-Revisado a Junio 2010*. Available at: http://www.mef.gob.pe/contenidos/pol_econ/marco_macro/Informe_Seguimiento_MMM2010_2012_Rev_ISEM.pdf [Retrieved September 25, 2010].

Ministerio de Economía y Finanzas. 2010b. *Marco Macroeconómico Multianual 2011–2013*. Available at: http://www.mef.gob.pe/contenidos/pol_econ/marco_macro/MMM2011_2013.pdf [Retrieved September 10, 2010].

Ministerio de Economía y Finanzas. 2010c. *Marco Macroeconómico Multianual Revisado 2011–2013 (actualizado al mes de agosto del 2010)*. Available at: http://www.bcrp.gob.pe/docs/Publicaciones/Programa-Economico/MMM-2011-2013-agosto. pdf [Retrieved September 25, 2010].

Ministerio de la Producción estima alcanzar las 100 mil mypes formalizadas en próximos 60 días, 2010, July 23. *Andina*. [online] Available at: http://www.andina.com. pe/Espanol/Noticia.aspx?id=AVi67/wmE0Y= [Retrieved on August 25, 2010].

Ministerio de Relaciones Exteriores del Perú. 2010a. *Convenios sobre inversiones*. Available at: http://www.rree.gob.pe/portal/Pbilateral.nsf/dd957cb673afb91a052 56c0c005e6bb5?OpenView&Start=1&Count=160&Expand=2.4#2.4 [Retrieved on August 25, 2010].

Ministerio de Relaciones Exteriores del Perú. 2010b. *Informe de la Secretaría – Parte C (Régimen de Política comercial: Marco y Objetivos)*. Available at: http://www.rree. gob.pe/portal/Multi.nsf/b8d39e730990725d05256bf3007d721c/2ed22005079319 2105256c290056e832?OpenDocument [Retrieved on August 25, 2010].

Moro, Diana (2010). *Experiencia y Resultados de la Nueva Administración Judicial. Juzgados Comerciales de Lima*. [PDF slides] Presentation at the VIII International Seminar on Judicial Management, held in Brasilia, 28–30 November 2010. Available at: http://www.cejamericas.org/ponenciasVIIIgestion/experienciayresultadosdelanue vaadmjudicial.pdf [Retrieved on August 22, 2010].

Olivera, Mario. 2002. "Sociología de la corrupción: una base científica para emprender reales políticas anticorrupción." Lima: Colegio de Sociólogos del Perú.

Organización Internacional para las Migraciones, Instituto Nacional de Estadística e Informática. 2009. "Migración Internacional en las Familias Peruanas y Perfil del Peruano Retornante." Lima. [online] Available at: http://www.oimlima.org.pe/docs/ publicacion2009-1.pdf [Retrieved August 5, 2010].

Peñaranda, César. 2010, August 24. *Importancia económica de la micro y pequeña empresa en el Perú.* [PowerPoint slides]. Presentation at the III Expopyme Alternativas de financiamiento para seguir creciendo frente a un entorno más competitivo, Cámara de Comercio de Lima. Available at: http://www.camaralima.org.pe/IIIExpoPyme/Manana/MYPEs%20-%20Dr%20Pe%C3%B1aranda.ppt [Retrieved on August 22, 2010].

Perry, G.E. and W.F. Maloney. 2007. "Overview: Informality: Exit and Exclusion." In G.E. Perry et al. (Eds), *Informality: Exit and Exclusion*, pp. 1–20. Washington: World Bank. [online]. Available at: http://books.google.com.pe/books?hl=es&lr=&id=JXIQ HXi_crAC&oi=fnd&pg=PR11&dq=Informality:+Exit+and+Exclusion&ots=m-qGk2B t2y&sig=wbWN6oEWBfEvGiwaMnwBbNWOR5I#v=onepage&q&f=false [Retrieved on August 23, 2010].

Perú obtiene otro reconocimiento: Calificadora Standard & Poor's le otorga grado de inversión. 2008, July 15. *El Peruano* pp. 3–4.

Perú y Unión Europea concluyen negociación de TLC bilateral. 2010, February 28. *Andina* [online]. Available at: http://www.andina.com.pe/espanol/Noticia.aspx?id= GSFgtRmqJIo= [Retrieved on August 28, 2010].

Pinilla, Susana. 2004. *Condiciones de éxito de los emprendedores emergentes de Lima en el contexto de globalización.* Tesina. Universidad Nacional Mayor de San Marcos. Facultad de Ciencias Sociales. Lima. Available at: http://sisbib.unmsm.edu.pe/bibvirtual/monografias/sociales/pinilla_cs/contenido.htm [Retrieved August 4, 2010].

Presidential Proclamation 8341: "To Implement The United States-Peru Trade Promotion Agreement and for Other Purposes." 74 Fed. Reg. 4105 (2009). Available at: http://edocket.access.gpo.gov/2009/pdf/E9-1573.pdf [Retrieved on August 12, 2010].

Proética. 2010. *Sexta Encuesta Nacional sobre percepciones de la corrupción en el Perú.* [PowerPoint slides]. Available at: http://www.proetica.org.pe/Descargas/sexta%20encuesta.ppt [Retrieved on September 17, 2010].

Projusticia. 2007. *Las inversiones y la estabilidad jurídica en el Perú.* Available at: http://www.projusticia.org.pe/downloads/documento/Inversiones%20y%20Estabilidad%20Juridica.doc [Retrieved August 26, 2010].

Promperú. 2006. "Perfil del Turista Extranjero 2005." [online] Available at: http://media.peru.info/IMPP/2010/TurismoReceptivo/Demanda%20Actual/Perfil%20del%20Turista%20Extranjero%202005/Publicación%20Perfil%20del%20Turista%20Ex tranjero%202005.pdf [Retrieved October 13, 2010].

Promperú. 2010a. "Nivel de Satisfacción del Turista Extranjero 2009." [online] Available at: http://media.peru.info/IMPP/2010/TurismoReceptivo/Demanda%20Actual/Nive l%20de%20Satisfacción%20del%20Turista%20Extranjero/Publicación%20NSTE%2 02009.pdf [Retrieved September 10, 2010].

Promperú. 2010b. "Perfil del turista extranjero 2009." [online] Available at: http://media.peru.info/IMPP/2010/TurismoReceptivo/Demanda%20Actual/Perfil%20de l%20Turista%20Extranjero%202009/Publicación%20PTE%202009.pdf [Retrieved September 04, 2010].

Razo, C. and F. Rojas. 2007. "Del monopolio de Estado a la convergencia tecnológica: evolución y retos de la regulación de telecomunicaciones en América Latina." Serie Desarrollo Productivo No. 185. CEPAL. Santiago de Chile. [online] Available at: http://www.eclac.org/publicaciones/xml/4/32434/Serie_DDPE_185.pdf [Retrieved on August 31, 2010].

Resolución Directoral No. 1066/INC. "Reconocen como especialidad culinaria perú-ana al 'Pollo a la brasa'." 2004, October 27. *El Peruano* 21 (8896): 279193.

Resolución Legislativa No. 25312. "Aprueban el 'Convenio Constitutivo del Organismo Multilateral de Garantía de Inversiones." April 3, 1991. *El Peruano*.

Resolución Ministerial No. 0441-2010-AG. "Declaran el tercer domingo de julio de cada año como 'El día del Pollo a la Brasa'." 2010, June 26. *El Peruano* 27 (11037): 421246.

Roky's. 2010. "Pollos y Parrilladas Roky's." [website] Available at: http://www.rokys. com/ [Retrieved September 13, 2010].

Ruiz, Gonzalo. 2010, August 23. "Perú, un nuevo punto en el mapa del turismo gastronómico mundial." *Diario ElPaís.cr.* [online] Available at: http://www.elpais. cr/articulos.php?id=30820 [Retrieved on September 10, 2010].

Santa María, H. 2010, April 5. "Siete razones por las que el Perú podría crecer 7% este año." *Gestión* p. 31. Available at: http://gestion.pe/impresa/edicion/2010-04-05/9169 [Retrieved August 25, 2010].

Serida, J., A. Borda, K. Nakamatsu, O. Morales, and P. Yamakawa. 2006. *Global Entrepreneurship Monitor: Perú 2004–2005*. ESAN. Lima. [online] Available at: http:// gemconsortium.org/download.asp?fid=455 [Retrieved September 3, 2010].

Serida, J., A. Borda, and K. Nakamatsu. 2007. *Global Entrepreneurship Monitor: Perú 2006*. Lima: ESAN. [online] Available at: http://gemconsortium.org/ download/1290017810180/gem_2006.pdf [Retrieved September 3, 2010].

Serida, J., A. Borda, L. Uehara, K. Nakamatsu, and J. Alzamora. 2009. *Global Entrepreneurship Monitor: Perú 2007*. Lima: ESAN. [online] Available at: http:// gemconsortium.org/download/1290017510321/GEM%20Peru%202007.pdf [Retrieved September 3, 2010].

Serida, J., K. Nakamatsu, and L. Uehara. 2010. *Global Entrepreneurship Monitor: Perú 2008*. Lima: ESAN. [online] Available at: http://gemconsortium.org/download. asp?fid=1042 [Retrieved September 3, 2010].

Serida, J., K. Nakamatsu, and L. Uehara. In press. *Global Entrepreneurship Monitor: Perú 2009*. Lima: ESAN.

Superintendencia de Banca, Seguros y AFP. 2010. *Peruvian Financial System, Liquidity Indicators Jan 2002–Sept 2008: Loan Loss Provisión, NPL Ratio of the Banking System, Credit to Private Sector, and Liquidity Ratio of the Banking System* [statistics]. Available at: http://www.sbs.gob.pe/0/modulos/JER/JER_Interna.aspx?ARE=0&PFL=0&JER=148 [Retrieved September 10, 2010].

Tam, Felipe. 2010. "Las microfinanzas bajo el microscopio." *Punto de Equilibrio* 18 (102). Available at: http://www.puntodeequilibrio.com.pe/punto_equilibrio/01i. php?pantalla=noticia&id=15814&bolnum_key=30&serv_key=2100 [Retrieved September 25, 2010].

Transparency International. 2009. *Corruption Perceptions Index 2009*. Transparency International's work. Berlin. Available at: http://www.transparency.org/policy_ research/surveys_indices/cpi/2009 [Retrieved on August 17, 2010].

United Nations Commission on International Trade Law. 2010. *Status 1958 Convention on the Recognition and Enforcement of Foreign Arbitral Awards – the "New York" Convention.* Available at: http://www.uncitral.org/uncitral/en/uncitral_texts/ arbitration/NYConvention_status.html [Retrieved September 2, 2010].

United Nations in Perú and Presidencia del Consejo de Ministros. 2009. *Informe de cumplimiento de los Objetivos de Desarrollo del Milenio. Perú 2008. Resumen Ejecutivo.* Oficina del Coordinador Residente.de las Naciones Unidas en el Perú. Secretaría Técnica de la Comisión Interministerial de Asuntos Sociales. Available at: http:// www.onu.org.pe/upload/documentos/IODM-Peru2008.pdf [Retrieved August 25, 2010].

Vargas Llosa, M. 2009, March 22. "El sueño del chef." *El Comercio* p. a4.

Verdera, F. 2010. *Perú, programa especial de reconversión laboral Revalora Perú. OIT Notas sobre la crisis.* Available at: http://www.oit.org.pe/2/wp-content/uploads/2009/10/09-Peru-esp.pdf [Retrieved August 7, 2010].

Vuletin, G. 2008. "Measuring the Informal Economy in Latin America and the Caribbean," Working Paper WP/08/102. International Monetary Fund. Available at: http://www.imf.org/external/pubs/ft/wp/2008/wp08102.pdf [Retrieved on August 22, 2010].

World Bank. 2008. *Doing Business 2009: Comparing Regulations in 181 Economies.* Washington, DC: World Bank Group. Available at: http://www.doingbusiness.org/~/media/FPDKM/Doing%20Business/Documents/Annual-Reports/English/DB09-FullReport.pdf [Retrieved September 20, 2010].

World Bank and International Finance Corporation. 2010. *Doing Business 2011: Making a Difference for Entrepreneurs.* Washington, DC: World Bank Group. Available at: http://www.doingbusiness.org/~/media/FPDKM/Doing%20Business/Documents/Annual-Reports/English/DB11-FullReport.pdf [Retrieved September 20, 2010].

World Bank. World Development Indicators. *Domestic Credit Provided by Banking Sector 2005–09 (% of GDP).* [Data file]. Available at: http://data.worldbank.org/indicator/FS.AST.DOMS.GD.ZS?display=map [Retrieved August 23, 2010].

9
Entrepreneurship in Venezuela: Case Study

Roberto Vainrub and Aramis Rodriguez
IESA

Entrepreneurs are driven by the need to make a living or by a vision of exploiting opportunity. Together, they weave a country's economic fabric; but those who strive for opportunity have the capacity to bring about innovation and change, to shape a flourishing economy. Sometimes entrepreneurs overshoot their target and their business flounders. Something of that ilk occurs when government leaders shape the context in which economies grow or decline, a paradox that is illustrated by Venezuela's entrepreneurial and political development.

This chapter begins by describing historical and cultural factors that have influenced entrepreneurial activity in Venezuela, and is followed by a review of economic and political developments that govern the country's business context. Measures of entrepreneurship during periods of economic, financial, and regulatory volatility are examined, and best practices by key players who grew their business under turbulent conditions are described. The chapter concludes by noting a series of challenges currently faced by investors in Venezuela, together with opportunities within reach of entrepreneurs with both vision and stamina.

Historical and cultural factors

Entrepreneurship in Venezuela has been shaped by the country's history. During three centuries of colonial rule Venezuela was part of Greater Colombia. As early as the sixteenth century German bankers sought gold and silver from Venezuela, which was open to the Caribbean and the world. In the 1730s the Spanish crown commissioned a Basque trading company to deter pirates from roaming the Venezuelan coast and ensure continued supply of the country's exquisite cocoa. Beginning in 1810 a Venezuelan, Simón Bolívar, liberated five countries from Spain in the quest for a grand South American union patterned on the one being shaped in North America; but

Venezuela soon became engulfed in conflicts led by military chiefs. The first strongman, José Antonio Páez, separated Venezuela from Colombia in 1830 and ruled intermittently until the 1860s. Yet Venezuela remained a magnet for people from faraway lands.

Europeans arriving in Venezuela in the nineteenth century included the Blohm, Boulton, Hellmund, and Vollmer ancestors of what decades later became leading family-owned companies. The first telegraph cable linking South America and Marseilles in the 1870s brought people from a dozen countries: Italians settling largely in eastern Venezuela and Sephardic Jews and people of Arab origin in the west – generally in sea coast communities. Coffee and cattle displaced cocoa, but discovery of oil in the 1920s abruptly altered Venezuela's future. Incipient but growing oil revenue enabled Juan Vicente Gómez to rule for 40 years – the first chieftain to put in place a strong central government in what remained a largely rural society.

As the state gained economic power, business and other social groups closely linked with government officials benefited. Largely overlooked were efforts to shape civilian political life and build strong governmental institutions of the kind that foster entrepreneurial development. The outcome was a system of personal political exchange among small social groups that left out the population at large. Business opportunity outside such groups was stifled, slowing the evolution of a body of law that would contain corruption.

Cultural factors also weighed heavily on entrepreneurial initiative. Latin America is considered relatively homogeneous from a cultural standpoint (Ogliastri et al. 1999: 49). Commonly shared values include elitism, low achievement motivation, little control over uncertainty, and unusually high loyalty to families and groups. Dealy (1992) holds that commonly shared beliefs and social affinities tend to differ from northern values – Latin Americans being less inclined to undertake efforts aimed at acquiring prestige or accumulating wealth. Unlike Latin Americans from more conservative, class-dominated societies, Venezuelans became uncommonly egalitarian (Uslar 1963: 121), an attribute that in neighboring Colombia has been linked with an urge for individual freedom, secularization, and consumerism (Cruz 1993).

Emergence of modern Venezuela

Following the Second World War, Venezuela's rising oil revenue and plans by strongman Marcos Pérez Jiménez to reshape the country's development by recruiting European immigrants brought skills to foster trade and industry, and build local infrastructure. Table 9.1 shows that almost two-thirds of Venezuelan immigrants were born in Europe, largely Spain, Italy, and Portugal (Baptista 2006). Population in urban centers across the country soared. The blend of migrants, landed elites, and local population spawned

Table 9.1 Venezuela's European immigration, 1936–81

	Total population A	Foreignborn B	B/A(%)	European immigrants	From Spain, Italy, and Portugal	% European of total immigrants	% from Spain, Italy, and Portugal
1936	3,364,347	47,026	1.4	22,916	8,432	48.7	36.8
1941	3,850,771	49,928	1.3	24,938	11,016	50.0	44.2
1950	5,034,380	206,767	4.1	134,076	92,902	64.8	69.3
1961	7,523,999	541,536	7.2	369,298	330,366	68.2	89.5
1971	10,721,522	596,455	5.6	329,850	298,426	55.3	90.1
1981	14,516,735	1,074,629	7.4	349,117	317,536	32.5	91.0

Source: Adapted from Pellegrini (1989).

an emerging middle class, shaping a social fabric that laid the foundations of Venezuela's entrepreneurial spirit.

In less than a decade, Venezuela underwent remarkable change. Nelson Rockefeller's International Basic Economy Corporation opened the first supermarkets in major cities, with scores of multinational and local companies supplying previously unavailable packaged goods. Immigrants soon dominated one trade or another (Gómez and Dezerega 1989): Italians generally ran the construction sector and part of the food chain, as in poultry and meatpacking; Portuguese opened neighborhood food shops that in time became supermarket chains; Spaniards from the Canary Islands and Galicia operated carpentry and metalworking shops, or served as taxi drivers who later organized road transport; Basques became academics; Jews from Eastern Europe helped build a textile and garment-making industry. Larger businesses and banks were led by the prevailing higher social classes and of skilled immigrants.

But prosperity did not spread throughout society, and income gaps widened. By the 1980s as much as one-half of Venezuela's labor force sought to make a living from the informal economy; micro-entrepreneurs operated atomized business units, largely in trade, services, and makeshift workshops, housed in sprawling urban slums prone to violence. Such entrepreneurial activities were driven by necessity, not business opportunity. Underlying such opportunity was the individualist character of Venezuelan entrepreneurs seeking to serve consumers anxious to access material goods.

Venezuela's mid-twentieth-century infant industry, as elsewhere in Latin America, was guided by policies led by the United Nations Economic Commission for Latin America, locally known by its Spanish acronym CEPAL. Markets in each Latin American country were protected from foreign competition. Only after borders were opened following the 1989 Washington Consensus,[1] did multinational or *multilatina* companies acquire family-owned firms throughout the region and close down undersized, inefficient plants (Gómez 1997); operations were gradually regrouped, manufacturing in larger markets and strengthening marketing support elsewhere (Penfold and Vainrub 2009). Few exports other than oil and iron ore were competitive. Venezuela's overvalued currency encouraged imports, and the country's fragile economy became dependent on oil prices.

Changing business and political context: Social and political forces

Recent decades have witnessed profound social, economic, and political change in Venezuela and throughout Latin America (Smith 2005, Tulchin and Brown 2002). Following the fall of Pérez Jiménez, a pact, signed in 1958, among political forces led by Rómulo Betancourt forged a vision of Venezuela as perhaps the region's leading democracy – prospects that were buttressed by soaring oil revenue in the 1970s. Expanding population, however, coupled with gross income inequality and poor coverage of basic public services, spawned social tensions. Oil revenue had been deployed to expand state-owned enterprises, with considerable wealth siphoned away by business, labor, and military insiders linked to political parties. When oil prices began a long decline in the 1980s, the country's political mood steadily worsened. In 1992, Lt Col. Hugo Chávez led a failed coup; and in 1998, angered citizens elected him president by a landslide vote.

Chávez started out by rewriting the Constitution, expanding presidential powers before turning to control of the economy by means of nationalizations, expropriations, direct subsidies, and heavy spending (Penfold and Corrales 2011). Nationalizations spanned a privately owned, publicly traded telecom firm together with power and light companies, four foreign-owned cement firms, and an Argentine-owned steelyard; expropriations included 74 oil service providers, rural and urban property, and more than 40 factories and firms, including the country's leading coffee processors (Álvarez 2006).

The outcome of these developments was unprecedented political and regulatory volatility that generated an unpropitious climate for launching business ventures. Figure 9.1 shows Venezuela had long been prey to recurrent periods of political instability, dictatorial rule, and revolutionary turbulence; and double-digit inflation had plagued the economy for years. In 1983, Venezuela suffered its first financial crisis in decades. This was followed by intermittent periods of currency exchange controls, civil riots and unrest, two coup attempts, the impeachment of President Carlos Andrés Pérez, and a restructuring of external debt. All this did not call a halt to opportunity-driven business. But unhappily for Venezuela, necessity-driven entrepreneurship became more relevant.[2]

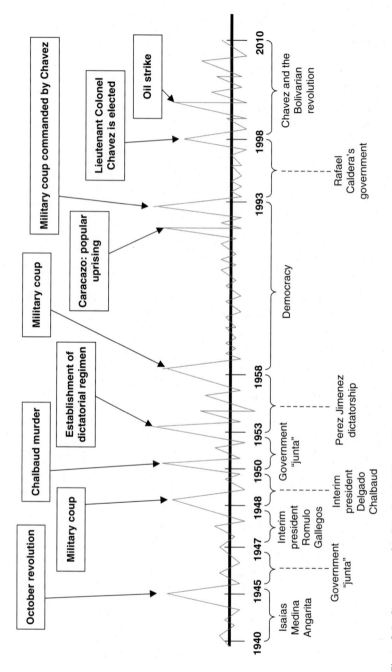

Figure 9.1 Sixty years of political volatility in Venezuela
Source: Author's elaboration.

Chávez's "Bolivarian revolution" based its legitimacy on successive electoral victories. Figure 9.2 shows that, on the average, as many as 14 elections were held in a span of less than 12 years. Despite certain electoral setbacks, each outcome was presented as a revolutionary victory, thus generating a climate of uncertainty for investors and entrepreneurs. In the last ten years, the political agenda has played a predominant role in lives of Venezuelans every year. Figure 9.3 depicts the high polarization as measured by confidence in President Chávez and confidence in his opposition. Although political party opposition is permitted, the country's oldest TV station, featuring by far the largest audience, was silenced in 2008 by not renewing its license; and state-owned broadcast media have greatly expanded.

Following an attempted coup against the regime in 2003, Chávez undertook to build voter support, especially among the poor. He succeeded in developing hard-core loyalty from about two-fifths of the country's voters, in large measure by delivering primary healthcare and subsidized food prices in slum communities by means of generously supported programs called missions.[3] For example, Mission Che Guevara (initially named *Vuelvan Caras* and aimed at the unemployed) offered vocational programs in agriculture, tourism, and construction, including cash stipends for participants deemed loyal to the regime. Interestingly enough, Chávez was unable to retain voter support in the country's largest urban areas in the 2010 parliamentary elections.

Social and economic impact during the last decade

After 12 years in power, the Chávez presidency weighs heavily on business as it does on social relations among ordinary Venezuelans. Chávez himself has declared (August 2010): "the Bolivarian revolution seeks to encourage and produce small and medium-sized businesses that seek to work for Venezuela"; yet he has also stated (June 17, 2010): "Fedecámaras [National Federation of Chambers of Commerce and Industry] members represent the most parasitic and monopolistic colonial form of capitalism," declaring them to be "enemies of the homeland." Such charges, reiterated on weekly radio and TV programs, and on national media hookups on prime time, have been coupled with heavy-handed land expropriations and business takeovers. Not surprisingly, investment in plant and equipment by privately owned firms has dwindled and local output of all goods, including foodstuffs, declined markedly; new ventures in recent years have centered largely on projects promising a handsome short-term return, such as importing expensive vehicles or opening first-class restaurants.

Government impact on business, and on professional and upper-middle-income groups generally have also affected the economy. Factories, including auto assembly plants, periodically close operations awaiting import

268

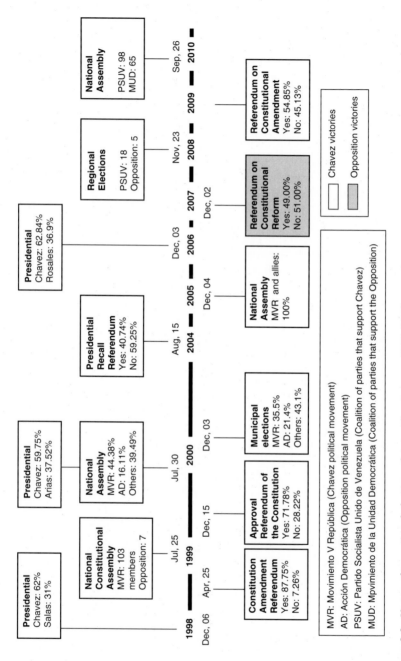

Figure 9.2 Venezuelan national elections dates and outcomes, 1998–2010
Source: Author's elaboration based on data from CNE (Consejo Nacional Electoral de Venezuela).

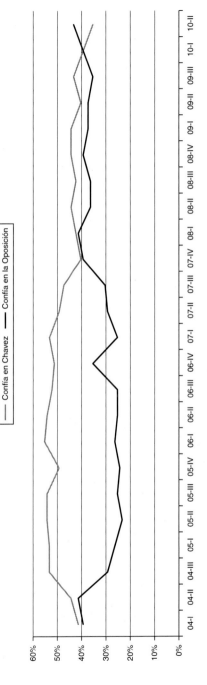

Figure 9.3 Polarization of confidence (Chávez *vs.* the Opposition)
Source: Consultores 21 (2010).
Consultores 21 is an important Venezuelan market research company.

licenses for key materials held up by public agency officials. Widespread shortages persist despite massive food imports by government agencies. Pork and poultry producers have shut down, unable to reach breakeven at controlled prices under high inflation. Food processors must limit their inventory lest they be accused of hoarding, risking confiscation of their goods. Butchers unable to sell sliced and pan-ready cuts of beef at retail prices set by the authorities have at times offered chunks of meat attached to hide and bone; some supermarkets simply closed the meat department. Consumers must visit several retail outlets in search of basic household staples, including coffee and toilet paper.

Despite rebounding oil prices, Venezuela's economy shrank by 5.8 percent in the first three months of 2010 compared to the same period in 2009 (Banco Central de Venezuela 2010). Figure 9.4 shows Venezuela recorded the highest inflation rate in Latin America – 30.4 percent (International Monetary Fund 2010). Meanwhile, government rhetoric vis-à-vis inflation, widespread shortages, and general discontent centers on more of the same: big business is blamed for destabilizing the economy.

Support is ostensibly offered to small business as a means of growing "twenty-first century socialism." As explained by President Chávez (2003), the social economy "brings together economic and social interests and gains

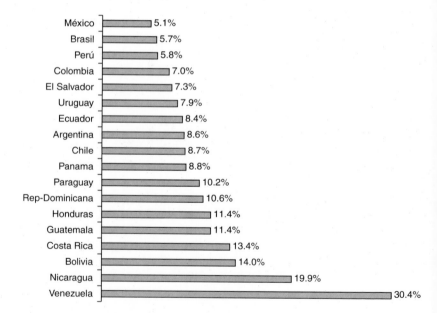

Figure 9.4 Inflation rate in Latin America, 2009
Source: Modified from International Monetary Fund (2010).

strength from dynamism in local communities featuring citizen and worker participation in alternative business, such as associative enterprises and self-managed micro-enterprises." Social production enterprises (EPSs)[4] are defined (Chávez 2005) as "economic entities dedicated to the production of goods or services in which work has its proper and authentic value, with no discrimination associated with any type of work, no privileges related to certain positions or hierarchies and with equality between its members, based on participative planning."

To forge a so-called social economy, massive resources have been lavished on setting up and financing operations by cooperatives. A first step was to relax requirements for registering cooperatives contained in legislation grounded in international practice. As a result, the number of cooperatives operating in Venezuela rose from 1336 in 2001 to 102,568 in 2005 (Bruni Celli 2009: 247). An in-depth study of a sample of nine cooperatives considered unusually successful by international donor organizations and other knowledgeable observers found that the best that could be said for them was their capacity to offer employment (an average of 24 members plus 10 employees each); significantly, four of the nine were unable to replace working capital and equipment required for operations, and the five that could were led by managers of above-average education (Bruni Celli 2009: 268). In short, vast resources channeled to cooperatives from 2001 onwards appear to have been largely wasted.

Venezuela has for the past four decades featured a business context that borders on the unpredictable as a result of the country's economic, financial, and regulatory volatility. Perhaps the clearest evidence of financial volatility is that despite price controls, the Venezuelan bolivar declined in value from 1975 to 2009 by a stunning 50,000 percent (Penfold and Vainrub 2009: 28). Admittedly, however, current threats to business enterprise are considered more severe than those experienced in the past.

Oil prices and politics

When Chávez was first elected in 1998, Venezuela's economy was in a shambles. Prices for Venezuelan oil had fallen to almost US$8 per barrel, the lowest in decades. GDP per capita had reverted to the level of the early 1950s; 58 percent of the population lived in poverty and 29 percent in extreme poverty (Banco Central de Venezuela 2010). At the start of President Chávez's administration, fiscal and monetary policy was conservative; contrary to what might have been expected, one of the first measures deployed was to cut back on social expenditures.

In the first five years of the Chávez administration, 1999–2003, the economy contracted – at first because of low oil prices, and later as a result of political uncertainty. By 2001 civic organizations, political parties, business

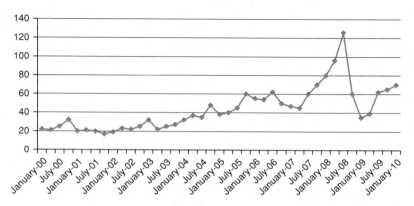

Figure 9.5 Oil prices (US$/barrel) – Venezuelan basket (2000–10)
Source: Banco Central de Venezuela (BCV in Spanish).

Table 9.2 Oil as percentage of total exports

Year	Oil exports	Other exports
1999	79.83	20.17
2000	83.30	16.87
2001	81.54	18.46
2002	80.40	19.60
2003	80.90	19.10
2004	82.87	17.13
2005	86.41	13.59
2006	88.40	11.60
2007	90.77	9.23
2008	93.68	6.32
2009	94.54	5.46

Source: BCV (Banco Central de Venezuela).

groups, and the media increasingly expressed discontent against the president. In April 2002 Chávez was removed from the presidency, albeit for only two days, and later that year a three-month-long work stoppage halted oil production. Other reasons for the economic decline were capital flight and a sharp fall in foreign investment. A stopgap measure undertaken early in 2003 was the reintroduction of exchange controls.[5]

As shown in Table 9.2, six years after Chávez's 2004 announcement of a new economic model, Venezuela's dependence on oil is greater than ever before. During the first four years of the Chávez administration oil represented roughly 80 percent of total exports, with other products accounting for the remaining 20 percent (Banco Central de Venezuela 2010). Following 2004, other exports declined steadily, to 13.6 percent in 2005, 9.2 percent in 2007, and a mere 5.5 percent in 2009 (Banco Central de Venezuela 2010).

An economic overview of the Chávez presidency reveals that Venezuela's oil exports reached, over a span of 12 years, nearly US$1 trillion. Figure 9.6 shows that much of this influx was channeled to consumption, with Venezuela importing about two-thirds of its food needs. Up to 2008, US firms exported US$1.6 billion worth of agricultural products, including wheat, corn, soybeans, soybean meal, cotton, animal fats, vegetable oils, and other items that render Venezuela an important market, within South America, for US exports (Banco Central de Venezuela 2010). But Venezuelan industrial output declined as political uncertainty, regulatory volatility, and high-handed government measures, combined with an overvalued official exchange rate that inhibits exports, shrank private investment. Other than oil, manufacturing in Venezuela came to consist mainly of cement, tires, paper, fertilizer, and vehicle assembly for both domestic and export markets.

Consider now the accumulated impact of Venezuela's political and business context on entrepreneurship.

Measures of entrepreneurship and current challenges

Year after year, Venezuela has ranked among the world's top countries in terms of early entrepreneurial activity as measured by the GEM.[6] Table 9.3 shows that, each year, as many as three million people, approximately 22.8 percent of Venezuelan adults, start a new business or run a recent start-up. Given the business context described above, how is this possible?

Table 9.3 shows that more than one-third of Venezuelans who start a new business do so out of necessity, as compared with about one-quarter of those starting a new business in other countries for which GEM data are available. Even under necessity, however, TEA has declined since 2003, the first year for which data are available. Some specialists consider this trend is simply an outcome of declining per capita income.[7] Nonetheless, entrepreneurial activity driven by opportunity increased during the same period. In 2003, 55.6 percent of business start-ups were classed as driven by opportunity; by 2009, this figure had climbed to 66 percent (Fernández et al. 2009, Vainrub and Arevalo 2003).

To shed light on what motivates Venezuelans to start a new business, either out of necessity or opportunity, a group of local specialists was convened (GEM 2003, 2005, 2007). These specialists concurred that both economic and political forces shape entrepreneurial activity. A majority considered high political uncertainty during the last decade as the main force defining these variables, with oil prices as a second determining factor. Figure 9.7 illustrates the impact of how, from 2002 to 2003, the work stoppage and a corresponding halt in oil production paralyzed the economy. Immediately afterwards, as the economy emerged from the crisis and oil prices soared in

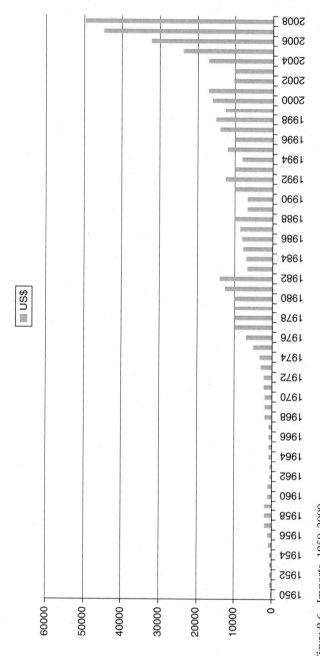

Figure 9.6 Imports, 1950–2009
Source: Banco Central de Venezuela (2010).

Table 9.3 Entrepreneurial activity in Venezuela

	2003	2005	2007	2009	Average
Total entrepreneurial activity (TEA, %)	27.3	25	20.2	18.7	22.75
Opportunity-driven (%)	55.6	59.6	61.6	66.84	60.91
Necessity-driven (%)	41.9	36.8	32.24	32.08	35.8
Opportunity/necessity	1.36	1.6	1.95	2.08	1.74

Sources: Fernández et al. (2009); Vainrub and Arevalo (2003).

2003–04, business opportunities flourished; but soon thereafter the prospect of another election at year-end 2004 brought on renewed political uncertainty, again slowing opportunity-driven entrepreneurship.

From 2005 to 2008, fiscal income from soaring oil prices triggered significant growth in household consumption, coupled with a perception of better times and improved business opportunity. Relatively few people considered themselves unemployed, thus curbing the pursuit of necessity-driven activities. Moreover, large numbers of Venezuelans participated in one or more social missions that entitled them to cash stipends that may have discouraged them from seeking employment.[8] TEA declined to 20.2 percent in 2007 (Fernández et al. 2009), and the proportion of opportunity-seeking entrepreneurs rose vis-à-vis those driven by necessity. During this period of frequent elections, opposition parties were perceived as lacking vision and public concern arose over control of the judiciary by the executive; confidence in business opportunity may have waned.

Despite vast opportunities that oil booms periodically generate for Venezuelan entrepreneurs, starting a business implies overcoming a number of challenges. Table 9.4 shows how Venezuela is rated by several world indices. By and large these measures assess the country's regulatory processes as being overly discretionary and slow, labor legislation as comparatively rigid, corruption as widespread, and government as overplaying its hand in business by, for example, expropriating companies and applying stringent price controls. Venezuela's banking system is considered relatively sophisticated, but capital markets offer firms few products to access financing; moreover, available options are invariably subject to arbitrary government intervention.

Nonetheless, most of sources for Table 9.4 point to certain competitive advantages that could be turned into opportunities for suitable entrepreneurs. Venezuela features a market that is comparatively sophisticated – given the legacy of so many immigrants and an overvalued currency that facilitates travel abroad – vis-à-vis other Latin American countries, with high consumption patterns for certain goods[9] and a large enough population. In terms of natural resources Venezuela is blessed as well, not only by oil but vast iron ore reserves,

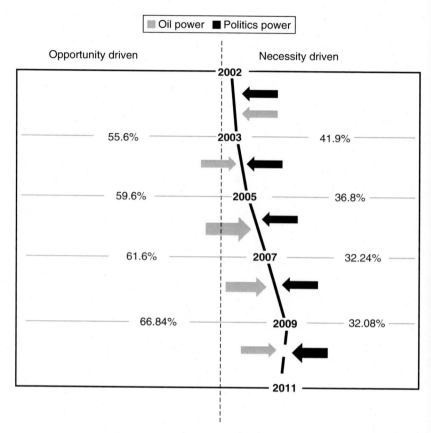

Figure 9.7 Forces and factors governing entrepreneurship in Venezuela, 2002–9
Source: Author's elaboration based on data from GEM.

Table 9.4 Venezuela's world competitiveness rankings

Competitive Index	Year	Organization	Countries ranked	Venezuela's rank
Global Competitive Index	2010	World Economic Forum	133	113
Competitive Index	2010	IMD	58	58
Doing business	2010	World Bank	183	177
Index of Economic Freedom	2010	Heritage Foundation	179	174

Sources: World Economic Forum (2010); Institute for Management Development (2010); Heritage Foundation (2010); World Bank (2010).

abundant water, an extensive coastline, a favorable climate, and a strategic geographical location. Fairly good infrastructure in terms of ports, airports, roads, and telecommunications is available in comparison with its neighbors.

Investors must of course balance opportunities at hand in light of threats surrounding a given project, let alone feasibility and sustainability. Some of those threats and opportunities include weak institutions, an inoperative labor market, and an inefficient bureaucracy.

Weak institutions

A weak institutional framework is perhaps the most frequently cited factor when gauging the feasibility of undertaking direct investments in emerging markets. Consider the following developments that have taken place in Venezuela in recent years (Penfold and Vainrub 2009).

In 2001, a new Lands and Agricultural Development Law was decreed that derogated the entire legal framework concerning agricultural land, imposing a regime allowing a public agency to assess land use. Following passage of this law thousands of acres of cattle ranches and sugarcane lands have been expropriated.

In 2007 and 2008, the government declared several industries to be strategic, and proceeded to nationalize scores of companies including a good many that, as noted earlier, were foreign-owned. These developments were taken as evidence that private property is at risk in Venezuela.

Venezuela is also noted for steep transaction costs that are due to a high crime rate and issues concerned with personal safety, water and power stoppages, regulatory volatility, lack of intellectual property rights, and judicial insecurity. Such factors raise the cost of doing business and fuel uncertainty among opportunity-driven entrepreneurs.

Inoperative labor market

Venezuela's business community views the country's labor legislation as a major hurdle. Since 2001 decrees have been recurrently promulgated to protect formally employed workers against layoffs; moreover, workers cannot be demoted or relocated unless authorized by a Labor Ministry work inspector. These labor law provisions raise contract or dismissal costs, and foster the practice of hiring temporary help (for less than three months) not covered by such protection.

Inefficient bureaucracy

Tables 9.5 and 9.6 show the bureaucratic and legal hurdles, including the number of procedures and time required for processing that must be overcome in Venezuela to register a new firm are greater than in any other region country.

Table 9.5   Number of procedures, time, and cost to start a business

Region and country	Procedures (numbers)	Time (days)	Cost (as % of per capita income)
Latin America and Caribbean	9.5	61.7	36.4
Venezuela	16	141	24

Source: adapted from Doing Business Ranking.

Table 9.6   Number of procedures to start a business in Latin American countries

Country	Number of procedures	Duration of longest procedure
Argentina	15	5 days – Public Register of Commerce
Bolivia	15	15 days – Register in national health insurance
Brazil	16	90 days – Operations permit
Chile	9	15 days – Obtain municipal working license (*patente municipal*)
Colombia	9	14 days – Register in social security system
Ecuador	13	29 days – Inspection from the municipality
Paraguay	7	25 days – Register in *Sistema Unificado de Apertura de Empresas*
Perú	9	15 days – Obtain municipal license
Uruguay	11	45 days – Obtain approval of company's by laws
Venezuela	16	90 days – Register for social security
Average	12	

Source: adapted from Doing Business Ranking.

According to the Heritage Foundation (2010), the overall freedom to start, operate, and close a business is seriously restricted under Venezuela's regulatory environment. Table 9.7 shows that starting a business takes around 141 days, compared to the world average of 35 days and 9.5 in Latin America and the Caribbean. On average, every entrepreneur must complete 16 procedures to start a business, with certain steps taking from 50 to 90 days.

By way of examples, registering with the social security office can take as long as six months; obtaining an industrial or commercial license from a competent municipality can take 50 days. To actually start a business the entrepreneur must file copies of registration, a sanitation certificate, a lease for the premises to be occupied, the latest balance sheet, and a declaration stating the number of employees.

Opportunity-driven Venezuelan entrepreneurs have in recent years overlooked the above business hurdles to seek what Prahalad and Hart (2002) termed the fortune at the bottom of the pyramid (BoP).

Table 9.7   Starting a business in Venezuela (number of procedures and days)

Procedure: registration requirements summary	Time to complete (days)
1 Reserve company name	1
2 Obtain approval for company name	3
3 Prepare and legalize company charter documents	5
4 Open bank account	1
5 Register at the local mercantile registry (Registro Mercantil)	30
6 Publish charter articles in a local newspaper (*Gaceta Forense del Registro Mercantil*)	3
7 Register company books	1
8 Register with national tax authority	1
9 Obtain tax clearance certificate at municipal level (Instituto Municipal de Aseo Urbano).	1
10 Register with the Ministry of Labor	1
11 Go through a labor inspection (Labor Inspectorate)	8
12 Register for social security at a local regional fund.	90
13 Register at the National Educational Cooperation Institute (INCE)	1
14 Obtain fire approval and undergo an inspection	28[†]
15 Obtain conformity of use certificate (zoning permit)	15[†]
16 Obtain industrial or commercial license from a competent municipality	50[†]

Source: World Bank Organization (2010) *Doing Business Ranking*. http://www.doingbusiness.org/economyrankings/ Consulted: sep 2010.
[†] Simultaneous with procedure 11.

BoP ventures

In Venezuela, BoP initiatives are particularly relevant because 80 percent of the population fall in lower-income brackets. In other words, Venezuela features a low-income market comprising more than 22 million people (4.4 million households) that, for the most part, have not been targeted by local companies (Jiménez and Puente 2009).

In part stemming from social redistribution of oil revenue under Venezuela's mission programs, the BoP market has become increasingly important – not only given its sheer size but also relative to other market segments. Companies entering this market driven by social entrepreneurship found that BoP markets feature a number of sub segments. Others have found that given appropriate strategies, the market should offer considerable long-term profit. But according to Auletta and Puente (2009), the huge BoP market potential can only be reached by deploying differentiated value propositions (as opposed to simply offering lightly adapted, low-quality, or lower-priced products), a practice that few companies have up to now undertaken in light of the investment required to probe consumer behavior patterns and assemble a suitable distribution system.

Venezuelan marketing specialists experienced in dealing with BoP consumers hold that to succeed in serving them, companies must deploy innovative approaches; a number of ventures aimed at serving these market segments have purportedly relied on stereotyped communication strategies based on misconceived or erroneous consumer profiles (Dakduk 2009).

Companies that have successfully ventured into Venezuelan BoP markets generally admit to having initially launched their effort with insufficient knowledge of key information areas such as low-income consumer lifestyle, buying and shopping habits, and product expectations (Jiménez and Puente 2009). On the other hand, by undertaking costly, trial-and-error investment to generate insights into strategies for catering to BoP consumers, companies such as Capriles (publisher of *Últimas Noticias,* a newspaper highlighting content drawn from poor communities), Día a Día (convenience stores in poor communities featuring high turnover goods at low prices), Cruzsalud (prepaid healthcare), and Confinanzas (microfinance) have become market pioneers and stand to gain considerable competitive advantage.

Balancing threats and opportunities

Changes in economic, political, and regulatory conditions altering Venezuela's business context have driven entrepreneurs towards either of the following strategies: search out unusually attractive ventures, or cautiously seek investment opportunities offering a quick return. The former may involve a fairly high-risk, long-term commitment with a potentially handsome payback – such as acquiring a distressed company operating in a fairly predictable market or undertaking a construction project. Quick returns can sometimes be obtained from imports or certain services.

Figure 9.8 shows a number of factors that influence the entrepreneurial balance between opportunities, threats, and the kind of business venture that may be launched.

GEM data for Venezuela report that 46.8 percent of ventures promising low potential growth are trade related, 34.7 percent are traditional services, and a scant 3.3 or 3.4 percent, respectively, are manufacturing and primary sector businesses. The most common types of venture include convenience stores, small restaurants, fast food chains, bakeries, ice cream parlors, retail household goods, clothing shops, telecom services, and beauty salons. Clearly, these activities do not add value to the economy as do those based on knowledge or materials transformation that are characteristic of more developed societies.

Data for 2005 show 27.3 percent of Venezuelan entrepreneurs seek to recover their investment in just six months, 35.7 percent in one year, and 19.7 percent in two years. In other words, more than four out of five investors seek a payback of less than two years.

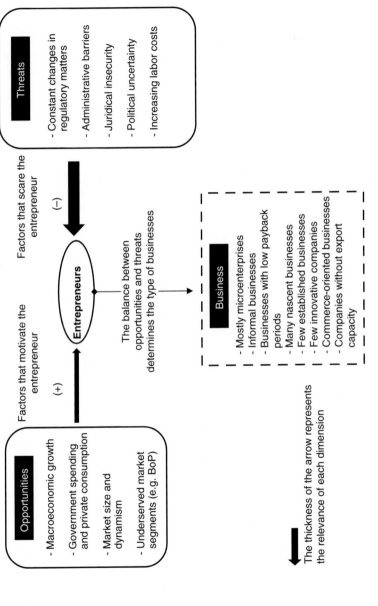

Figure 9.8 Balancing entrepreneurial opportunities, threats, and kinds of business
Source: Author's elaboration.

Also significant is that roughly 50 percent of Venezuelan entrepreneurs report they have no customers outside the country, thus showing they have little or no interest in exporting.

An appalling figure is that only one out of every four Venezuelan start-ups has survived for at least 3.5 years. In countries such as Argentina, Brazil, Chile, Spain, and Portugal every other one survives, whereas start-ups remain in business longer in Japan, Italy, Sweden, and Holland (Fernández et al. 2006). These figures suggest early TEA in Venezuela hardly suffices to build sizable companies, and there is little or no entrepreneurial activity that significantly contributes to economic development.

Navigating successfully amidst turbulence

How do firms determined to stay in business and operate profitably overcome the current economic, financial, and regulatory challenges they confront in Venezuela? Consider first the example of Casa Hellmund.

Casa Hellmund

This family-owned company has been doing business in Venezuela since 1862 (Rodríguez and Vidal 2007). Casa Hellmund[10] is known for its versatility in running different kinds of business. Up to 1930 the firm exported coffee and cocoa, served as a general agent for a steamship line, and imported foodstuffs. During the past 80 years Casa Hellmund has specialized in photography, focusing on capturing, processing, and printing images, and representing leading photocopy companies in Venezuela – including Fujifilm, Canon, Sony, Leica, and Xerox. Yet at one point the firm represented a line of sporting goods.

Events that took place in the course of Casa Hellmund's long history, including being cut off from suppliers during the Second World War, have strongly impacted the company. Again and again, operations had to be suspended and business rebuilt. Moreover, in recent decades the company had to deal with abrupt economic, financial, and regulatory changes in Venezuela's business context.

Exchange controls put in place in 2003 became a major hurdle, as products could no longer be purchased overseas at reasonable prices. Multinational companies operating in Venezuela – such as Eastman Kodak – took undue advantage of this situation by shipping goods to their local subsidiaries at headquarters price. To overcome this source of unfair competition and maintain access to its suppliers, Casa Hellmund stepped up attendance at international photo fairs, cultivated its worldwide network of contacts, and searched for new business opportunities.

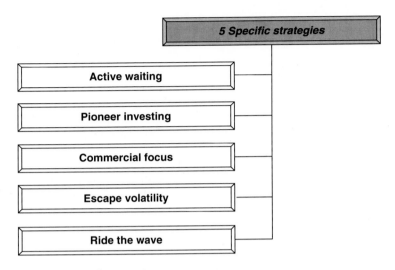

Figure 9.9 Five specific strategies
Source: Author's elaboration.

During the Chávez regime, from 2000 onwards, Casa Hellmund's excellent relations with its employees helped shield it from the impact of legal issues arising from some 36 changes in labor regulations. Violation of a regulation could have closed down the company for days or weeks on grounds of non-compliance. The company estimates the total cost of these regulations increased the cost of doing business by almost 80 percent. To offset such costs, employees have been offered the opportunity to become shareholders and obtain Casa Hellmund franchises for photo developing stores. This has made employees feel more involved and valued. Such practices have enabled the company to handle the increased costs resulting from new laws and regulations.

Other companies have survived by stepping up corporate entrepreneurship. Figure 9.9 shows five types of strategies deployed by Venezuelan companies to expand operations in recent years as a means of overcoming economic, financial, and regulatory volatility: standing watch, pioneer investing, focus on marketing, escaping volatility, and riding the wave.

Standing watch

To deploy this strategy, a company must prepare itself managerially and financially to seize golden opportunities, usually by means of mergers and acquisitions. The strategy has been widely used by local companies operating in the financial and food sectors, and is generally unsuited for MNCs insofar as decisions must be made quickly. Consider two examples.

Empresas Polar is Venezuela's largest privately owned conglomerate. There follows a chronological summary of acquisitions made by this company over the past 50 years:

- 1960: When most large Venezuelan companies were concerned with the nation's economy and avoided major investments, Empresas Polar acquired a major beer competitor; by significantly expanding output, the company repositioned itself to benefit from soaring oil prices following 1974, reaching 85 percent market share.
- 1983: A financial crisis led to the imposition of exchange controls and slowed raw material imports. Polar averted the crisis by purchasing a small mill to produce cornmeal.
- 1988: During another crisis year, Polar acquired nine processing companies with prestige brands belonging to US-based Beatrice Foods, thus significantly expanding output.
- 1999–2000: Despite a weak economy and poor political outlook, Polar entered a joint venture with PepsiCo to produce soft drinks and snacks.
- 2001: Polar acquired Mavesa, a leading margarine, vegetable oil, soap and detergent maker, turning the company into Venezuela's largest food producer.

Banesco is one of Venezuela's largest banks, and leveraged growth through timely acquisitions of several competitors during a period of economic uncertainty that adversely impacted the financial sector.

Pioneer investing

To deploy this strategy, companies identify a market with unsatisfied demand where product innovation is possible, aiming to achieve high profitability. Unlike the standing watch strategy, implemented by means of mergers and acquisitions, pioneer investment pursues growth in a new market segment. This strategy has most commonly been observed in telecommunications, pharmaceutical retailing, and shopping malls. Two examples follow.

Grupo Sambil is the largest private construction company in Venezuela. Until 1997 the company's portfolio was largely focused on office and residential property. Sambil then began building and operating shopping centers. Venezuela's first Sambil Mall revolutionized the shopping center industry in Venezuela and the Caribbean by featuring a wide variety of shops, services, and entertainment facilities. The same concept was replicated in cities across Venezuela.

Farmatodo is Venezuela's largest drugstore chain, with South America's highest sales volume. At the close of the 1990s the company capitalized on lagging investment in the retail pharmacy sector by launching self-service drugstores combined with convenience stores, operated on a 24-hour basis. Innovations were also made in marketing, pricing, store design, branding, logistics, and the company's business relationship with suppliers. Farmatodo came to open almost one store per month over a span of four years, and has expanded to neighboring Colombia.

Focus on marketing

In highly volatile business contexts, companies may seek to move their manufacturing facilities to a more stable economy and focus on marketing. Investing in market research and consumer behavior analysis, together with a well-trained sales and service staff, can prove highly profitable. Following is the experience of Mexican-owned MABE, Venezuela's largest home appliance company.

MABE had for years manufactured appliances in Venezuela under its own brand and General Electric, importing parts from its plant in Mexico. When the Chávez administration renounced a trade agreement with Colombia and Mexico, the Venezuelan plant was closed and moved to Colombia. By focusing on marketing and taking advantage of Venezuela's huge growth in consumer demand, MABE market share grew by 10 points to 60 percent in 2005. To achieve this growth, MABE invested heavily in advertising and knowledge of low-income consumers. Customers were guaranteed long-term after-sales service by means of a network of support facilities manned by highly trained staff.

Locatel is one of Venezuela's most successful health product retailers. To reduce risk and shore up growth, franchises were granted to a large number of local investors. Self-service shopping was employed, as at Farmatodo, but customers were offered a wider variety of health products including rentals of wheelchairs and other medical equipment. Stores were established in leading Venezuelan cities and in neighboring Colombia.

Escaping volatility

Escaping volatility implies reducing exposure to risk by organizing business abroad. Few Venezuelan companies have set up international operations. Mergers and acquisitions are an effective route for operational risk diversification, but entail developing the organizational capabilities employed by MNCs. Building export markets diversifies commercial risk, but the operational risk posed by economic and regulatory volatility remains. Consider the following examples.

Chocolates El Rey was founded in 1929 as a family business making cocoa tablets, and in recent years became a highly successful chocolate manufacturer. For decades, company growth was inhibited by regulatory practices, ostensibly to protect cocoa growers; but following 1990 exports were encouraged. Chocolates El Rey defined its mission as producing premium chocolate for local and international markets, evoking Venezuela's eighteenth-century role. A major effort was made to develop business-to-business food services, aimed at makers of other products requiring high-quality chocolate as an ingredient. The company also innovated by drawing on the experience of European wine and cheese makers, applying the *appellation controlée* concept to cocoa. Chefs and food critics from the US and Europe were invited to visit the company's cocoa plantation and manufacturing plant – a less expensive strategy than advertising in noted gourmet magazines. Also, local cocoa growers were offered technical assistance to improve quality. Following these efforts the company dominated the local market and exports grew to 810 tons in 2005–6.

Organización Diego Cisneros (ODC) was founded in 1920 and is among the five largest MNCs in Latin America. ODC is the Venezuelan group that has been best able to compete in the global economy based on a worldwide strategy of mergers, acquisitions, and joint ventures, chiefly in telecoms and the media. Interest in business abroad stemmed from Venezuelan market size limitations and concern over future regulatory changes. ODC still operates a TV channel and a brewery in Venezuela.

Riding the wave

"Riding the wave" is Venezuelan slang for companies that grow by exploiting close relations with government agencies to take advantage of public spending. The practice has been employed by several construction, finance, and insurance companies, but is not considered a valid competitive strategy.

Building on local tradition

Companies sometimes overlook opportunities for building on local traditions to develop new product concepts. For generations, Venezuelans patronized street-cart peddlers to drink a sweet rice-and-sugar beverage known as *chicha*. But sales declined as consumers became more aware of vendors' poor hygienic conditions, and the packaged, pasteurized product sold in supermarkets and other shops did not entirely fulfill taste expectations. In 2000, two Venezuelan entrepreneurs came up with the idea of selling a freshly made, high-quality version of the product in small, fast-service retail franchises named after a street peddler, Juan Chichero. In less than two years as many as 160 outlets were in operation across the country, in addition to those set up by competitors who copied the concept. What appeared to be a burgeoning market burst in December 2002 as a result of Venezuela's three-month work stoppage protesting against Chávez; in February 2003 only 40 of the franchisees remained in business, and all competitors closed. Thanks to strong brand recognition, in recent years Juan Chichero slowly recovered much of its lost ground.

Gleaning the outlook for entrepreneurship in Venezuela

For some years the prospects for entrepreneurship in Venezuela will likely remain fairly much as at present: highly uncertain in light of political issues, and subject to economic, financial, and regulatory volatility. Accordingly, quick-return projects pursued by relatively few entrepreneurs holding ready cash will be coupled with a much larger number of necessity-driven ventures by Venezuelans from all levels of society: small-scale businesses centered on food preparation, light manufacturing and services, some of which will fulfill the Chávez regime's criteria for promoting a social enterprise economy. A determining factor will no doubt be oil prices and output levels; but even if oil prices fail to rise and Venezuelan oil output remains stagnant, as it has for some years, significant resources will continue to flow into Venezuela – and in all likelihood, sooner or later much more will come.

In 2010 the US Geological Survey announced Venezuela's oil reserves could double the supplies of Saudi Arabia, a far more optimistic assessment than even the best-case scenario put forward by President Hugo Chávez (http://news.bbc.co.uk/2/hi/8476395.stm – consulted October 2010). Venezuela's Orinoco Tar Belt oil may be heavy and require processing, but is far easier and cheaper to extract than that from Brazil's offshore fields lying deep under ocean salt beds, and doing so does not threaten the environment – as in Alaska, Canada's Athabasca tar sands and, perhaps too, the South Atlantic.

Current Venezuelan government efforts to promote oil ventures with companies from China, Russia, and Iran have been accompanied by overtures to Western oil companies, suggesting terms that will accommodate their demands. As these projects materialize – and resources flowing into Venezuela rise – a new configuration of investors stands to emerge. Multinational companies that offer services no government can do without, such as data processing and telecommunications, could be the first to invest in upgrading what they have to offer. A second investment tier could come from multinationals the government views as politically neutral, producing goods and services not considered strategic. Perhaps rapprochement could even be reached with certain large privately owned firms such as Empresas Polar, given its importance in ensuring food supply.

Other opportunity-driven investors could sprout from a coterie of business people close to the government. Some would likely be wave riders, the term employed earlier to describe Venezuelan companies who seek close ties with whatever government is in power and offer it support; others could emerge from within government party circles, financed from obscure sources.

In other words, if the Chávez government were to continue in power for several years, a return to opportunity-driven entrepreneurship in Venezuela should not be discarded. But in the event Venezuela's political outlook changes – another factor that cannot be discarded – entrepreneurship might again flourish. Generations of Venezuelans, long before Chávez, have stashed funds abroad for safekeeping. Thousands of Venezuelans now work as managers for oil companies in several countries, and are credited with steering Colombia's impressive growth in oil output. Additionally, a number of Venezuelan firms in banking, engineering services, and other fields that continue doing business in Venezuela have in recent years set up operations abroad. By doing so they have retained their most valuable asset, human capital and know-how.

Lastly, once the country's political climate stabilizes, the human factor must also be considered. In the 1970s Venezuela recorded the highest GDP growth rate in all Latin America, and featured the largest middle-income consumer market – one that has since been overtaken by fast-growth economies such as Brazil and Chile. Oil prices and large-scale immigration shaped Venezuela's entrepreneurial success. If this country served as a magnet for so many in the past, all the more reason why hundreds of thousands of Venezuelans now living abroad could return and increase the entrepreneurial skills required to rebuild their homeland and draw on its burgeoning oil wealth.

Notes

1. A set of economic policy reforms promoted for crisis-wrought developing countries by Washington-based institutions such as the International Monetary Fund (IMF), World Bank, and the US Treasury Department.
2. In turbulent times, opportunities appear, but expected payback periods are low (Fernández et al. 2006), preventing the creation of real and sustainable economic prosperity.
3. Mission Che Guevara, focused on skills for the unemployed, is one of 25 such programs. Healthcare services missions span Barrio Adentro (primary healthcare), Mission Miracle (eye disorders), and Mission Smile (dentistry). Others include Barrio Mothers Mission (care for women in poverty), Mission Negra Hipólita (care for children, adolescents, and homeless or physically challenged adults, named after Simón Bolívar's black nanny), Barrio Adentro Deportivo (promotion of physical exercise, use of leisure time in the training of sports promoters), Mission Habitat (home building and remodeling), and Mission Mercal (consumer staple retail outlets in poor communities featuring subsidized prices).
4. A series of documents define EPSs as "community production units, constituted under the appropriate legal form, for the fundamental purpose of producing goods and provide services to meet the basic needs of communities and their environment, drawing on men and women from the missions, privileging solidarity, cooperation, complementariness, reciprocity, fairness, and sustainability values over the values of profit or gain" (Framework Agreement for the Promotion, Encouragement and Development of Social Production Enterprises, Ciudad Guayana, Sept. 2005). An EPS must necessarily include in its articles of

incorporation the modality of associated labor and collective property enterprise, with social production as its mission; hence the model can be applied by a cooperative (given its collective nature) or a business.

5. Venezuela employed exchange controls for the first time following the February 1983 financial crisis. On January 23, 2003, in an attempt to support the bolivar and bolster the government's declining level of international reserves, as well as to mitigate the adverse impact from the oil industry work stoppage on the financial system, the Ministry of Finance and the Central Bank suspended foreign exchange trading. On February 6, the government established CADIVI, a currency control board charged with handling foreign exchange procedures. The board set the US dollar exchange rate at 1596 bolivars to the dollar for purchases and 1600 to the dollar for sales.

6. GEM gauges entrepreneurial activity in 46 countries. The main GEM indicator is TEA, based on the number of people starting a new firm and those starting a new business within an established company. Since 2003, the Institute of Advanced Studies in Administration (IESA), a local business school, has compiled GEM data for Venezuela.

7. According to Acs (2007), early entrepreneurship activity is directly related to per capita income. Countries with low incomes generally show high early entrepreneurial activity.

8. According to figures obtained from http://www.barrioadentro.gov.ve/ (consulted in March 2009) 2,800,000 people were enrolled in the Misión Robinson (1 y 2) literacy programs, and 200,000 people in Misión Rivas, a secondary education program for school dropouts. Additionally, 265,000 participated in Misión Vuelvan Caras, presumably obtaining cash stipends for being unemployed or starting up cooperatives (see Bruni Celli 2009).

9. Venezuelans who moved to Colombia as political conditions worsened often express surprise at the relative absence of fresh mozarella and ricotta cheese (Italian influence), fresh (i.e., not frozen) fish and shellfish (Spanish influence) and watercress or other produce grown in Venezuela by Portuguese farmers.

10. The Casa Hellmund case was described in detail by Rodriguez and Vidal (2007) within the frame of the STEP methodological guidelines (Nordqvist and Zellweger 2010).

References

Acs, Z. J. 2007. "How Is Entrepreneurship Good for Economic Growth?" *Innovations* 1, no. 1.

Álvarez, A. 2006. "Social Cleavages, Political Polarization and Democratic Breakdown in Venezuela." In Richard O. Lalander (Ed.), *Venezuelan Politics and Society in Times of Chavismo* (pp. 18–28). Stockholm University Institute of Latin American Studies.

Auletta, N., and R. Puente. 2009. "Innovación y mercadeo un mapa de utilidad par alas mayorías." *Debates IESA* 14, no. 1.

Baptista, A. 2006. "Los números de Europa, Venezuela y la inmigración europea." In K. Krispin (Ed.), *De Europa a Venezuela: la inmigración europea a Venezuela desde lo que es hoy la Unión Europea entre los años 1936 y 2006* (pp. 15–20). Caracas, Venezuela: Unión Europea.

Banco Central de Venezuela. 2010. http://www.bcv.org.ve/excel/5_2_4.xls?id=332. [Retrieved September, 2010].

Bruni Celli, J. 2009. "Viabilidad económica y desempeño cooperativo: ¿cuán exitosa es la experiencia venezolana?" In M. Penfold and R. Vainrub (Eds.), *Estrategias en tiempos de turbulencia: las empresas venezolanas*. Caracas: Ediciones IESA.

Chacón, E (2010) Presidente llama a pequeñas empresas privadas a trabajar por el socialismo. www.alopresidente.gob.ve Feb 2012. http://www.alopresidente.gob.ve/informacion/2/1784/presidente_llama_a.html.

Chávez, H. 2003. *Aló Presidente No. 164: Transcription of TV Program No. 164*. September 14. Caracas: Palacio de Miraflores.

Chávez, H. 2005. *Aló Presidente No. 240: Transciption of TV Program No. 240*. November 20. Caracas: Palácio de Miraflores.

Consultores 21. 2010. *Perfil 21*, no. 82, June.

Cruz, F. 1993. "La Cultura y la Modernidad de las Organizaciones." In R. D. Echeverry, A. Chanla, and C. Davila, *En busca de una administración para America Latina* (pp. 43–52). Cali, Colombia: Universidad del Valle.

Dakduk, S. 2009. "¿Cómo aprenden los consumidores de las mayorías?" *Debates IESA* 14, no. 1.

Dealy, G. C. 1992. *The Latin Americans: Spirit and Ethos*. Boulder, CO: The Westview Press.

Fernández F., A. Rodríguez, and R. Vidal. 2006. *Global Entrepreneurship Monitor. Informe Venezuela 2005*. Caracas: IESA Entrepreneurship Center.

Fernández F., A. Rodríguez, and R. Vidal. 2009. *Global Entrepreneurship Monitor. Informe Venezuela 2007–08*. Caracas: IESA Entrepreneurship Center.

Global Entrepreneurship Monitor. 2003, 2005, 2007. *Informe Venezuela*. Caracas: IESA Entrepreneurship Center.

Gómez, H., and V. Dezerega. 1989. "Chispa y acierto: la iniciativa que se emprende." In M. Naím (Ed.), *Las Empresas Venezolanas: su gerencia* (pp. 413–55). Caracas: Ediciones IESA.

Gómez, H. 1997. "The Globalization of Business in Latin America." *The International Executive* 39, no. 2: 225–54.

Heritage Foundation. 2010. *Index of Economic Freedom Report*. Washington, DC.

Institute for Management Development. 2010. *World Competitiveness Yearbook*. Lausanne, Switzerland.

International Monetary Fund (2010). *World Economic Outlook*. Washington, DC.

Jiménez, C., and R. Puente. 2009. "Un mundo poco conocido: el consumidor del mercado de las mayorías." *Debates IESA* 14, no. 1.

Nordqvist, M., and T. Zellweger. 2010. *Transgenerational Entrepreneurship: Exploring Growth and Performance of Family Firms across Generations*. Cheltenham: Edward Elgar.

Ogliastri, E., C. McMillen, C. Altschul, M. E. Arias, C. de Bustamante, C. Dávila, P. Dorfman, M. Ferreira de la Coletta, C. Fimmen, J. Ickis, and S. Martínez. 1999. "Cultura y liderazgo organizacional en 10 países de América Latina." *Academia-Revista Latinoamericana de Administración* 22: 29–57.

Patrescu, D. (2010) Chavez Orders Autoseat de Venezuela Takeover. www.autoevolution.com. feb 2012. http://www.autoevolution.com/news/chavez-orders-autoseat-de-venezuela-takeover-21498.html.

Pellegrini, A. (1989). *Historia de la Inmigración en Venezuela, siglo XIX y XX*. Caracas, Venezuela.

Penfold, M., and X. Corrales. 2011. *Dragon in the Tropics: Hugo Chávez and the Political Economy of Revolution in Venezuela*. Washington, DC: The Brookings Institution (forthcoming).

Penfold M., and R. Vainrub (Eds). 2009. *Estrategias en tiempos de turbulencia: las empresas venezolanas.* Caracas: Ediciones IESA.

Prahalad, C. K., and S. Hart. 2002. "The Fortune at the Bottom of the Pyramid." *Strategy + Business* 1, no. 26.

Rodríguez, A., and R. Vidal. 2007. "The Casa Hellmund Case." Master case presented in Babson College STEP Seminar. San Jose, Costa Rica: INCAE.

Smith, Peter. 2005. *Democracy in Latin America: Political Change in Comparative Perspective.* New York: Oxford University Press.

Tulchin, J., and A. Brown. 2002, *Democratic Governance and Social Inequality.* Boulder, CO: Lynne Rienner Publishers.

Uslar, A. 1963. "La imagen pública de la empresa privada en Venezuela." In Seminario Internacional de Ejecutivos, *La responabilidad empresarial en el progreso social de Venezuela.* Caracas: Cromotip.

Vainrub, R., and G. Arevalo. 2003. *Global Entrepreneurship Monitor. Informe Venezuela 2003.* Caracas: IESA Entrepreneurship Center.

World Bank. 2010. "Doing Business Ranking." http://www.doingbusiness.org/economyrankings/. [Retrieved September, 2010].

World Economic Forum. 2010. *World Competitiveness Report* 2010–2011. [Retrieved October, 2010].

10
Conclusion

Esteban R. Brenes
INCAE Business School

Jerry Haar
Florida International University

During the first decade of the twenty-first century, during the boom years of 2005–9 and the "Great Recession" and "Anemic Recovery" stages that followed, entrepreneurship stood front and center as both opportunity and necessity entrepreneurs harnessed the spirit of enterprise to create something of their very own. Regardless of political orientation – socialist, capitalist, or mixed – many countries have been promoting entrepreneurship through a variety of policy mechanisms and program delivery vehicles. Malaysia, Singapore, China, India, Vietnam, Chile, Brazil, Colombia, and many others have seen their governments evolve and adopt "business-friendly" policies. As examples, India is making it easy for Indians living abroad to come back to their country and develop a new business, and China's Community Central Party School offers courses on entrepreneurship. While Mao Tse-tung is most likely turning over in his grave, the entrepreneurial bug has caught on in the People's Republic of China and pragmatism has chipped away at ideological purity in a country that remains authoritarian but perhaps with a looser grip on the reins of power and control.

Globalizing trends

While many forces and factors shape entrepreneurship, macroeconomic stability and inflation control are among the most important elements for creating the right environment. Globalization has facilitated many won-drous things – innovation processes, access to technology, larger market opportunities, and the existence of a new group of entrepreneurs, one that is more knowledgeable, more technologically oriented, and more aggressive. Trade and investment across nations are booming and will continue unabated, despite periodic bouts of protectionism, mainly in agriculture and labor-intensive manufacturing. International trade agreements (ITAs) have been growing; and whether multilateral, plurilateral, or bilateral, regional or subregional, the trend continues and shows no sign of waning. As of 2011, 297 regional trade agreements were in force, of which 90 percent were FTAs of partial scope. This opens up the opportunity to institutionalize policy stability and provide predictability, to access new markets and technologies, and to become more efficient and customer-oriented given the competitiveness challenge found in ITAs.

New consumer demographics

The growth of the middle class and the consequent behavior of the bottom of the pyramid are interesting changes, particularly in developing economies. Both groups are growing at a very fast pace. They are open to more consumption as they become wealthier. Female emancipation is another force that is shaping entrepreneurship. Most are self-employed; and worldwide there are many support programs – public, private, and non-profit – that reinforce female entrepreneurship. Still another expanding development is immigration-related entrepreneurship. As citizens cross borders for political, economic, religious, ethnic, or family reasons (for example, Venezuelans to Colombia, Haitians to Miami, Vietnamese to Montreal, Pakistanis to London), many turn to entrepreneurial pursuits, usually with the support of family and the community enclaves to which they migrate.

There are forces and factors that threaten and challenge entrepreneurship. The first factor is local in nature and has to do with government and political challenges. Government bureaucracy affects the health and growth of entrepreneurship; and corruption, which is considered as the best proxy for institutional failure, creates uncertainty and instability to potential local and foreign entrepreneurs. Other threats are deficient physical infrastructure such as roads, airports, ports, water, electricity, and communication systems, especially in developing economies. Beyond physical infrastructure, some countries also lack direct government support and interest, business support services, financial support, information services and university–business collaboration.

New businesses today are moving away from a low-skilled workforce towards a knowledge-based economy that relies more and more on technically adept human capital. Therefore poor education systems are a major factor threatening entrepreneurship, given the difficulties in getting the right people for new enterprises. Labor flexibility is another challenge as many countries try to protect employment by increasing the difficulties in hiring and firing workers. Such possibilities hamper the productivity and performance of SMEs in particular.

Credit is yet another barrier. The initial years of operation, usually with losses or low profits, hinder new enterprises from securing bank loans. In addition, mistrust of financial institutions, not enough income to save, underdeveloped financial markets, lack of business angels and venture capitalists, and short-term investment cultures are major problems faced by entrepreneurs in many emerging economies. The need to develop or strengthen business angels, venture capitalists, investment bankers, and capital markets are imperative for success.

Paying taxes is a fact for every business. However, for new businesses especially, taxation is a major administrative headache. Administratively complicated tax systems are sometimes more costly than the taxes actually paid.

The case of Latin America

As stated in the Introduction, the Washington Consensus drew (and in some cases "pushed") Latin American economies towards neo-liberal economic policies. The objective was to help these economies recover from the "lost decade" of the 1980s. Privatization, economic liberalization, FTAs, and many other pro-market policies were implemented throughout the region. That process boosted entrepreneurship through the measures that improved the economic environment. However, that has not been enough. Entrepreneurs need to band together to remove the distortions currently present in their markets, encourage human capital development, allocate scarce resources through market processes, and provide employment alternatives to the public sector.

Fortunately, the vast majority of countries in Latin America follow policies oriented towards improving stability, healthy growth, and democracy. However, there has been a backlash in Venezuela, Bolivia, Nicaragua, and Ecuador, which introduced certain reforms towards what some call "the new twenty-first-century socialism." Reversing privatizations, partially closing the economies to international trade, distorting markets and prices, and failure to create political and legal transparency, are among the factors that, in the balance, have negatively affected entrepreneurial development in the region.

At times overlooked, or at least underestimated, Latin American families have been essential for entrepreneurial growth throughout the centuries. Today, transgenerational entrepreneurship research has demonstrated that families are very effective in promoting new business development and spreading the spirit of entrepreneurship among their members. Business expansion happens today not only within the family firm's core business, but it is common to see them entering into different fields either under the umbrella of the corporation or outside.

An interesting element that is changing the structure of the industries and shaping a new type of entrepreneur is OFDI. Many firms, especially but not exclusively from Mexico (Gruma), Brazil (Gerdau), and Chile (LAN), are investing heavily in other countries. Other examples are Pollo Campero from Guatemala, Techint (Argentina), and Astrid y Gastón (Peru). This is a relatively new phenomenon. In the past, companies invested most of their excess cash in their home markets either in the same company or through diversification. Firms are expanding to other countries of the region as they understand them better, as macroeconomic and political environments are more stable, as logistics have improved, and as successful business models in their home countries can be expanded easily to countries with similar conditions.

In the following section examples that confirm some of the observations made above are extracted from the country chapters.

Argentina's macroeconomic and political stability has contributed to an important increase in FDI from other countries of the region. The arrival of some venture capital institutions has been key for promoting entrepreneurship. Firms that have internationalized their operations are growing faster thanks to globalization. Opportunity entrepreneurship is bigger than necessity entrepreneurship, indicating that the country, today, is in better shape for developing new firms. Unfortunately, the inflation rate is growing again, the bureaucracy is highly inefficient, regulations are complicated and cumbersome, and there is public antipathy towards entrepreneurs among large classes of Argentines (for example, labor unions, civil servants, the lower-level salaried workers).

Brazil's economic transformation started in the 1990s and today it offers very special conditions for the development of entrepreneurship. It has a dynamic domestic market, new laws to simplify tax procedures in particular for SMEs and for R&D and innovation, and is fourth in the world in business incubators. Brazil has a strong culture that supports and admires entrepreneurs, and during the past ten years has witnessed the emergence of deeper capital markets, angel investors, and venture capital and private equity firms. Indeed, opportunity entrepreneurship is the highest in the region just after Uruguay. However, Brazil still has work to do to overcome bureaucratic, regulatory, and financial impediments that stifle entrepreneurship. The nation still ranks lower than Peru, Chile, and Colombia in the number of days it takes to start up a new business, its R&D and innovation achievements are modest at best, and for all its alleged export prowess, Brazil possesses low levels of internationalization.

Chile initiated a unilateral process of economic openness before any other country in the region. That process has improved the country's business environment, and today Chilean companies are very competitive locally and internationally. Chile's government is transparent, norms and regulations are stable and predictable; bureaucratic procedures relatively efficient (opening a new company is easy); and corruption is under control. In fact,

Chile possesses one of the best legal systems in the region. The government has many programs to promote entrepreneurship, such as business incubators, science and technology parks, and support for consulting, networking, and economic resources. Chile allocates copper taxes proceeds, among other sources, to promote entrepreneurship. Today, 70 percent of new firms come from opportunity entrepreneurship, and SMEs represent 38 percent of total employment.

Colombia is a country in which entrepreneurship has been a major policy issue for the national government in the first decade of this century. Laws to promote entrepreneurship (Law 1014, 2006) and to raise the status of the national science and technology agency, Colciencias (Law 1286, 2009) were passed, and institutions within the government have taken on special roles in the promotion of entrepreneurship. One of them is the Servicio Nacional de Aprendizaje (SENA), a technical education institution for blue-collar workers that trains them to be entrepreneurs through a designated source of funding – Fondo Emprendedor. Law 1286 elevated Colciencias to a cabinet-level agency, creating a mandate for supporting the development of high-technology and high-impact entrepreneurship. One interesting aspect of the process in Colombia has been the support of the media in fostering a culture of entrepreneurship, identifying role models, and helping entrepreneurs access information and resources. GEM survey results reveal that opportunity and necessity entrepreneurship has the same prevalence today, and the government has recognized the need for differentiated policies to promote both of them. One in five people in the country are involved in some entrepreneurial activity and 12.2 percent of the population owns a business. However, some obstacles are still present, most notably financing, generally regarded as one of the biggest barriers to the development of entrepreneurial ventures in Colombia. This is especially true with respect to high-potential ventures that require larger sums of start-up capital. The country is currently making only timid advances in promoting the development of venture capital and business angel institutions. The relationship between firms and universities is weak; and while most entrepreneurial activity begins in the informal sector, after three years less than 50 percent join the formal sector.

Costa Rica is a country that is moving from a knowledge society to knowledge-based economy in which innovation is a key element and IT entrepreneurship is growing. A well-trained and educated population, impressive health indicators, an open economy, economic, political, and regulatory stability, and strong institutions make Costa Rica a safe place to invest. This is an emerging economy that reinvented itself by diversifying its portfolio of exports and today is the third largest per capita exporter in the world. Unfortunately, Costa Rica records unimpressive GDP growth levels (most likely related to government inefficiency), a burdensome bureaucracy, underdeveloped capital markets, and a lackluster banking sector. Although SME financing is developed and strongly supported by two public banks, private banks are risk averse in financing the kinds of technology projects necessary for Costa Rica to build on the strong platform created by Intel and the start-up (and now established) firms linked to it and other IT multinationals. Unfortunately, angel investors and venture capitalists are in short supply.

Mexico is a nation where entrepreneurship is widespread and widely celebrated. Some contributing factors are: an open economy, with 11 FTAs encompassing 41 countries; a bureaucracy which, although still problematic for entrepreneurs, has been steadily improving; a positive image held by the public of entrepreneurs; and strong networks internally and externally, such as support from family and friends. The motivations for a new venture in the case of Mexican entrepreneurs are better income (49 percent) and independence (39 percent). Apparently, self-employment is a better opportunity for Mexicans. Formal employment is not regularly available and usually does not pay well, in many cases the benefits of self-employment are greater than those of being an employee. In general, informal businesses in Mexico have very low barriers to entry – 40 percent of GDP comes from informal businesses. Conversely, Mexico faces important obstacles for the development of entrepreneurship: inequality – half of the population is in poverty; corruption and weak institutions; drug trafficking and gang violence; insufficient innovation, usually concentrated in formal and large firms; and informality – most firms are born informal and continue to be so indefinitely.

Peru is an interesting case of recent transformation for the better vis-à-vis entrepreneurship. Immersed in guerrilla war, political instability and turmoil in the 1980s, the country is now stable and an attractive locale for doing business, with the GDP per capita having doubled in the last ten years. Poverty and inequality are down, and the middle class is growing. Some elements that contribute to entrepreneurship are: prudent neo-liberal economic policies, legal reforms, and investor protection laws. A law passed in 2008 to promote competitiveness, and public and private sector grants to both rural and urban areas for micro and small business development are yielding very positive results. Nevertheless, Peru continues to face obstacles to entrepreneurial activities, and business informality still represents around 42 percent of GDP, accounting for 98.5 percent of the firms, and only 9.2 percent of employees work in formal companies. Informality impedes businesses from accessing training, public purchases, health protection, and pension funds, therefore new legislation to formalize those firms was issued.

Venezuela, despite its status as an oil-rich nation, is faring poorly economically. In fact, not even state-owned companies are performing well.

Since 1997, the production levels of PDVSA, the national oil company, have declined by 50 percent, yet the economy remains totally dependent on oil (95 percent of the nation's exports). The authoritarian government of President Hugo Chávez has created an environment vehemently hostile to capitalism and, therefore, to entrepreneurship. Chavez's socialist policies include nationalization of companies and expropriations – a real threat to property rights; subsidies that distort the market; exchange rate controls; costly and rigid labor legislation that makes entrepreneurs less willing to hire new employees; corrupt and weak institutions including the judicial system; bureaucratic obstruction of businesses and costly access to credit. Nevertheless, 22.8 percent of the adult population or 3 million people have started a new business during the last ten years. However, two-thirds were necessity entrepreneurs, implying two things – jobs are not available and there are not many opportunities for entrepreneurs in this country. The main questions are: How is it that established firms decided to stay in business? How do they survive? How do they operate profitably in the face of the current economic, financial, and regulatory challenges that confront Venezuela? A number of firms in Venezuela are either buying other companies to diversify or sending their operations abroad, developing new local products based on customs or traditions, or improving relations with institutions to do business with the government, taking advantage of increased government spending.

Recommendations for the future of entrepreneurship in Latin America

The future of entrepreneurship in Latin America will depend on government policies as well as actions taken and leadership provided by the private sector – not to mention the "spirit of enterprise," as George Gilder coins the phrase, among individual entrepreneurs. Throughout the book we have seen many opportunities to create a positive environment for entrepreneurship and the forces, factors, and drivers of entrepreneurship. These include liberal economic policies, governmental efficiency, the rule of law, access to, and affordability of, credit, and public safety.

Some specific actions that governments should consider are: promoting policies and laws to support entrepreneurship and innovation; establishing credible and predictable policies; creating strong laws for corruption control; protecting laws for private investment; putting into effect a transparent judicial system; investing in physical infrastructure; educating, from an early age, about the importance of entrepreneurship for the country's development; creating national prizes for entrepreneurs and for innovation; developing and implementing banking policies to facilitate funding for

SMEs; funding SMEs for research and innovation; promoting the creation of rural and municipal savings institutions; facilitating the attraction of venture capital; formalizing the informal firms; and committing to measurement methodologies such as participating in GEM.

The private sector as a key player should consider: collaborating with the government in the creation of national prizes; supporting policies for corruption control; working as a team with universities and research centers; securing media support to motivate entrepreneurial activities to improve entrepreneurial culture and make entrepreneurship a good career choice; creating angel investor networks with the support of regional banking institutions; and promoting the formulation of rules or protocols to assure the long-term life of family businesses.

Most important of all, however, is the individual entrepreneur. What happens at the firm level is paramount. Regardless of external forces, factors, and drivers, the entrepreneur has the greatest influence on his or her destiny. The firm's principal reason for existing, how it produces its goods or services and its portfolio of functions – management and organization, financial management, marketing, human resource management, supply chain (including sourcing), and customer relations – are all within the domain of the entrepreneur.

Entrepreneurship is a dynamo – some would say the prime one – of democratic capitalism. Its future in Latin America will be determined by government, business associations, civil society, and individuals cooperating and collaborating towards a common good – one that provides tangible benefits to enterprises large and small and to both producers and consumers.

Mahatma Gandhi said, "Be the change you wish to see in the world." Whether through choice or necessity, Latin America's entrepreneurs are dedicated to fulfill this task.

Index